Hello, Amélie here. I was just
thinking it was kinda chilly, and
now something crazy happened
outside. Everything turned white!
Did you think something like
that would be enough to make
me hesitate? I couldn't care less!
Chaaaaaarge!!
...Wait a second, lady. This stuff
is weirdly crunchy and I'm sinking!
And it's cooooold! Let's go
home. I'll jump on the old
guy who's still in bed!!

YŪKI TABATA

was born in Fukuoka Prefecture
and got his big break in the 2011
Shonen Jump Golden Future Cup
with his winning entry, *Hungry*
Joker. He started the magical fantasy
... 015.

BLACK CLOVER
VOLUME 15
SHONEN JUMP Manga Edition

Story and Art by YŪKI TABATA

Translation ✤ SARAH NEUFELD, HC LANGUAGE SOLUTIONS, INC.

Touch-Up Art & Lettering ✤ ANNALIESE CHRISTMAN

Design ✤ SHAWN CARRICO

Editor ✤ ALEXIS KIRSCH

Printed in the U.S.A.

Published by VIZ Media, LLC
P.O. Box 77010
San Francisco, CA 94107

10 9 8 7 6 5 4 3 2 1
First printing, May 2019

ratings.viz.com
RATED T TEEN

PARENTAL ADVISORY
BLACK CLOVER is rated T for Teen and is recommended for ages 13 and up. This volume contains realistic and fantasy violence.

VIZ MEDIA
viz.com

SHONEN JUMP
shonenjump.com

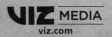

SHONEN JUMP MANGA

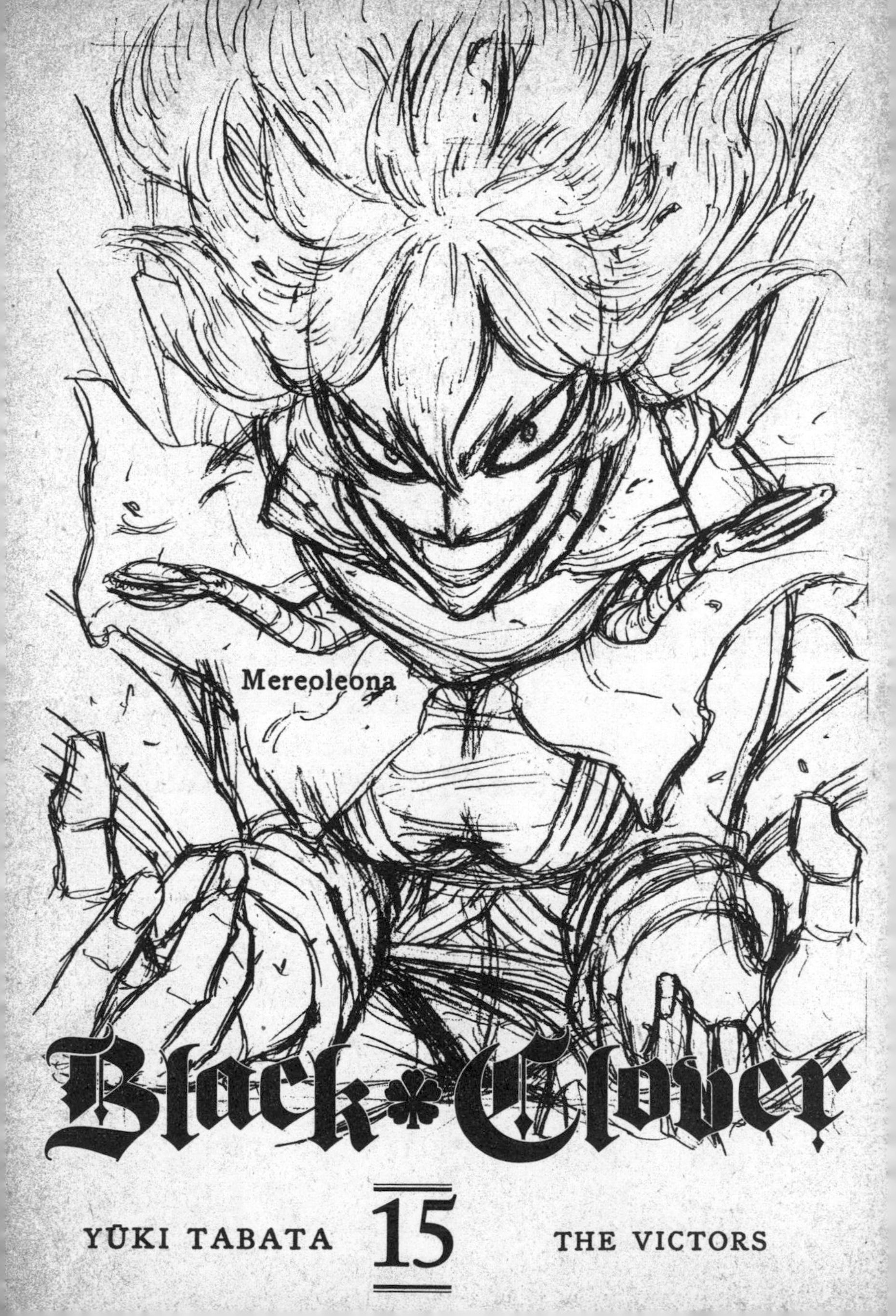
Mereoleona

Black ♣ Clover

YŪKI TABATA

15

THE VICTORS

Characters

Yuno

Member of: The Golden Dawn | Magic: Wind

Asta's best friend, and a good rival who's also been working to become the Wizard King. He controls Sylph, the spirit of wind.

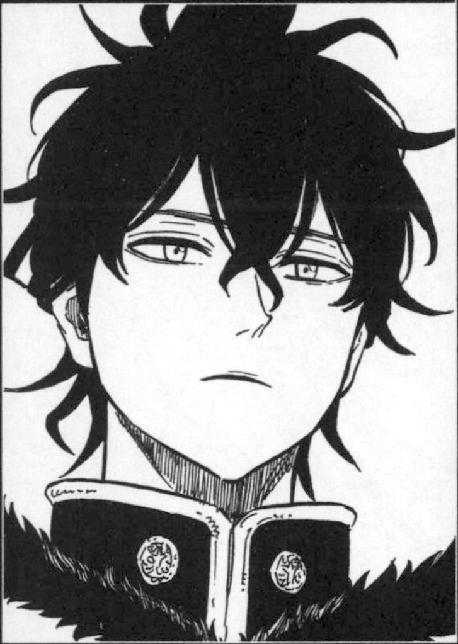

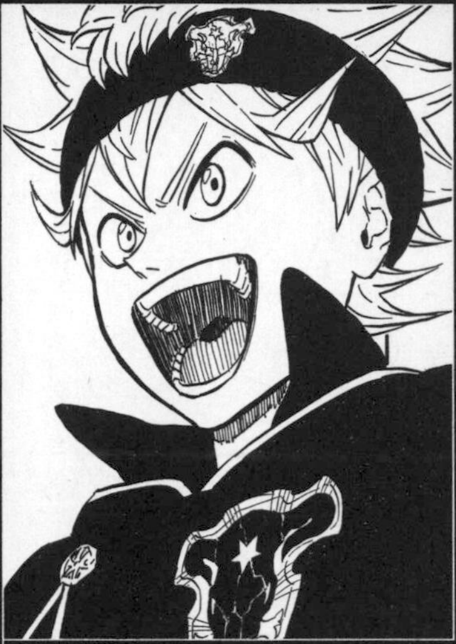

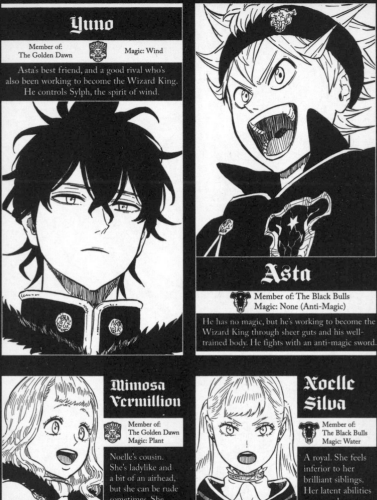

Asta

Member of: The Black Bulls
Magic: None (Anti-Magic)

He has no magic, but he's working to become the Wizard King through sheer guts and his well-trained body. He fights with an anti-magic sword.

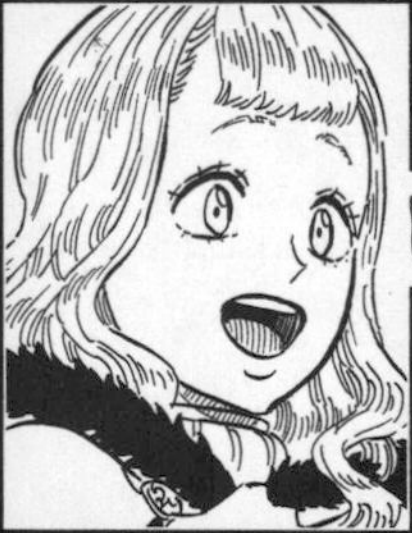

Mimosa Vermillion

Member of: The Golden Dawn
Magic: Plant

Noelle's cousin. She's ladylike and a bit of an airhead, but she can be rude sometimes. She might like Asta...

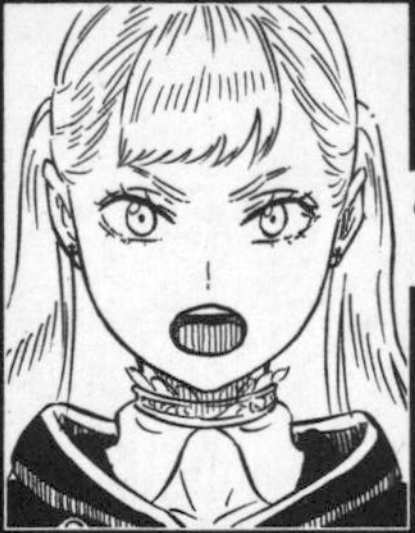

Noelle Silva

Member of: The Black Bulls
Magic: Water

A royal. She feels inferior to her brilliant siblings. Her latent abilities are an unknown quantity.

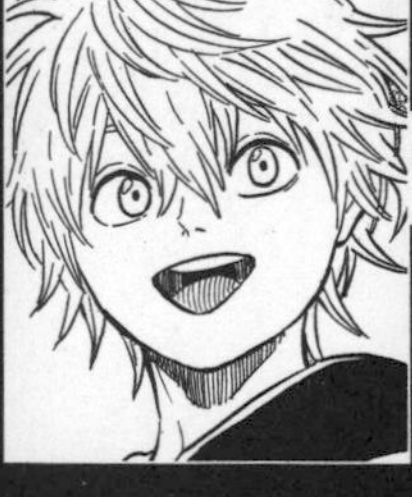

Luck Voltia

Member of: The Black Bulls
Magic: Lightning

A battle maniac. Once he starts fighting, he gets totally absorbed in it. Smiles constantly.

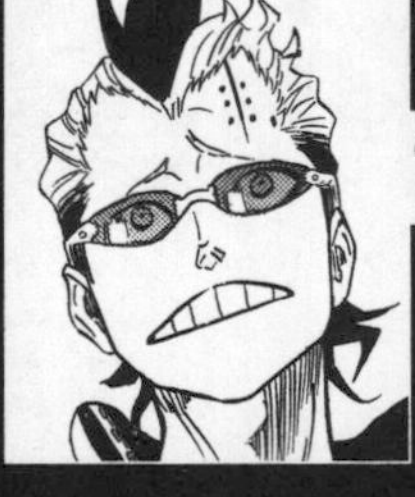

Magna Swing

Member of: The Black Bulls
Magic: Flame

He has the temperament of a delinquent, but he's quite courageous and does the right thing. Good at taking care of his companions.

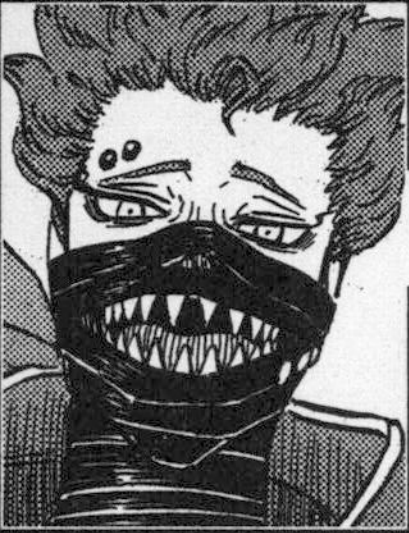

Zora Ideale

Member of: ?
Magic: Ash

He idolizes his father, who was a Magic Knight, and he's particularly good at trap spells. Has a cynical personality.

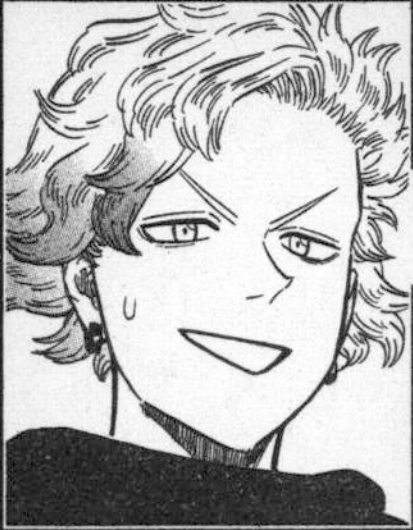

Finral Roulacase

Member of: The Black Bulls
Magic: Spatial

A flirt who immediately chats up any woman he sees. He can't attack, but he has high-level abilities.

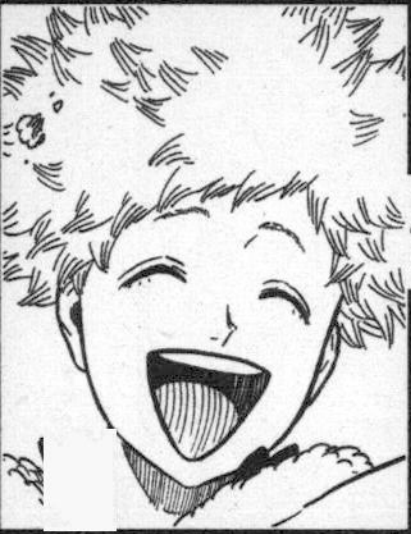

Bill Boismortier

Member of: The Aqua Deer
Magic: Picture

He has outstanding talent, and became a captain at an exceptionally young age. He made a surprise appearance as a contestant in the selection test.

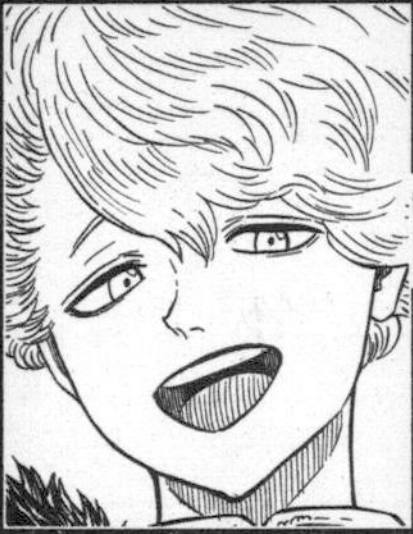

Langris Vaude

Member of: The Golden Dawn
Magic: Spatial

Finral's younger half brother. He isn't fond of Finral, who folded under the pressure of becoming head of their family.

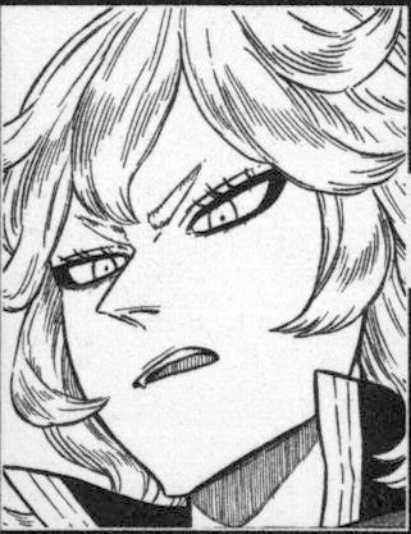

Mereoleona Vermillion

Member of: The Crimson Lion Kings
Magic: Flame

A brand-new captain. She has a stormy personality, and her high combat abilities are universally acknowledged.

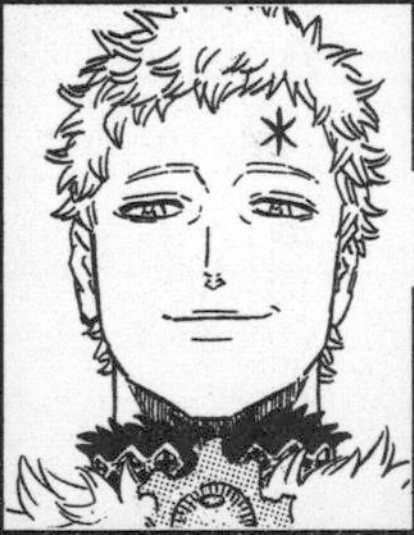

Julius Novachrono

Wizard King

The strongest man in the Clover Kingdom. Also a peerless magic fanatic. Hugely popular with the kingdom's citizens.

STORY

In a world where magic is everything, Asta and Yuno are both found abandoned on the same day at a church in the remote village of Hage. Both dream of becoming the Wizard King, the highest of all mages, and they spend their days working toward that dream.

The year they turn 15, both receive grimoires, magic books that amplify their bearer's magic. They take the entrance exam for the Magic Knights, nine groups of mages under the direct control of the Wizard King. Yuno, whose magic is strong, joins the Golden Dawn, an elite group, while Asta, who has no magic at all, joins the Black Bulls, a group of misfits. With this, the two finally take their first step toward becoming the Wizard King…

In the second round of the selection test, the brothers Finral and Langris face off and Langris wins. However, when he tries to strike a finishing blow, Asta flies into a rage. Their conflict gets out of control and it is decided that their fight will be counted as a third-round match. Who will win this fierce battle?!

CONTENTS

BLACK ✿ CLOVER

15

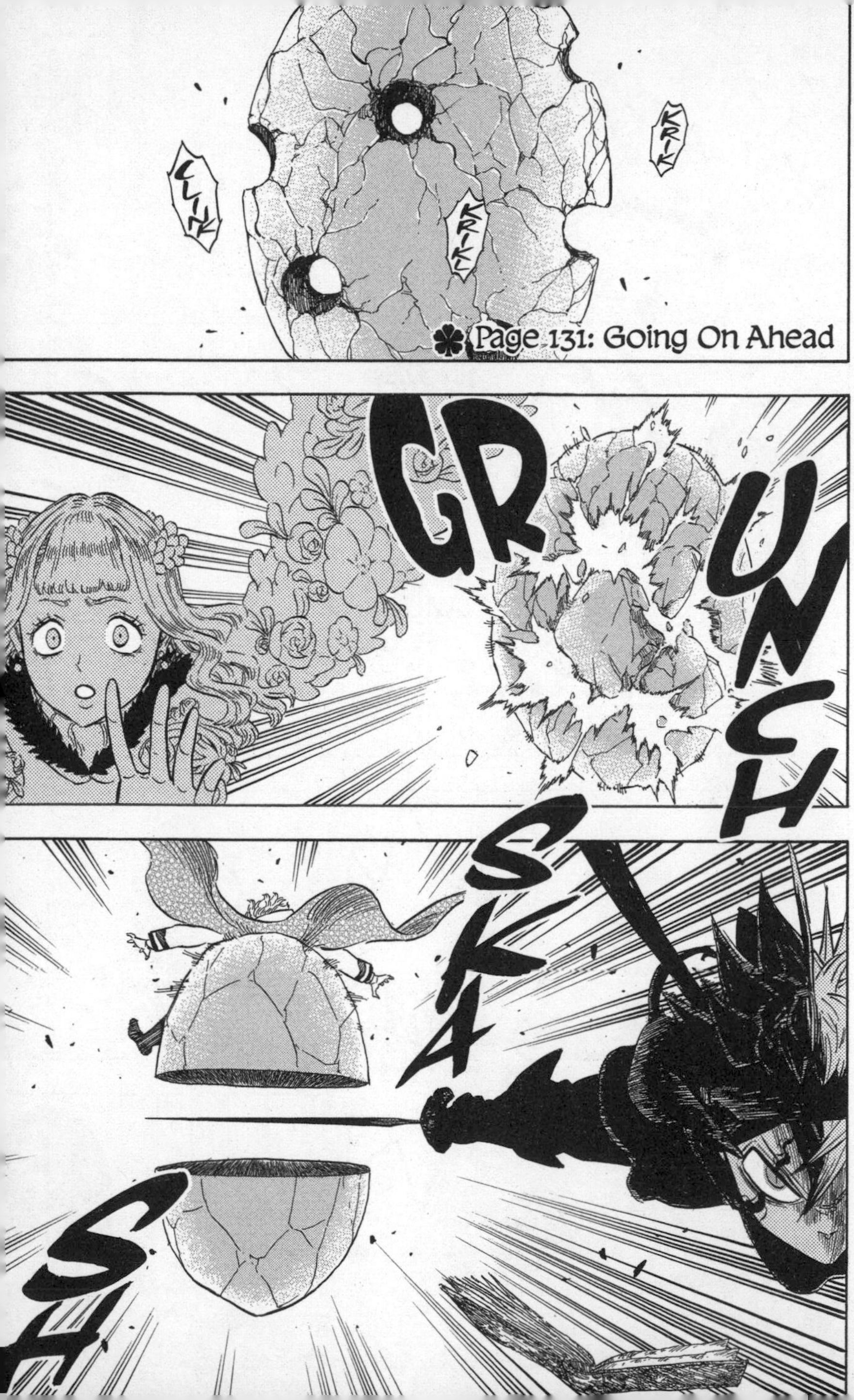

KRIK
KRIK
CLINK
Page 131: Going On Ahead
GRUNCH
SKA
SH

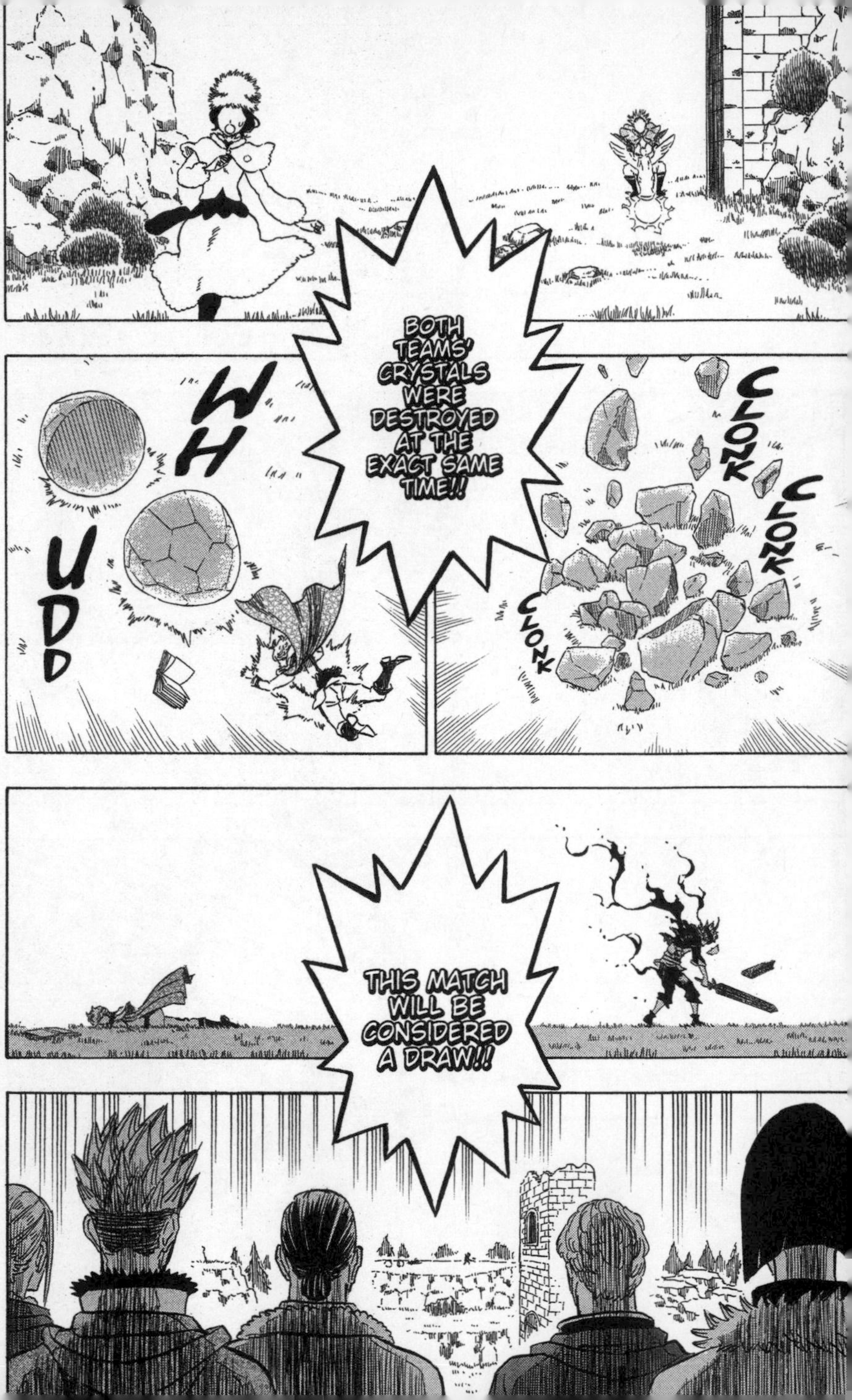
BOTH TEAMS' CRYSTALS WERE DESTROYED AT THE EXACT SAME TIME!!
CLONK
CLONK
CLONK
WHUDD
THIS MATCH WILL BE CONSIDERED A DRAW!!

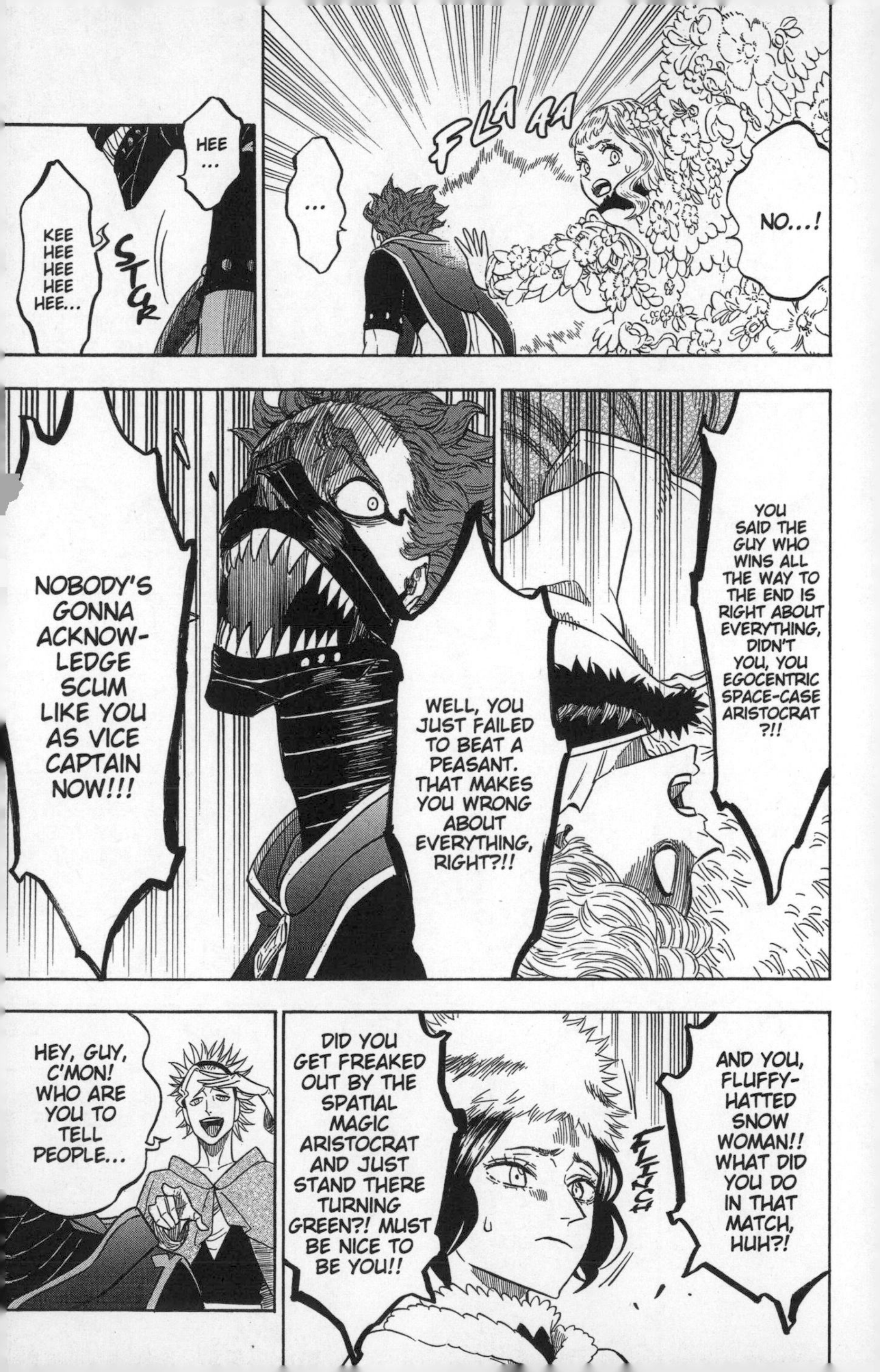
NO...!
FLA AA
...
HEE ...
KEE HEE HEE HEE HEE...
YOU SAID THE GUY WHO WINS ALL THE WAY TO THE END IS RIGHT ABOUT EVERYTHING, DIDN'T YOU, YOU EGOCENTRIC SPACE-CASE ARISTOCRAT ?!!
WELL, YOU JUST FAILED TO BEAT A PEASANT. THAT MAKES YOU WRONG ABOUT EVERYTHING, RIGHT?!!
NOBODY'S GONNA ACKNOW-LEDGE SCUM LIKE YOU AS VICE CAPTAIN NOW!!!
AND YOU, FLUFFY-HATTED SNOW WOMAN!! WHAT DID YOU DO IN THAT MATCH, HUH?!
DID YOU GET FREAKED OUT BY THE SPATIAL MAGIC ARISTOCRAT AND JUST STAND THERE TURNING GREEN?! MUST BE NICE TO BE YOU!!
HEY, GUY, C'MON! WHO ARE YOU TO TELL PEOPLE...

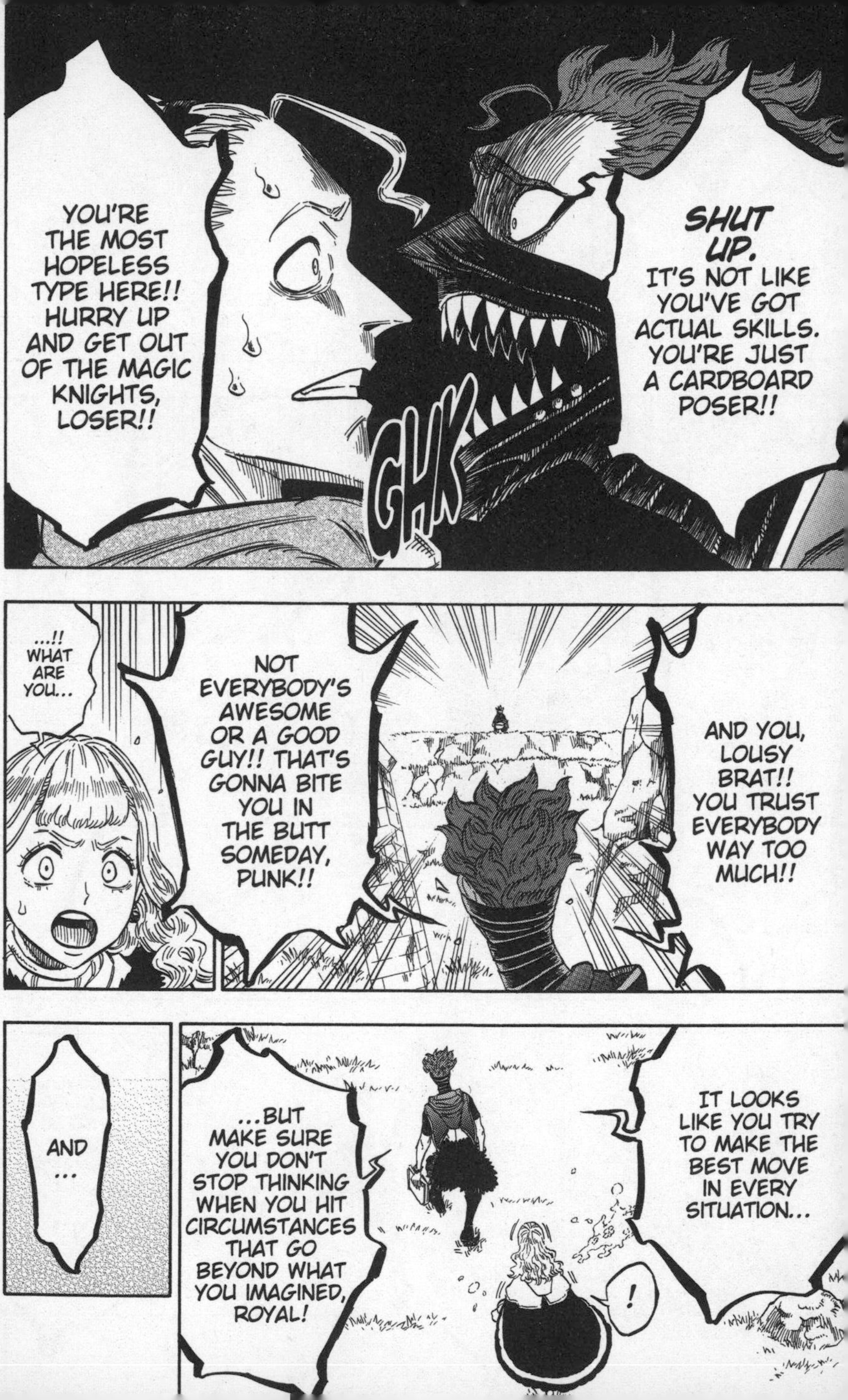
SHUT UP.
IT'S NOT LIKE YOU'VE GOT ACTUAL SKILLS. YOU'RE JUST A CARDBOARD POSER!!
GHK
YOU'RE THE MOST HOPELESS TYPE HERE!! HURRY UP AND GET OUT OF THE MAGIC KNIGHTS, LOSER!!
AND YOU, LOUSY BRAT!! YOU TRUST EVERYBODY WAY TOO MUCH!!
NOT EVERYBODY'S AWESOME OR A GOOD GUY!! THAT'S GONNA BITE YOU IN THE BUTT SOMEDAY, PUNK!!
...!! WHAT ARE YOU...
IT LOOKS LIKE YOU TRY TO MAKE THE BEST MOVE IN EVERY SITUATION...
...BUT MAKE SURE YOU DON'T STOP THINKING WHEN YOU HIT CIRCUMSTANCES THAT GO BEYOND WHAT YOU IMAGINED, ROYAL!
!
AND ...

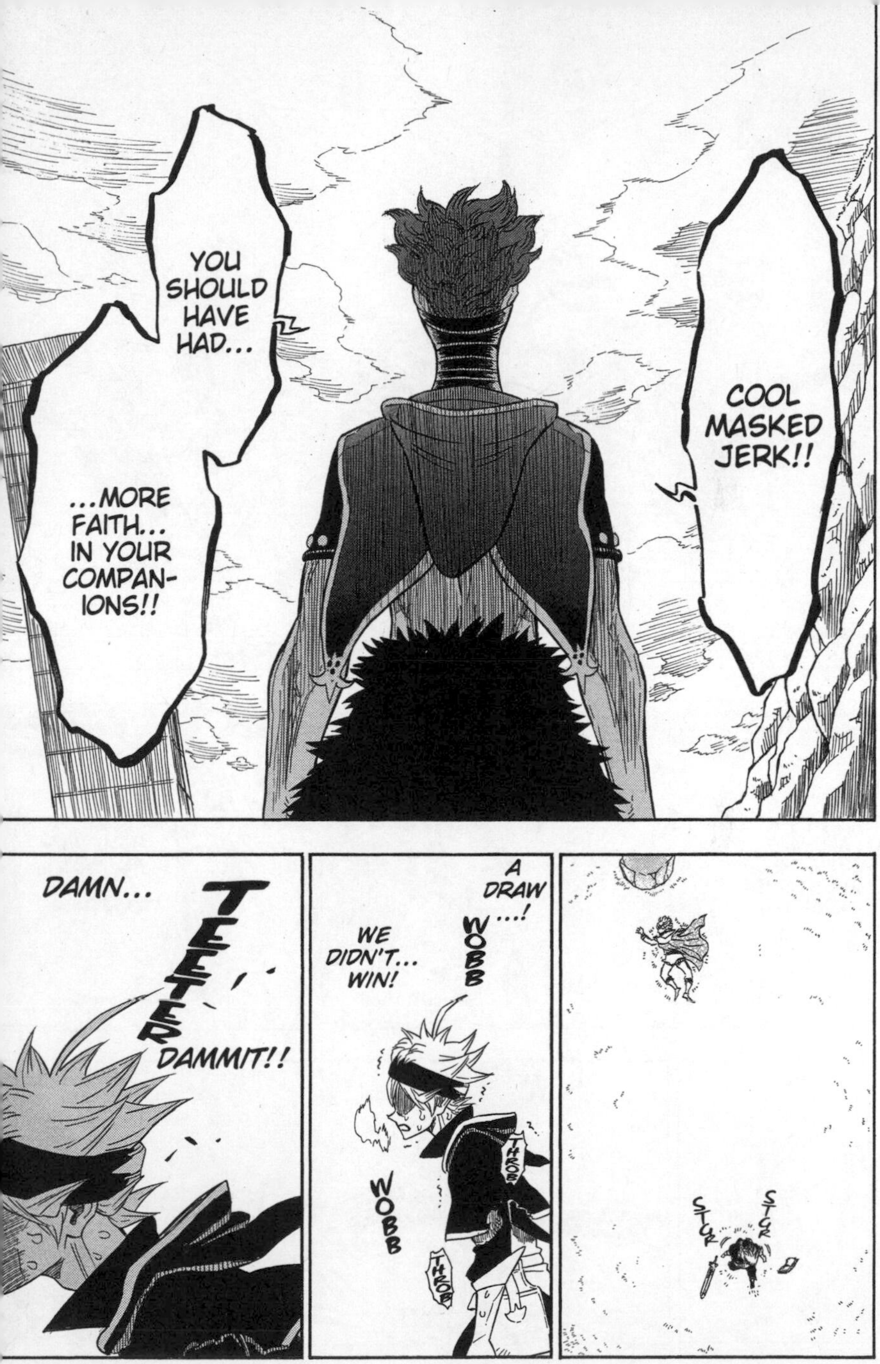
YOU SHOULD HAVE HAD...
...MORE FAITH... IN YOUR COMPAN- IONS!!
COOL MASKED JERK!!
STGR
STGR
A DRAW ...!
WOBB
WE DIDN'T... WIN!
THROB
WOBB
THROB
TEETER
DAMN...
DAMMIT!!

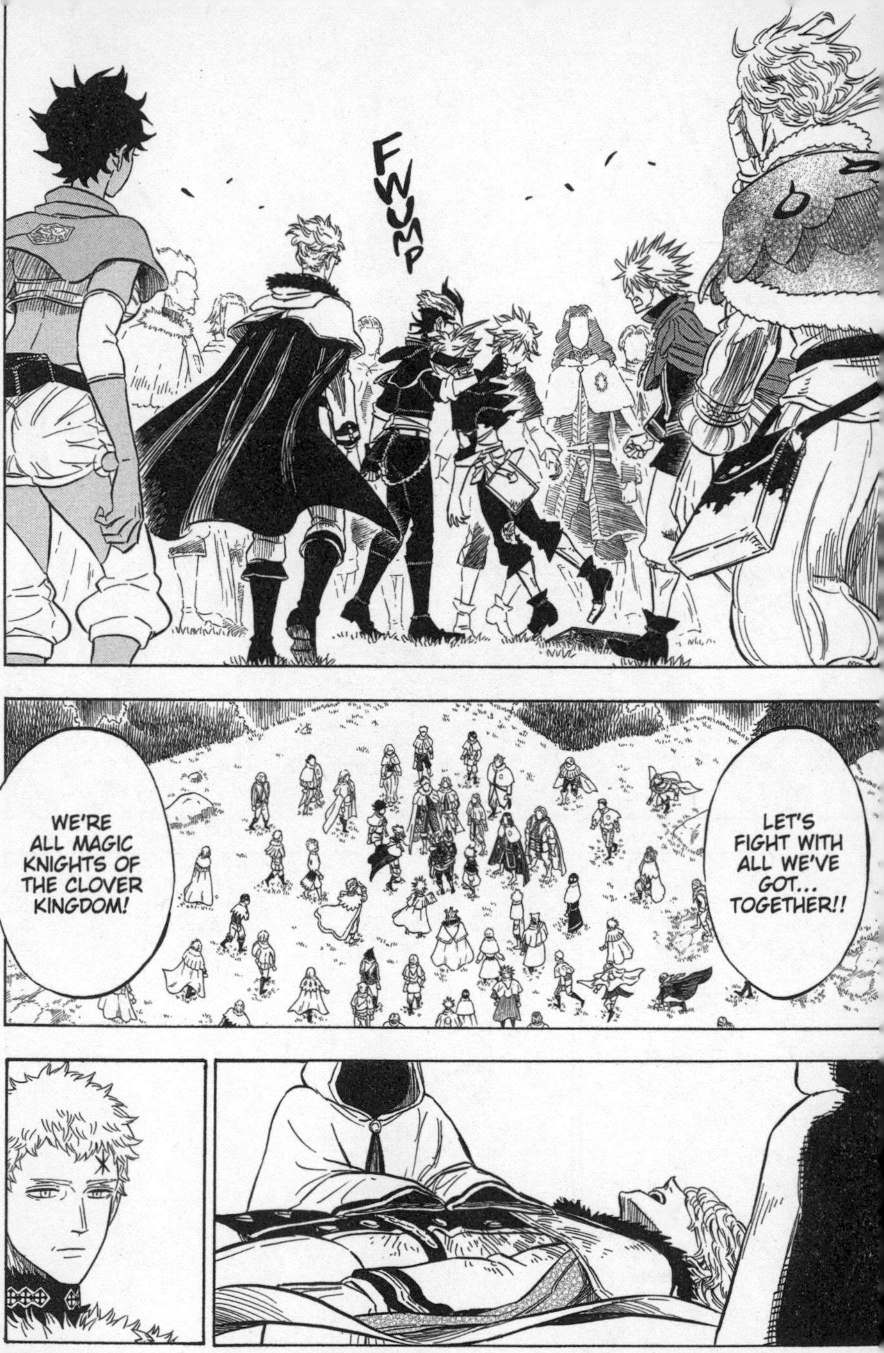
FWUMP
LET'S FIGHT WITH ALL WE'VE GOT... TOGETHER!!
WE'RE ALL MAGIC KNIGHTS OF THE CLOVER KINGDOM!

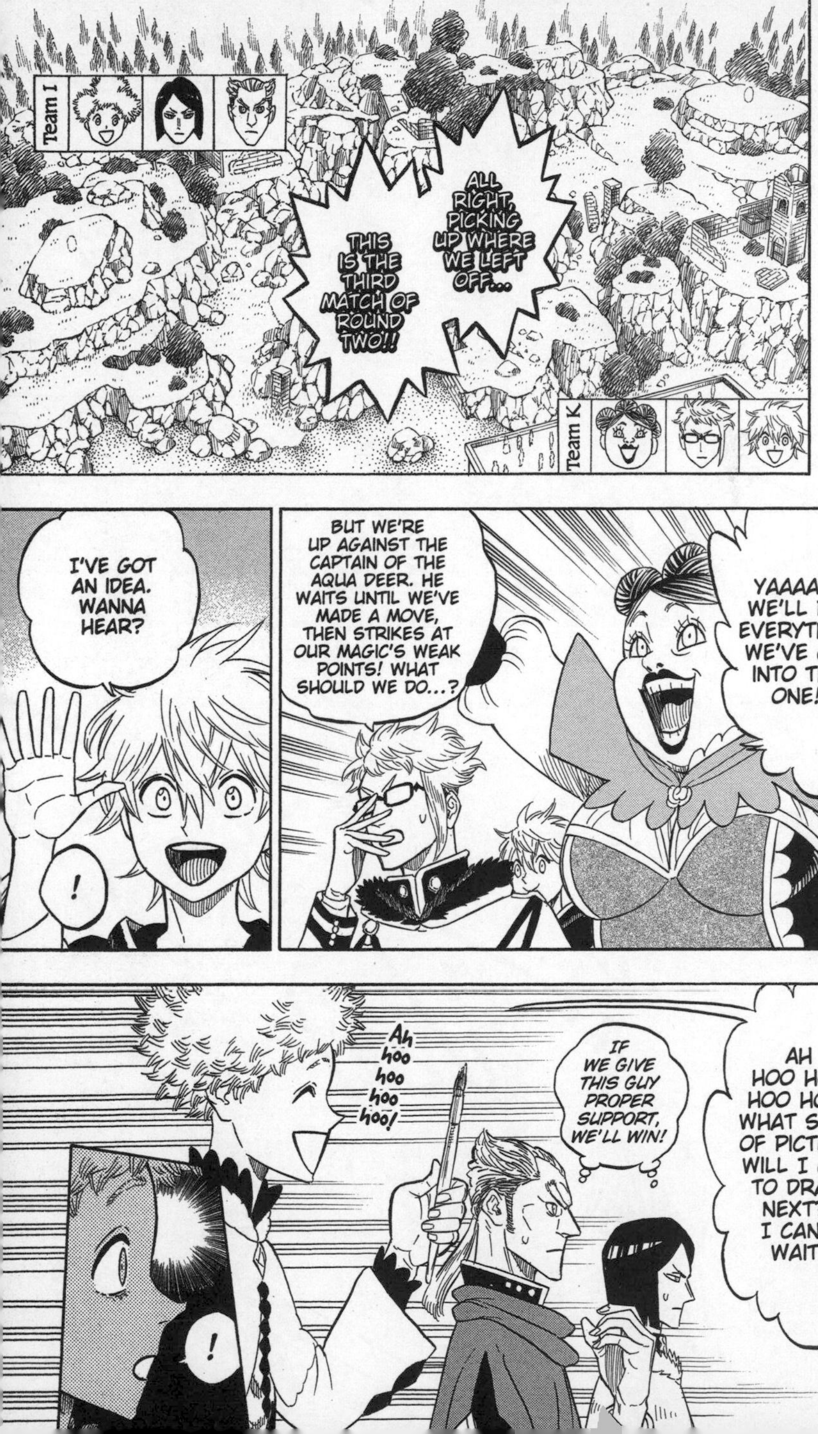
Team I
ALL RIGHT, PICKING UP WHERE WE LEFT OFF...
THIS IS THE THIRD MATCH OF ROUND TWO!!
Team K
YAAAAY!! WE'LL PUT EVERYTHING WE'VE GOT INTO THIS ONE!!
BUT WE'RE UP AGAINST THE CAPTAIN OF THE AQUA DEER. HE WAITS UNTIL WE'VE MADE A MOVE, THEN STRIKES AT OUR MAGIC'S WEAK POINTS! WHAT SHOULD WE DO...?
I'VE GOT AN IDEA. WANNA HEAR?
!
AH HOO HOO HOO HOO! WHAT SORT OF PICTURE WILL I GET TO DRAW NEXT?! I CAN'T WAIT!
IF WE GIVE THIS GUY PROPER SUPPORT, WE'LL WIN!
Ah hoo hoo hoo hoo!
!

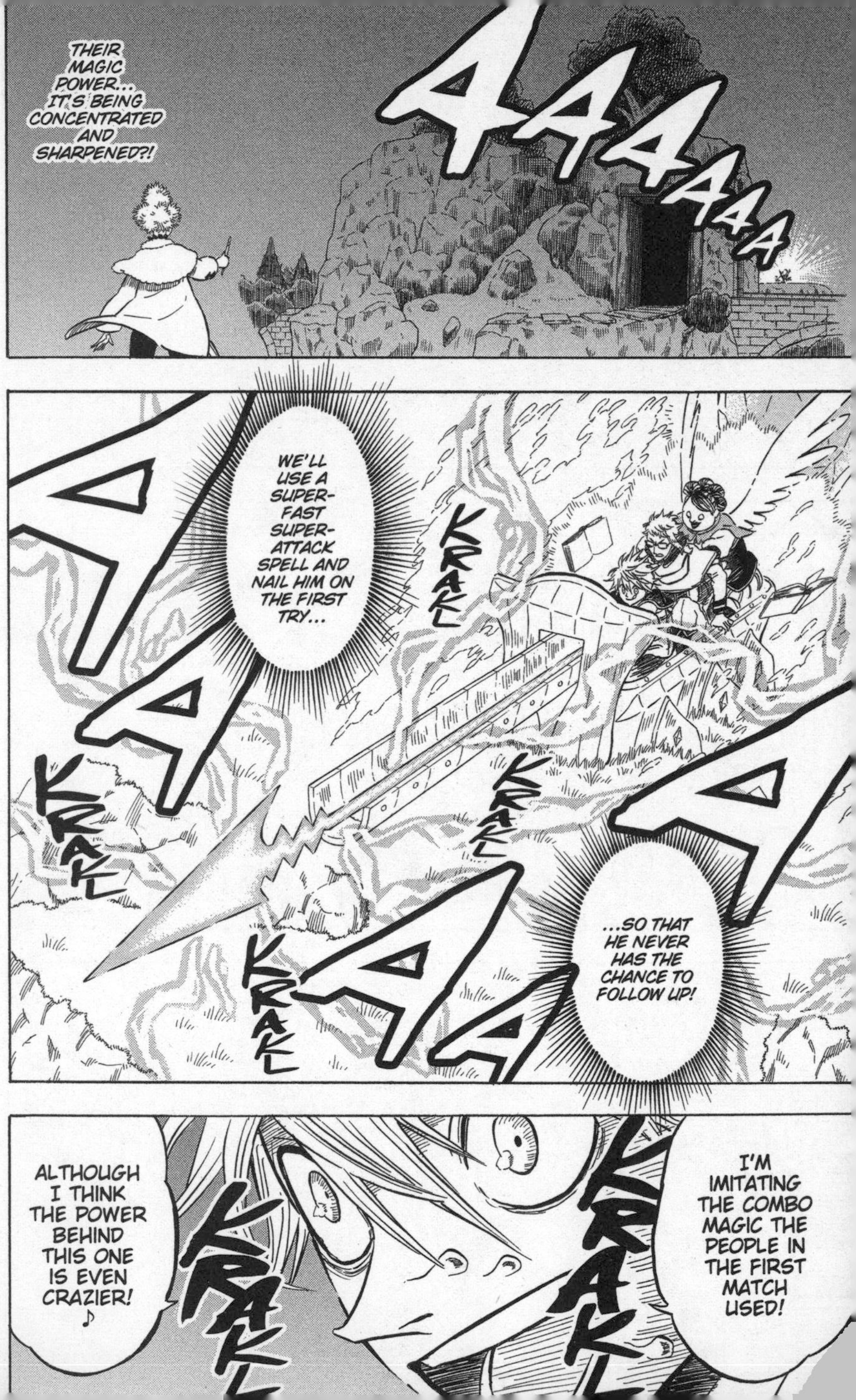
AAAAAAA
THEIR MAGIC POWER... IT'S BEING CONCENTRATED AND SHARPENED?!
AAAA
KRAKL
WE'LL USE A SUPER-FAST SUPER-ATTACK SPELL AND NAIL HIM ON THE FIRST TRY...
KRAKL
KRAKL
KRAKL
...SO THAT HE NEVER HAS THE CHANCE TO FOLLOW UP!
I'M IMITATING THE COMBO MAGIC THE PEOPLE IN THE FIRST MATCH USED!
KRAKL
KRAKL
ALTHOUGH I THINK THE POWER BEHIND THIS ONE IS EVEN CRAZIER! ♪

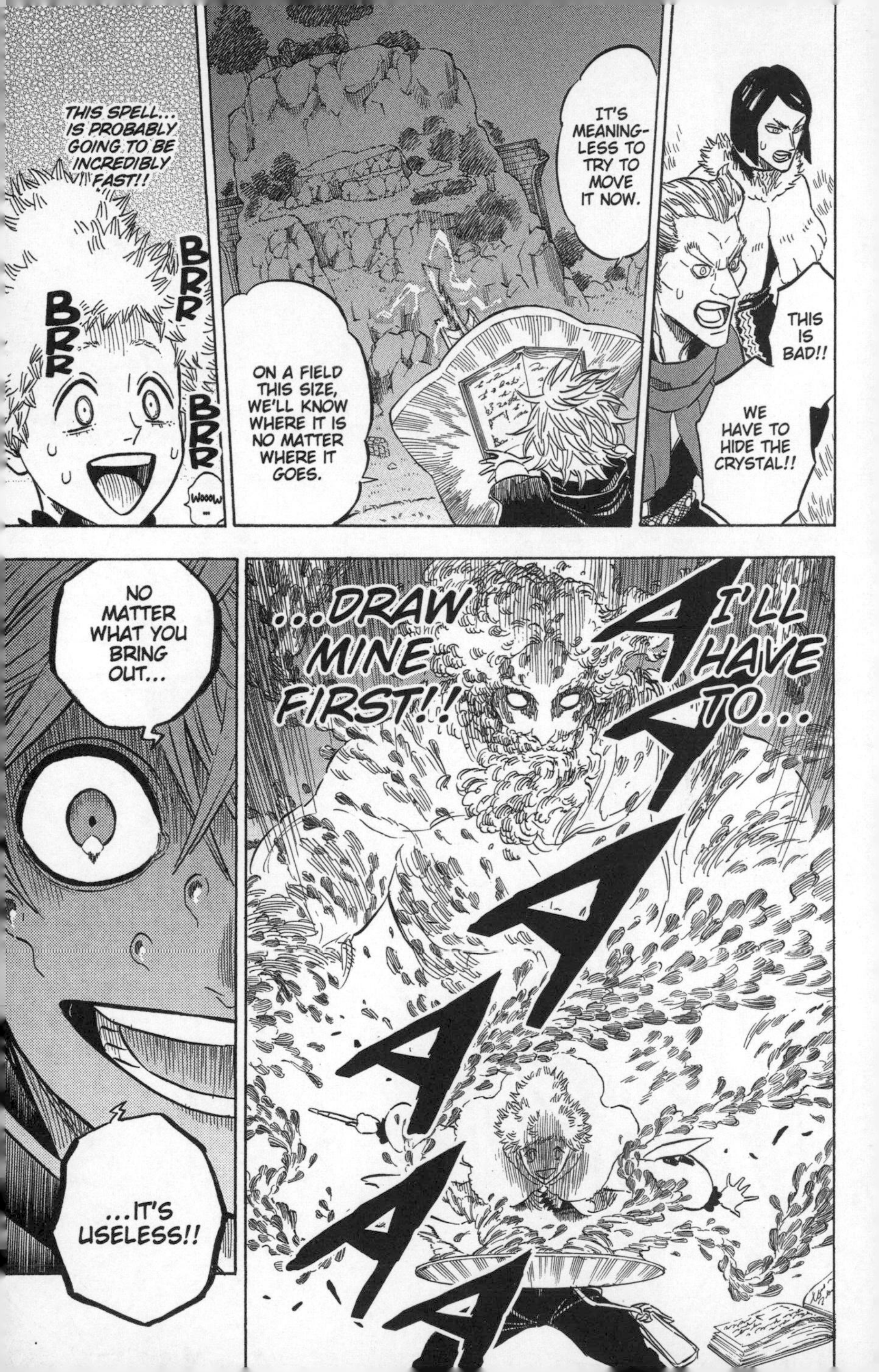
THIS IS BAD!!
WE HAVE TO HIDE THE CRYSTAL!!
IT'S MEANINGLESS TO TRY TO MOVE IT NOW.
ON A FIELD THIS SIZE, WE'LL KNOW WHERE IT IS NO MATTER WHERE IT GOES.
THIS SPELL... IS PROBABLY GOING TO BE INCREDIBLY FAST!!
BRR
BRR
BRR
WOOOW...
I'LL HAVE TO...
...DRAW MINE FIRST!!
AAAAAAAA
NO MATTER WHAT YOU BRING OUT...
...IT'S USELESS!!

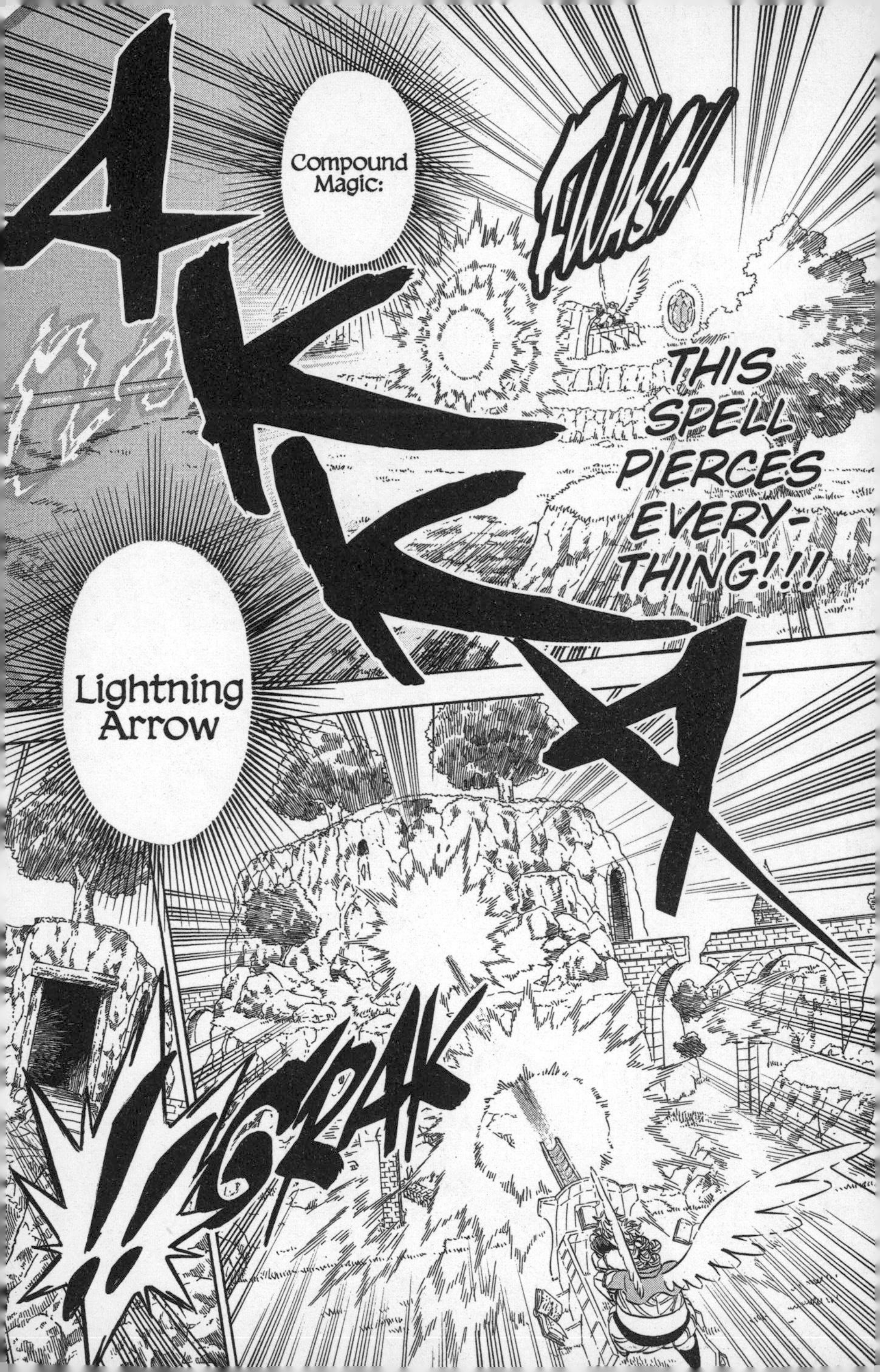
Compound Magic:
Lightning Arrow
THIS SPELL PIERCES EVERY-THING!!!

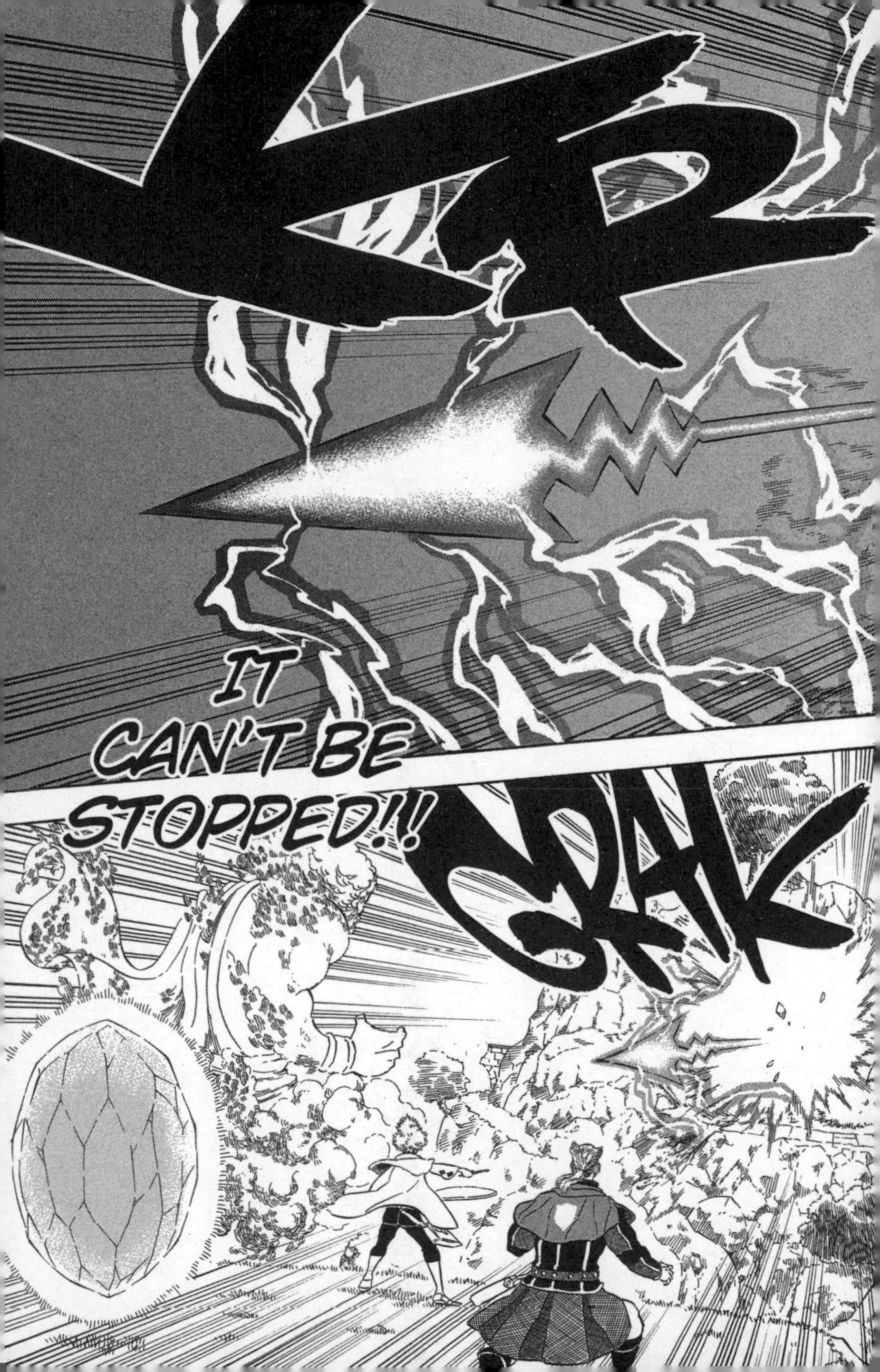
IT CAN'T BE STOPPED!!
CRAK

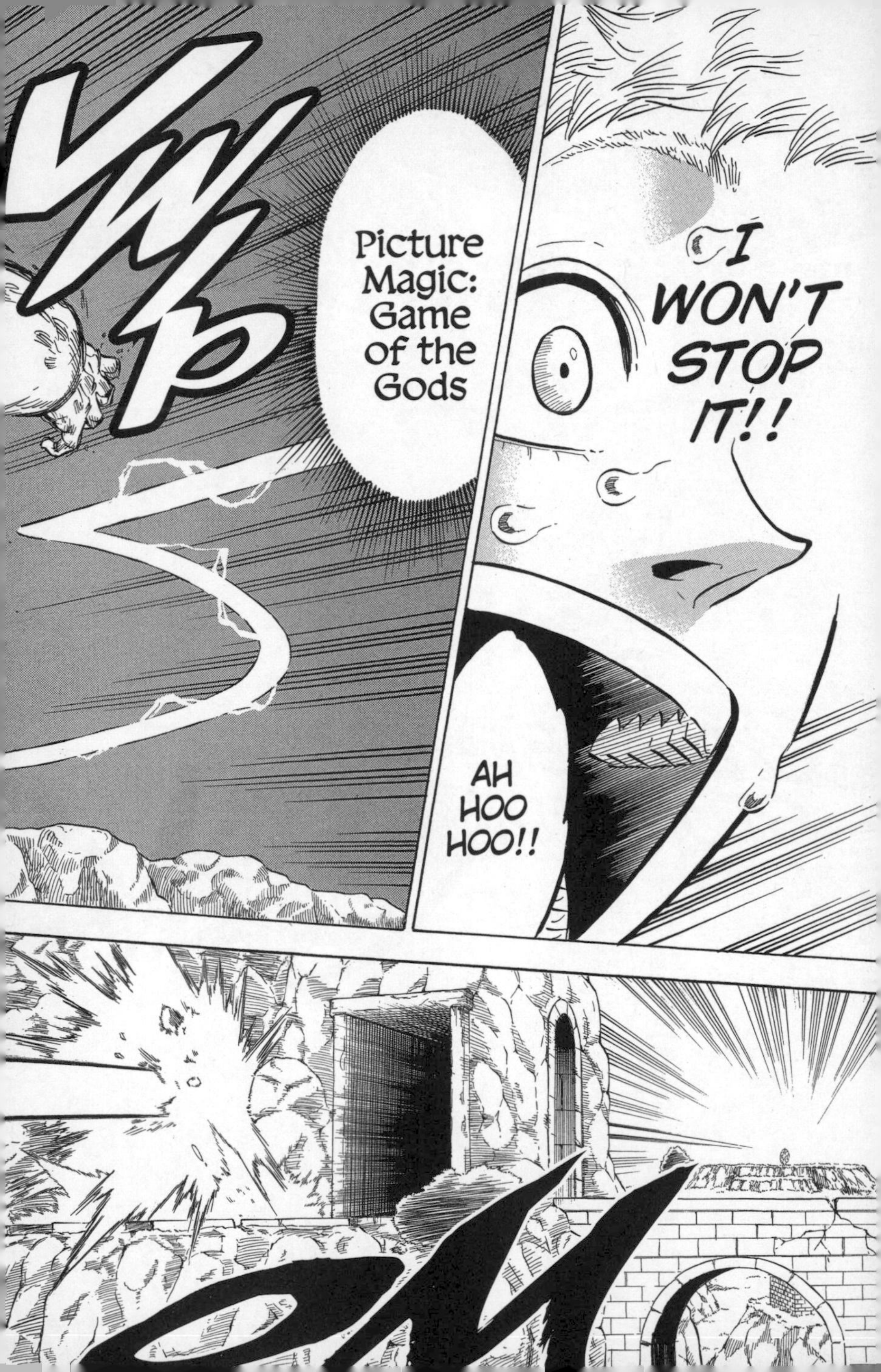
I WON'T STOP IT!!
AH HOO HOO!!
Picture Magic: Game of the Gods

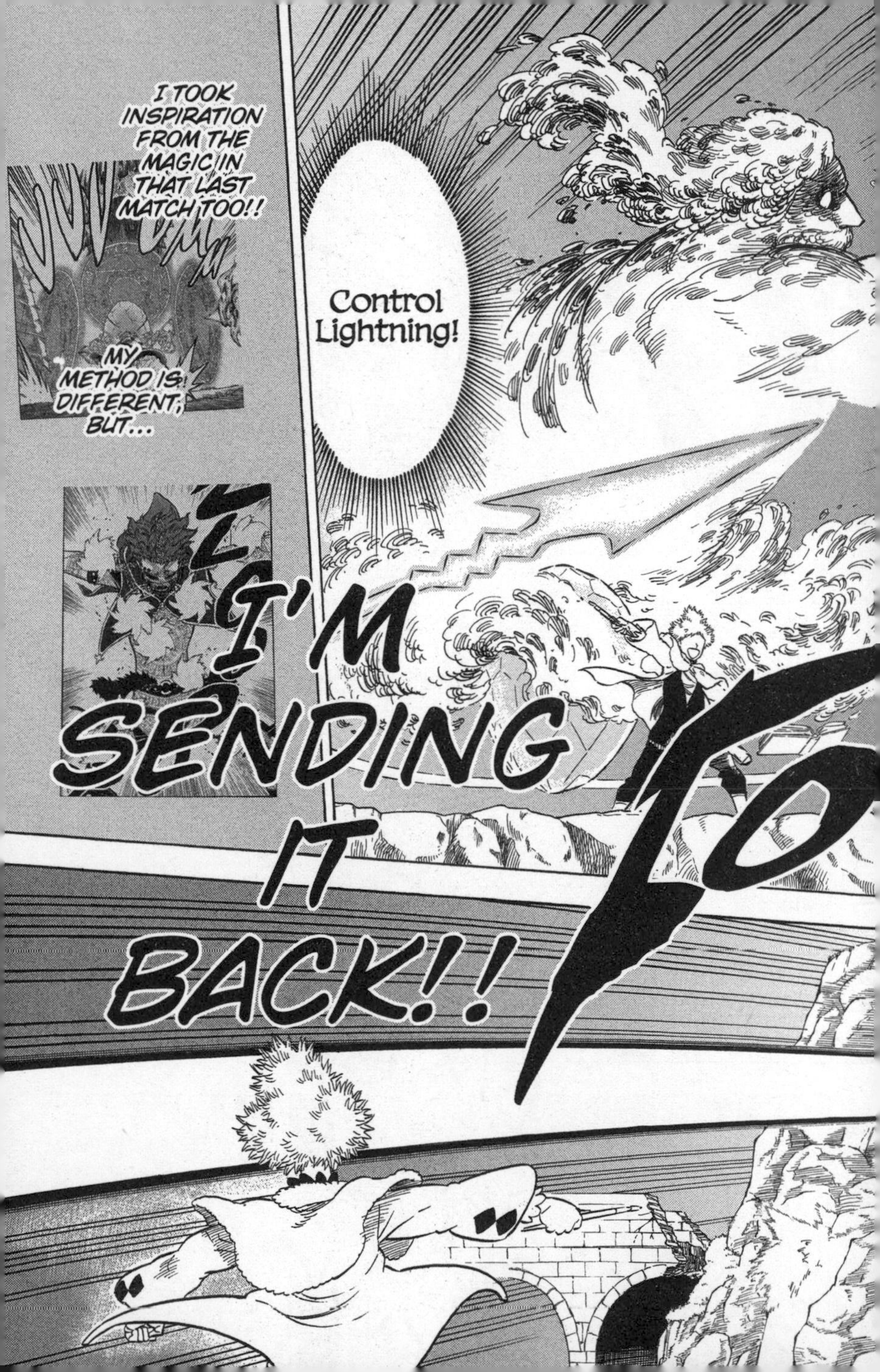
Control Lightning!
I TOOK INSPIRATION FROM THE MAGIC IN THAT LAST MATCH TOO!!
MY METHOD IS DIFFERENT, BUT...
I'M SENDING IT BACK!!

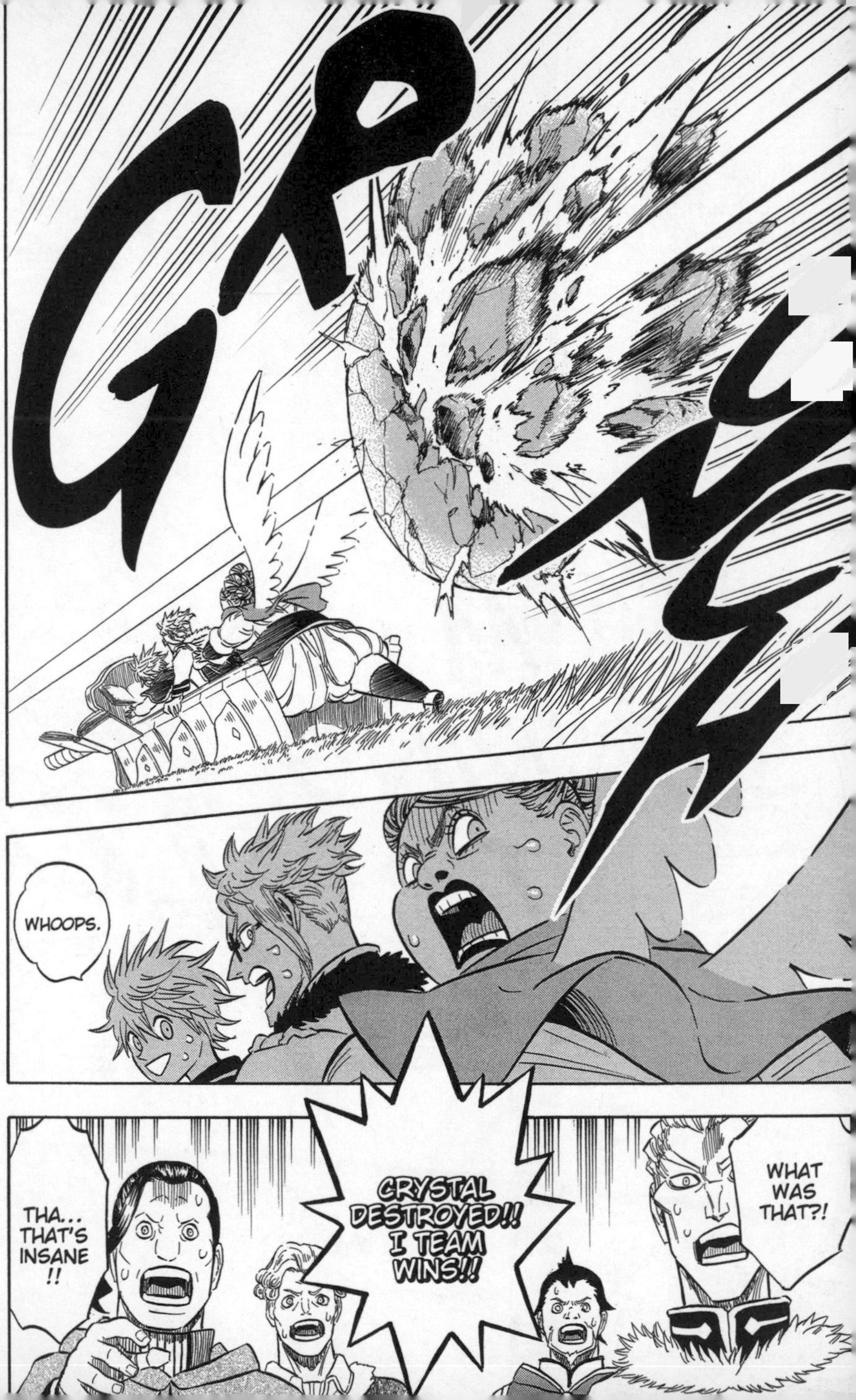
GRASH
WHOOPS.
WHAT WAS THAT?!
CRYSTAL DESTROYED!! I TEAM WINS!!
THA... THAT'S INSANE!!

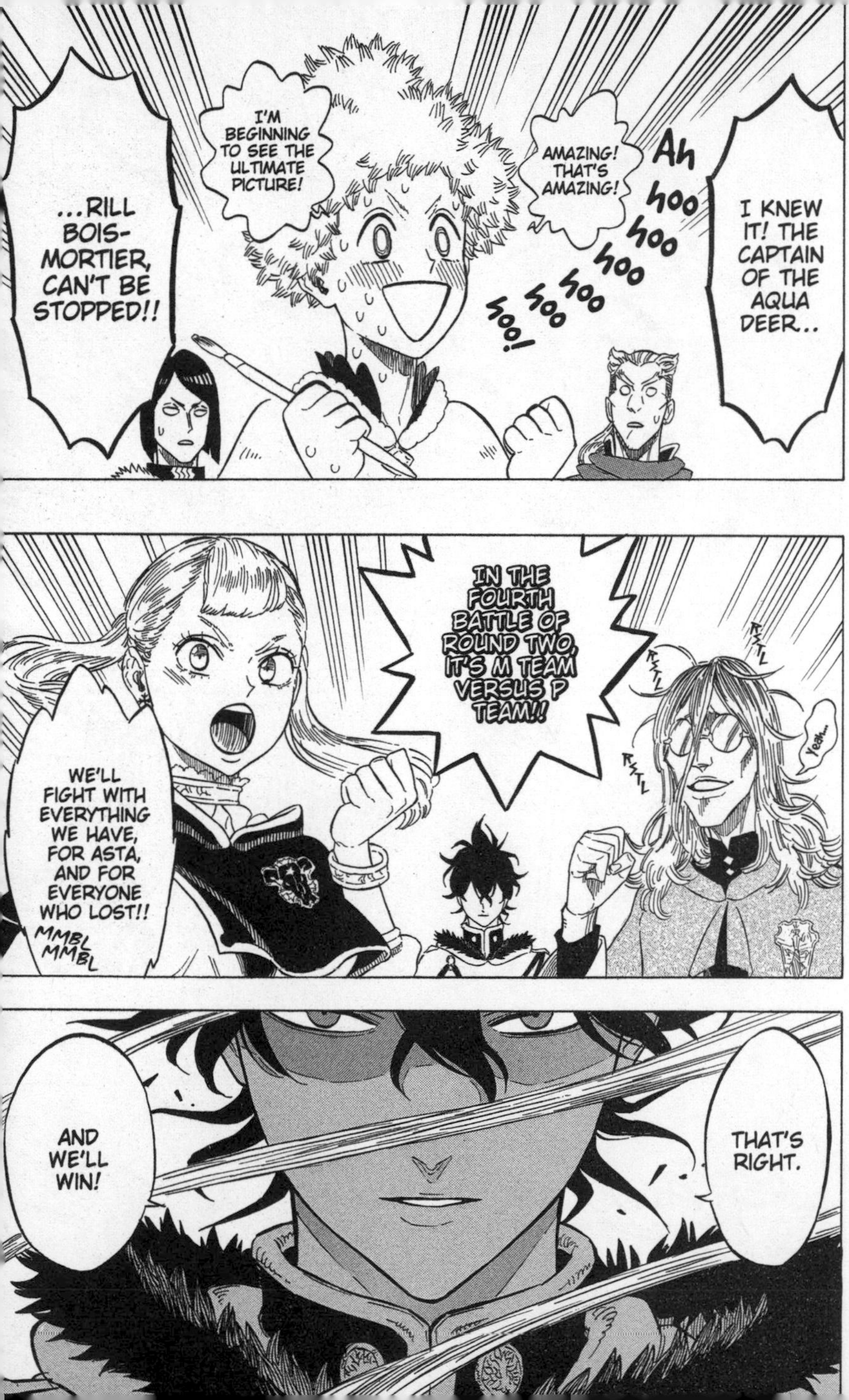
I KNEW IT! THE CAPTAIN OF THE AQUA DEER...
Ah hoo hoo hoo hoo hoo hoo!
AMAZING! THAT'S AMAZING!
I'M BEGINNING TO SEE THE ULTIMATE PICTURE!
...RILL BOIS-MORTIER, CAN'T BE STOPPED!!
RSTL
RSTL
RSTL
Yeah...
IN THE FOURTH BATTLE OF ROUND TWO, IT'S M TEAM VERSUS P TEAM!!
WE'LL FIGHT WITH EVERYTHING WE HAVE, FOR ASTA, AND FOR EVERYONE WHO LOST!!
MMBL MMBL
THAT'S RIGHT.
AND WE'LL WIN!

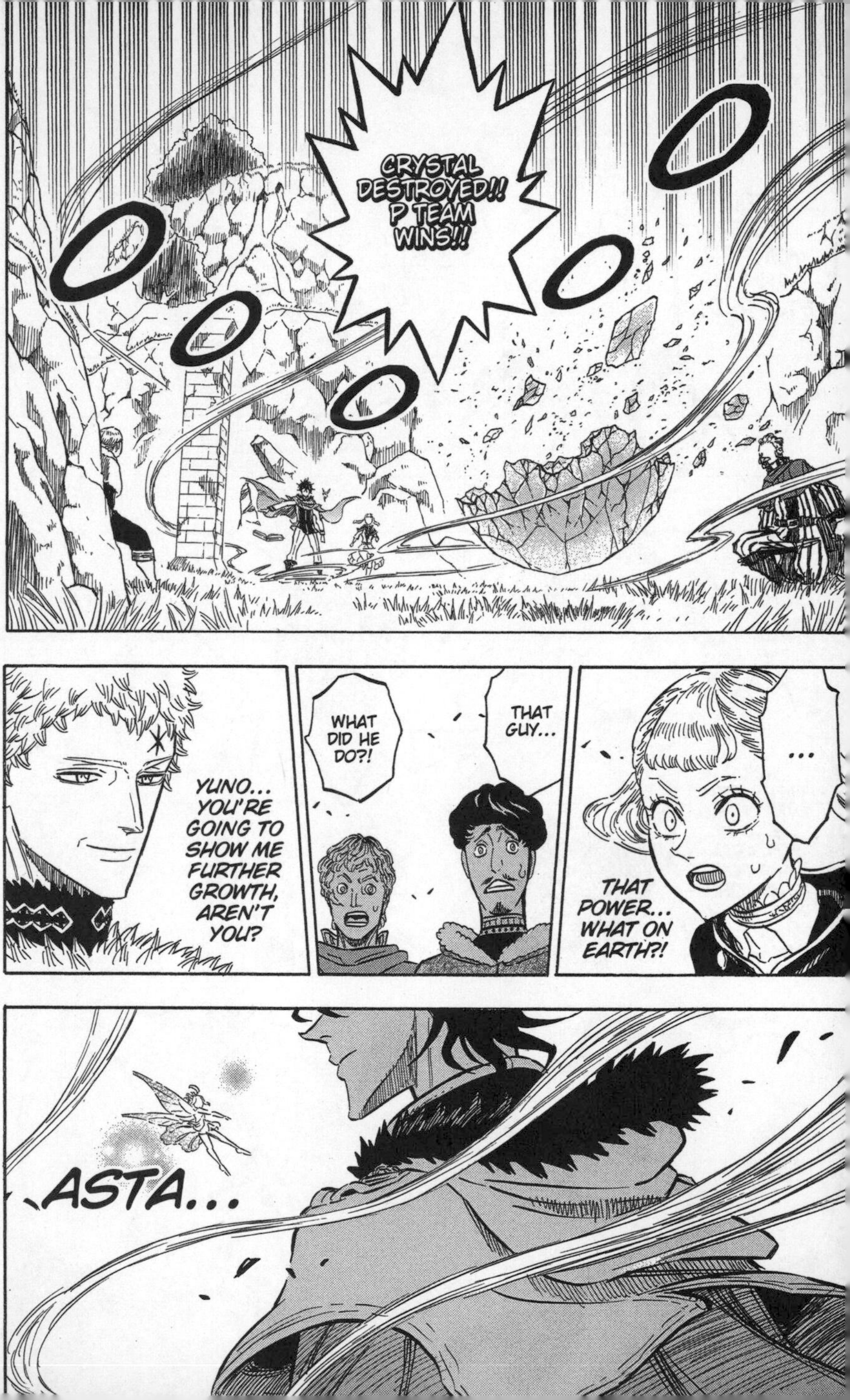
CRYSTAL DESTROYED!! P TEAM WINS!!
...
THAT POWER... WHAT ON EARTH?!
THAT GUY...
WHAT DID HE DO?!
YUNO... YOU'RE GOING TO SHOW ME FURTHER GROWTH, AREN'T YOU?
ASTA...

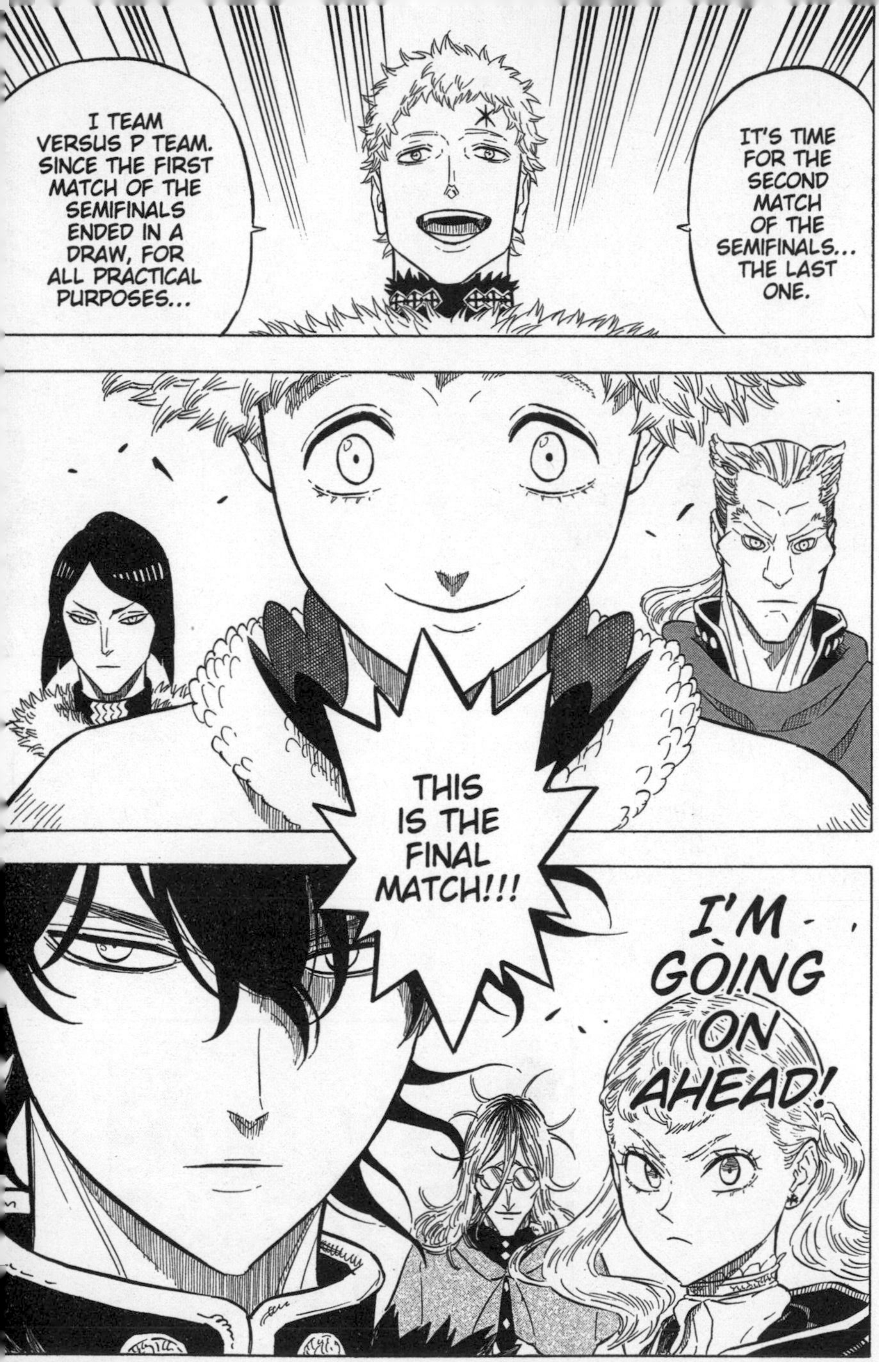
IT'S TIME FOR THE SECOND MATCH OF THE SEMIFINALS... THE LAST ONE.
I TEAM VERSUS P TEAM. SINCE THE FIRST MATCH OF THE SEMIFINALS ENDED IN A DRAW, FOR ALL PRACTICAL PURPOSES...
THIS IS THE FINAL MATCH!!!
I'M GOING ON AHEAD!

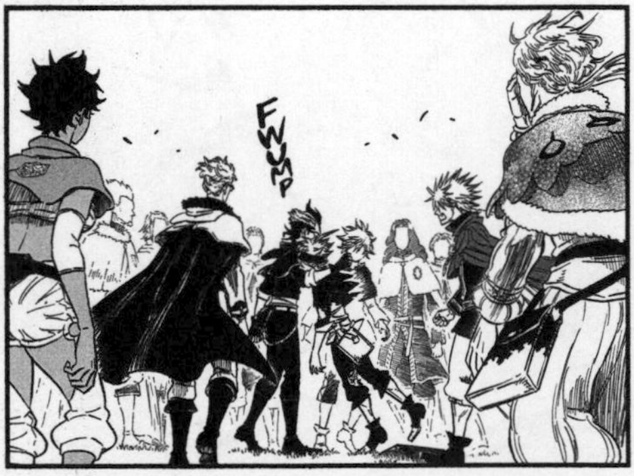
FWUMP

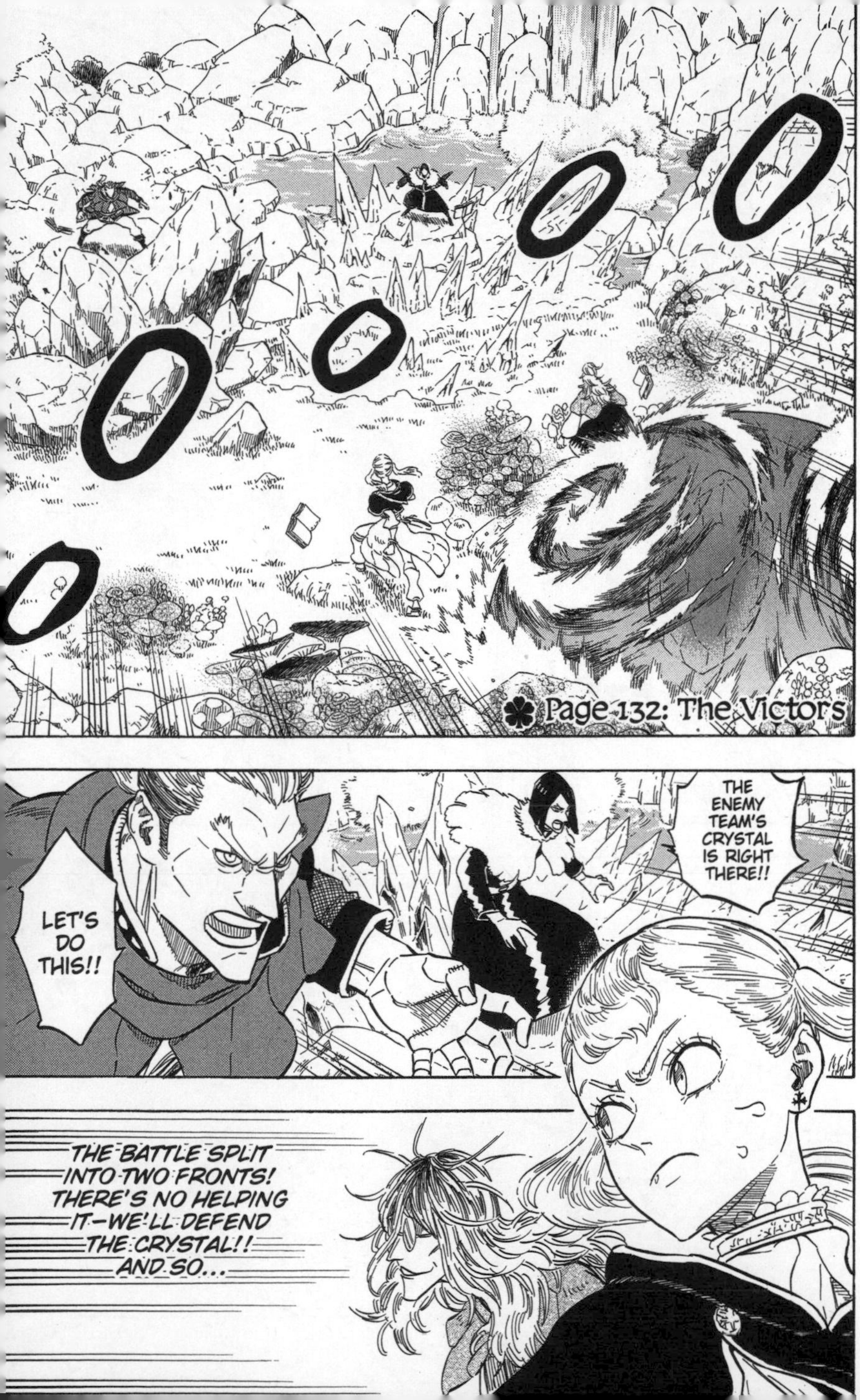
Page 132: The Victors
THE ENEMY TEAM'S CRYSTAL IS RIGHT THERE!!
LET'S DO THIS!!
THE BATTLE SPLIT INTO TWO FRONTS! THERE'S NO HELPING IT—WE'LL DEFEND THE CRYSTAL!! AND SO...

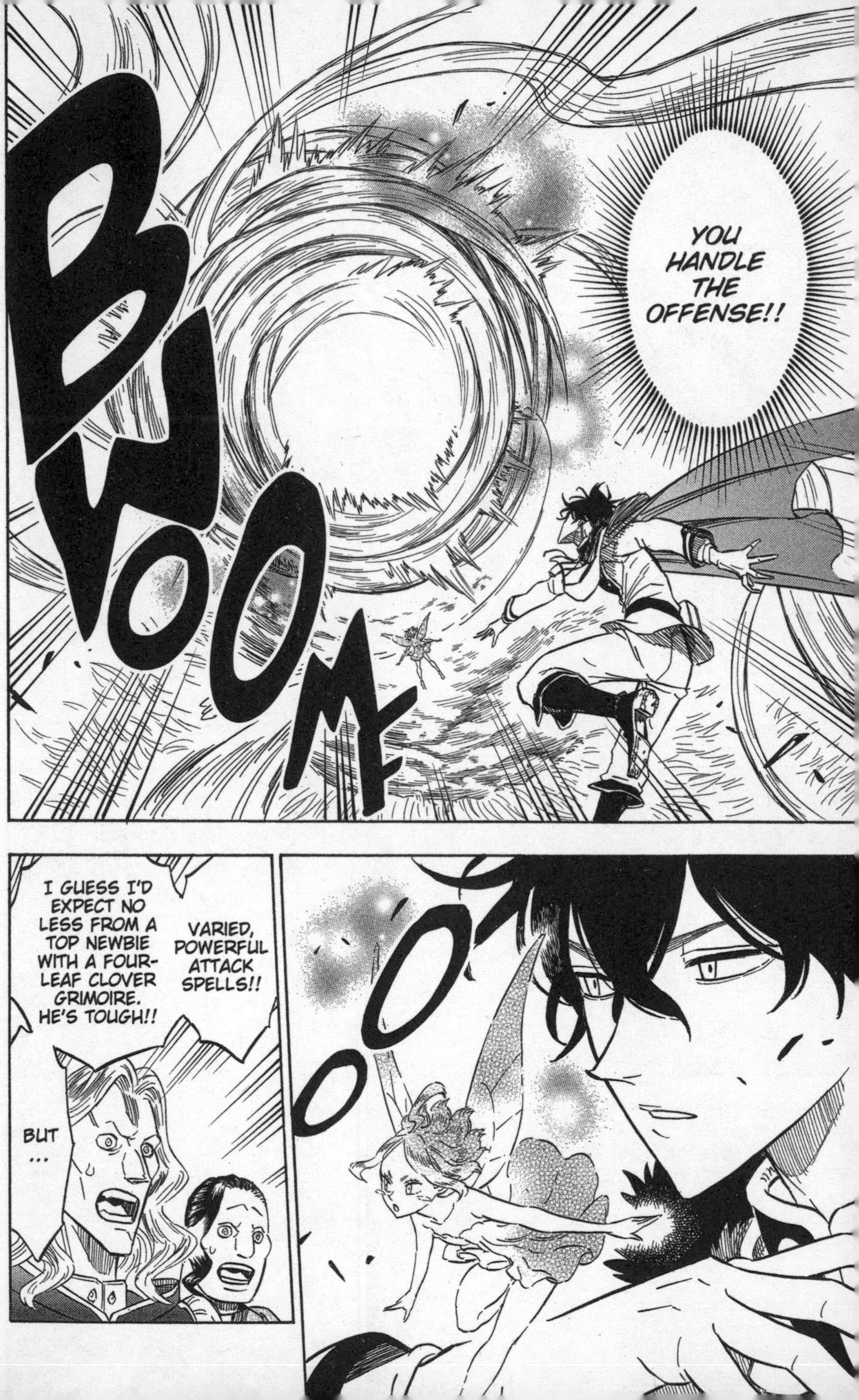
BWOOOM
YOU HANDLE THE OFFENSE!!
VARIED, POWERFUL ATTACK SPELLS!!
I GUESS I'D EXPECT NO LESS FROM A TOP NEWBIE WITH A FOUR-LEAF CLOVER GRIMOIRE. HE'S TOUGH!!
BUT...

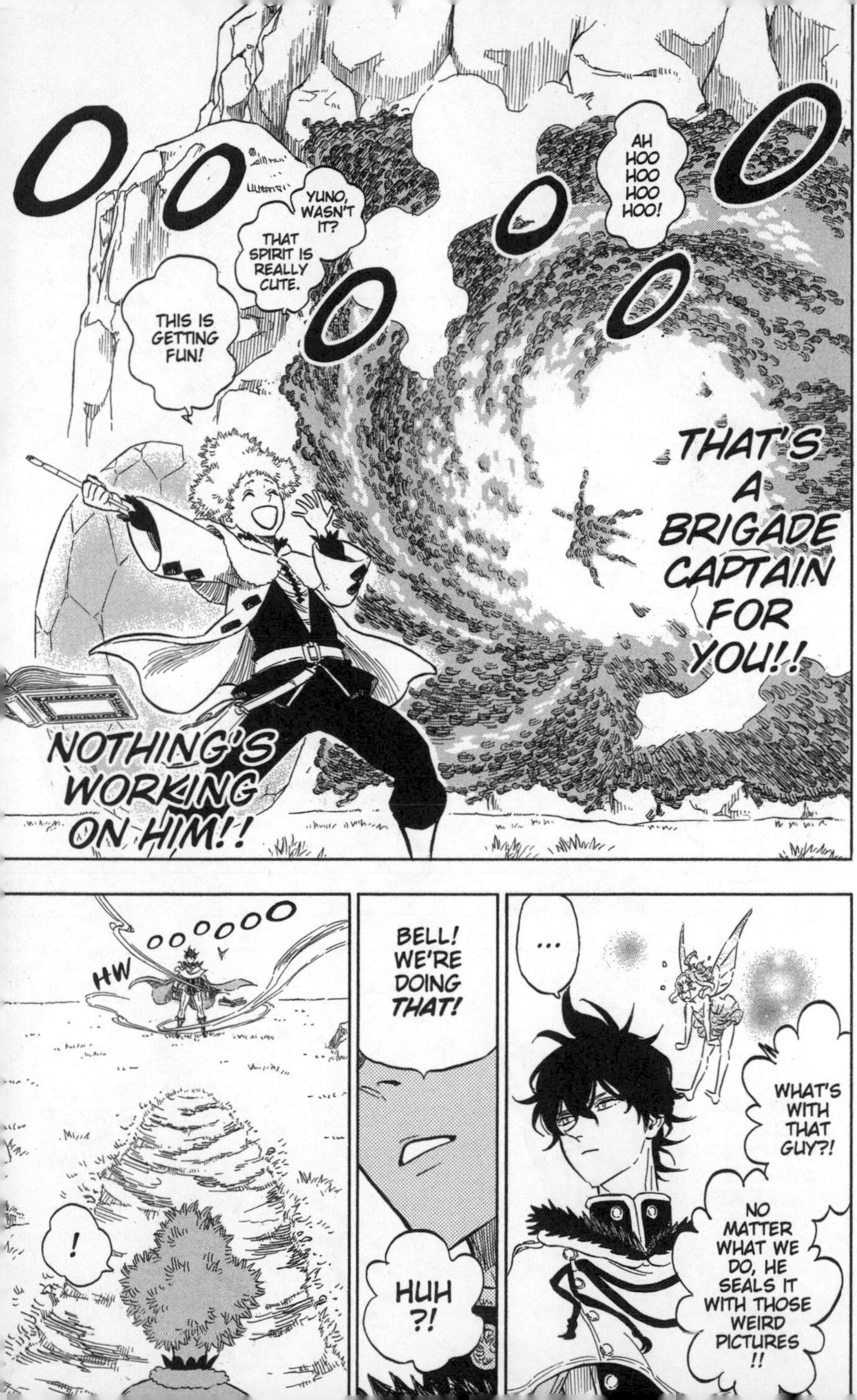
OOOOOO
AH HOO HOO HOO HOO!
YUNO, WASN'T IT?
THAT SPIRIT IS REALLY CUTE.
THIS IS GETTING FUN!
THAT'S A BRIGADE CAPTAIN FOR YOU!!
NOTHING'S WORKING ON HIM!!
...
WHAT'S WITH THAT GUY?!
NO MATTER WHAT WE DO, HE SEALS IT WITH THOSE WEIRD PICTURES!!
BELL! WE'RE DOING THAT!
HUH?!
HW
OOOOOOO
!

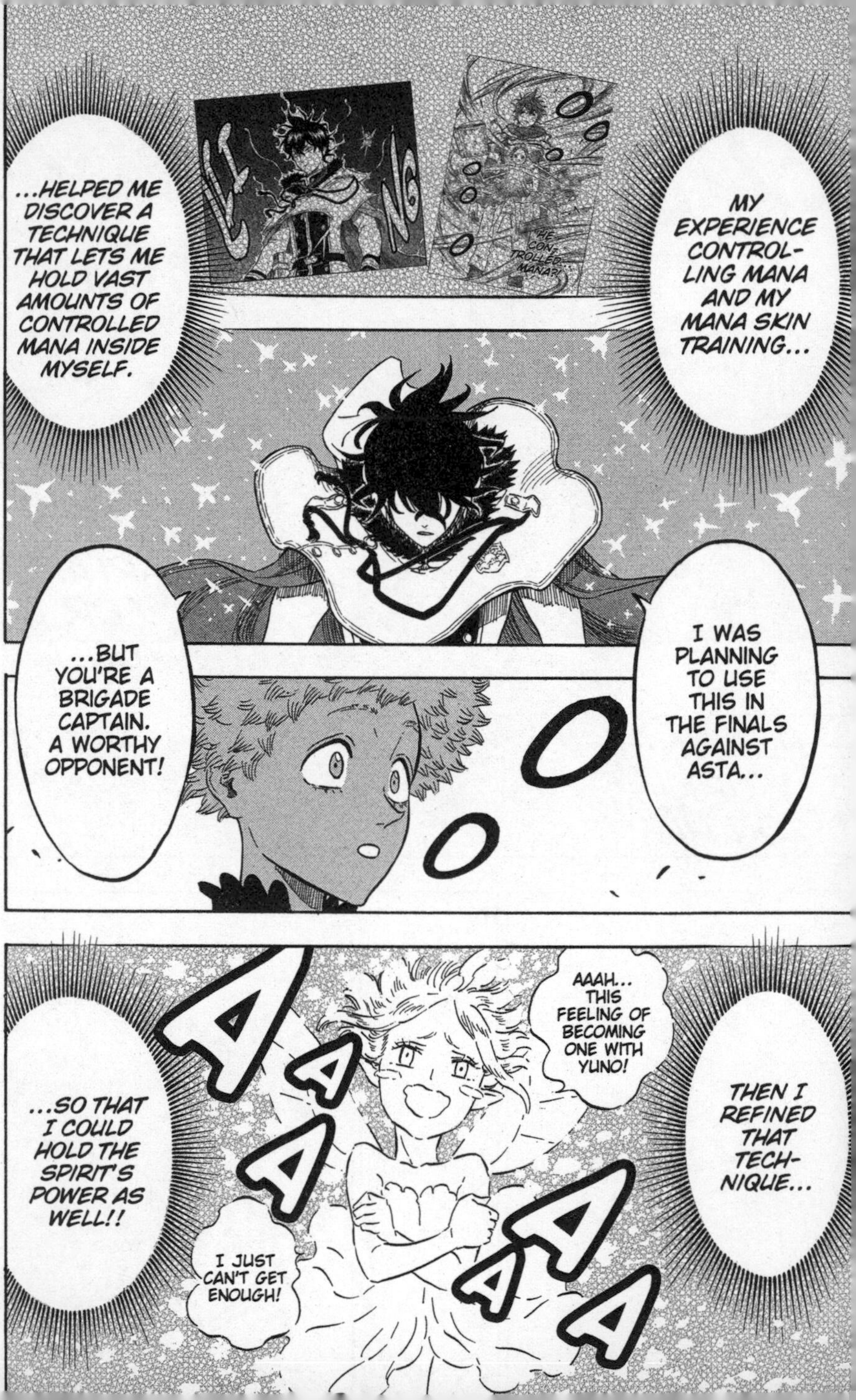
MY EXPERIENCE CONTROLLING MANA AND MY MANA SKIN TRAINING...
HE CONTROLLED... MANA?!
...HELPED ME DISCOVER A TECHNIQUE THAT LETS ME HOLD VAST AMOUNTS OF CONTROLLED MANA INSIDE MYSELF.
I WAS PLANNING TO USE THIS IN THE FINALS AGAINST ASTA...
...BUT YOU'RE A BRIGADE CAPTAIN. A WORTHY OPPONENT!
THEN I REFINED THAT TECHNIQUE...
AAAH... THIS FEELING OF BECOMING ONE WITH YUNO!
...SO THAT I COULD HOLD THE SPIRIT'S POWER AS WELL!!
I JUST CAN'T GET ENOUGH!
AAAAAAA

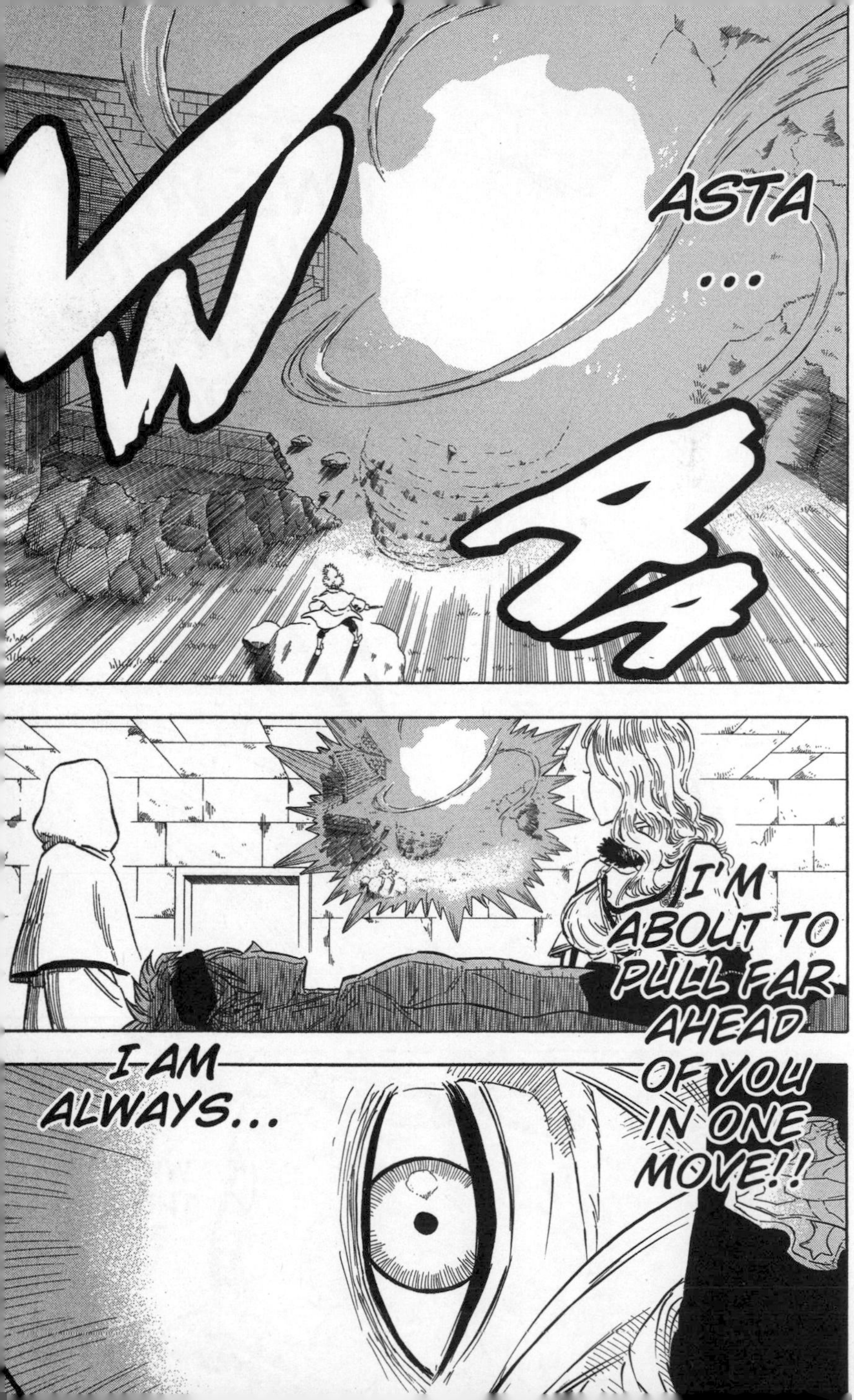
ASTA
...
I'M ABOUT TO PULL FAR AHEAD OF YOU IN ONE MOVE!!
I AM ALWAYS...

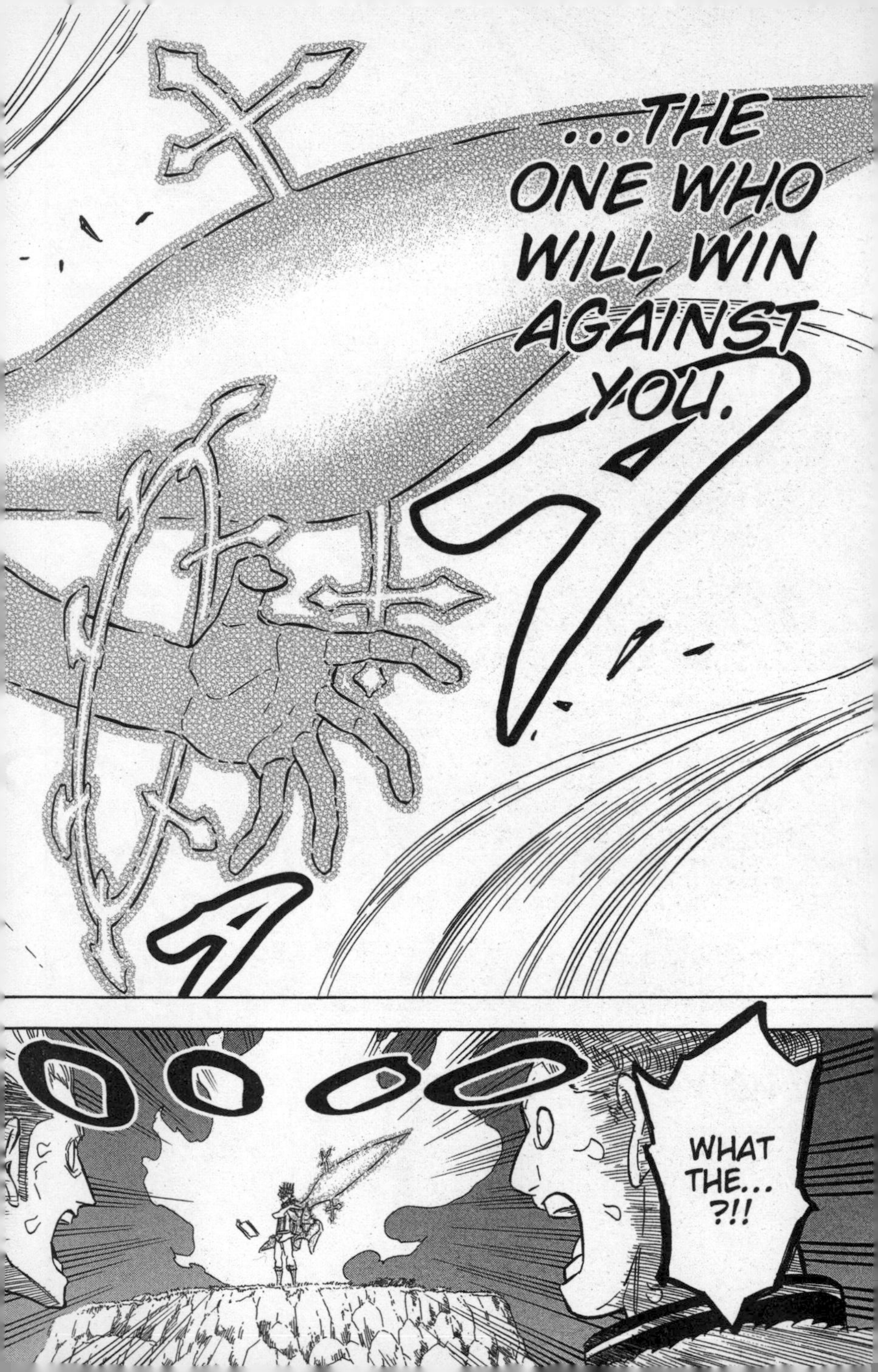
...THE ONE WHO WILL WIN AGAINST YOU.
WHAT THE... ?!!

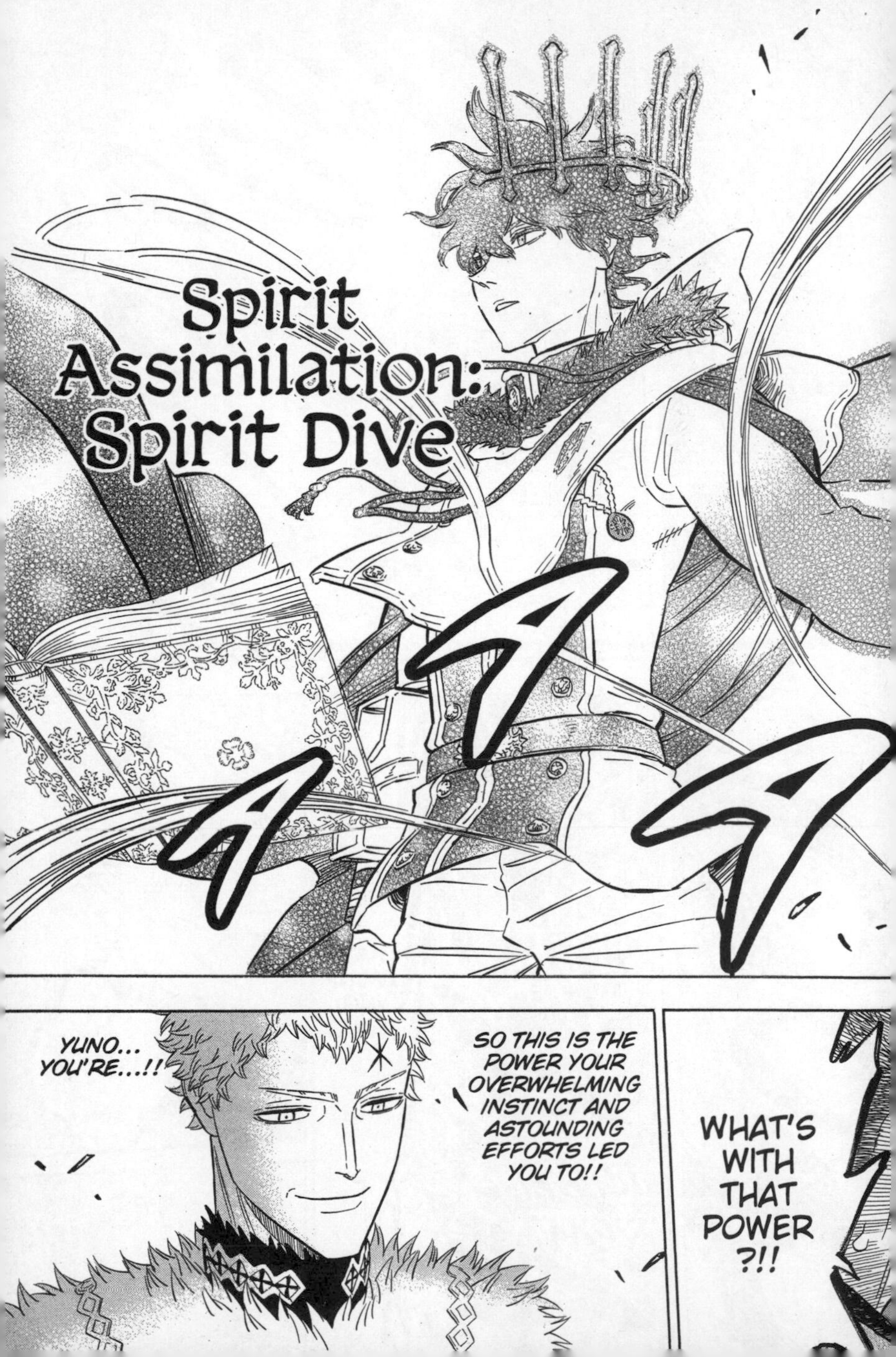
Spirit Assimilation: Spirit Dive
WHAT'S WITH THAT POWER ?!!
SO THIS IS THE POWER YOUR OVERWHELMING INSTINCT AND ASTOUNDING EFFORTS LED YOU TO!!
YUNO... YOU'RE...!!

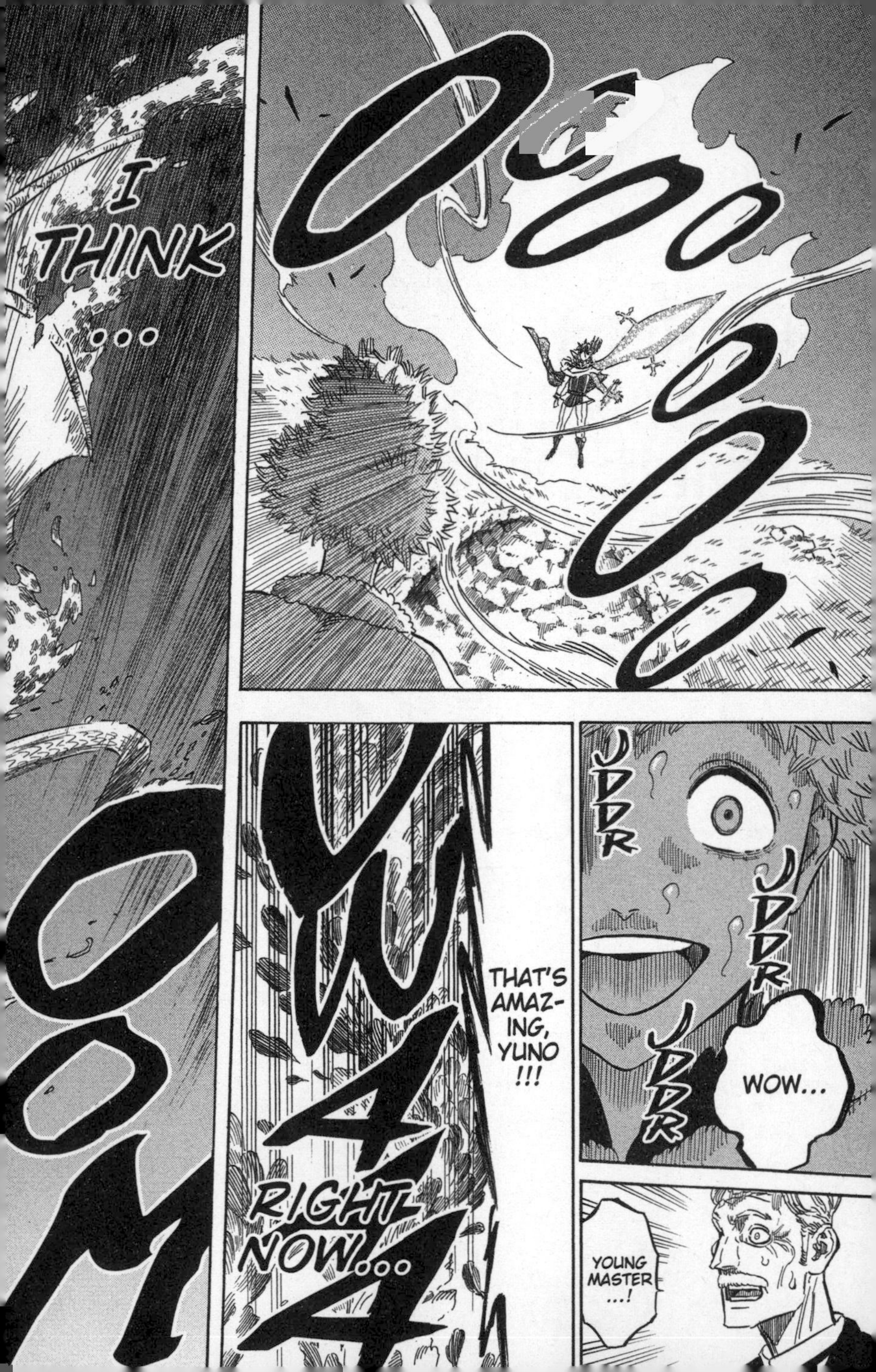
JDDR
JDDR
JDDR
WOW...
YOUNG MASTER ...!
THAT'S AMAZ-ING, YUNO !!!
RIGHT NOW...
I THINK ...

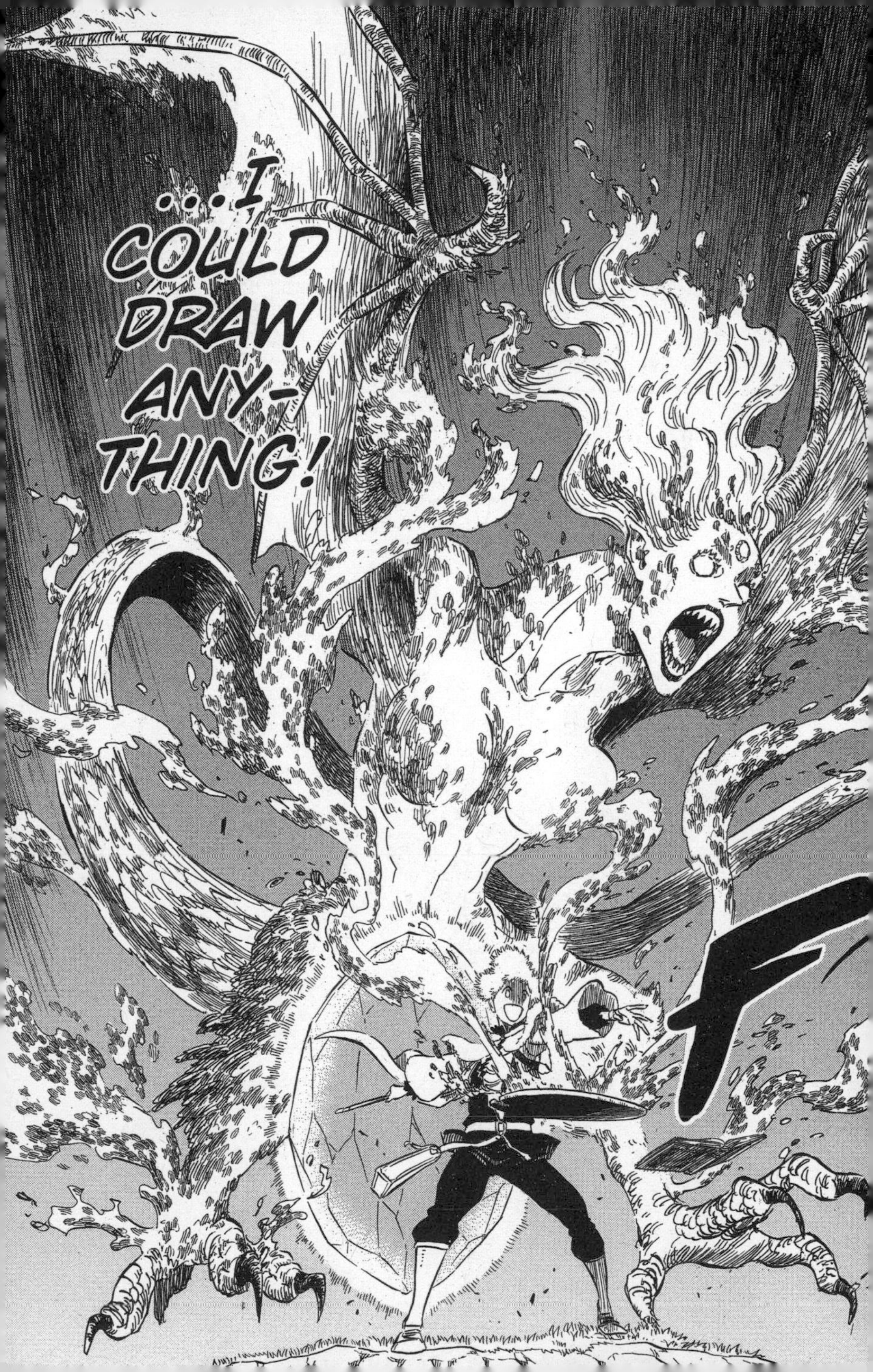
...I COULD DRAW ANY-THING!

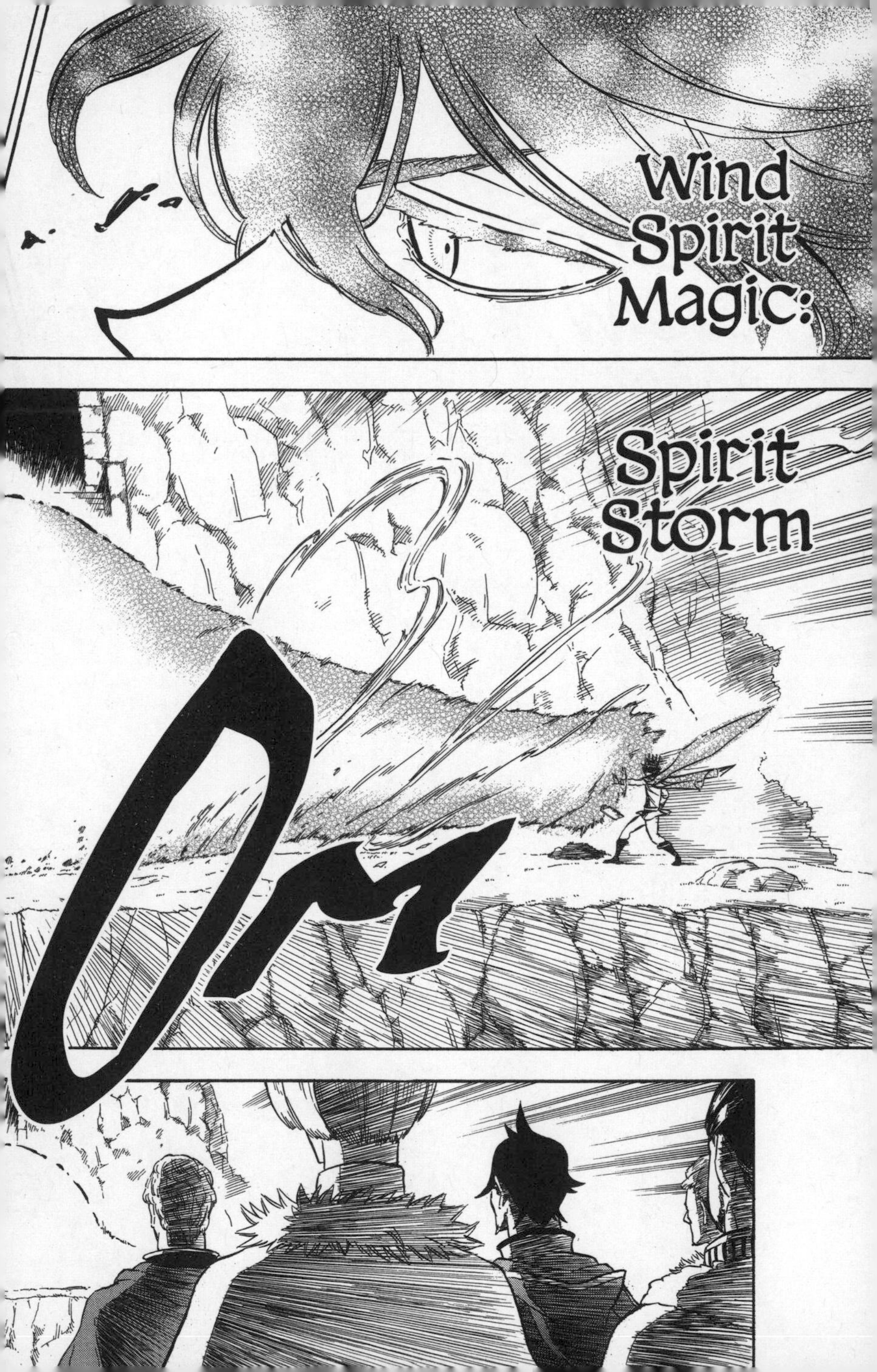
Wind Spirit Magic:
Spirit Storm

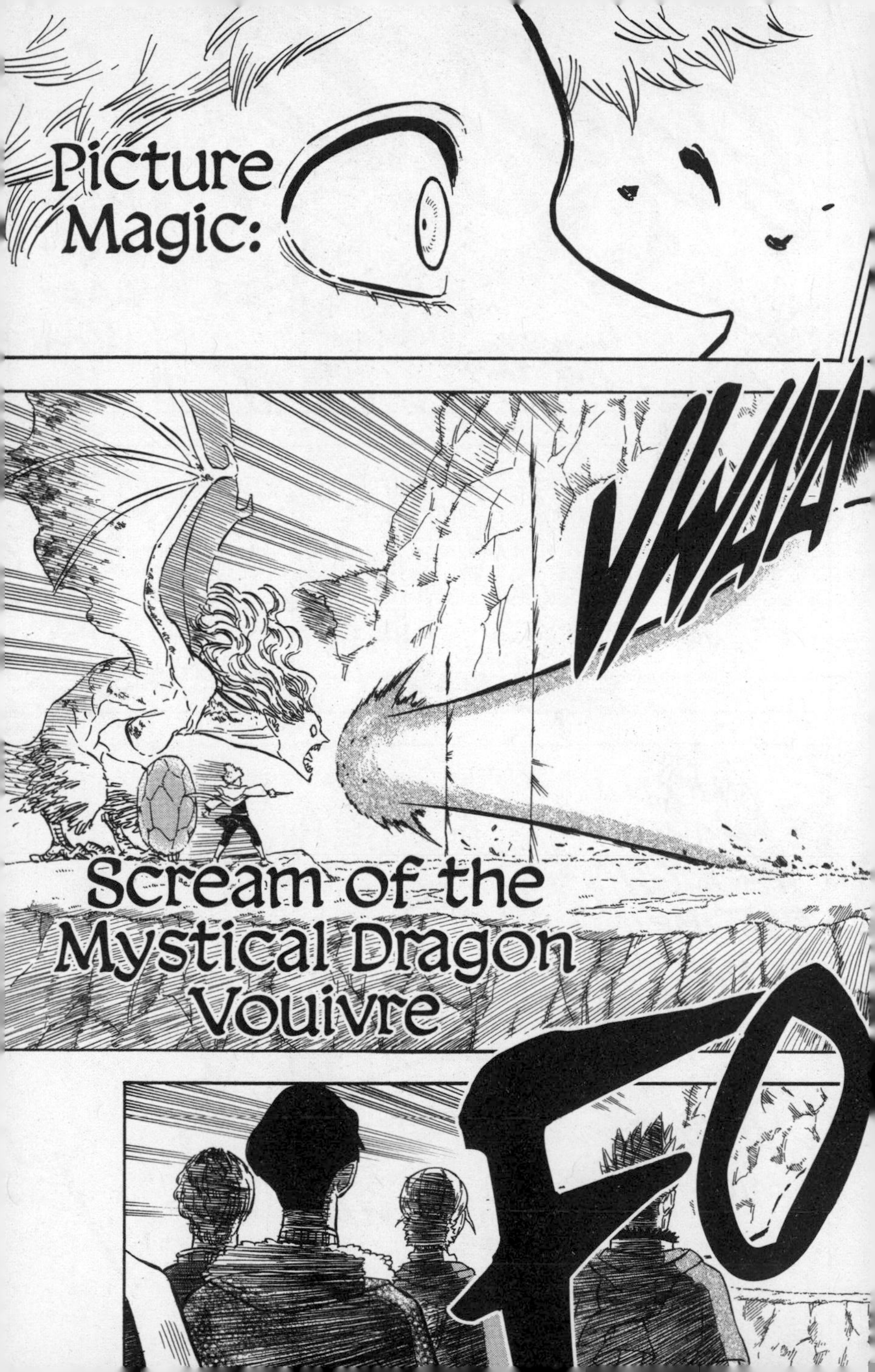
Picture Magic:
VWAA
Scream of the Mystical Dragon Vouivre
FO

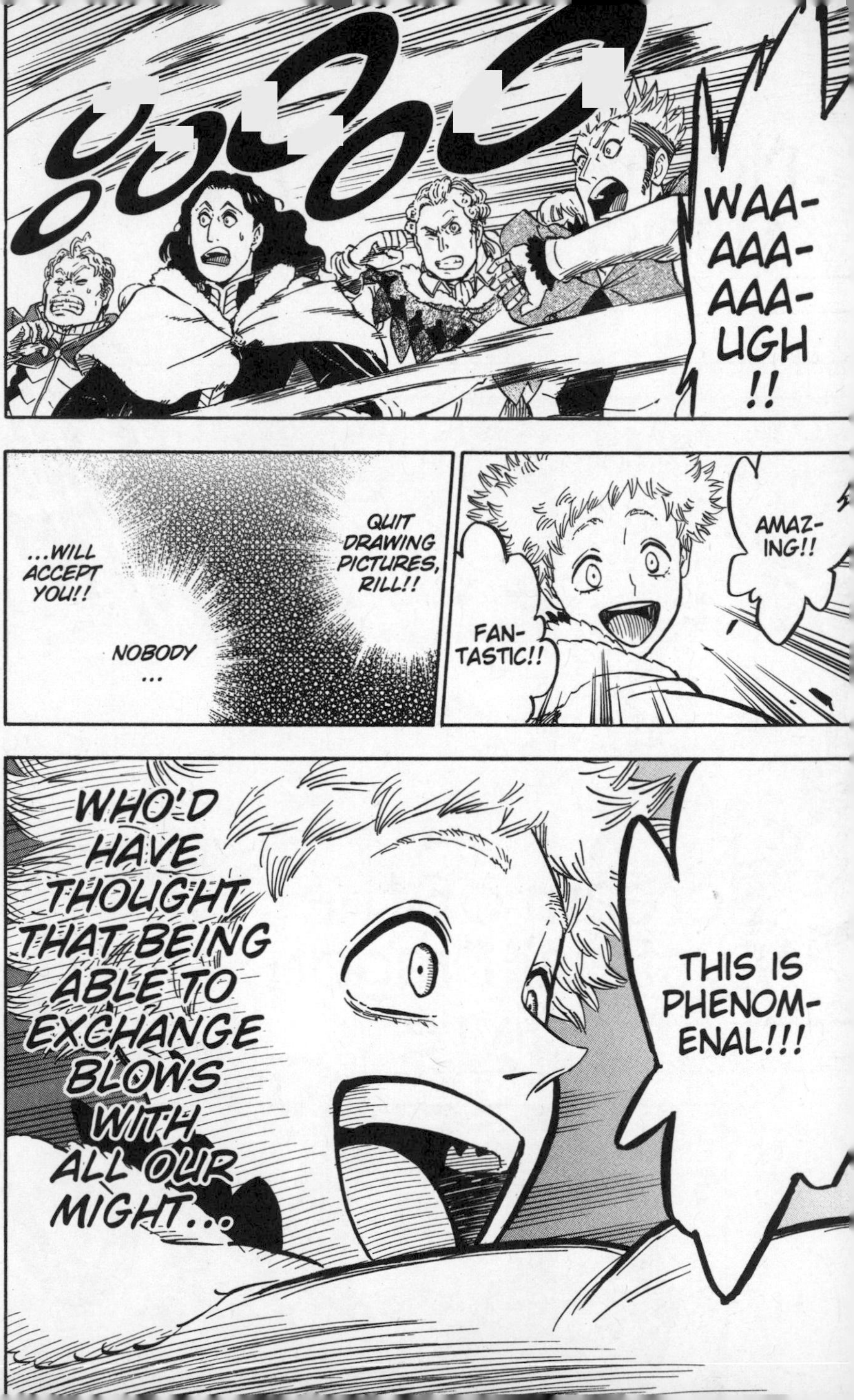
WAAAAAAAAAUGH!!
AMAZING!!
FANTASTIC!!
QUIT DRAWING PICTURES, RILL!!
NOBODY...
...WILL ACCEPT YOU!!
THIS IS PHENOMENAL!!!
WHO'D HAVE THOUGHT THAT BEING ABLE TO EXCHANGE BLOWS WITH ALL OUR MIGHT...

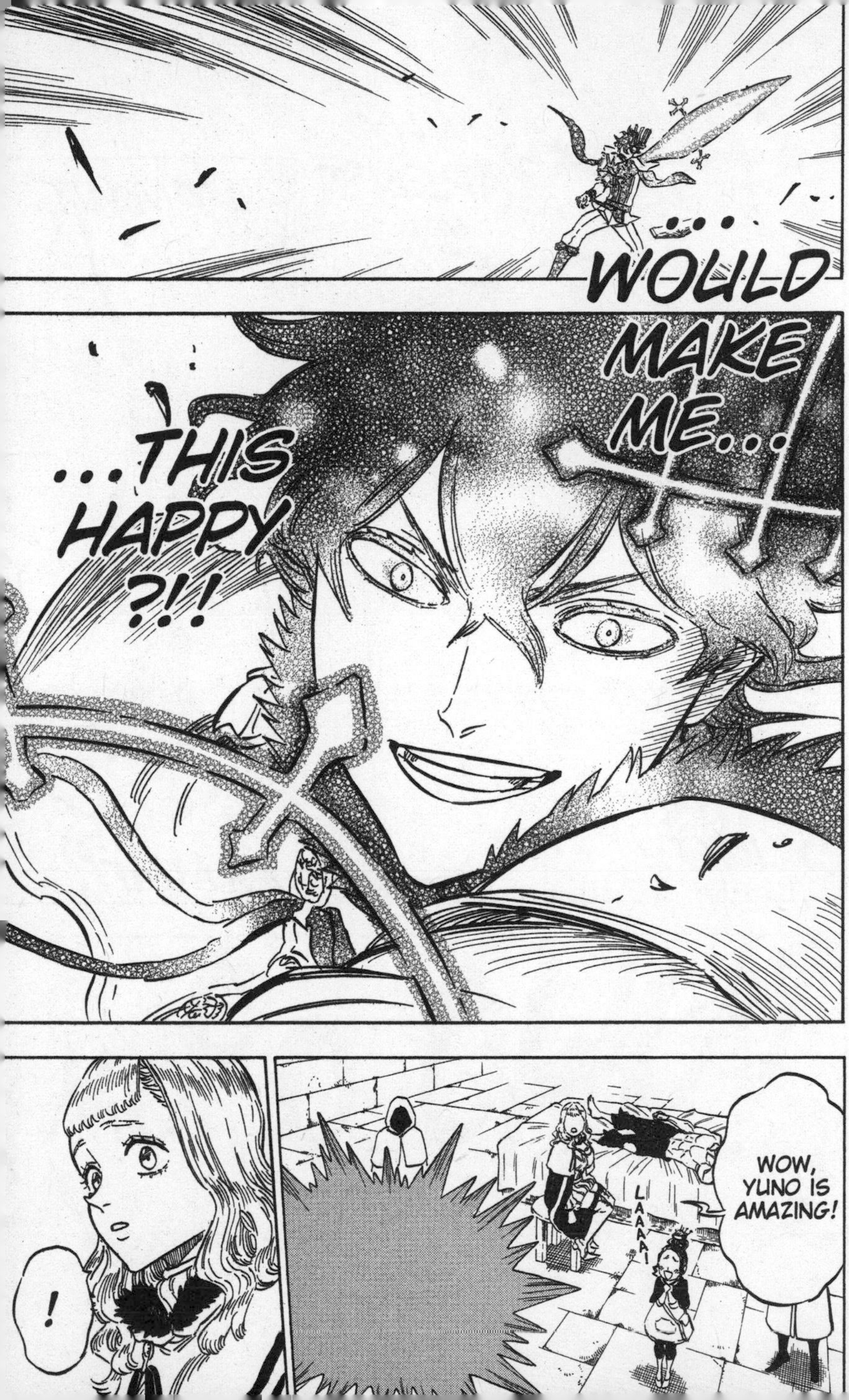
...WOULD MAKE ME...
...THIS HAPPY?!!
WOW, YUNO IS AMAZING!
LAAAA!
!

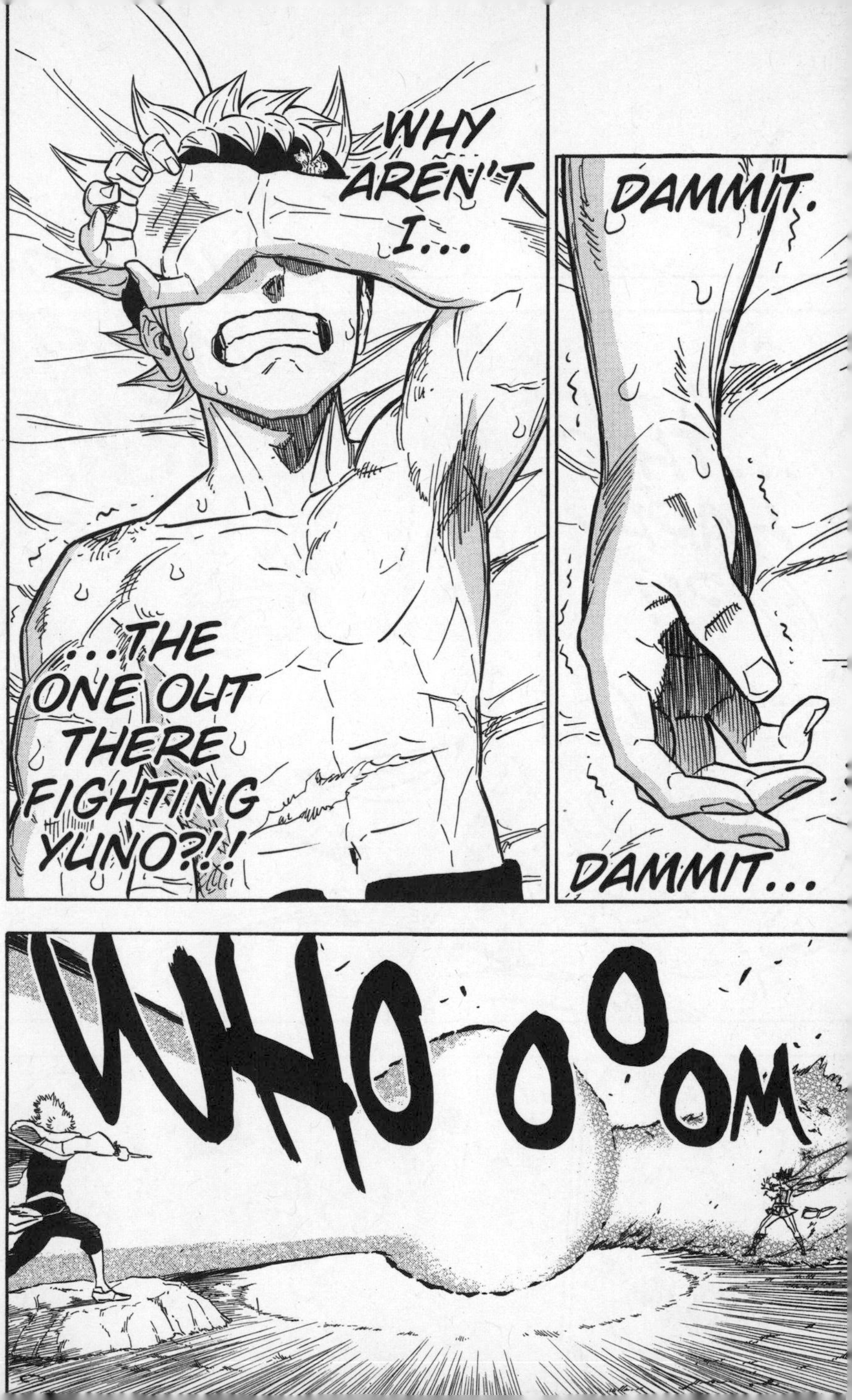
DAMMIT.
DAMMIT...
WHY AREN'T I...
...THE ONE OUT THERE FIGHTING YUNO?!!
WHOOOOM

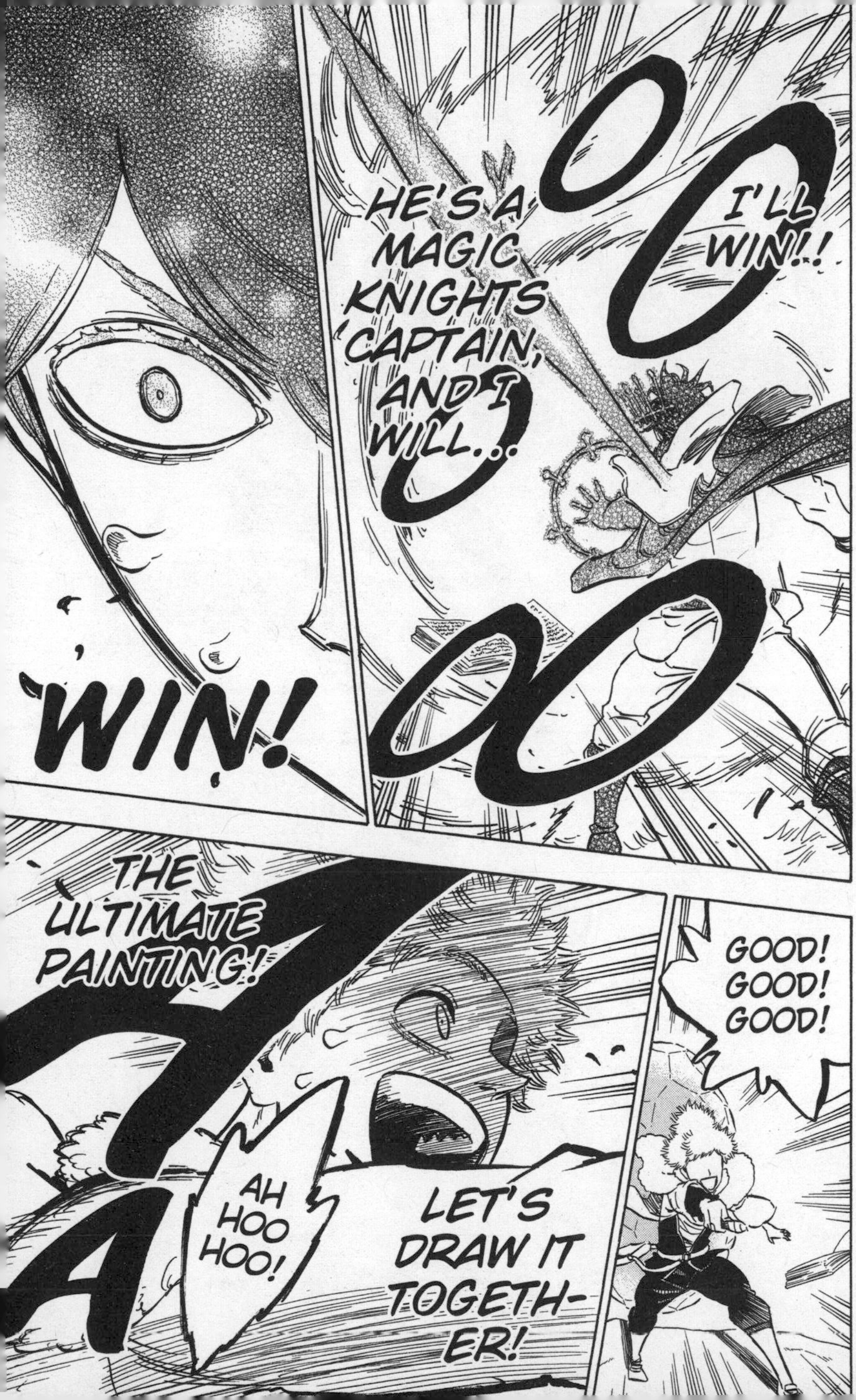
I'LL WIN!!
HE'S A MAGIC KNIGHTS CAPTAIN, AND I WILL...
WIN!
GOOD! GOOD! GOOD!
LET'S DRAW IT TOGETH-ER!
AH HOO HOO!
THE ULTIMATE PAINTING!

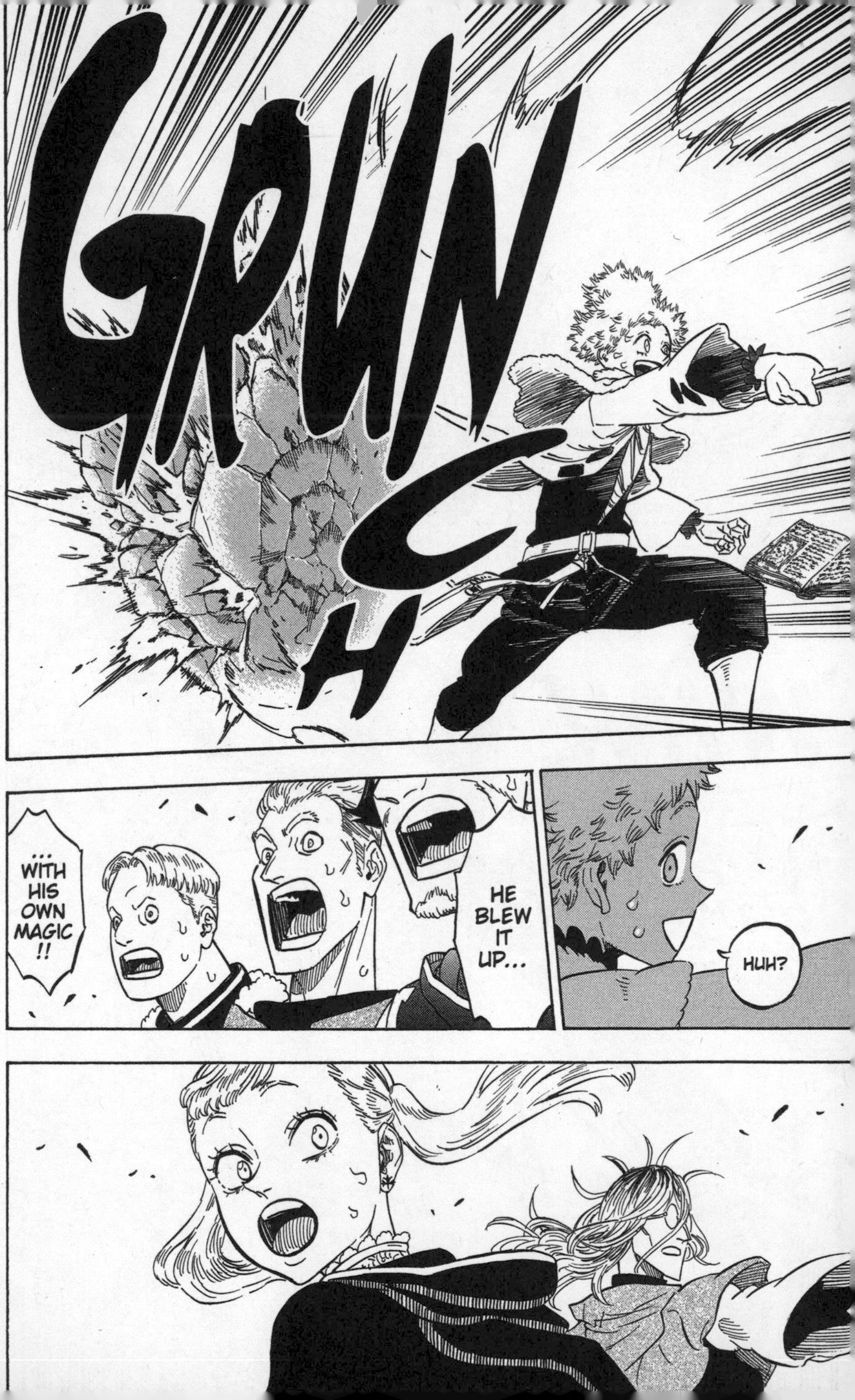
GRUNCH
HUH?
HE BLEW IT UP...
...WITH HIS OWN MAGIC!!

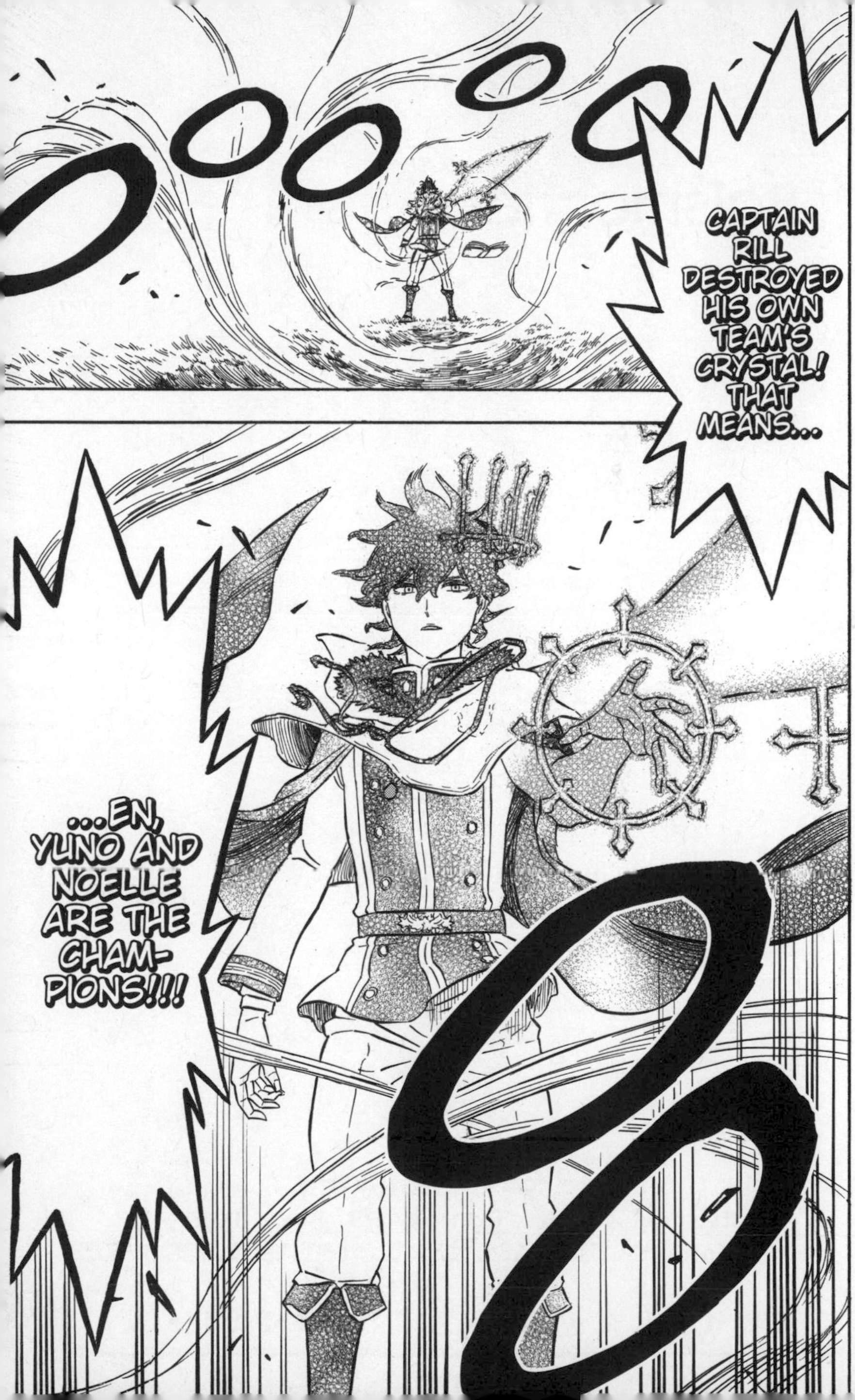
CAPTAIN RILL DESTROYED HIS OWN TEAM'S CRYSTAL! THAT MEANS...
...EN, YUNO AND NOELLE ARE THE CHAM-PIONS!!!

Rill Boismortier

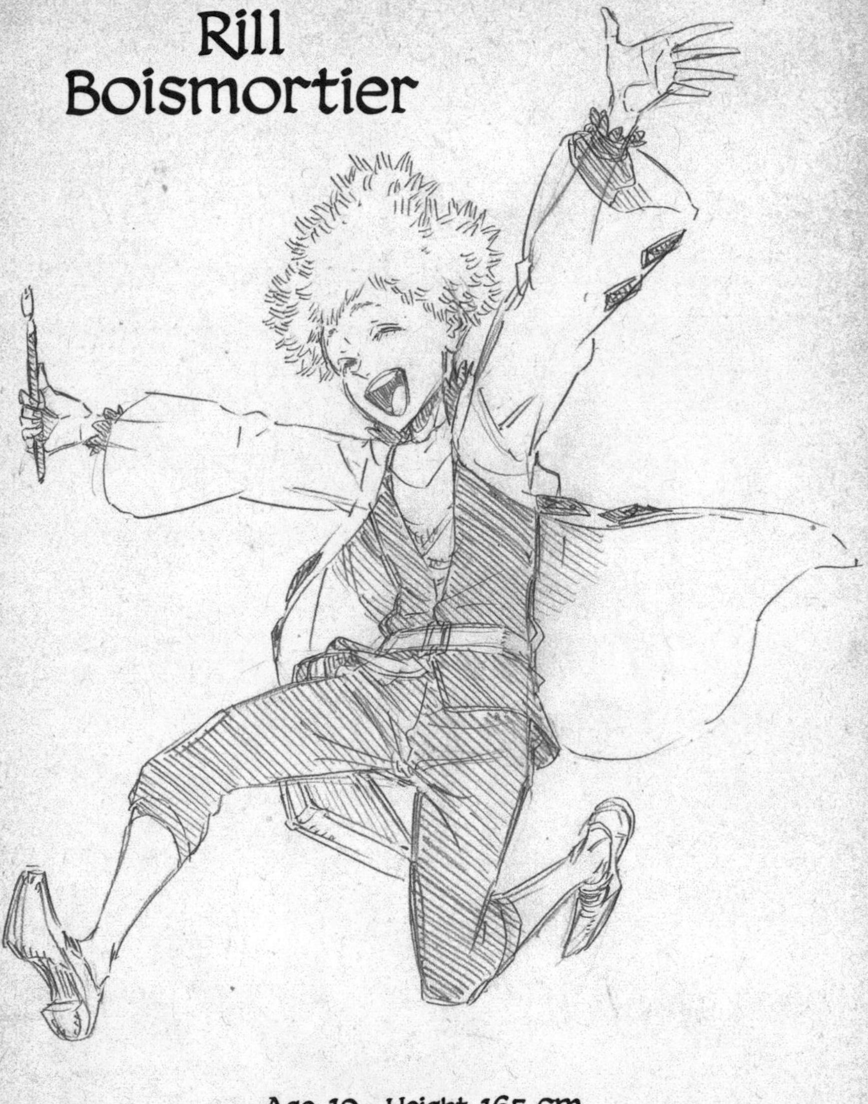

Age: 19 Height: 165 cm
Birthday: March 16 Sign: Pisces Blood Type: AB
Likes: Drawing pictures, waffles, the tea his butler makes

Character Profile

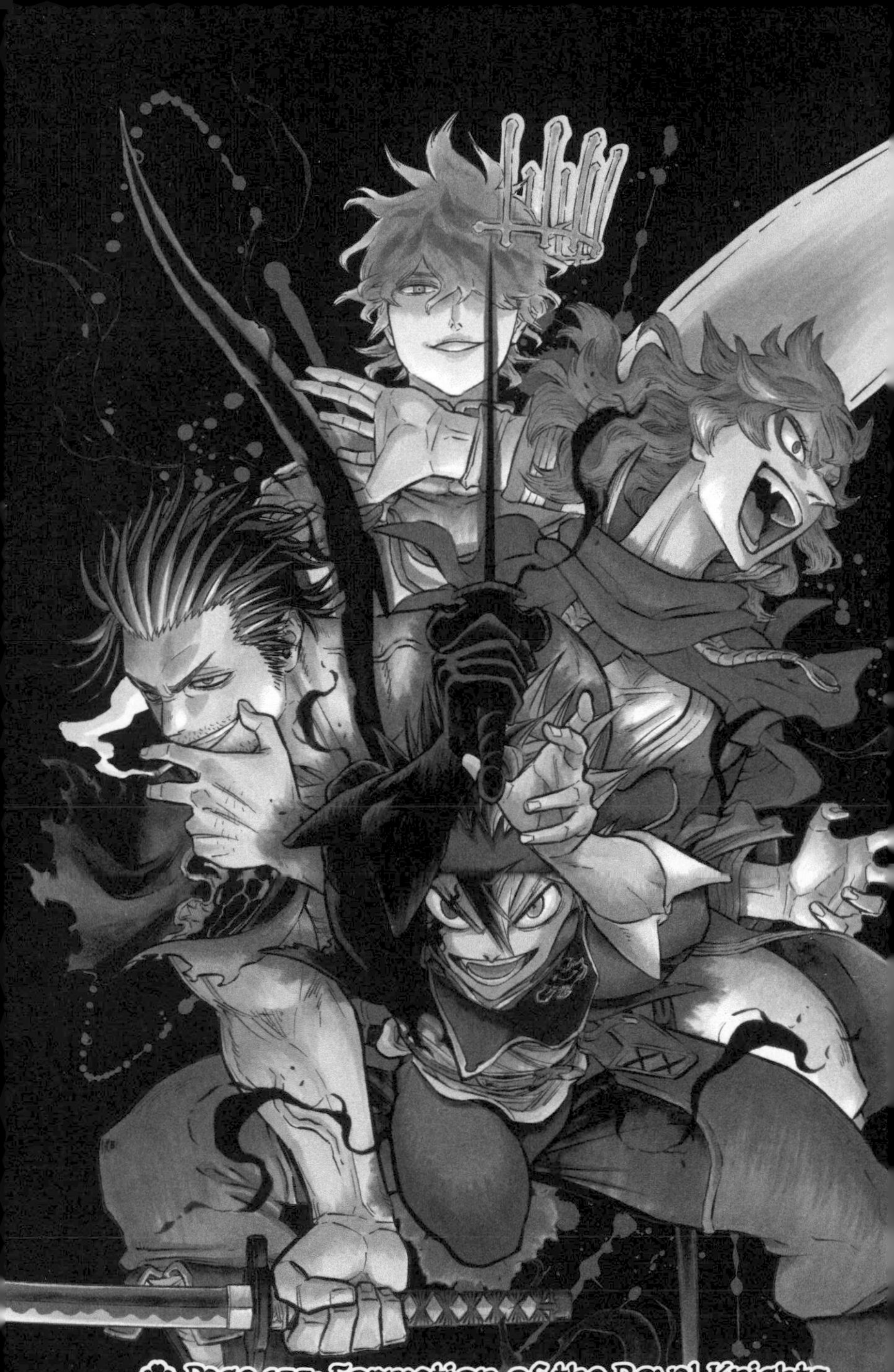

Page 133: Formation of the Royal Knights

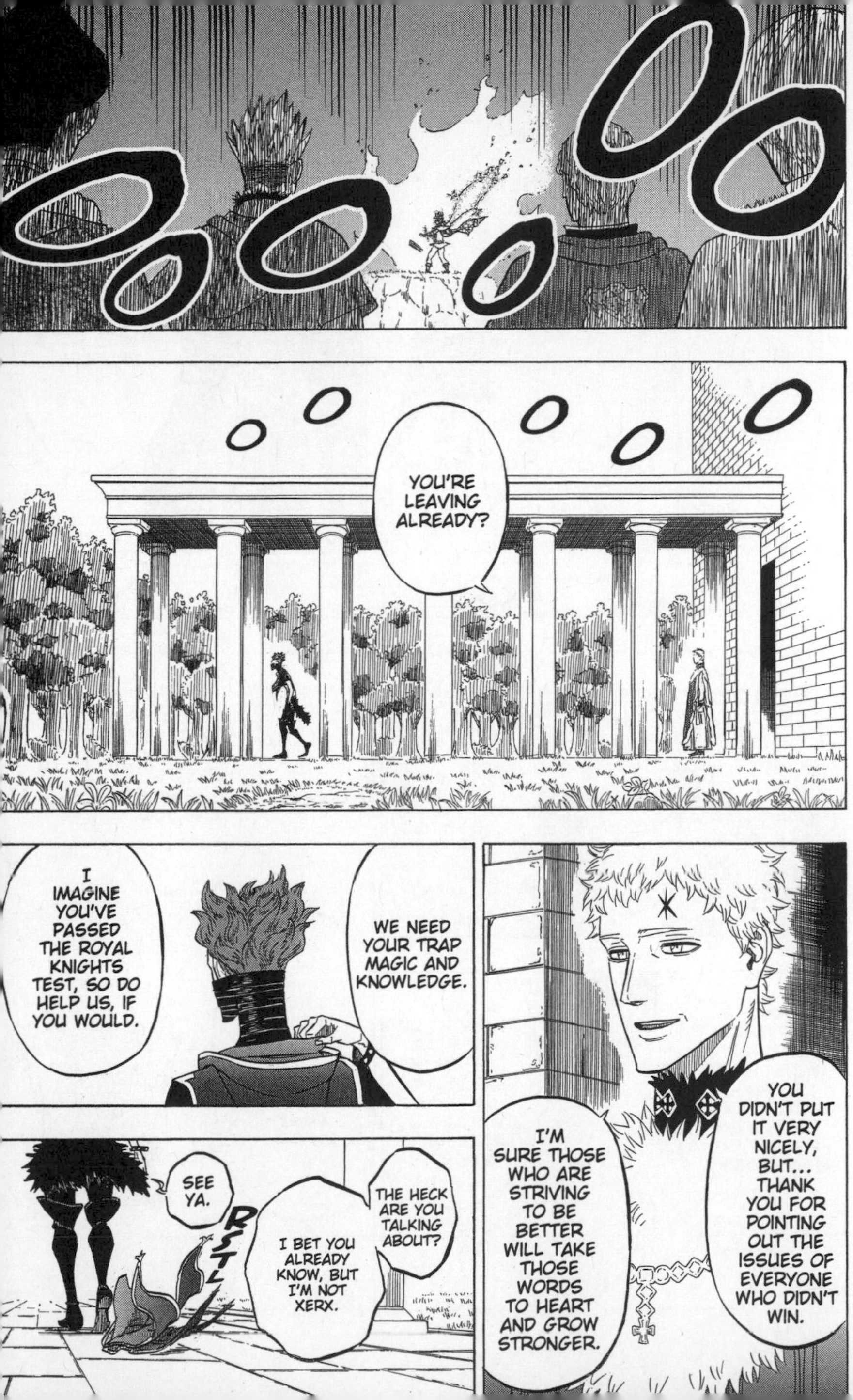
YOU'RE LEAVING ALREADY?
YOU DIDN'T PUT IT VERY NICELY, BUT... THANK YOU FOR POINTING OUT THE ISSUES OF EVERYONE WHO DIDN'T WIN.
I'M SURE THOSE WHO ARE STRIVING TO BE BETTER WILL TAKE THOSE WORDS TO HEART AND GROW STRONGER.
WE NEED YOUR TRAP MAGIC AND KNOWLEDGE.
I IMAGINE YOU'VE PASSED THE ROYAL KNIGHTS TEST, SO DO HELP US, IF YOU WOULD.
THE HECK ARE YOU TALKING ABOUT?
I BET YOU ALREADY KNOW, BUT I'M NOT XERX.
SEE YA.
RSTL

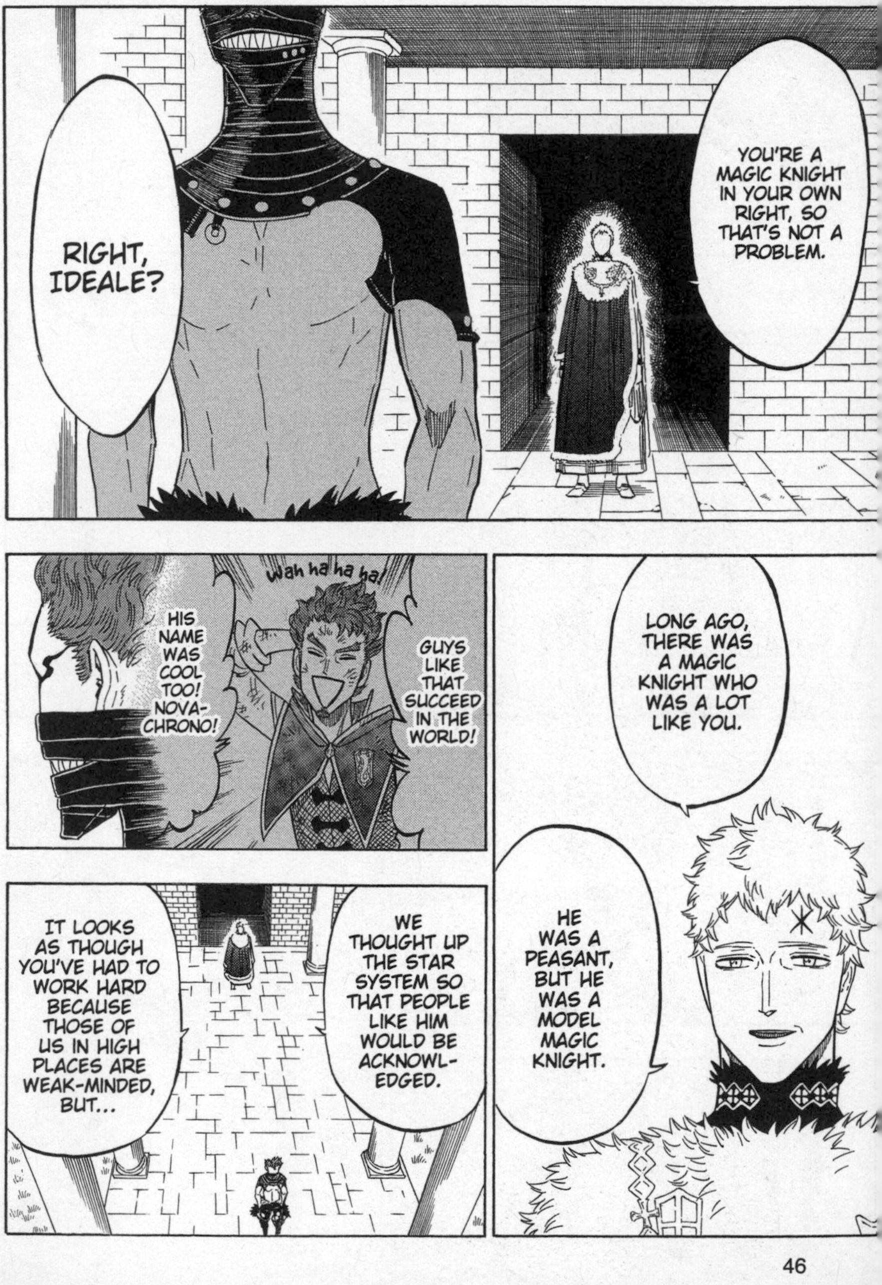
YOU'RE A MAGIC KNIGHT IN YOUR OWN RIGHT, SO THAT'S NOT A PROBLEM.
RIGHT, IDEALE?
LONG AGO, THERE WAS A MAGIC KNIGHT WHO WAS A LOT LIKE YOU.
HE WAS A PEASANT, BUT HE WAS A MODEL MAGIC KNIGHT.
Wah ha ha ha!
GUYS LIKE THAT SUCCEED IN THE WORLD!
HIS NAME WAS COOL TOO! NOVA-CHRONO!
WE THOUGHT UP THE STAR SYSTEM SO THAT PEOPLE LIKE HIM WOULD BE ACKNOWL-EDGED.
IT LOOKS AS THOUGH YOU'VE HAD TO WORK HARD BECAUSE THOSE OF US IN HIGH PLACES ARE WEAK-MINDED, BUT...

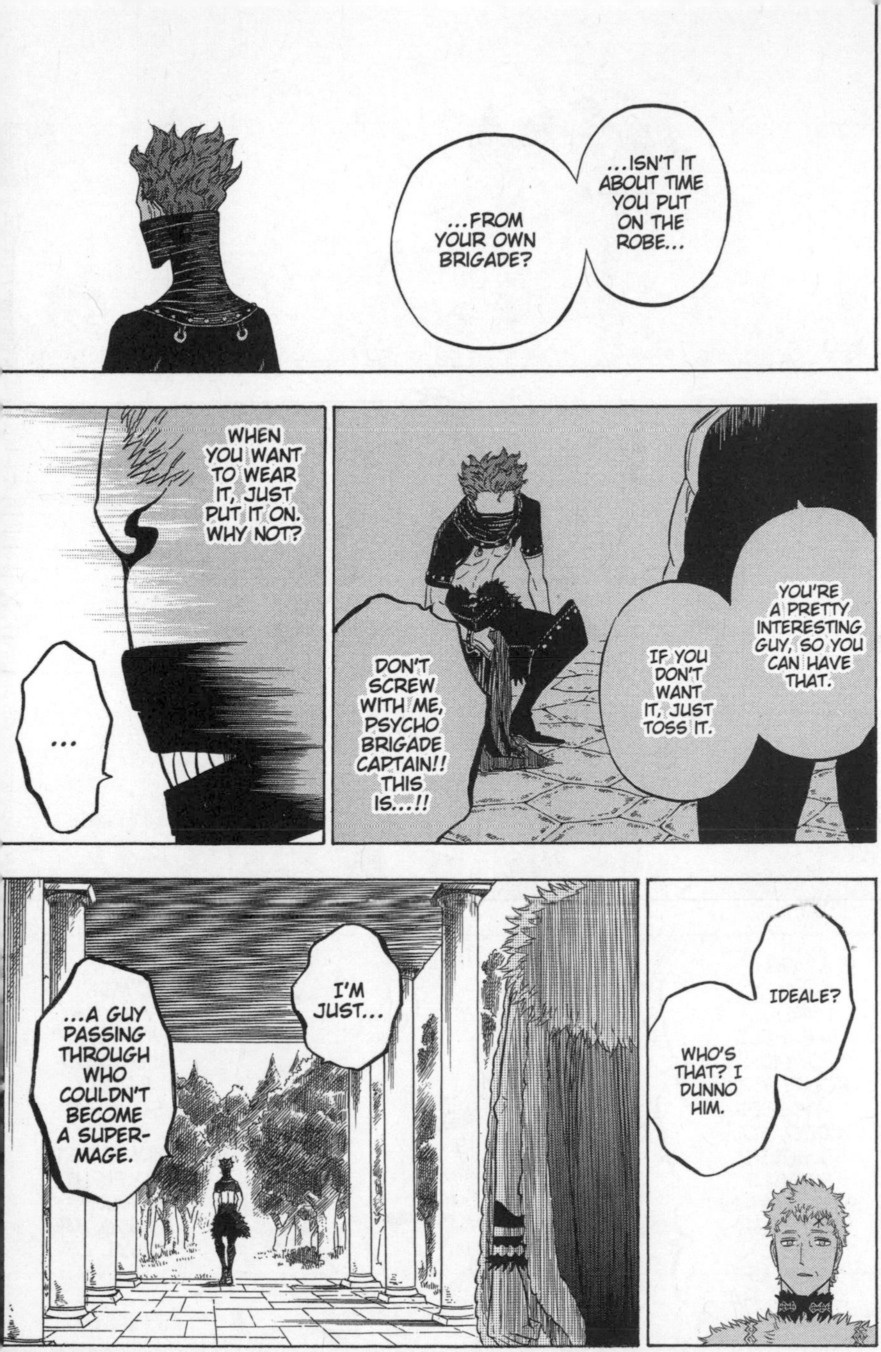
...ISN'T IT ABOUT TIME YOU PUT ON THE ROBE...
...FROM YOUR OWN BRIGADE?
YOU'RE A PRETTY INTERESTING GUY, SO YOU CAN HAVE THAT.
IF YOU DON'T WANT IT, JUST TOSS IT.
DON'T SCREW WITH ME, PSYCHO BRIGADE CAPTAIN!! THIS IS...!!
WHEN YOU WANT TO WEAR IT, JUST PUT IT ON. WHY NOT?
...
IDEALE?
WHO'S THAT? I DUNNO HIM.
I'M JUST...
...A GUY PASSING THROUGH WHO COULDN'T BECOME A SUPER-MAGE.

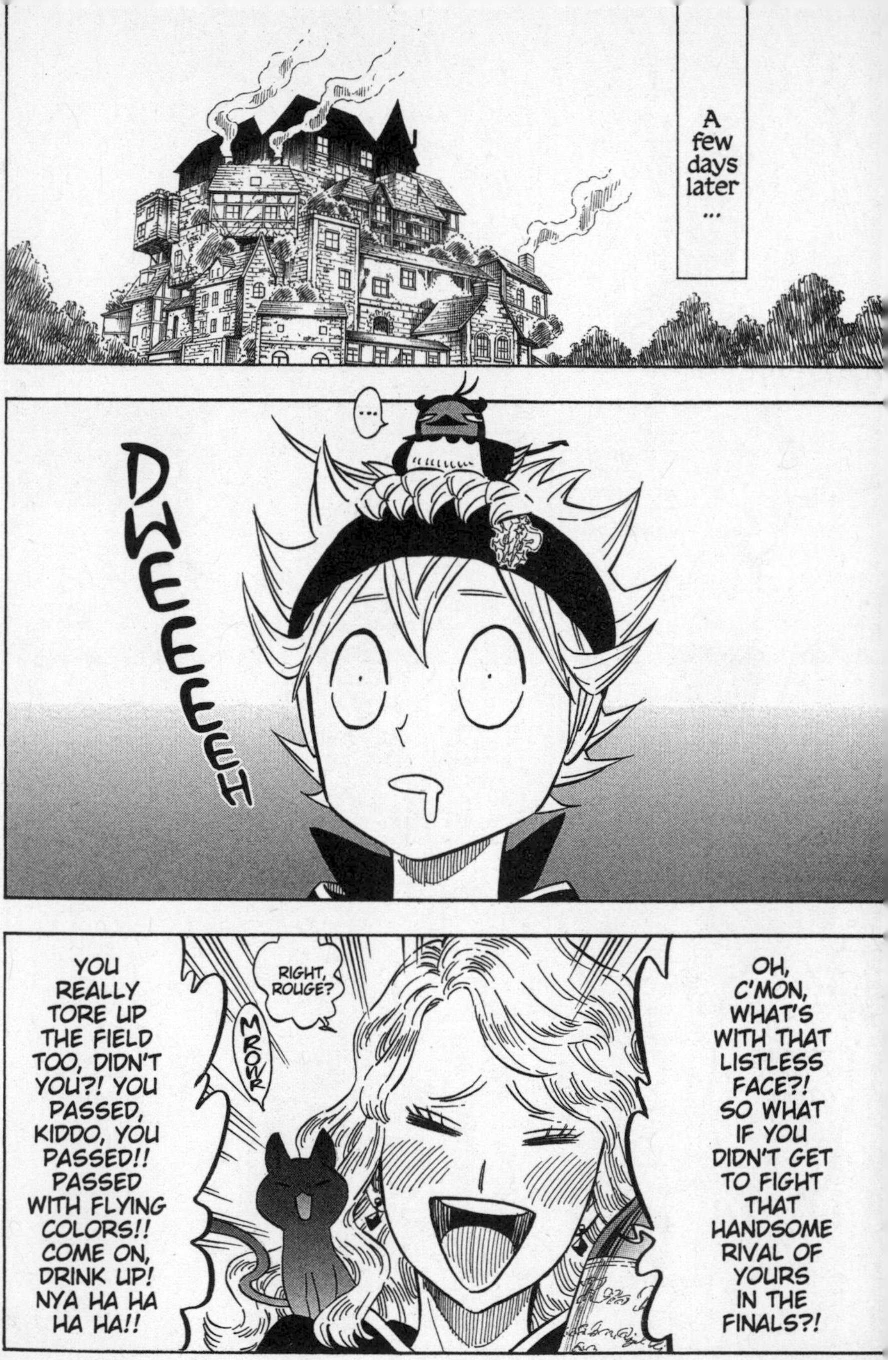

A few days later ...
...
DWEEEEEH
OH, C'MON, WHAT'S WITH THAT LISTLESS FACE?! SO WHAT IF YOU DIDN'T GET TO FIGHT THAT HANDSOME RIVAL OF YOURS IN THE FINALS?!
YOU REALLY TORE UP THE FIELD TOO, DIDN'T YOU?! YOU PASSED, KIDDO, YOU PASSED!! PASSED WITH FLYING COLORS!! COME ON, DRINK UP! NYA HA HA HA HA!!
RIGHT, ROUGE?
MROWR

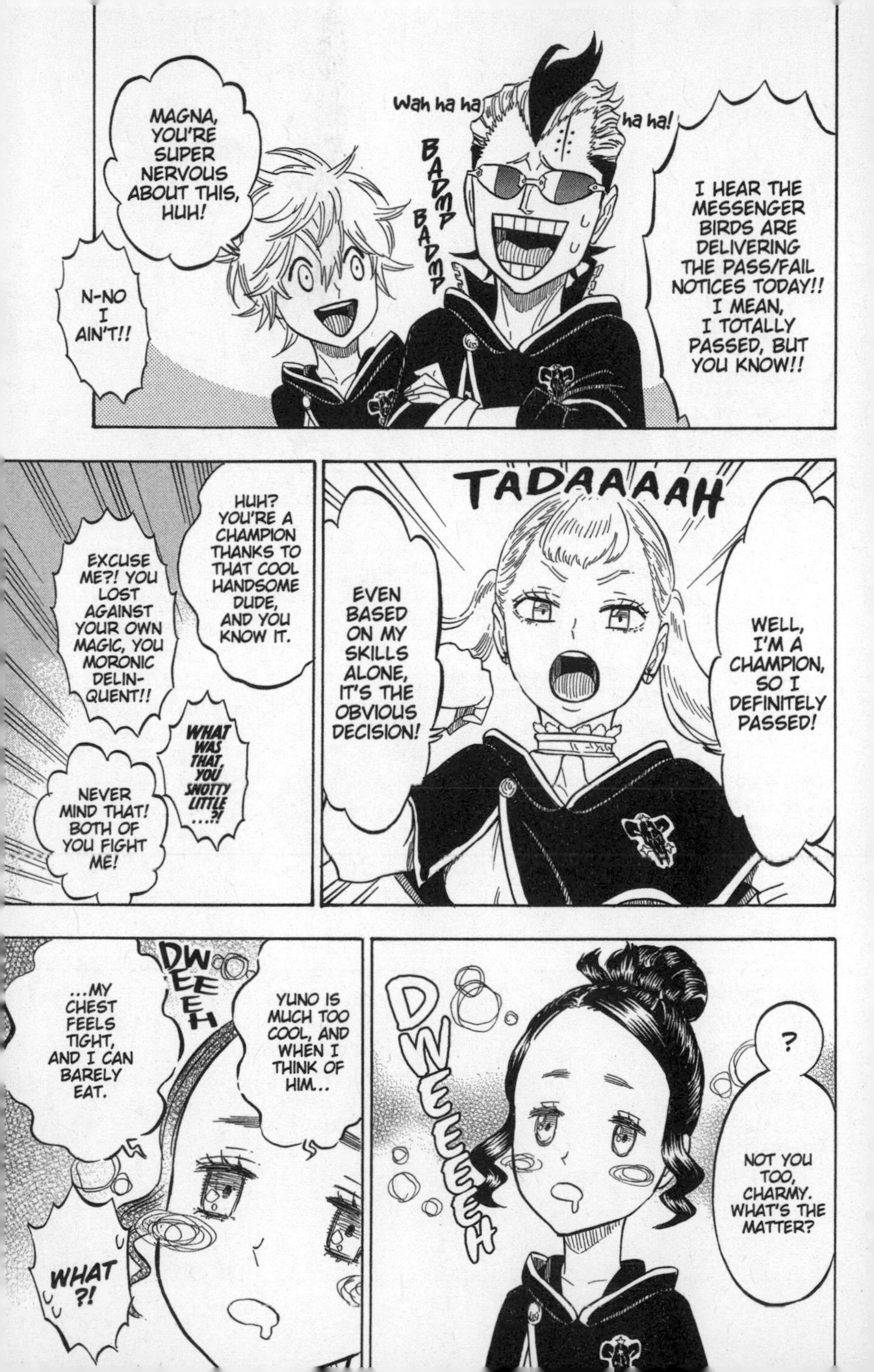
I HEAR THE MESSENGER BIRDS ARE DELIVERING THE PASS/FAIL NOTICES TODAY!! I MEAN, I TOTALLY PASSED, BUT YOU KNOW!!
Wah ha ha
ha ha!
BADMP BADMP
MAGNA, YOU'RE SUPER NERVOUS ABOUT THIS, HUH!
N-NO I AIN'T!!
TADAAAAH
WELL, I'M A CHAMPION, SO I DEFINITELY PASSED!
EVEN BASED ON MY SKILLS ALONE, IT'S THE OBVIOUS DECISION!
HUH? YOU'RE A CHAMPION THANKS TO THAT COOL HANDSOME DUDE, AND YOU KNOW IT.
EXCUSE ME?! YOU LOST AGAINST YOUR OWN MAGIC, YOU MORONIC DELIN-QUENT!!
WHAT WAS THAT, YOU SNOTTY LITTLE ...?!
NEVER MIND THAT! BOTH OF YOU FIGHT ME!
?
NOT YOU TOO, CHARMY. WHAT'S THE MATTER?
DWEEEEH
YUNO IS MUCH TOO COOL, AND WHEN I THINK OF HIM...
DWEEEH
...MY CHEST FEELS TIGHT, AND I CAN BARELY EAT.
WHAT?!

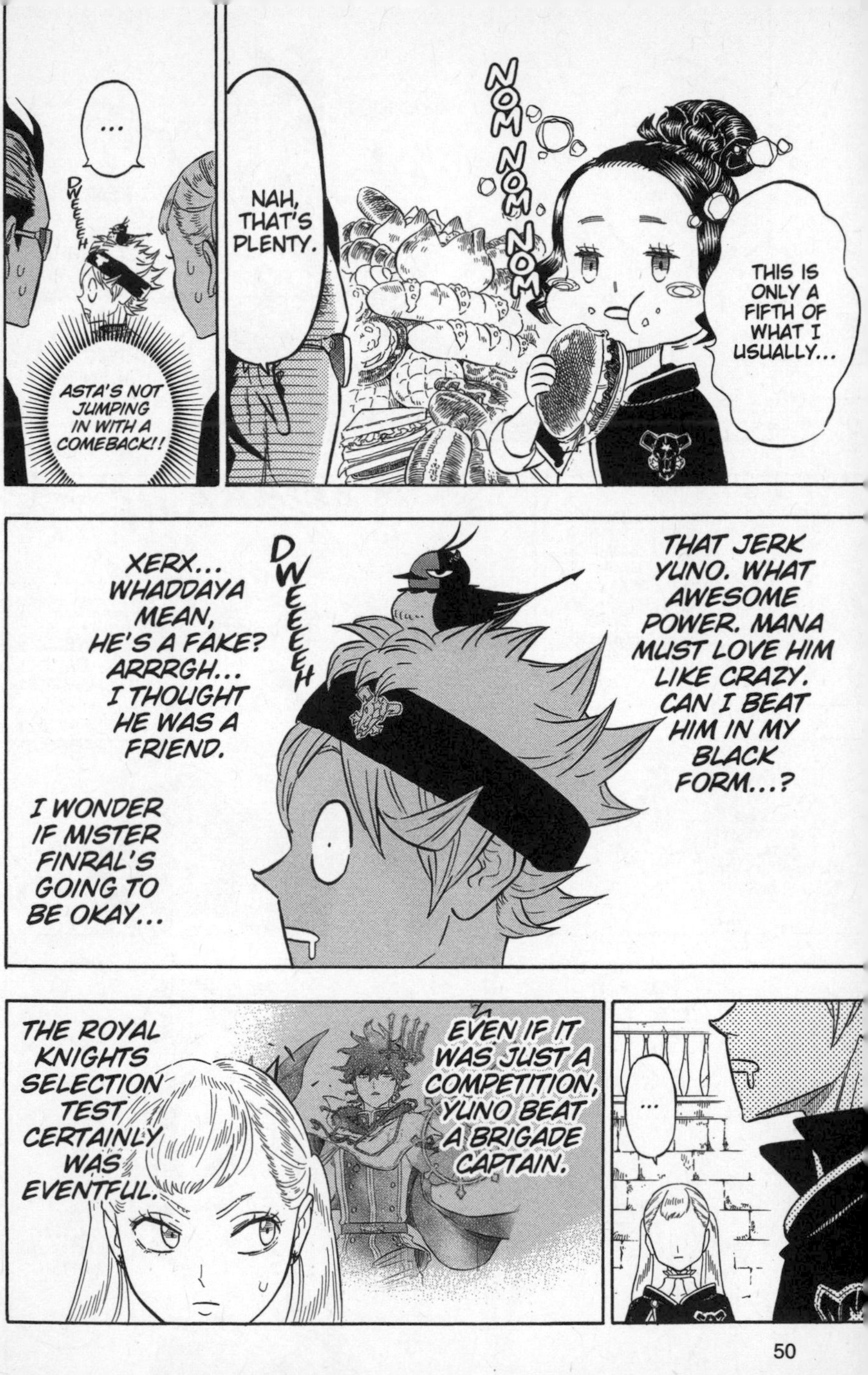
NOM NOM NOM NOM
THIS IS ONLY A FIFTH OF WHAT I USUALLY...
NAH, THAT'S PLENTY.
...
DWEEEEH
ASTA'S NOT JUMPING IN WITH A COMEBACK!!
THAT JERK YUNO. WHAT AWESOME POWER. MANA MUST LOVE HIM LIKE CRAZY. CAN I BEAT HIM IN MY BLACK FORM...?
DWEEEEH
XERX... WHADDAYA MEAN, HE'S A FAKE? ARRRGH... I THOUGHT HE WAS A FRIEND.
I WONDER IF MISTER FINRAL'S GOING TO BE OKAY...
...
EVEN IF IT WAS JUST A COMPETITION, YUNO BEAT A BRIGADE CAPTAIN.
THE ROYAL KNIGHTS SELECTION TEST CERTAINLY WAS EVENTFUL.

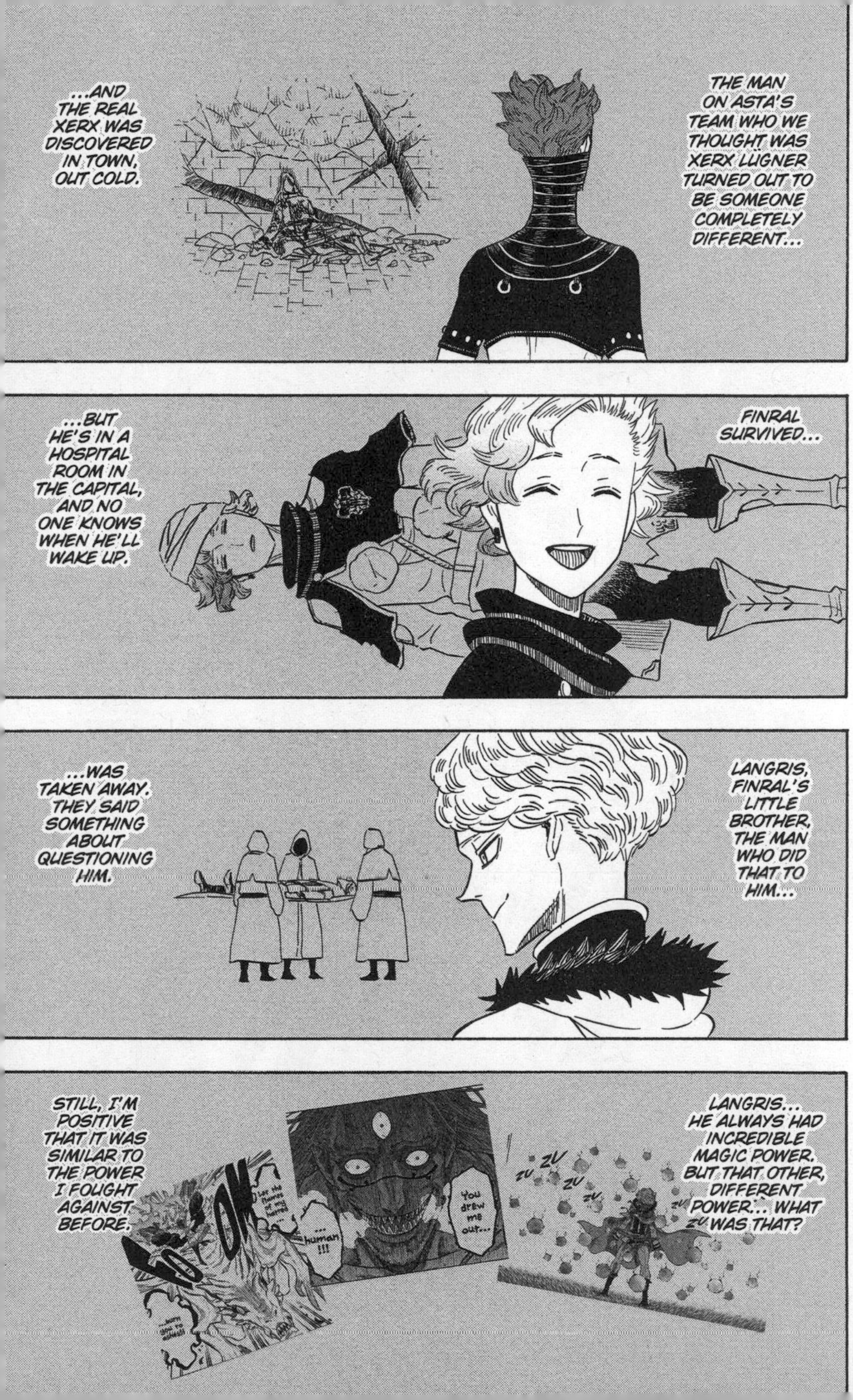
THE MAN ON ASTA'S TEAM WHO WE THOUGHT WAS XERX LÜGNER TURNED OUT TO BE SOMEONE COMPLETELY DIFFERENT...
...AND THE REAL XERX WAS DISCOVERED IN TOWN, OUT COLD.
FINRAL SURVIVED...
...BUT HE'S IN A HOSPITAL ROOM IN THE CAPITAL, AND NO ONE KNOWS WHEN HE'LL WAKE UP.
LANGRIS, FINRAL'S LITTLE BROTHER, THE MAN WHO DID THAT TO HIM...
...WAS TAKEN AWAY. THEY SAID SOMETHING ABOUT QUESTIONING HIM.
LANGRIS... HE ALWAYS HAD INCREDIBLE MAGIC POWER. BUT THAT OTHER, DIFFERENT POWER... WHAT WAS THAT?
ZU ZU ZU ZU ZU ZU
You drew me out...
...human!!!
Let the flames of my hatred...
GOOM
STILL, I'M POSITIVE THAT IT WAS SIMILAR TO THE POWER I FOUGHT AGAINST BEFORE.

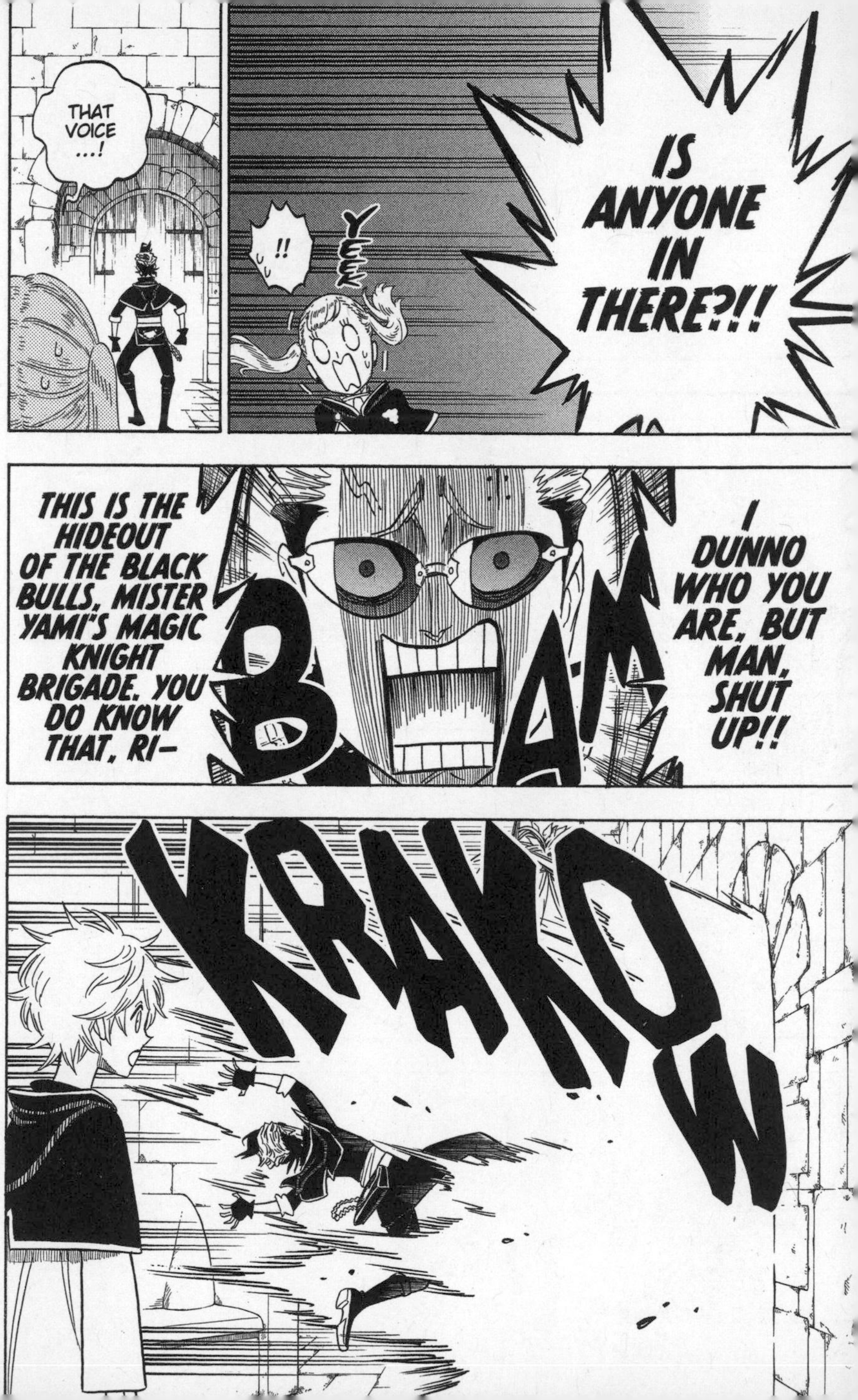
IS ANYONE IN THERE?!!
YEEK
!!
THAT VOICE ...!
I DUNNO WHO YOU ARE, BUT MAN, SHUT UP!!
THIS IS THE HIDEOUT OF THE BLACK BULLS, MISTER YAMI'S MAGIC KNIGHT BRIGADE. YOU DO KNOW THAT, RI-
BAM
KRAKOW

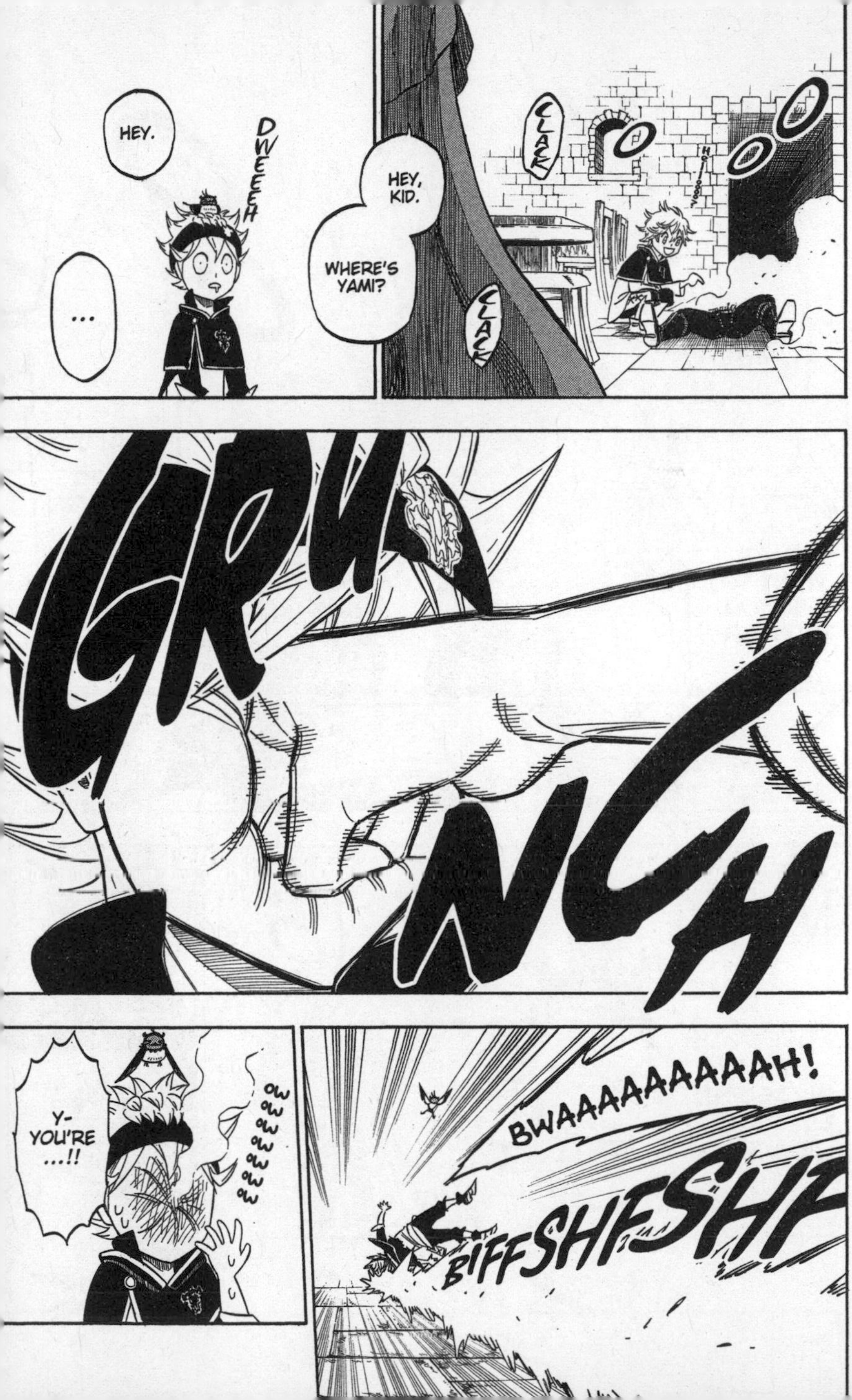
CLACK
HEY, KID.
WHERE'S YAMI?
CLACK
HEY.
DWEEEEH
...
GRUNCH
BWAAAAAAAAAH!
BIFF
SHF SHF
Y- YOU'RE ...!!
OW OW OW OW OW OW OW

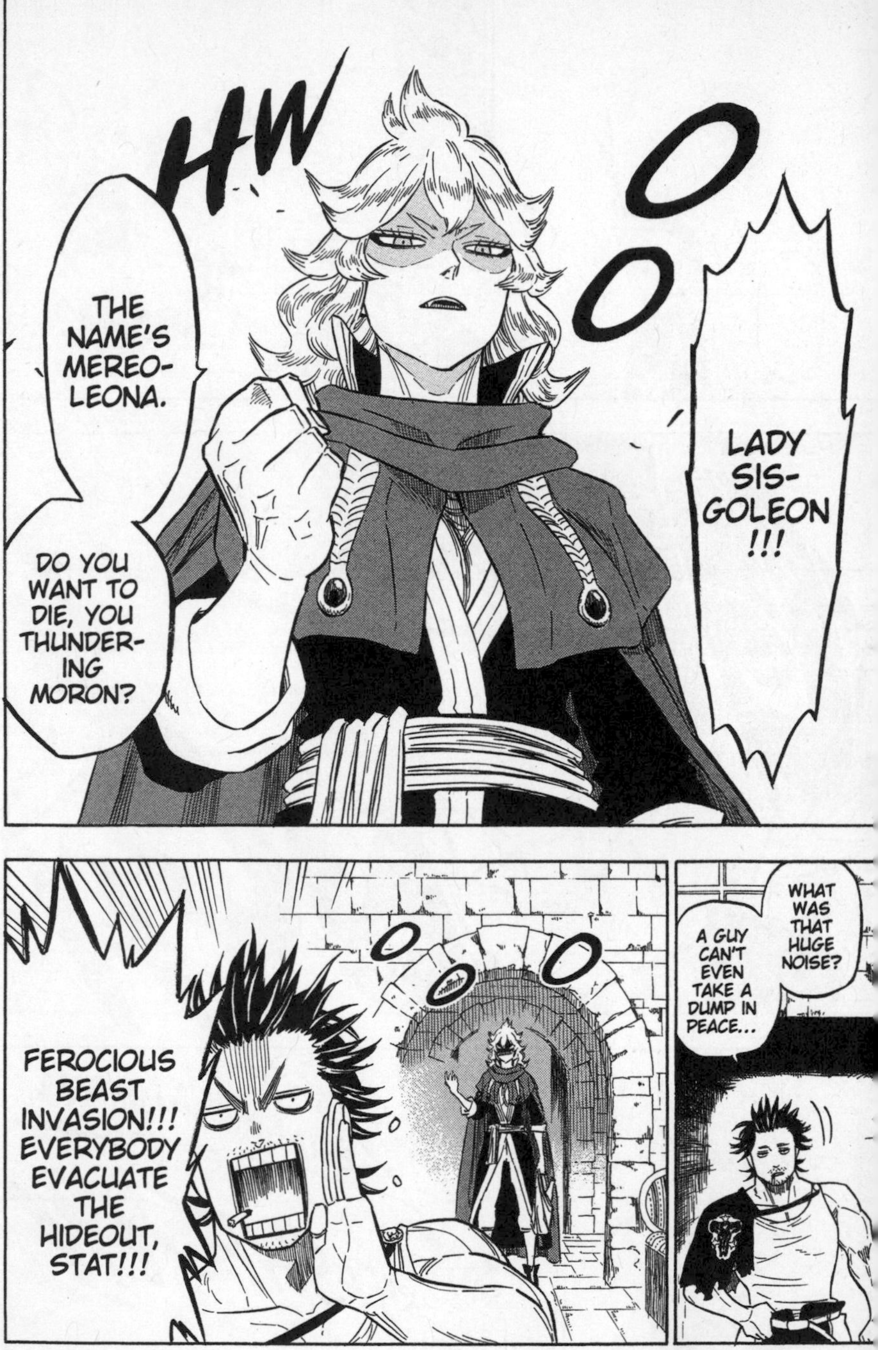
HWOOO
LADY SIS-GOLEON!!!
THE NAME'S MEREO-LEONA.
DO YOU WANT TO DIE, YOU THUNDERING MORON?
WHAT WAS THAT HUGE NOISE?
A GUY CAN'T EVEN TAKE A DUMP IN PEACE...
FEROCIOUS BEAST INVASION!!! EVERYBODY EVACUATE THE HIDEOUT, STAT!!!

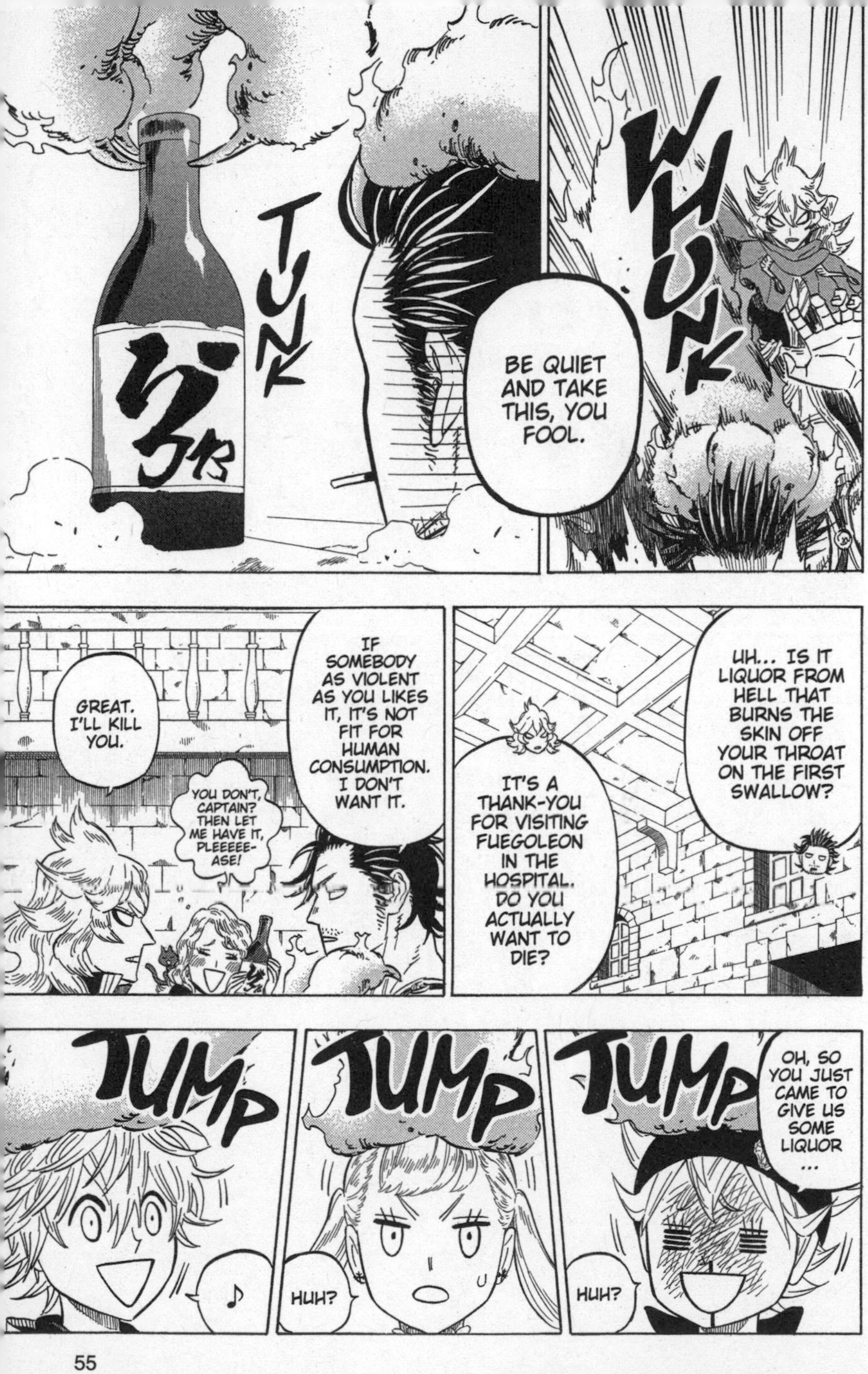
WHUNK
BE QUIET AND TAKE THIS, YOU FOOL.
TUNK
UH... IS IT LIQUOR FROM HELL THAT BURNS THE SKIN OFF YOUR THROAT ON THE FIRST SWALLOW?
IT'S A THANK-YOU FOR VISITING FUEGOLEON IN THE HOSPITAL. DO YOU ACTUALLY WANT TO DIE?
IF SOMEBODY AS VIOLENT AS YOU LIKES IT, IT'S NOT FIT FOR HUMAN CONSUMPTION. I DON'T WANT IT.
GREAT. I'LL KILL YOU.
YOU DON'T, CAPTAIN? THEN LET ME HAVE IT, PLEEEEE-ASE!
TUMP
OH, SO YOU JUST CAME TO GIVE US SOME LIQUOR...
HUH?
TUMP
HUH?
TUMP
♪

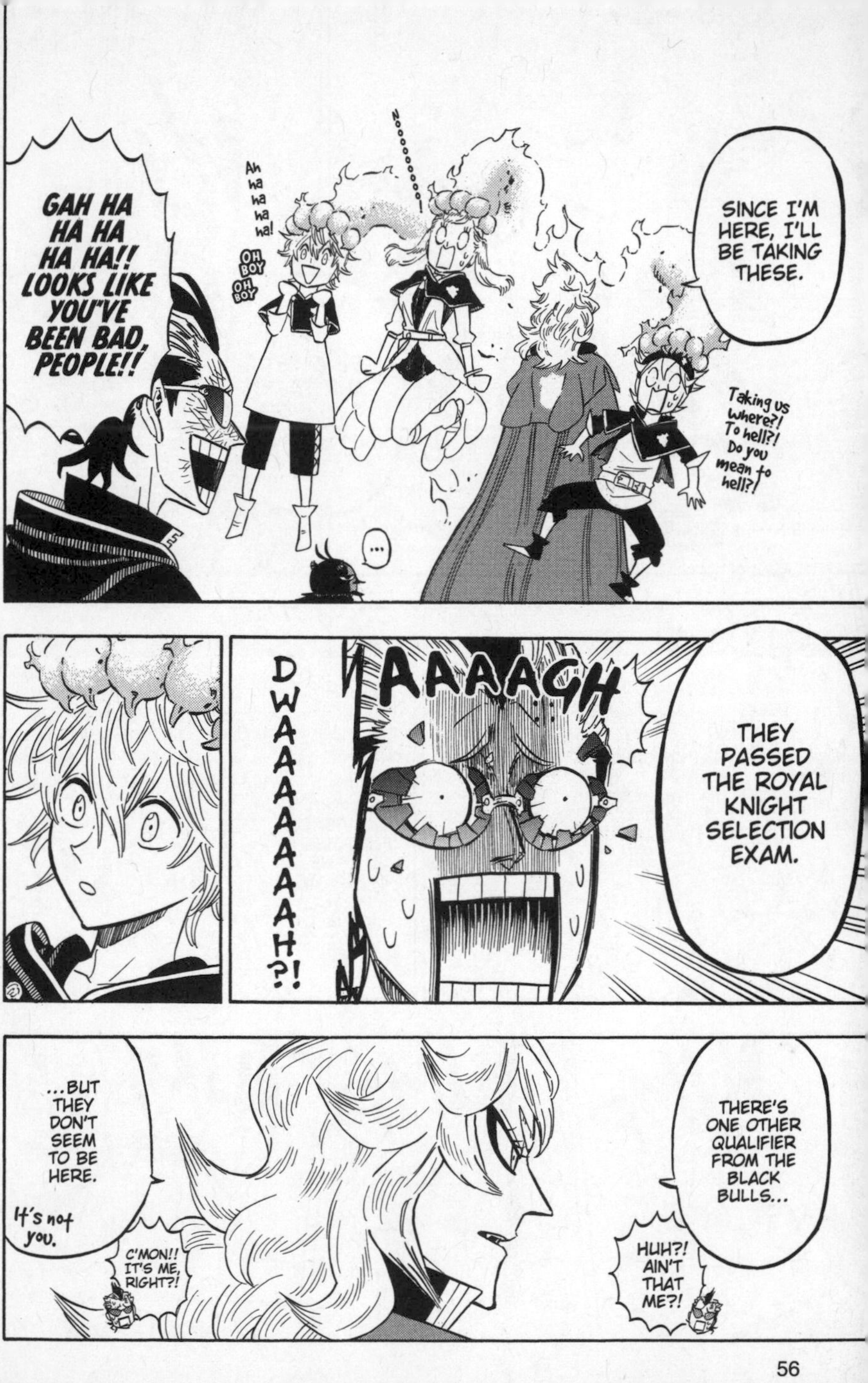
SINCE I'M HERE, I'LL BE TAKING THESE.
Taking us where?! To hell?! Do you mean to hell?!
NOOOOOOOOO!
Ah ha ha ha ha!
OH BOY OH BOY
GAH HA HA HA HA HA!! LOOKS LIKE YOU'VE BEEN BAD, PEOPLE!!
...
THEY PASSED THE ROYAL KNIGHT SELECTION EXAM.
AAAAGH
DWAAAAAAAAAH?!
THERE'S ONE OTHER QUALIFIER FROM THE BLACK BULLS...
HUH?! AIN'T THAT ME?!
...BUT THEY DON'T SEEM TO BE HERE.
C'MON!! IT'S ME, RIGHT?!
It's not you.

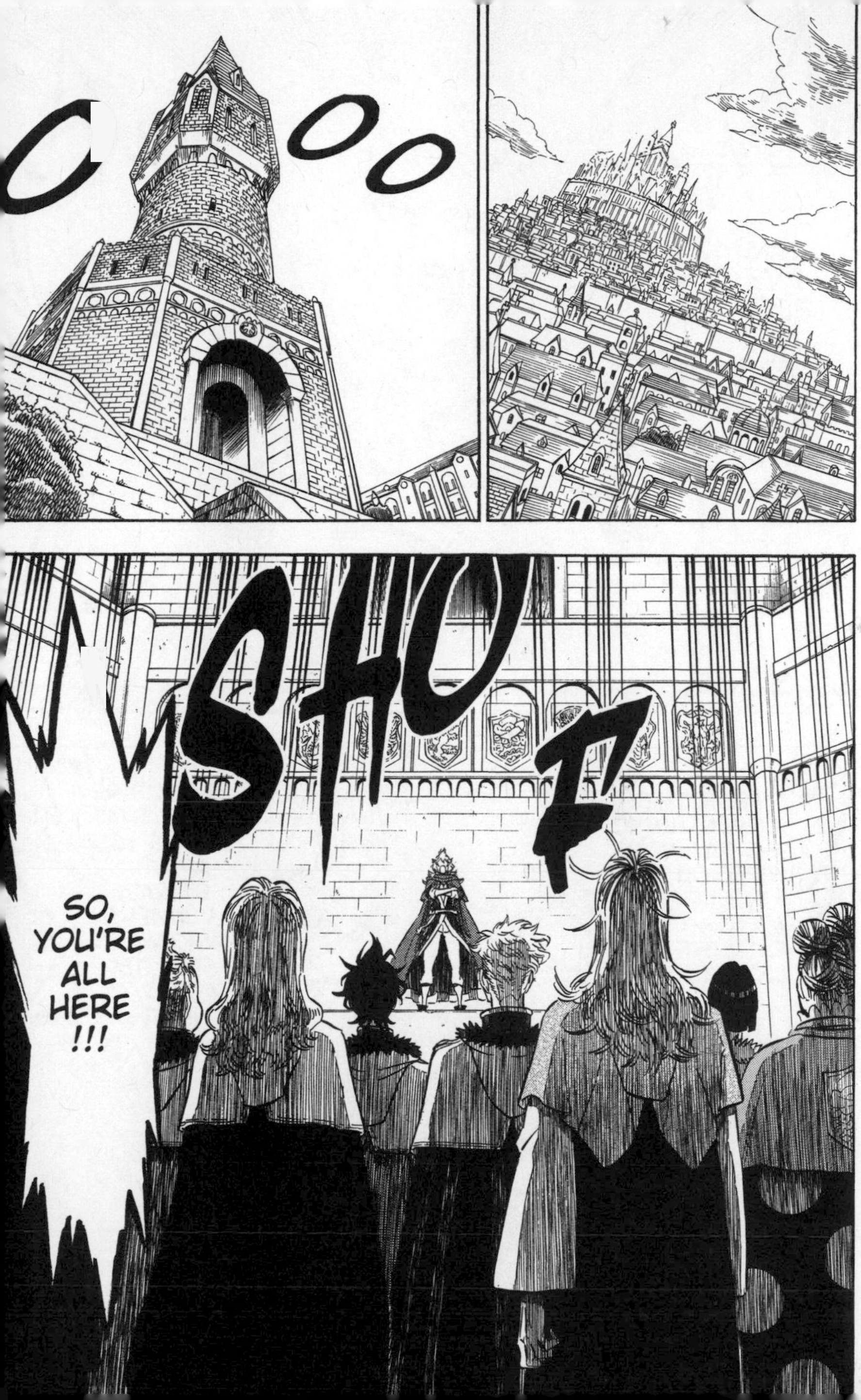
SO, YOU'RE ALL HERE!!!

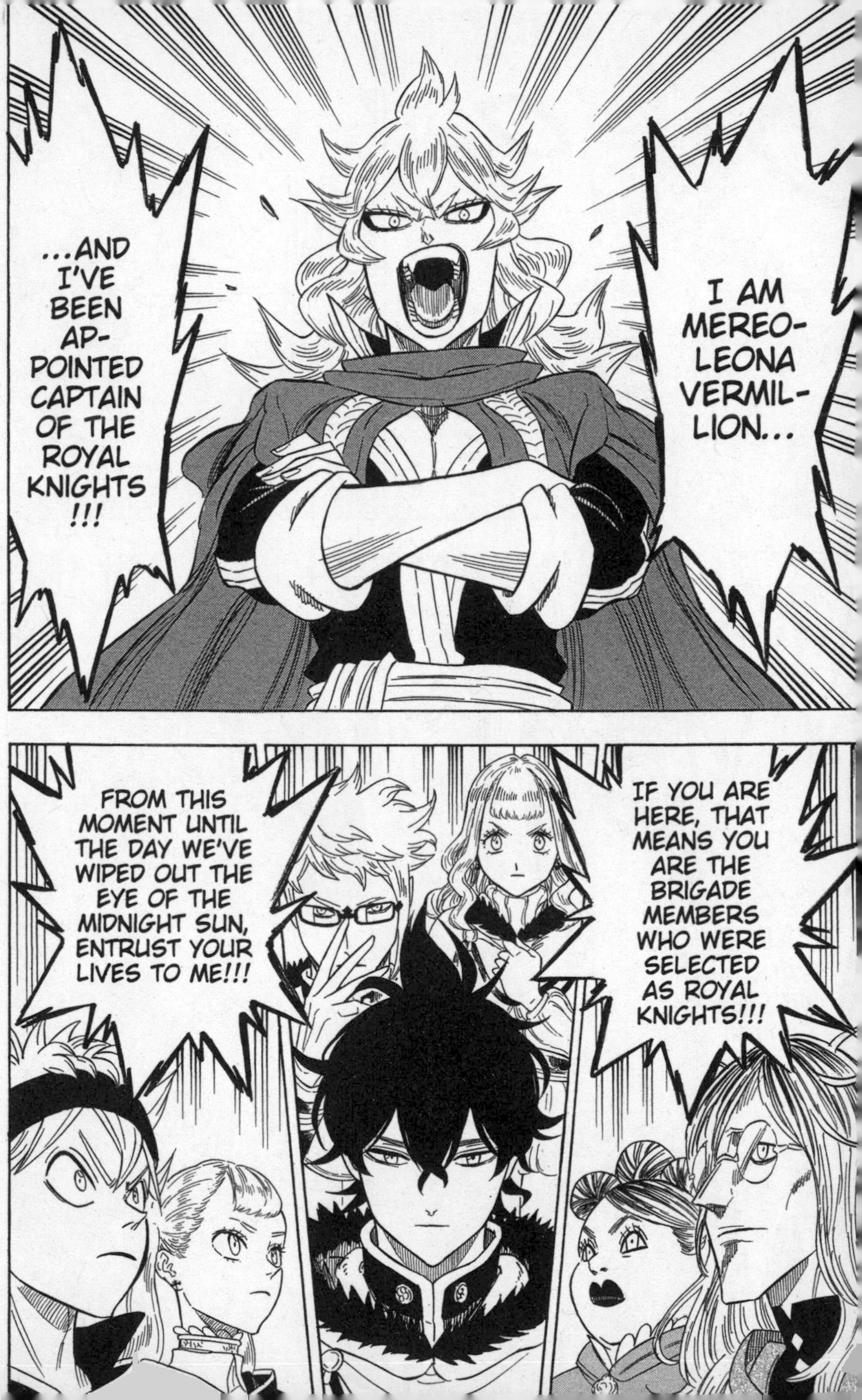
I AM MEREO-LEONA VERMIL-LION...
...AND I'VE BEEN AP-POINTED CAPTAIN OF THE ROYAL KNIGHTS !!!
IF YOU ARE HERE, THAT MEANS YOU ARE THE BRIGADE MEMBERS WHO WERE SELECTED AS ROYAL KNIGHTS!!!
FROM THIS MOMENT UNTIL THE DAY WE'VE WIPED OUT THE EYE OF THE MIDNIGHT SUN, ENTRUST YOUR LIVES TO ME!!!

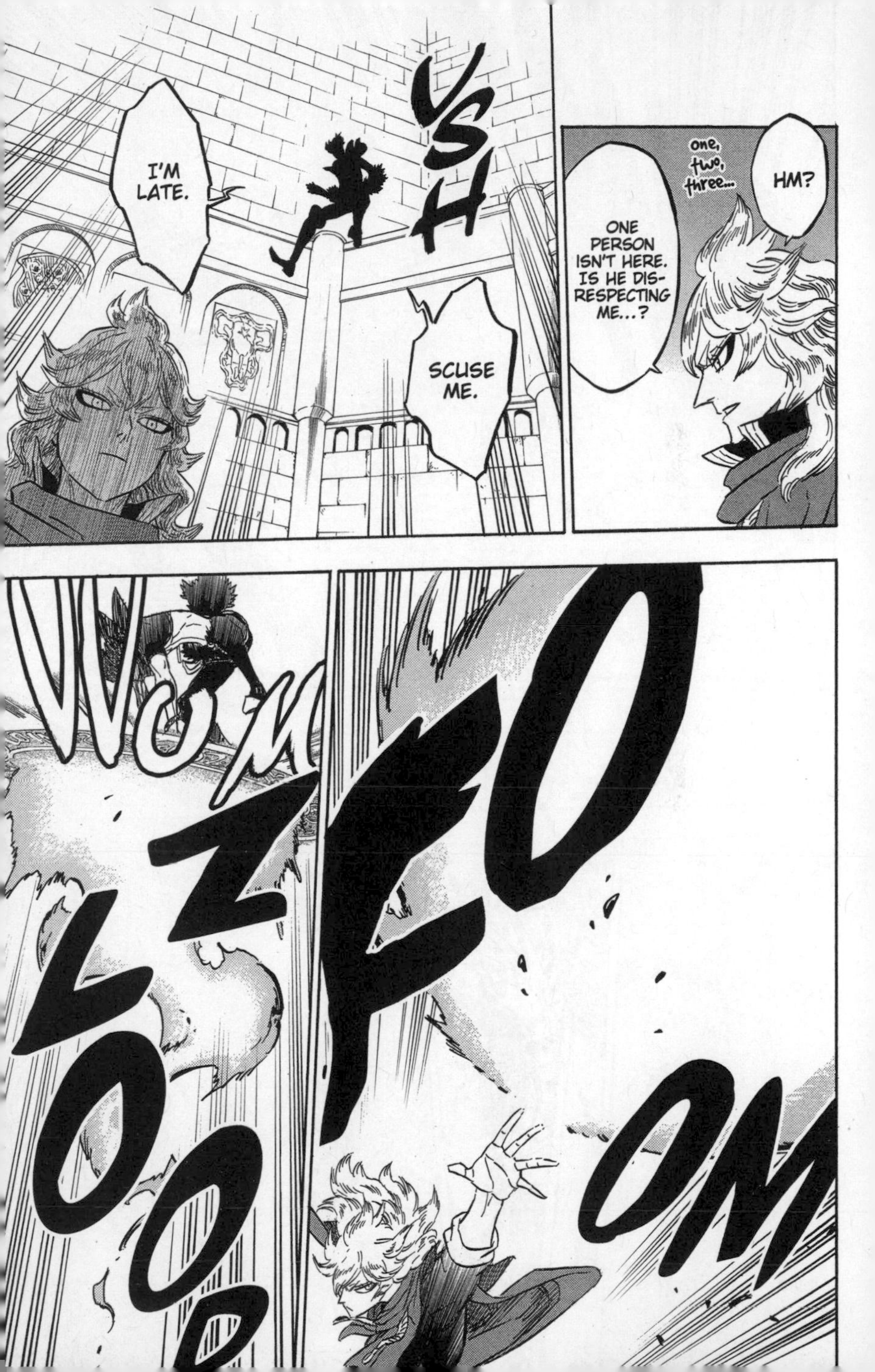
HM?
one, two, three...
ONE PERSON ISN'T HERE. IS HE DIS-RESPECTING ME...?
VSH
SCUSE ME.
I'M LATE.

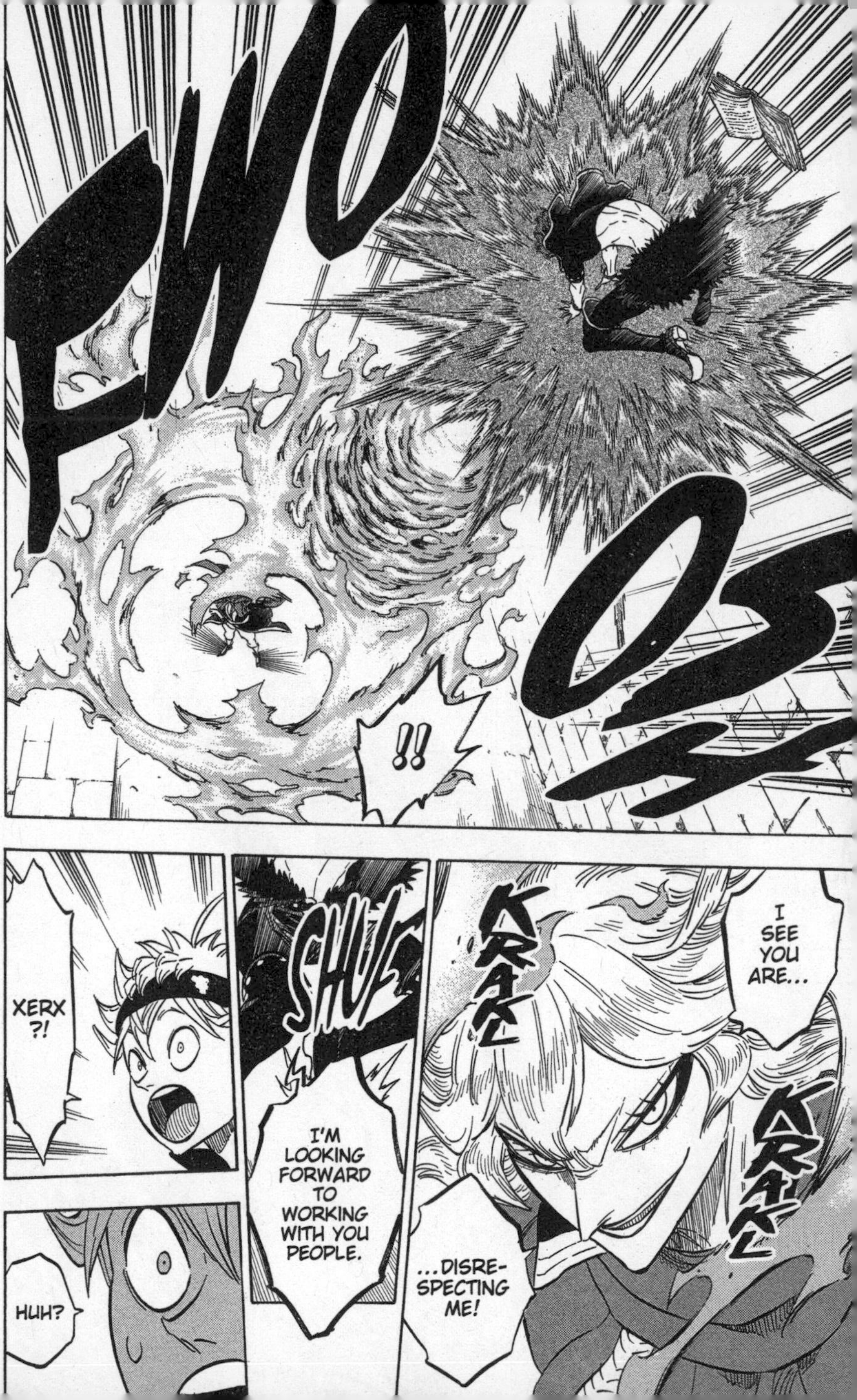
FWO
OSH
!!
I SEE YOU ARE...
KRAK
KRAK
...DISRE-SPECTING ME!
SHUK
I'M LOOKING FORWARD TO WORKING WITH YOU PEOPLE.
XERX ?!
HUH?

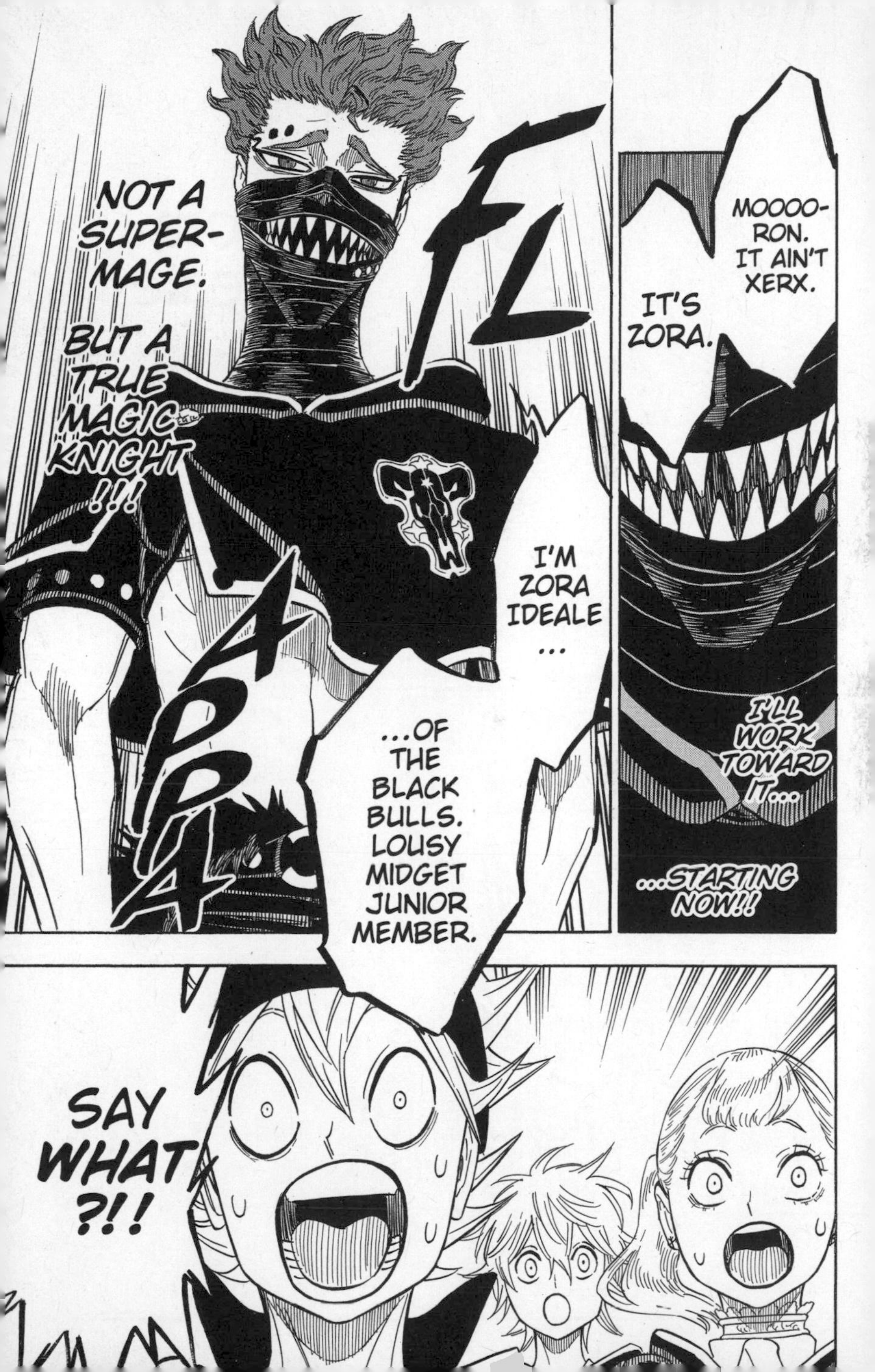
MOOOO-RON. IT AIN'T XERX.
IT'S ZORA.
I'LL WORK TOWARD IT...
...STARTING NOW!!
NOT A SUPER-MAGE.
BUT A TRUE MAGIC KNIGHT!!!
I'M ZORA IDEALE...
...OF THE BLACK BULLS. LOUSY MIDGET JUNIOR MEMBER.
SAY WHAT?!!

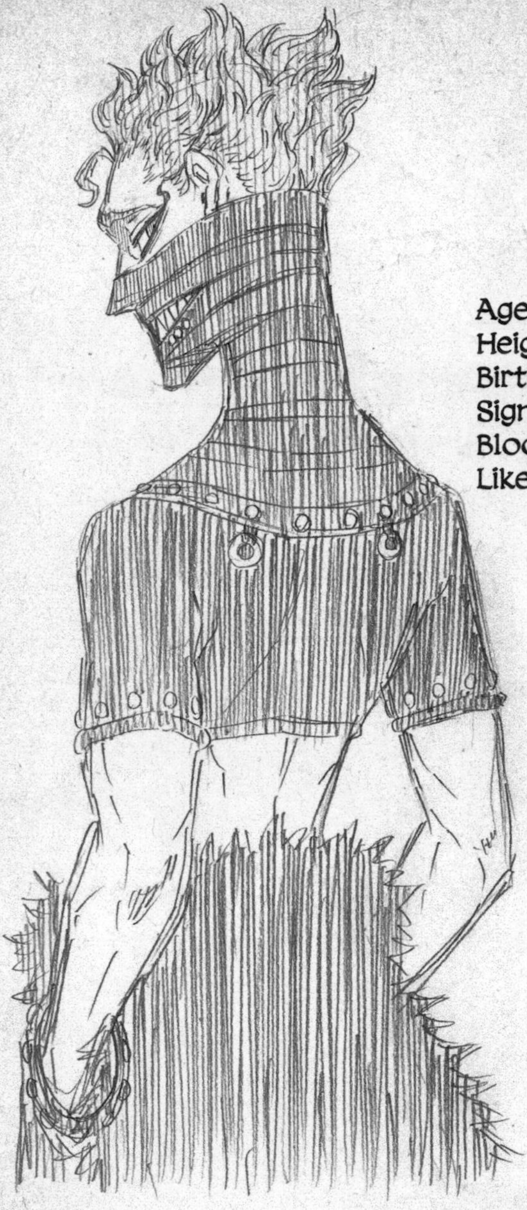

Zora Ideale

Age: 25
Height: 176 cm
Birthday: December 19
Sign: Sagittarius
Blood Type: A
Likes: Stew, his dad

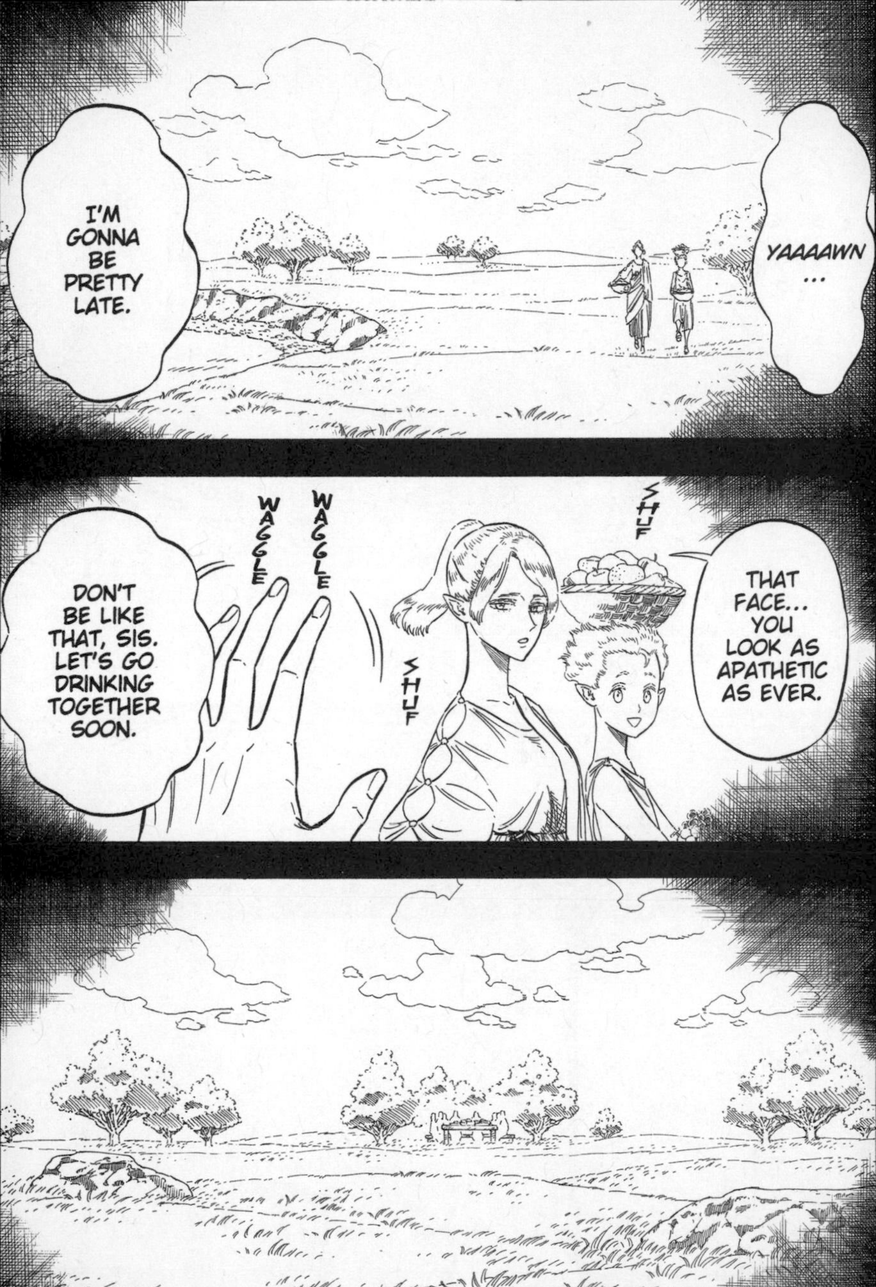
YAAAAWN...
I'M GONNA BE PRETTY LATE.
SHUF
THAT FACE... YOU LOOK AS APATHETIC AS EVER.
SHUF
WAGGLE
WAGGLE
DON'T BE LIKE THAT, SIS. LET'S GO DRINKING TOGETHER SOON.

Page 134: Dream

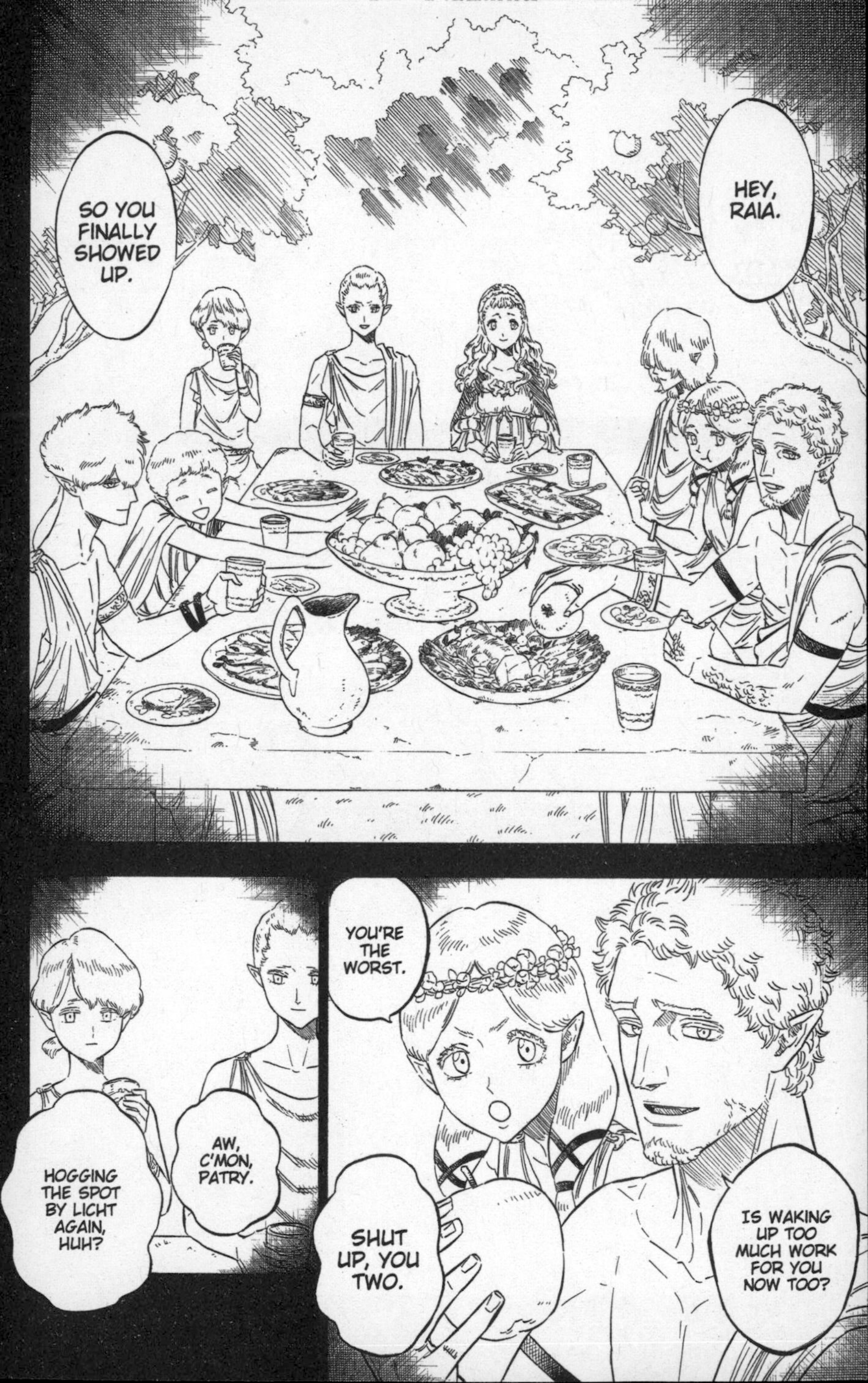
HEY, RAIA.
SO YOU FINALLY SHOWED UP.
YOU'RE THE WORST.
IS WAKING UP TOO MUCH WORK FOR YOU NOW TOO?
SHUT UP, YOU TWO.
AW, C'MON, PATRY.
HOGGING THE SPOT BY LICHT AGAIN, HUH?

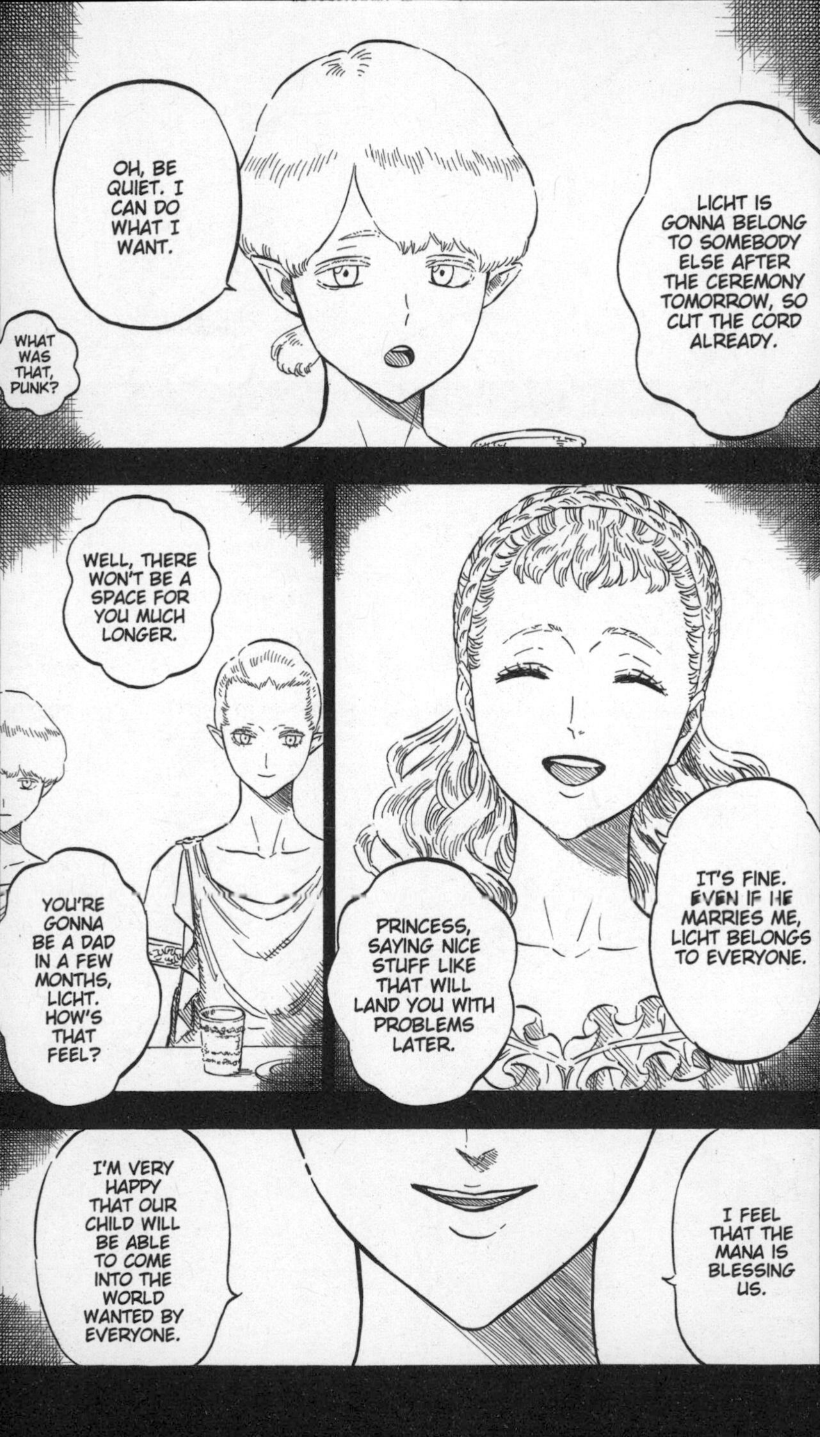
LICHT IS GONNA BELONG TO SOMEBODY ELSE AFTER THE CEREMONY TOMORROW, SO CUT THE CORD ALREADY.
OH, BE QUIET. I CAN DO WHAT I WANT.
WHAT WAS THAT, PUNK?
IT'S FINE. EVEN IF HE MARRIES ME, LICHT BELONGS TO EVERYONE.
PRINCESS, SAYING NICE STUFF LIKE THAT WILL LAND YOU WITH PROBLEMS LATER.
WELL, THERE WON'T BE A SPACE FOR YOU MUCH LONGER.
YOU'RE GONNA BE A DAD IN A FEW MONTHS, LICHT. HOW'S THAT FEEL?
I FEEL THAT THE MANA IS BLESSING US.
I'M VERY HAPPY THAT OUR CHILD WILL BE ABLE TO COME INTO THE WORLD WANTED BY EVERYONE.

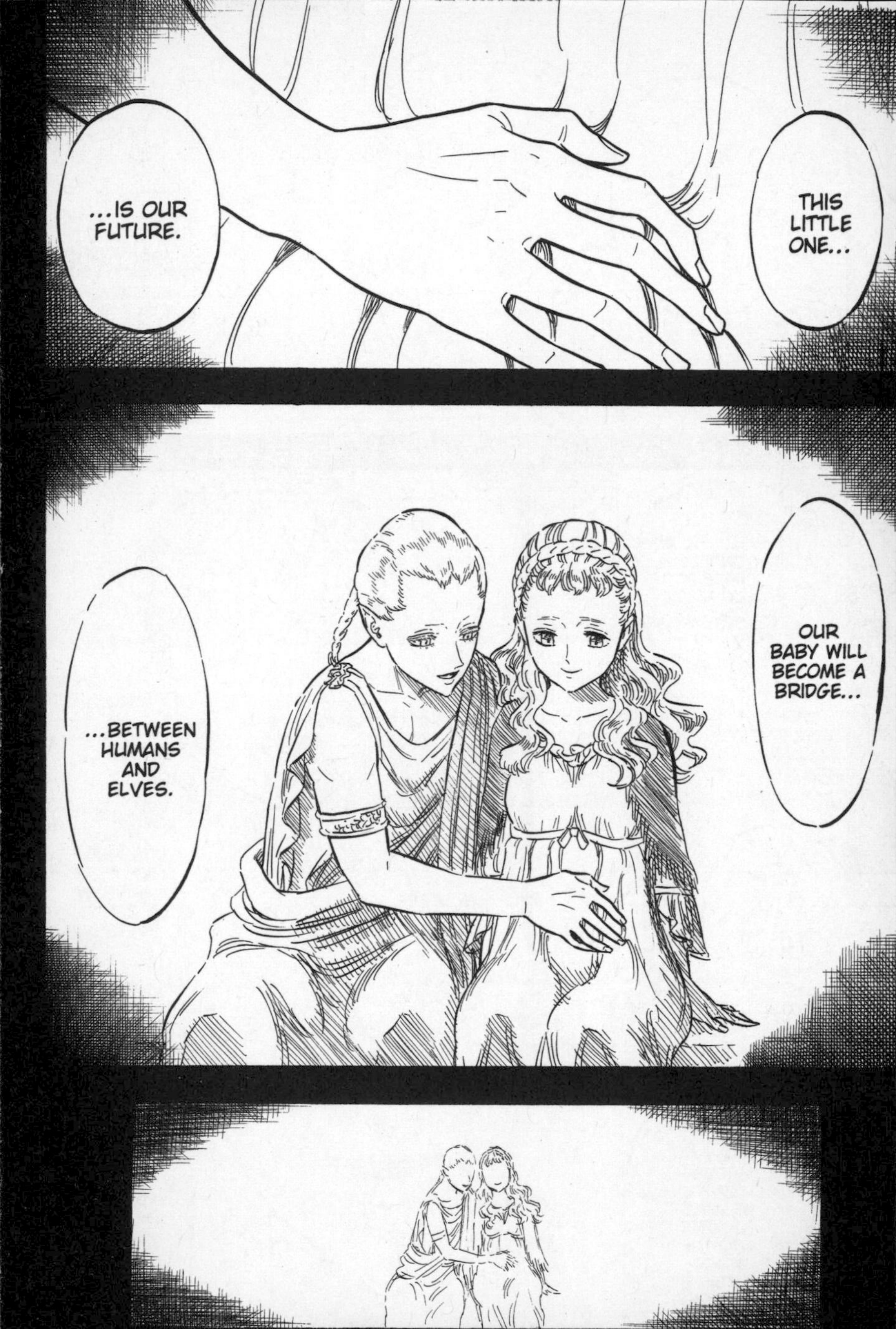
THIS LITTLE ONE...
...IS OUR FUTURE.
OUR BABY WILL BECOME A BRIDGE...
...BETWEEN HUMANS AND ELVES.

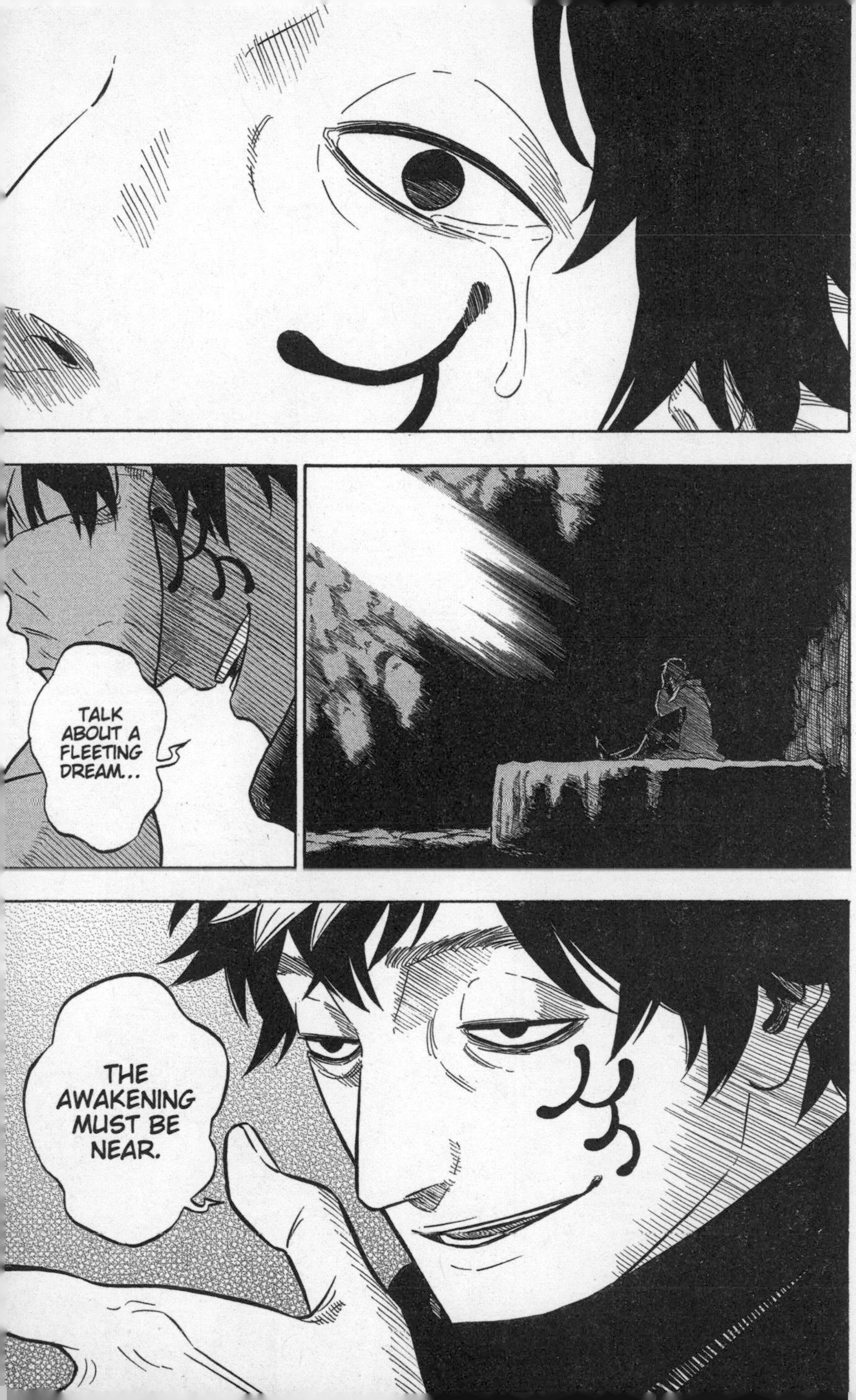
TALK ABOUT A FLEETING DREAM...
THE AWAKENING MUST BE NEAR.

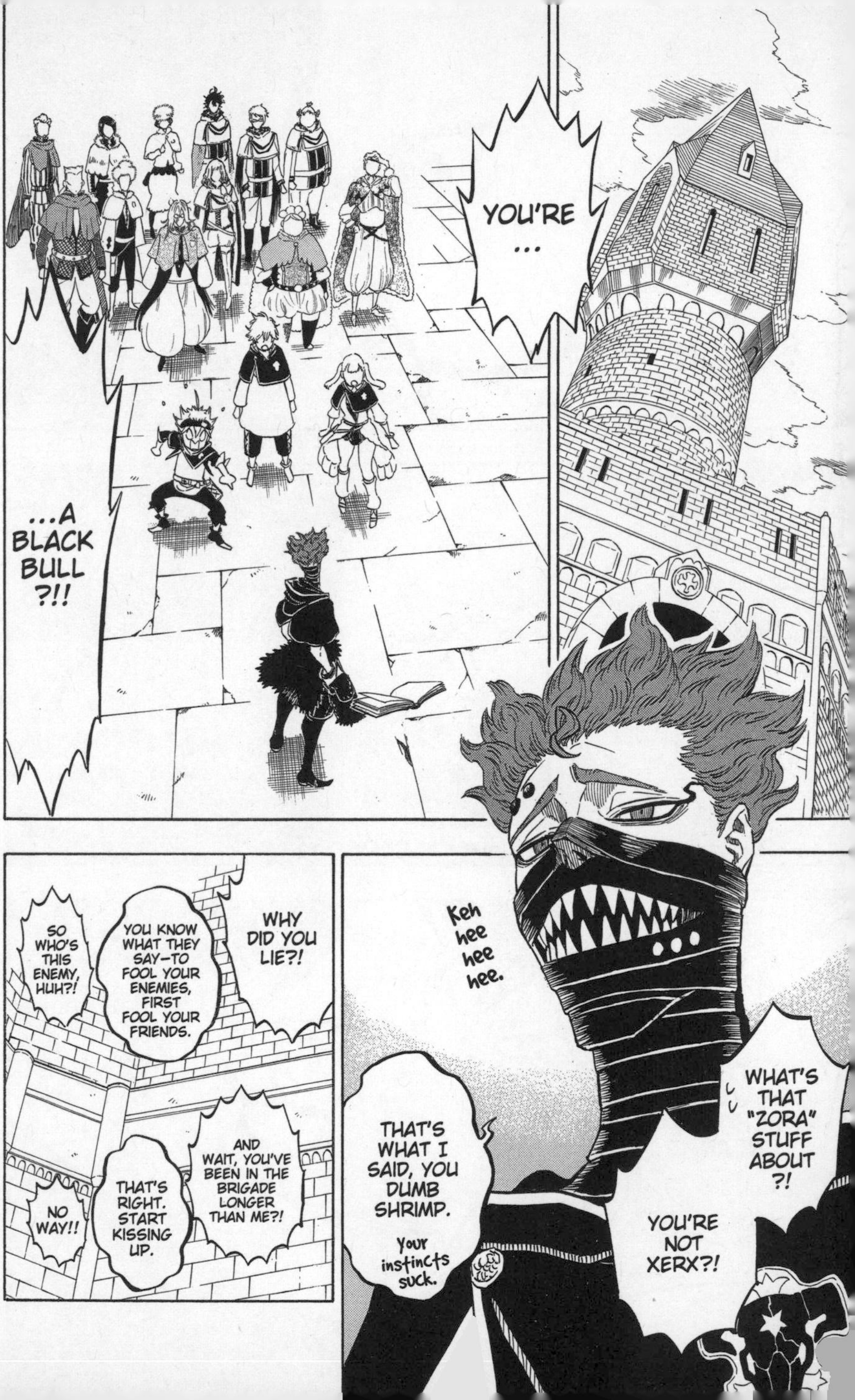
YOU'RE ...
...A BLACK BULL ?!!
Keh hee hee hee.
WHAT'S THAT "ZORA" STUFF ABOUT ?!
YOU'RE NOT XERX?!
THAT'S WHAT I SAID, YOU DUMB SHRIMP.
Your instincts suck.
WHY DID YOU LIE?!
YOU KNOW WHAT THEY SAY—TO FOOL YOUR ENEMIES, FIRST FOOL YOUR FRIENDS.
SO WHO'S THIS ENEMY, HUH?!
AND WAIT, YOU'VE BEEN IN THE BRIGADE LONGER THAN ME?!
THAT'S RIGHT. START KISSING UP.
NO WAY!!

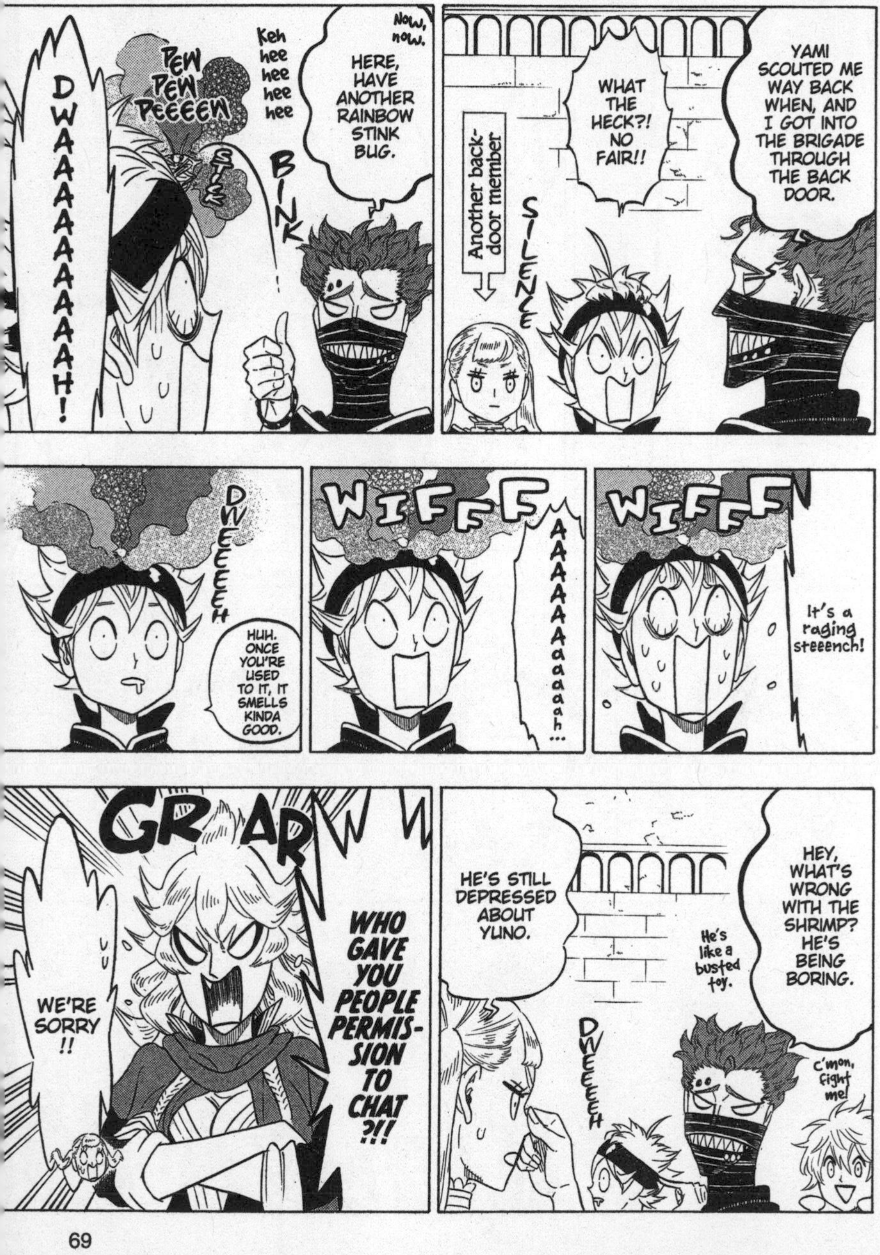
YAMI SCOUTED ME WAY BACK WHEN, AND I GOT INTO THE BRIGADE THROUGH THE BACK DOOR.
WHAT THE HECK?! NO FAIR!!
SILENCE
Another back-door member
Now, now.
HERE, HAVE ANOTHER RAINBOW STINK BUG.
Keh hee hee hee hee
BINK
STICK
PEW PEW PEEEEW
DWAAAAAAAAAAAH!
WIFFF
It's a raging steeench!
WIFFF
AAAAAAAAaaaah...
DWEEEEH
HUH. ONCE YOU'RE USED TO IT, IT SMELLS KINDA GOOD.
HEY, WHAT'S WRONG WITH THE SHRIMP? HE'S BEING BORING.
C'mon, fight me!
He's like a busted toy.
HE'S STILL DEPRESSED ABOUT YUNO.
DWEEEEH
GRAR
WHO GAVE YOU PEOPLE PERMISSION TO CHAT?!!
WE'RE SORRY!!

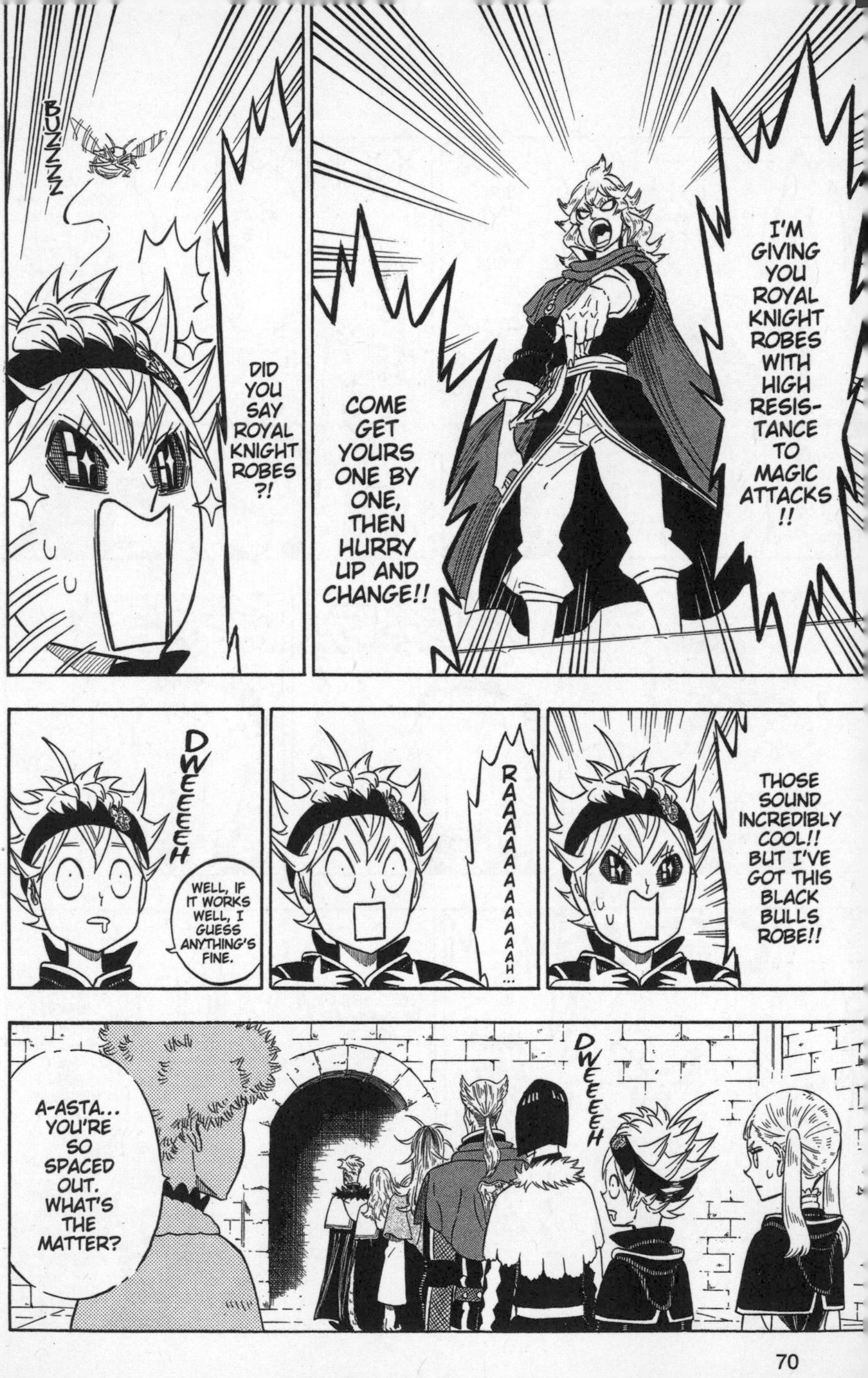
I'M GIVING YOU ROYAL KNIGHT ROBES WITH HIGH RESIS-TANCE TO MAGIC ATTACKS!!
COME GET YOURS ONE BY ONE, THEN HURRY UP AND CHANGE!!
BUZZZZ
DID YOU SAY ROYAL KNIGHT ROBES?!
THOSE SOUND INCREDIBLY COOL!! BUT I'VE GOT THIS BLACK BULLS ROBE!!
RAAAAAAAAAAAH...
DWEEEEEH
WELL, IF IT WORKS WELL, I GUESS ANYTHING'S FINE.
DWEEEEH
A-ASTA... YOU'RE SO SPACED OUT. WHAT'S THE MATTER?

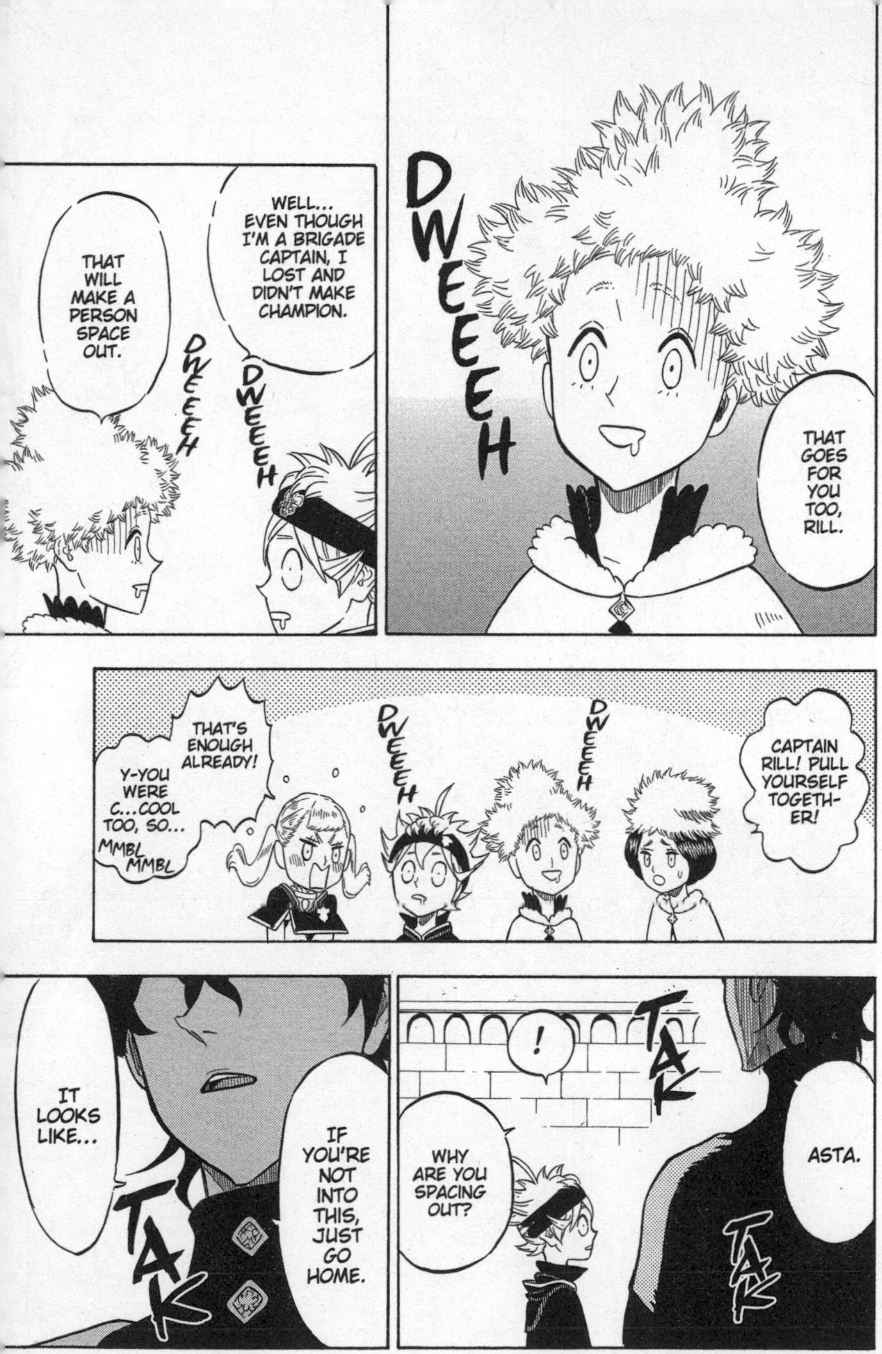
THAT GOES FOR YOU TOO, RILL.
DWEEEH
WELL... EVEN THOUGH I'M A BRIGADE CAPTAIN, I LOST AND DIDN'T MAKE CHAMPION.
DWEEEH
THAT WILL MAKE A PERSON SPACE OUT.
DWEEEH
CAPTAIN RILL! PULL YOURSELF TOGETH-ER!
DWEEEH
DWEEEH
THAT'S ENOUGH ALREADY!
Y-YOU WERE C...COOL TOO, SO...
MMBL MMBL
ASTA.
TAK
!
TAK
WHY ARE YOU SPACING OUT?
IF YOU'RE NOT INTO THIS, JUST GO HOME.
IT LOOKS LIKE...
TAK

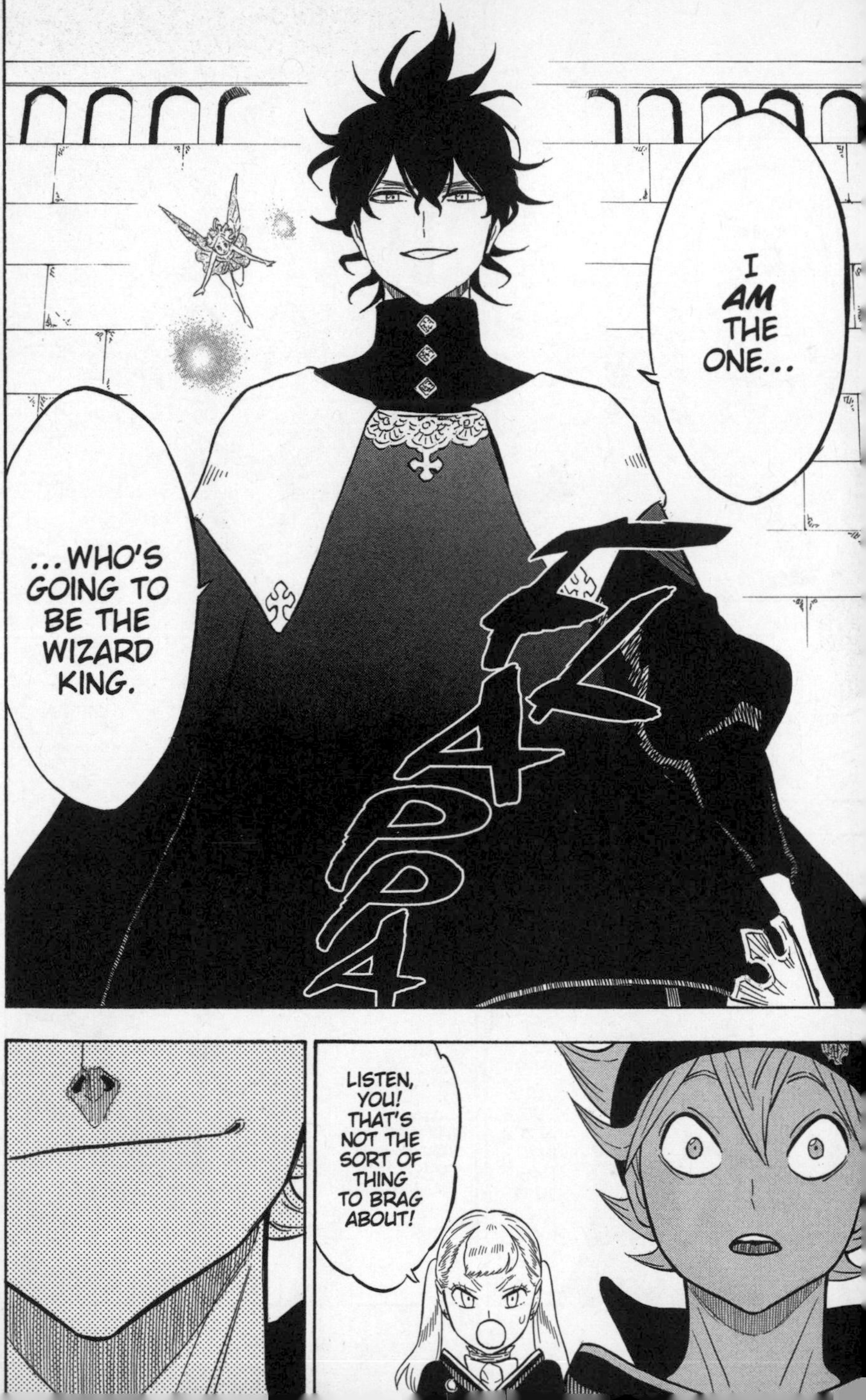
I AM THE ONE...
...WHO'S GOING TO BE THE WIZARD KING.
LISTEN, YOU! THAT'S NOT THE SORT OF THING TO BRAG ABOUT!

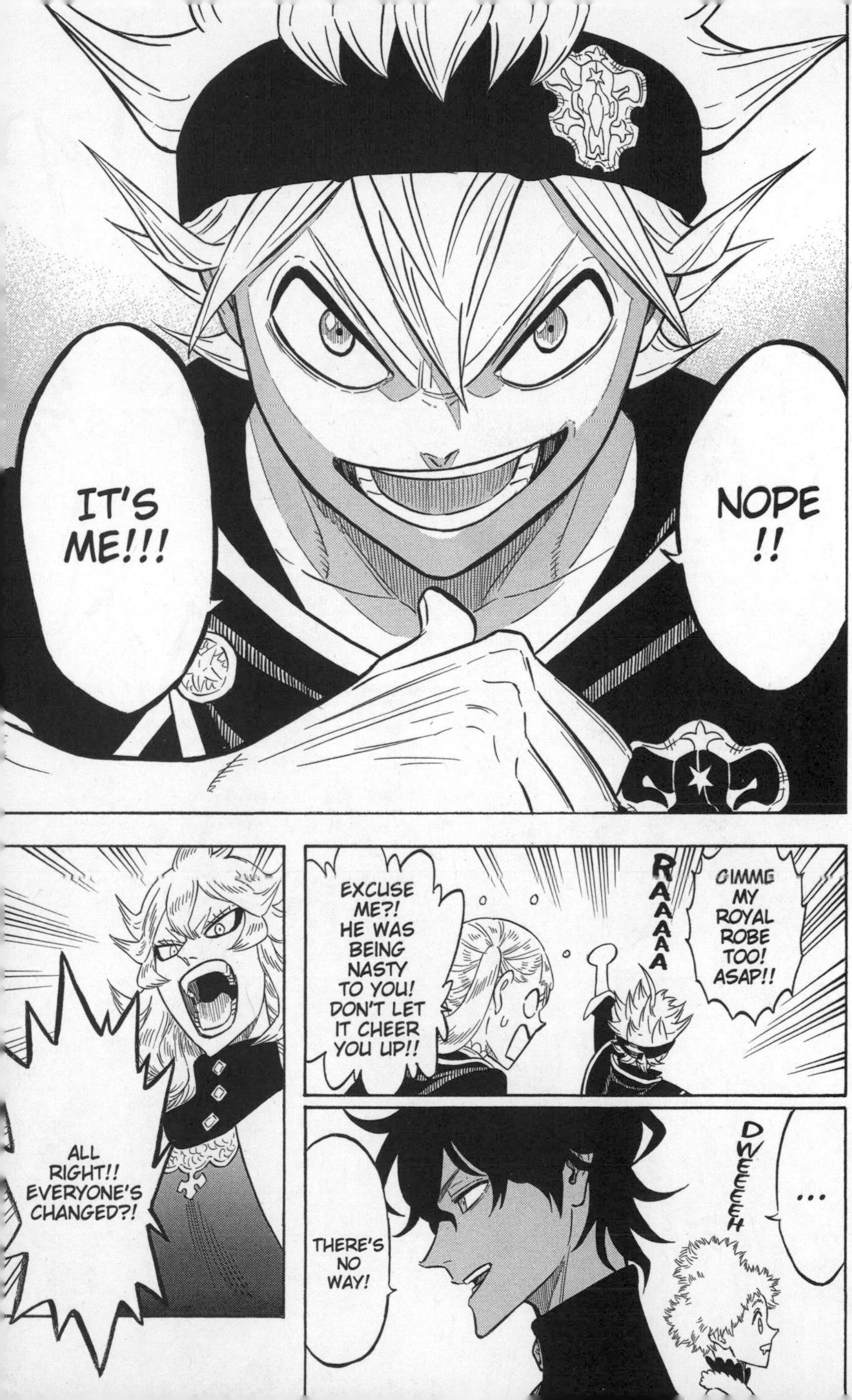
NOPE !!
IT'S ME!!!
GIMME MY ROYAL ROBE TOO! ASAP!!
RAAAAA
EXCUSE ME?! HE WAS BEING NASTY TO YOU! DON'T LET IT CHEER YOU UP!!
DWEEEEH
...
THERE'S NO WAY!
ALL RIGHT!! EVERYONE'S CHANGED?!

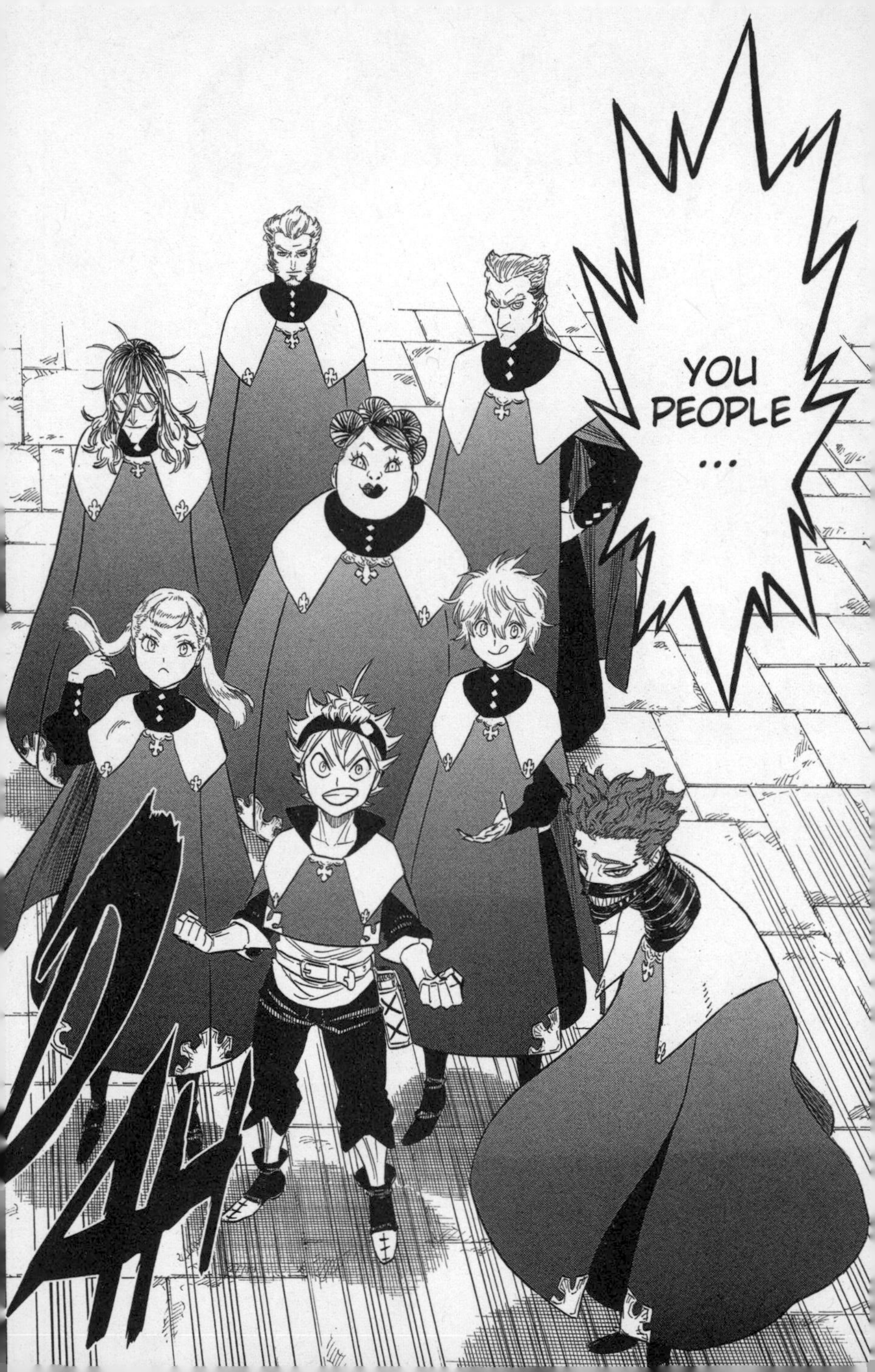
YOU PEOPLE ...

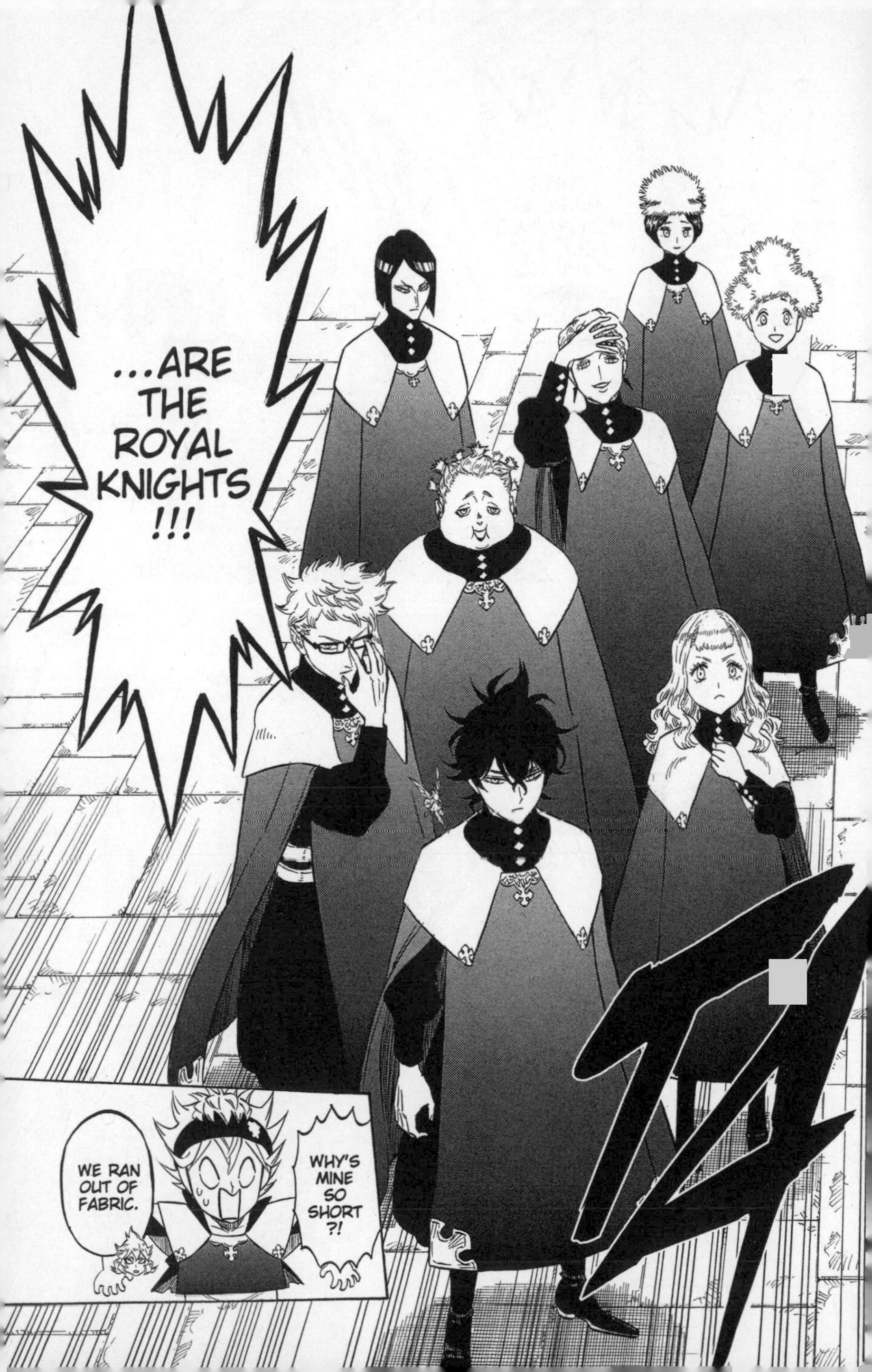
...ARE THE ROYAL KNIGHTS!!!
WHY'S MINE SO SHORT?!
WE RAN OUT OF FABRIC.

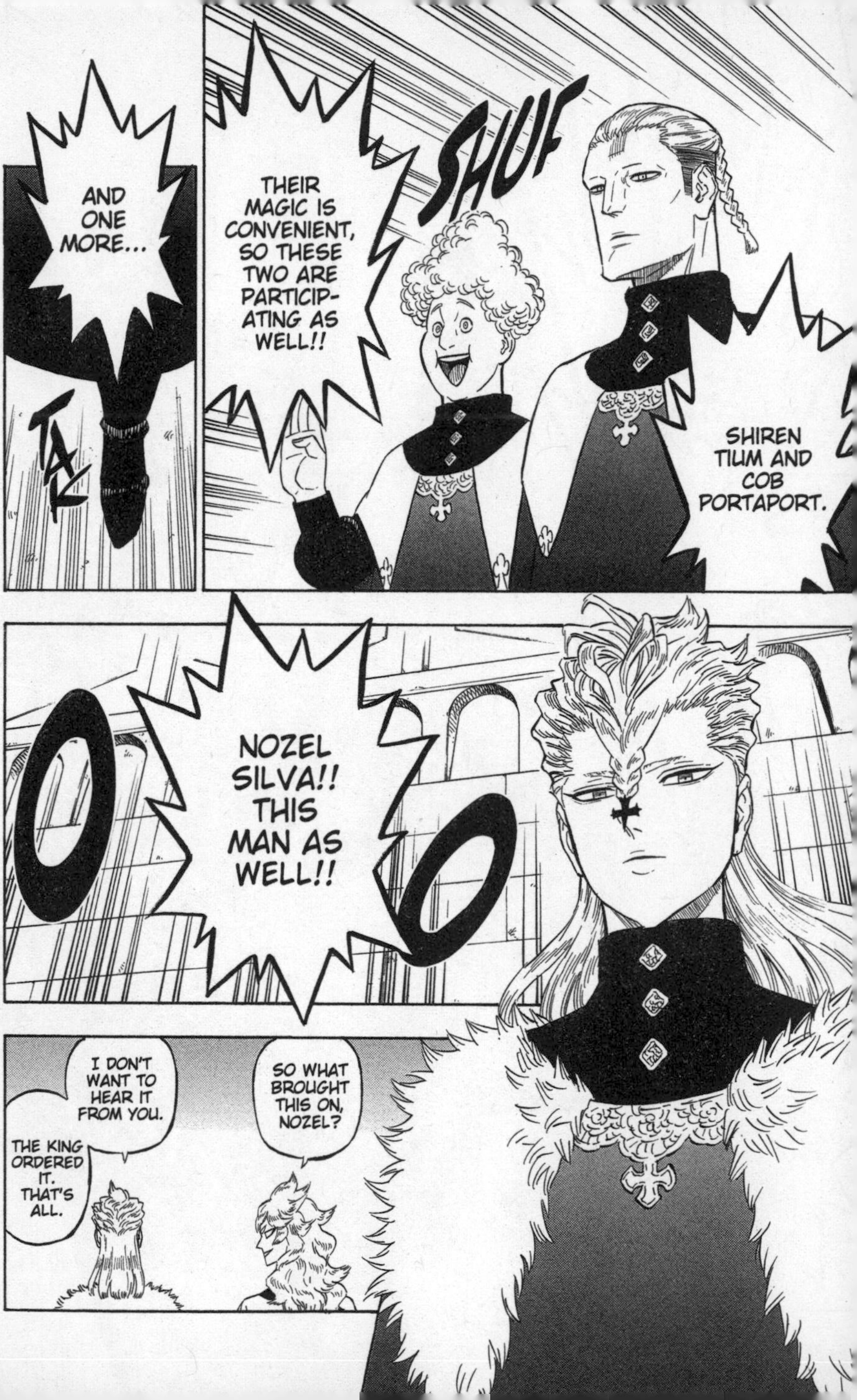
SHUF
SHIREN TIUM AND COB PORTAPORT.
THEIR MAGIC IS CONVENIENT, SO THESE TWO ARE PARTICIP-ATING AS WELL!!
AND ONE MORE...
TAK
NOZEL SILVA!! THIS MAN AS WELL!!
SO WHAT BROUGHT THIS ON, NOZEL?
I DON'T WANT TO HEAR IT FROM YOU.
THE KING ORDERED IT. THAT'S ALL.

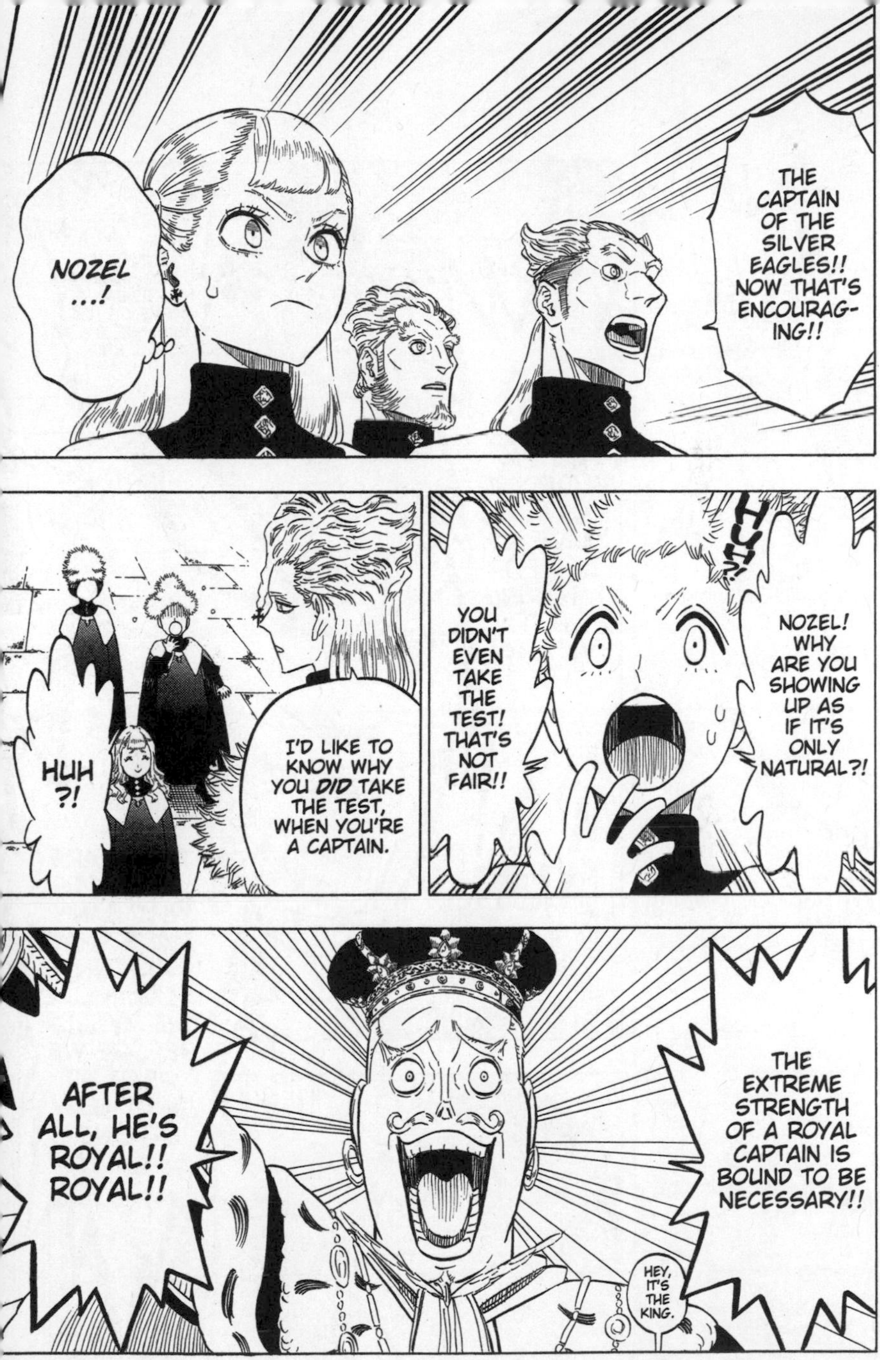
THE CAPTAIN OF THE SILVER EAGLES!! NOW THAT'S ENCOURAGING!!
NOZEL ...!
HUH?!
NOZEL! WHY ARE YOU SHOWING UP AS IF IT'S ONLY NATURAL?!
YOU DIDN'T EVEN TAKE THE TEST! THAT'S NOT FAIR!!
I'D LIKE TO KNOW WHY YOU *DID* TAKE THE TEST, WHEN YOU'RE A CAPTAIN.
HUH?!
THE EXTREME STRENGTH OF A ROYAL CAPTAIN IS BOUND TO BE NECESSARY!!
HEY, IT'S THE KING.
AFTER ALL, HE'S ROYAL!! ROYAL!!

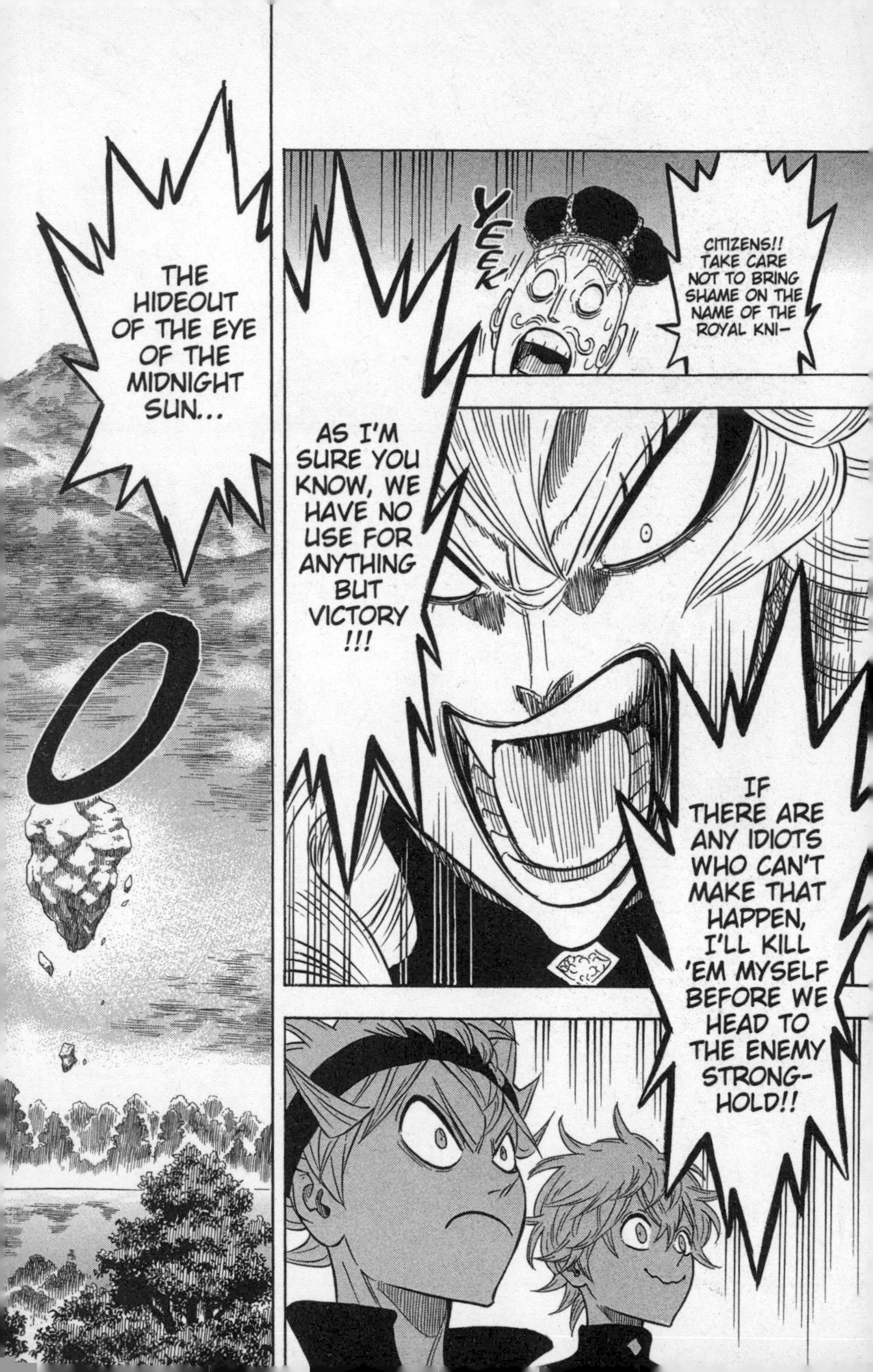
CITIZENS!! TAKE CARE NOT TO BRING SHAME ON THE NAME OF THE ROYAL KNI–
YEEK
AS I'M SURE YOU KNOW, WE HAVE NO USE FOR ANYTHING BUT VICTORY !!!
IF THERE ARE ANY IDIOTS WHO CAN'T MAKE THAT HAPPEN, I'LL KILL 'EM MYSELF BEFORE WE HEAD TO THE ENEMY STRONG-HOLD!!
THE HIDEOUT OF THE EYE OF THE MIDNIGHT SUN...

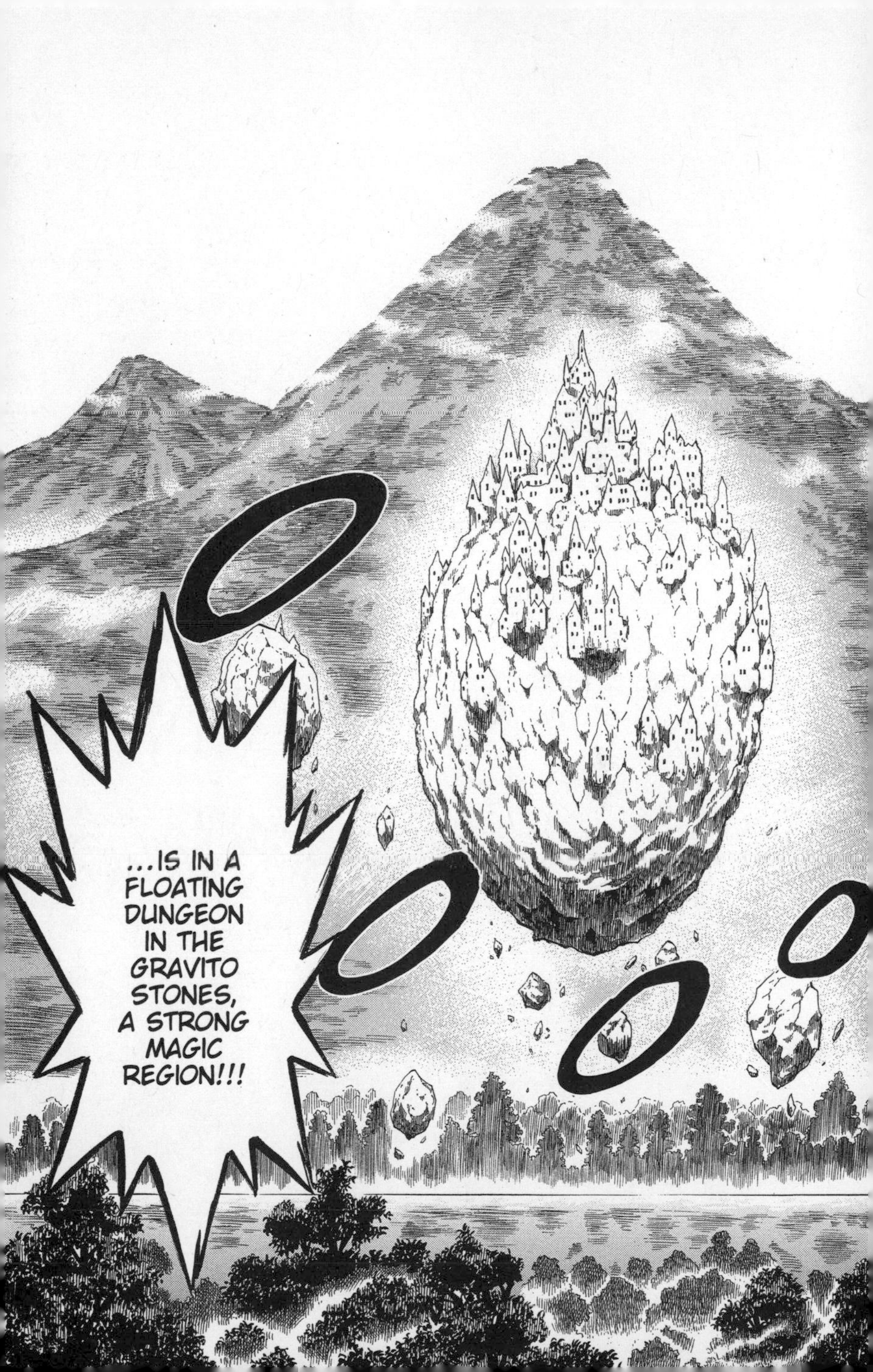
...IS IN A FLOATING DUNGEON IN THE GRAVITO STONES, A STRONG MAGIC REGION!!!

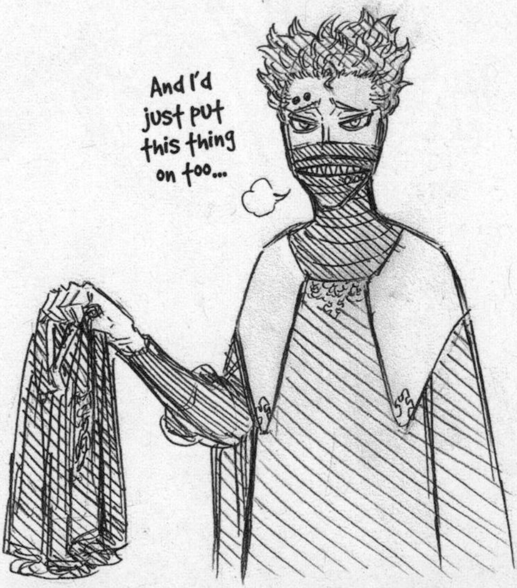
And I'd just put this thing on too...

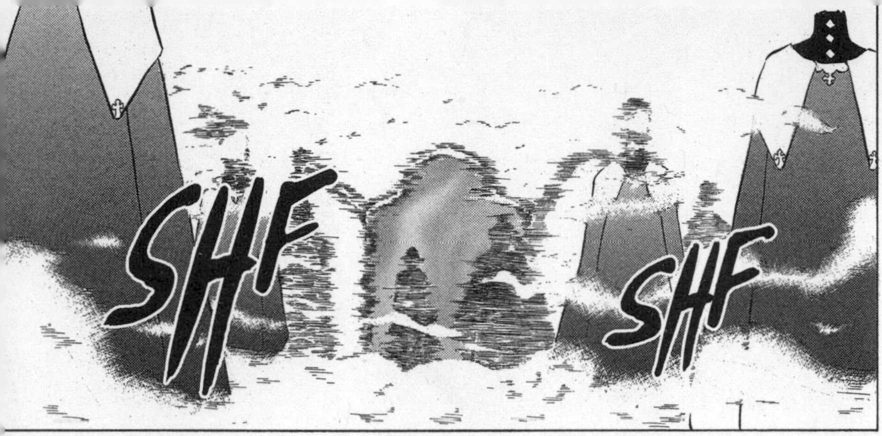
SHF
SHF
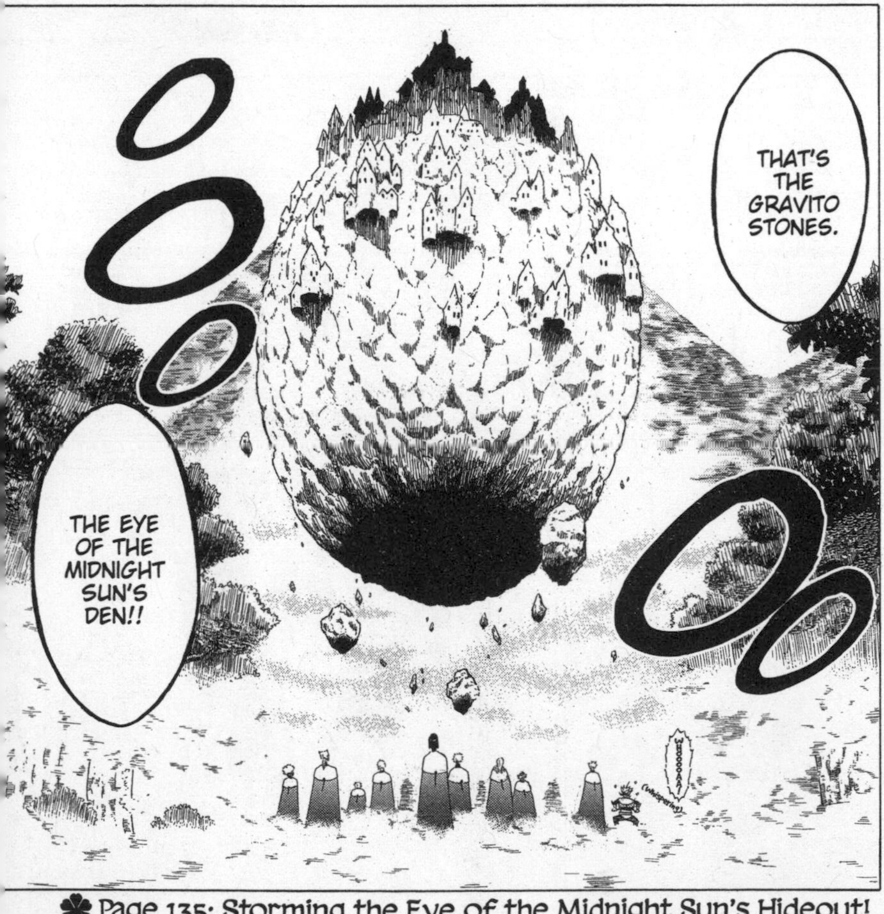
THAT'S THE GRAVITO STONES.
OOOO
THE EYE OF THE MIDNIGHT SUN'S DEN!!
OOOO
WHOOOOAA!
(whispering)

Page 135: Storming the Eye of the Midnight Sun's Hideout!

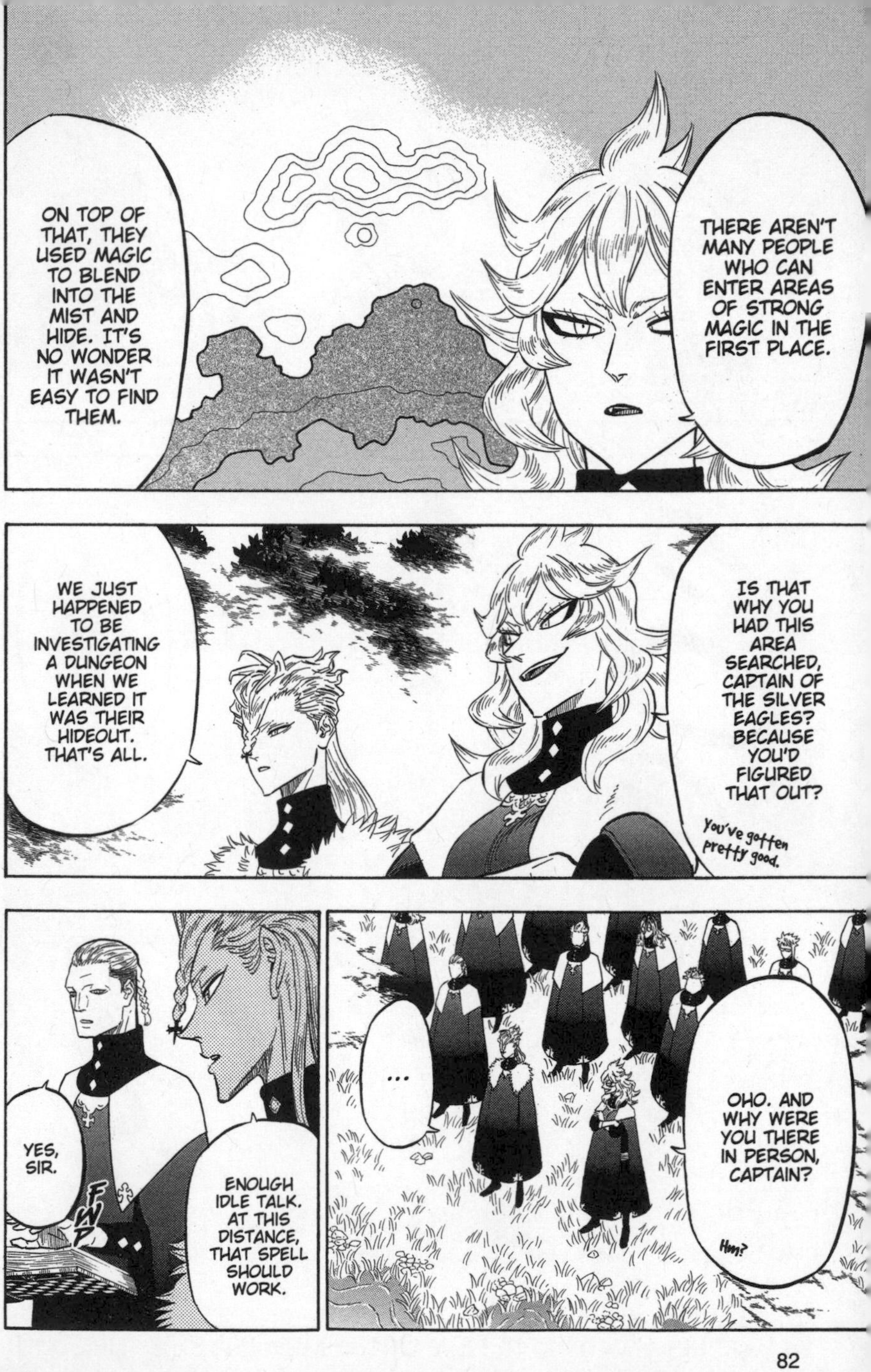
THERE AREN'T MANY PEOPLE WHO CAN ENTER AREAS OF STRONG MAGIC IN THE FIRST PLACE.
ON TOP OF THAT, THEY USED MAGIC TO BLEND INTO THE MIST AND HIDE. IT'S NO WONDER IT WASN'T EASY TO FIND THEM.
IS THAT WHY YOU HAD THIS AREA SEARCHED, CAPTAIN OF THE SILVER EAGLES? BECAUSE YOU'D FIGURED THAT OUT?
You've gotten pretty good.
WE JUST HAPPENED TO BE INVESTIGATING A DUNGEON WHEN WE LEARNED IT WAS THEIR HIDEOUT. THAT'S ALL.
OHO. AND WHY WERE YOU THERE IN PERSON, CAPTAIN?
Hm?
...
ENOUGH IDLE TALK. AT THIS DISTANCE, THAT SPELL SHOULD WORK.
FWP
YES, SIR.

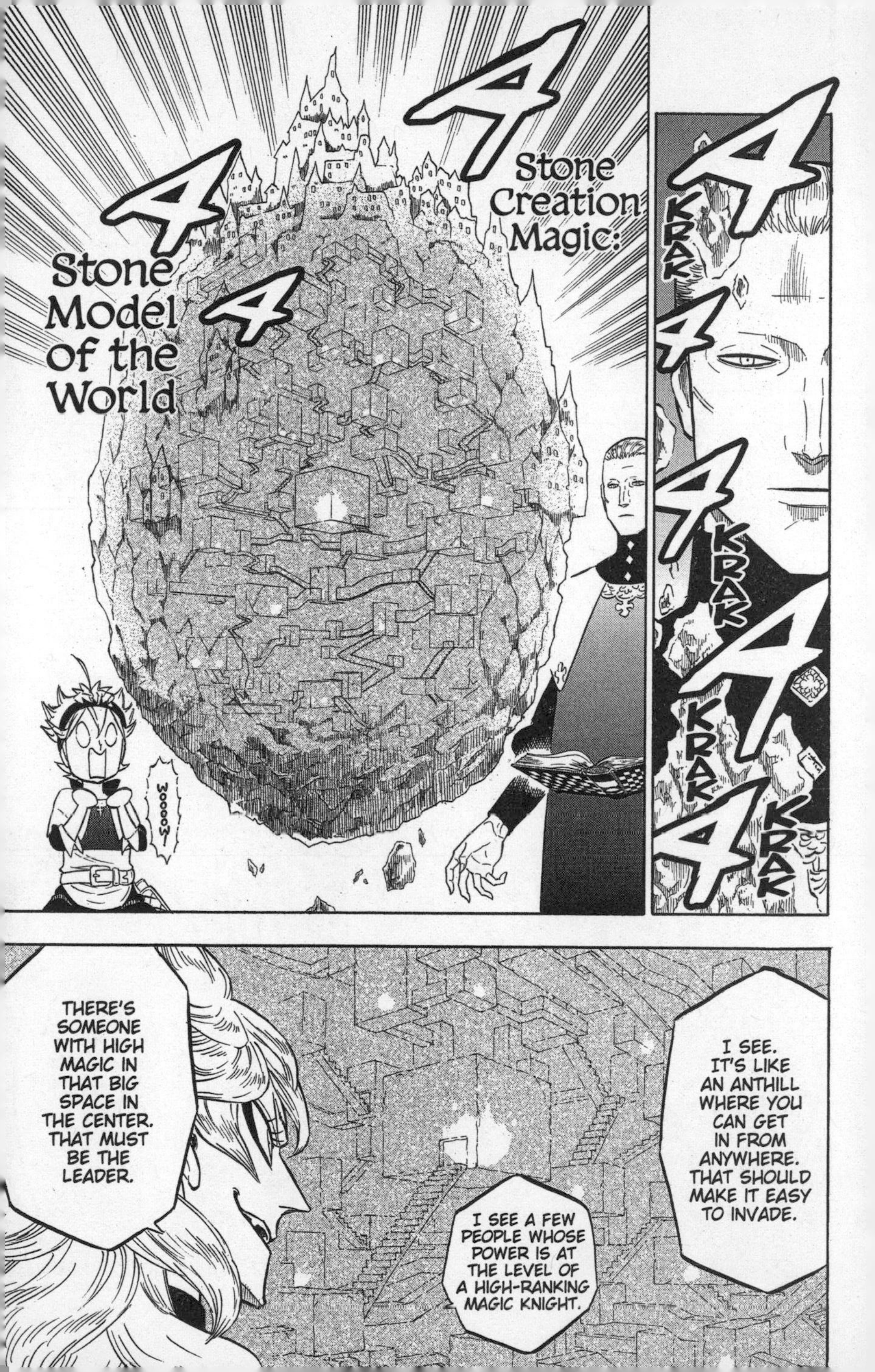
KRAK
KRAK
KRAK
KRAK
KRAK
KRAK
Stone Creation Magic:
Stone Model of the World
WOOOOW!
I SEE. IT'S LIKE AN ANTHILL WHERE YOU CAN GET IN FROM ANYWHERE. THAT SHOULD MAKE IT EASY TO INVADE.
I SEE A FEW PEOPLE WHOSE POWER IS AT THE LEVEL OF A HIGH-RANKING MAGIC KNIGHT.
THERE'S SOMEONE WITH HIGH MAGIC IN THAT BIG SPACE IN THE CENTER. THAT MUST BE THE LEADER.

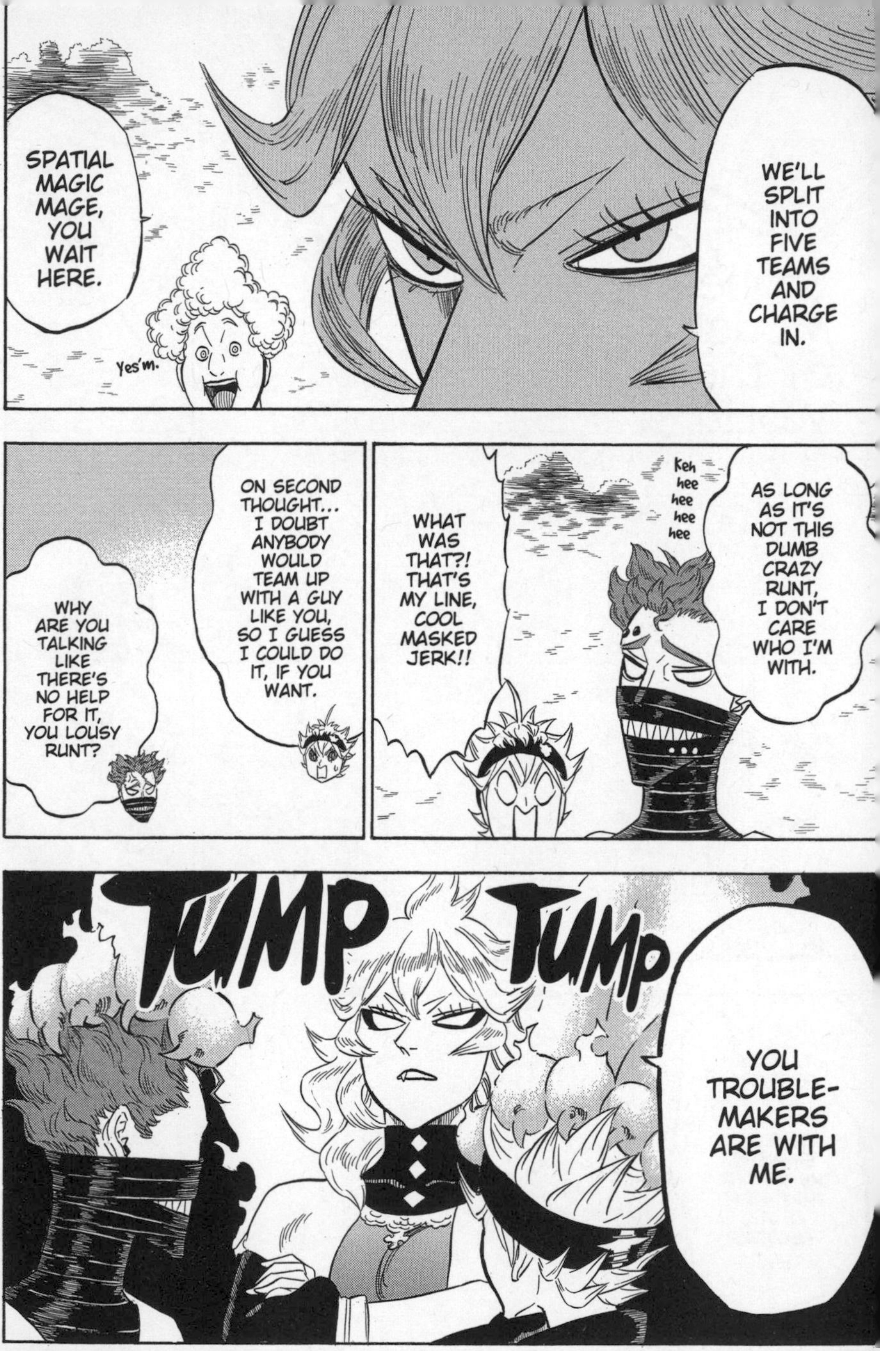
WE'LL SPLIT INTO FIVE TEAMS AND CHARGE IN.
SPATIAL MAGIC MAGE, YOU WAIT HERE.
Yes'm.
AS LONG AS IT'S NOT THIS DUMB CRAZY RUNT, I DON'T CARE WHO I'M WITH.
Keh hee hee hee hee
WHAT WAS THAT?! THAT'S MY LINE, COOL MASKED JERK!!
ON SECOND THOUGHT... I DOUBT ANYBODY WOULD TEAM UP WITH A GUY LIKE YOU, SO I GUESS I COULD DO IT, IF YOU WANT.
WHY ARE YOU TALKING LIKE THERE'S NO HELP FOR IT, YOU LOUSY RUNT?
TUMP TUMP
YOU TROUBLE-MAKERS ARE WITH ME.

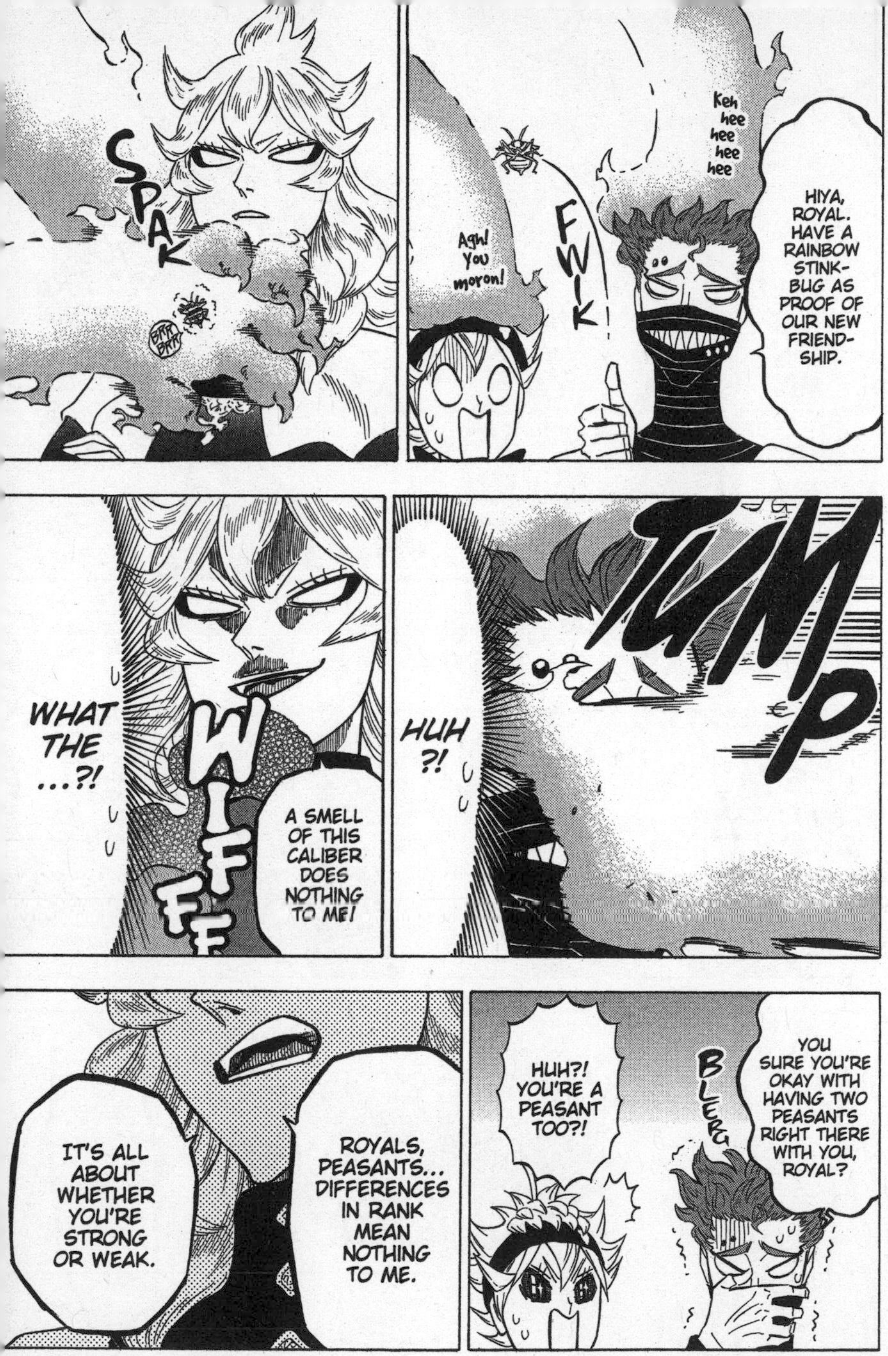
Keh hee hee hee hee
HIYA, ROYAL. HAVE A RAINBOW STINK-BUG AS PROOF OF OUR NEW FRIEND-SHIP.
FWIK
Agh! You moron!
SPAK
BRR BRR
TUMP
HUH ?!
WHAT THE ...?!
WIFFFF
A SMELL OF THIS CALIBER DOES NOTHING TO ME!
YOU SURE YOU'RE OKAY WITH HAVING TWO PEASANTS RIGHT THERE WITH YOU, ROYAL?
BLERG
HUH?! YOU'RE A PEASANT TOO?!
ROYALS, PEASANTS... DIFFERENCES IN RANK MEAN NOTHING TO ME.
IT'S ALL ABOUT WHETHER YOU'RE STRONG OR WEAK.

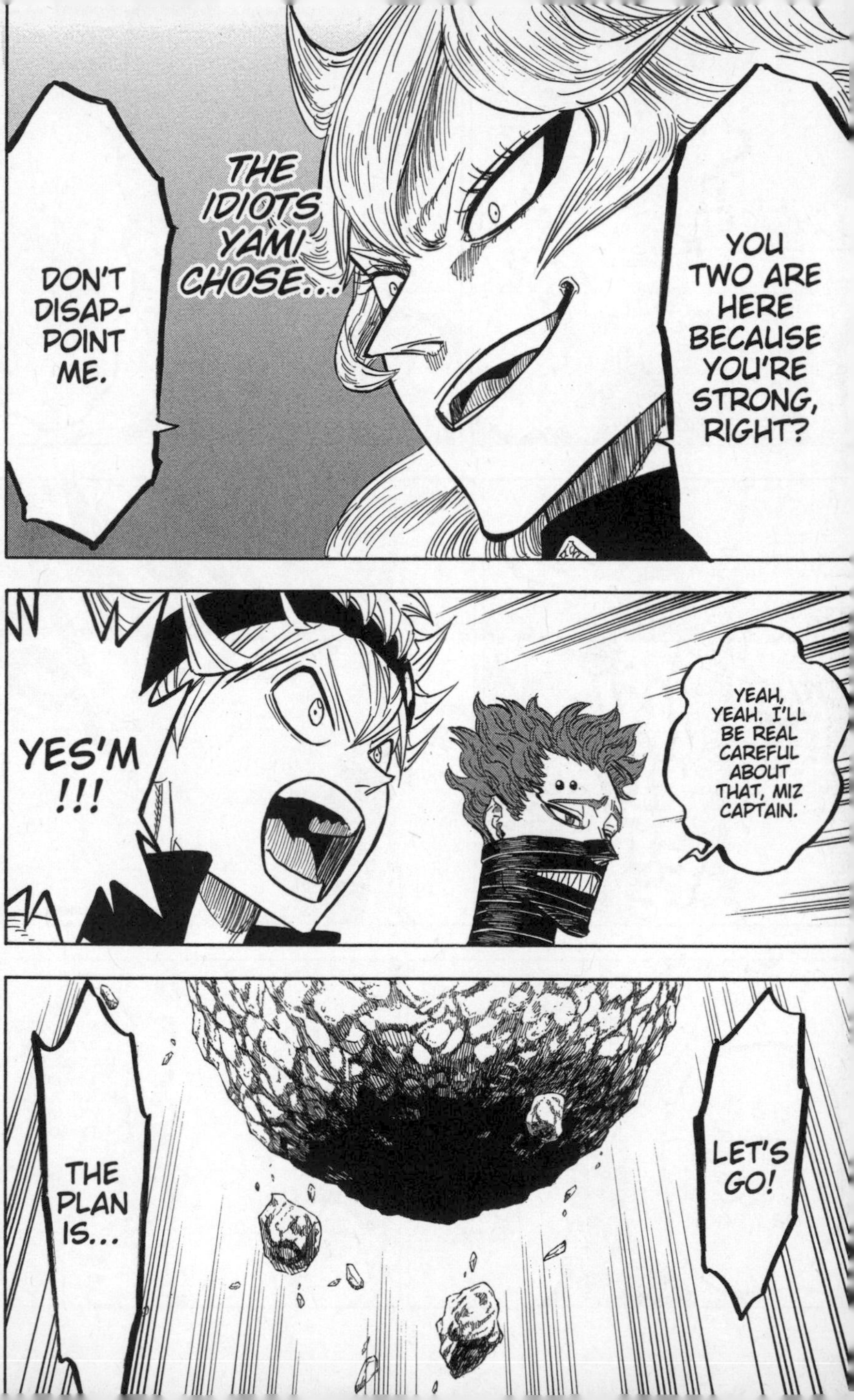
YOU TWO ARE HERE BECAUSE YOU'RE STRONG, RIGHT?
THE IDIOTS YAMI CHOSE...
DON'T DISAP-POINT ME.
YEAH, YEAH. I'LL BE REAL CAREFUL ABOUT THAT, MIZ CAPTAIN.
YES'M!!!
LET'S GO!
THE PLAN IS...

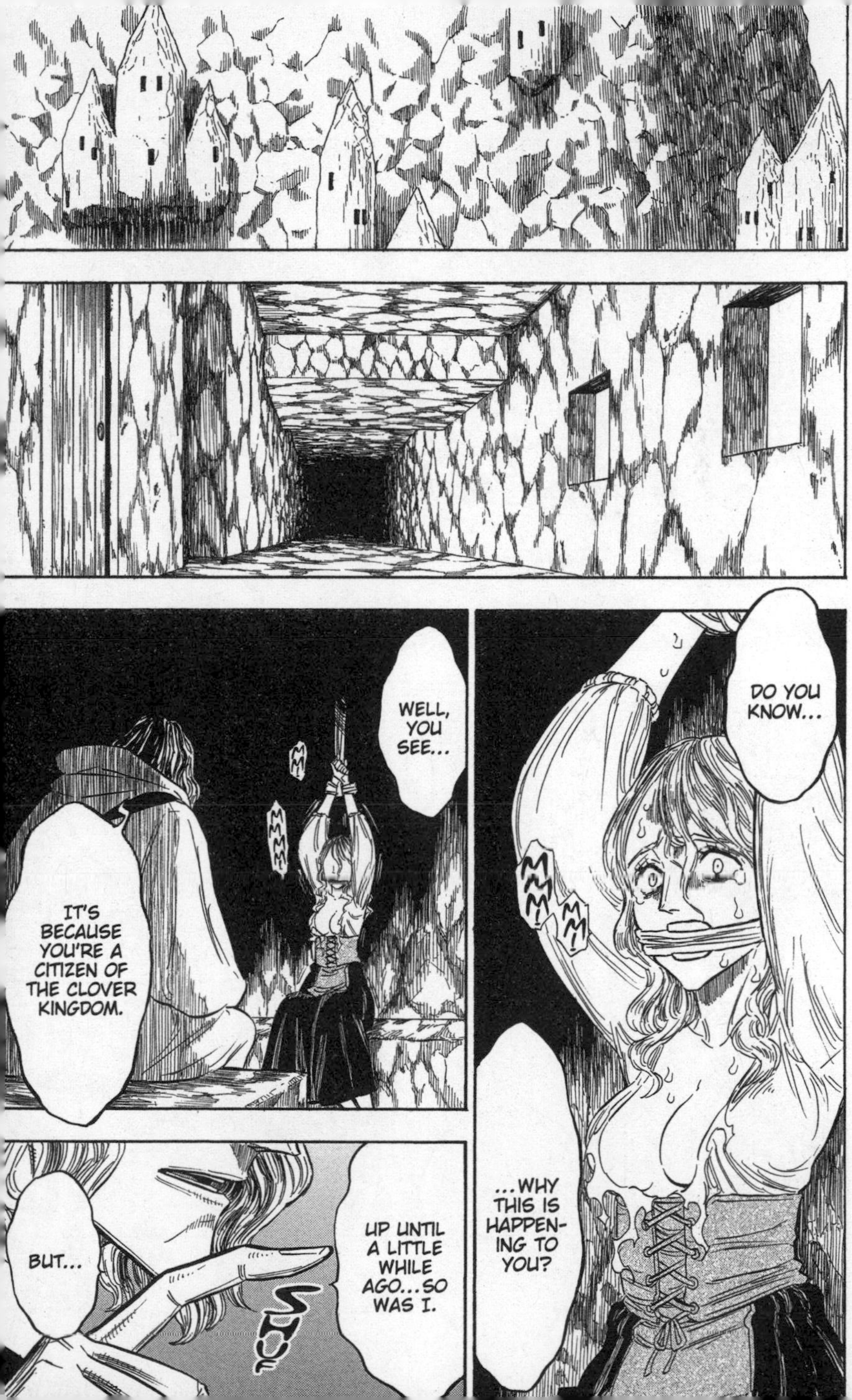
DO YOU KNOW...
MMM!
MM!
...WHY THIS IS HAPPEN-ING TO YOU?
WELL, YOU SEE...
MM!
MMMM
IT'S BECAUSE YOU'RE A CITIZEN OF THE CLOVER KINGDOM.
UP UNTIL A LITTLE WHILE AGO...SO WAS I.
BUT...

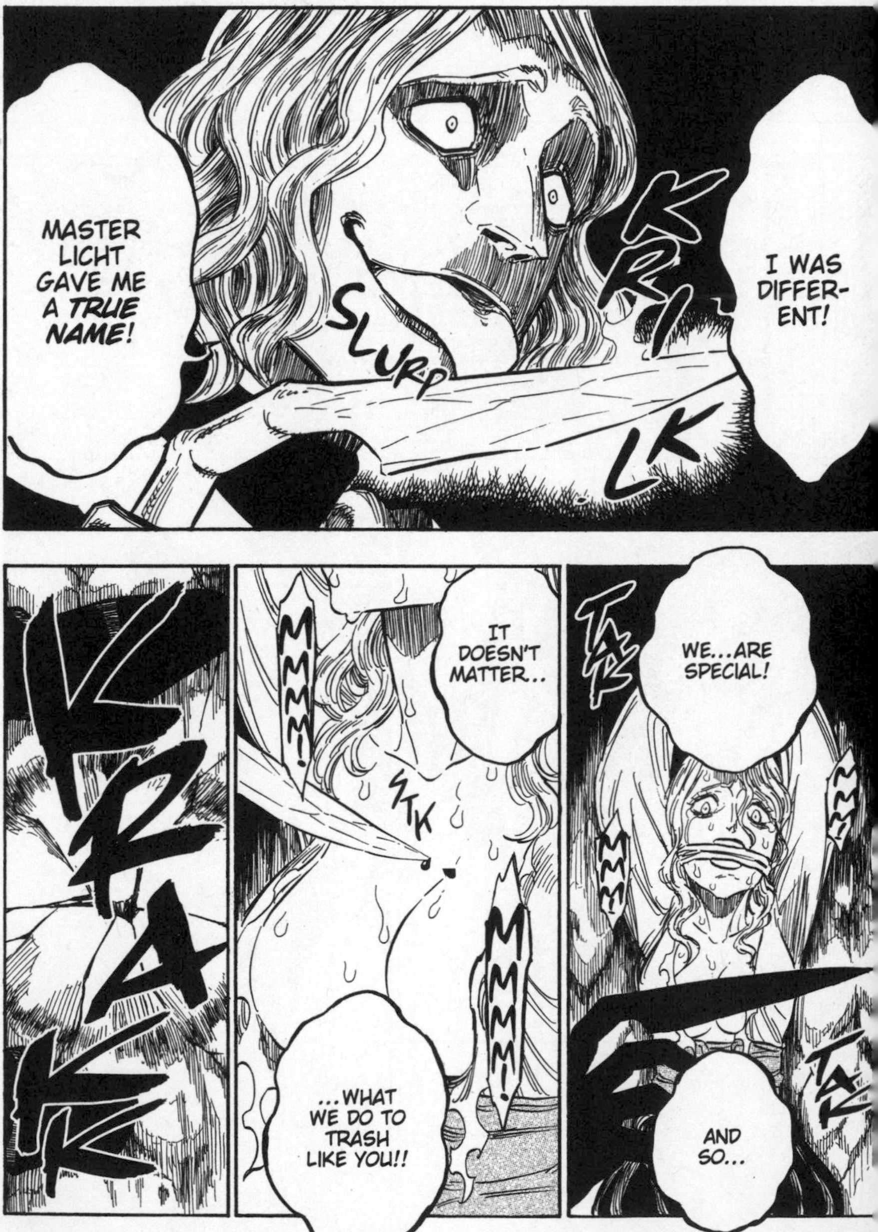
I WAS DIFFER-ENT!
KRILK
SLURP
MASTER LICHT GAVE ME A *TRUE NAME!*
TAK
WE...ARE SPECIAL!
MMM!
MMMM
AND SO...
TAK
IT DOESN'T MATTER...
MMMM!
STK
MMMMM!
...WHAT WE DO TO TRASH LIKE YOU!!
KRAK

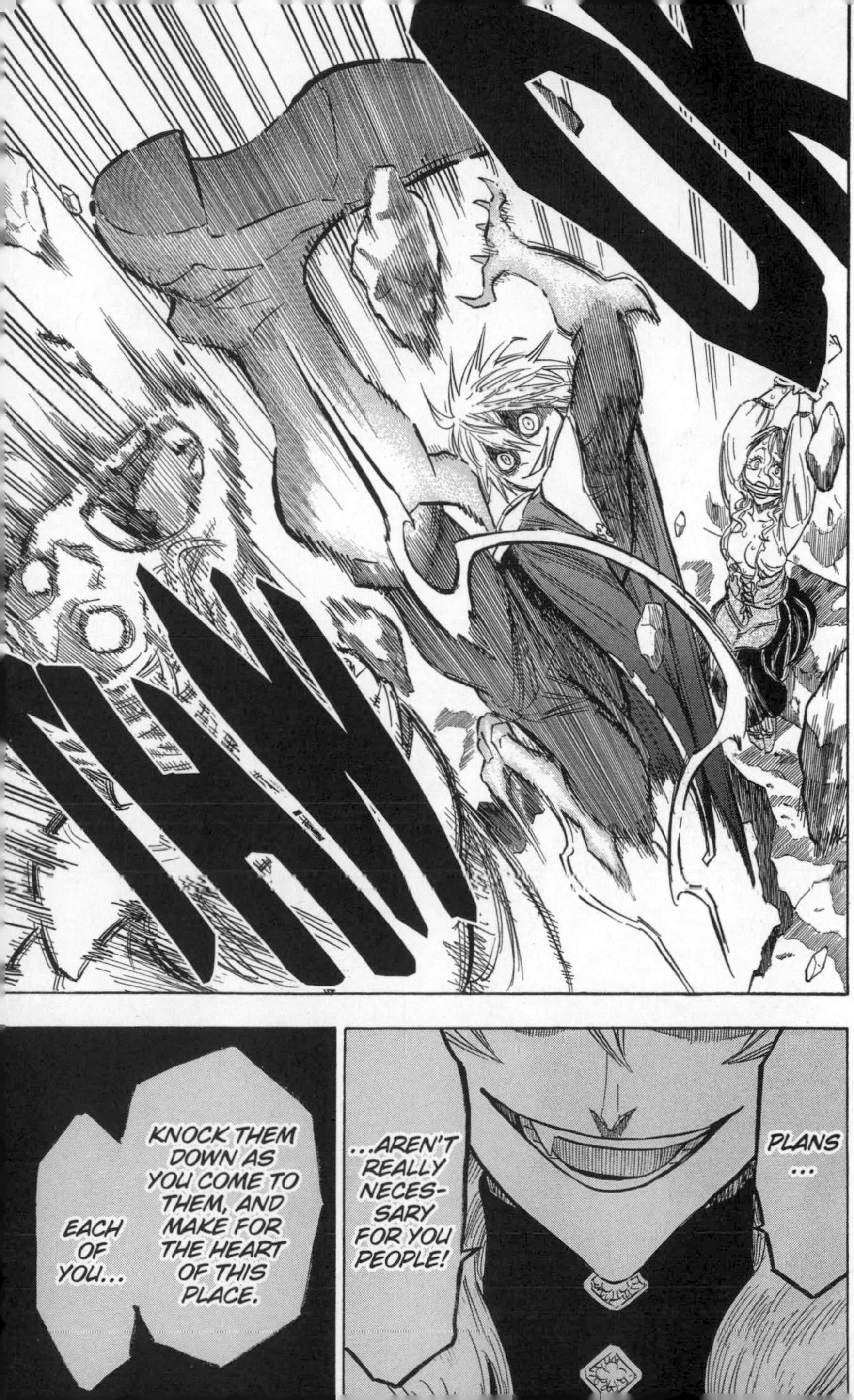
PLANS ...
...AREN'T REALLY NECES-SARY FOR YOU PEOPLE!
KNOCK THEM DOWN AS YOU COME TO THEM, AND MAKE FOR THE HEART OF THIS PLACE.
EACH OF YOU...

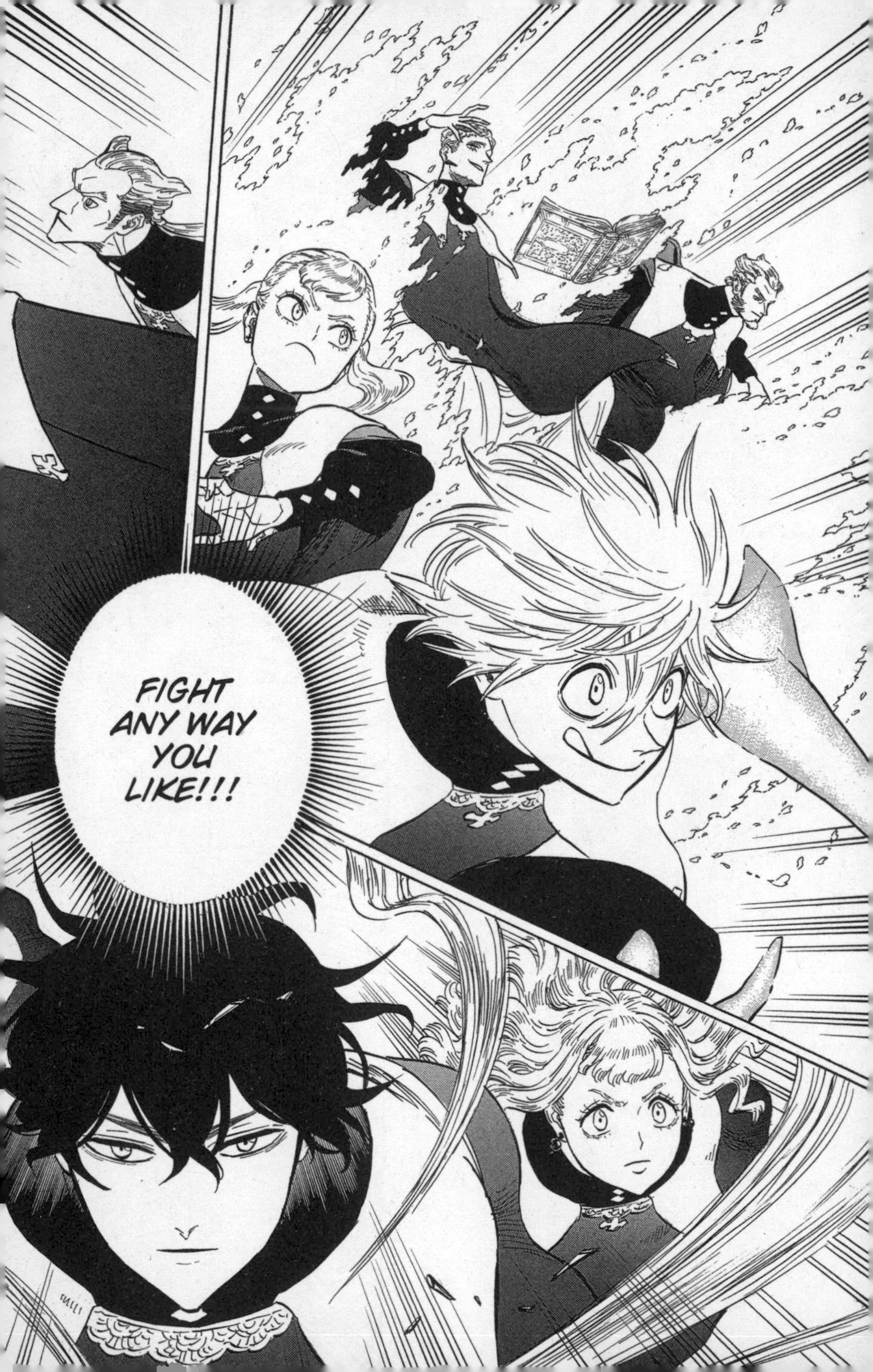
FIGHT ANY WAY YOU LIKE!!!

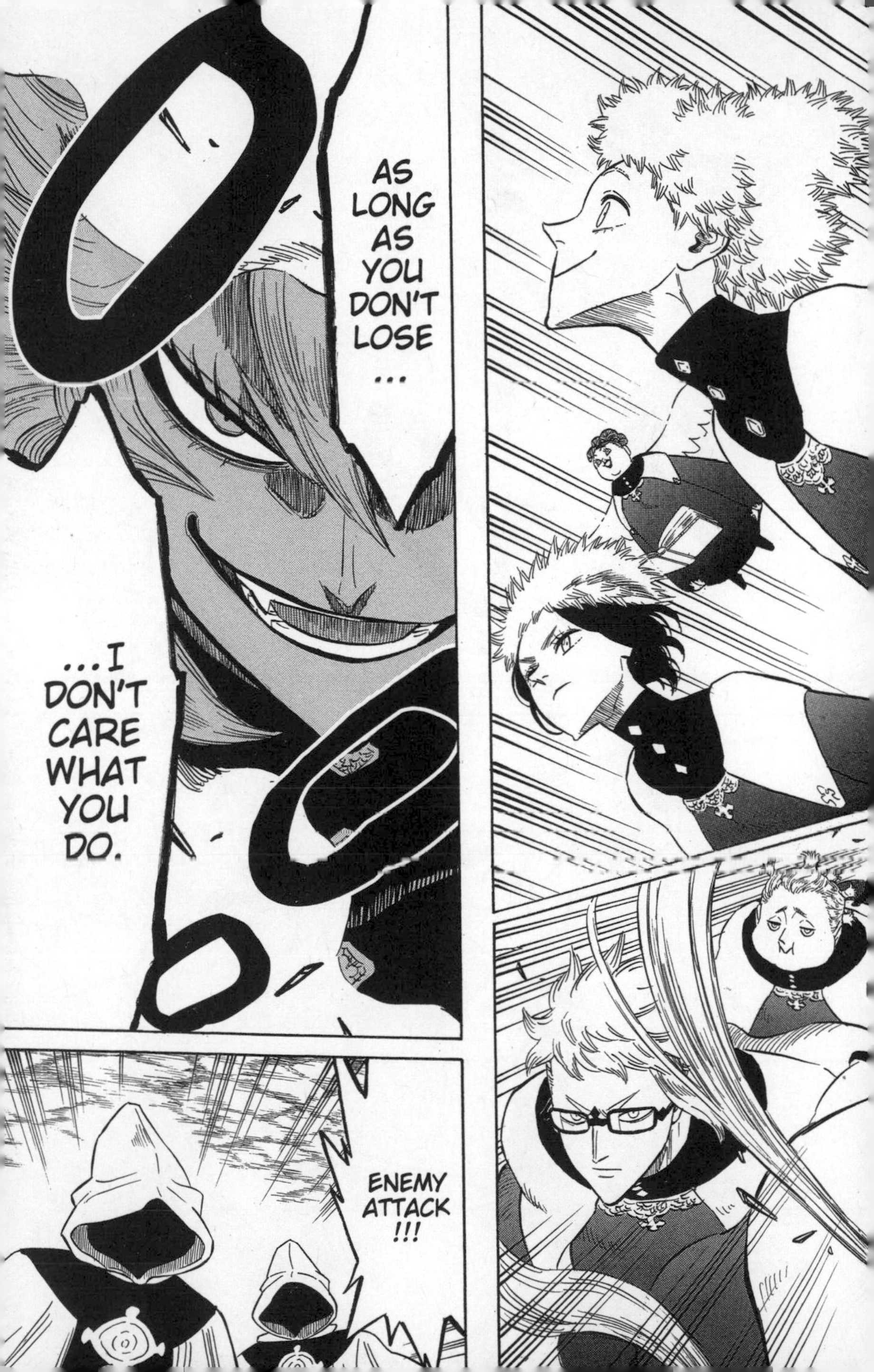
AS LONG AS YOU DON'T LOSE...
...I DON'T CARE WHAT YOU DO.
ENEMY ATTACK!!!

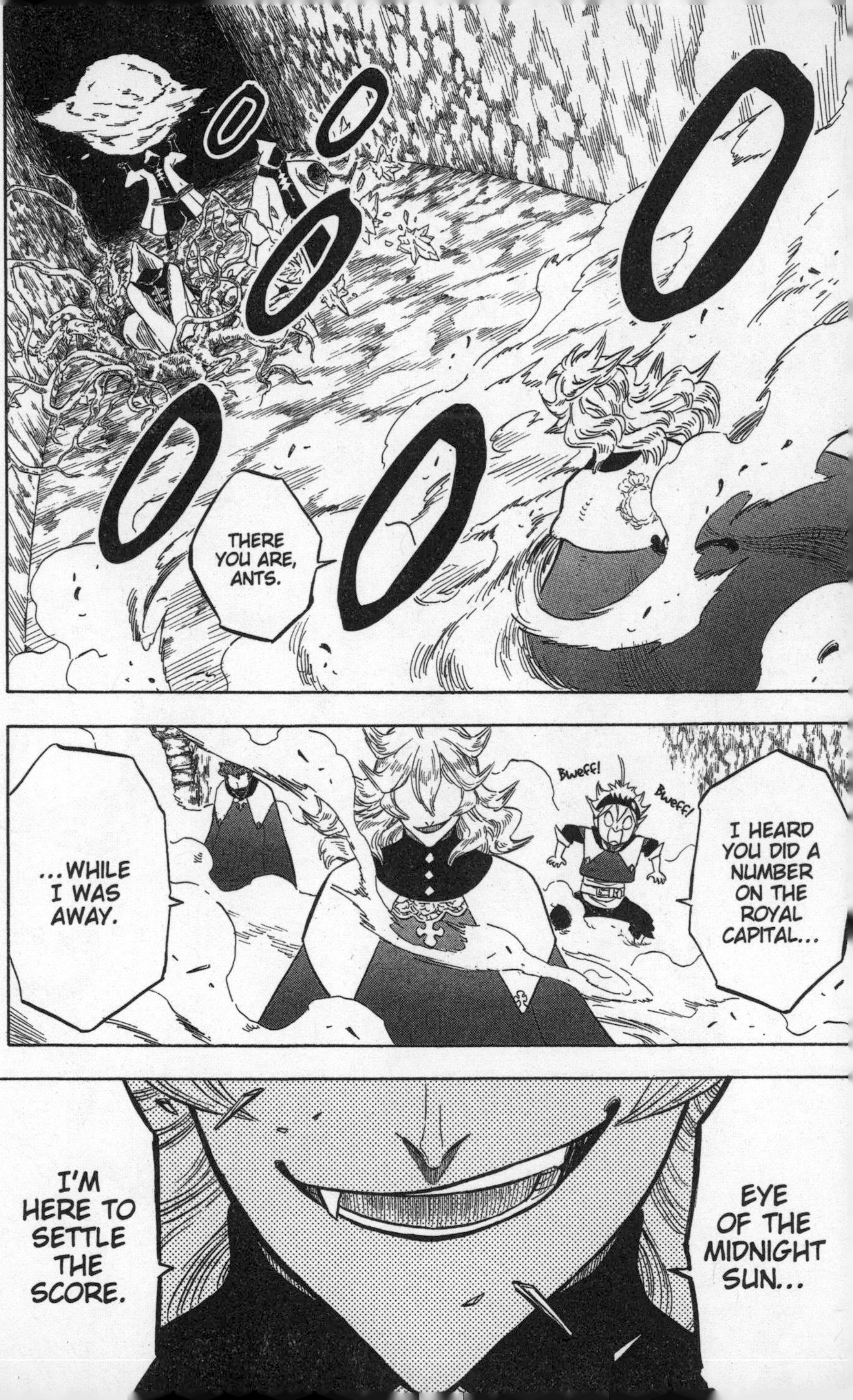
THERE YOU ARE, ANTS.
I HEARD YOU DID A NUMBER ON THE ROYAL CAPITAL...
Bweff!
Bweff!
...WHILE I WAS AWAY.
EYE OF THE MIDNIGHT SUN...
I'M HERE TO SETTLE THE SCORE.

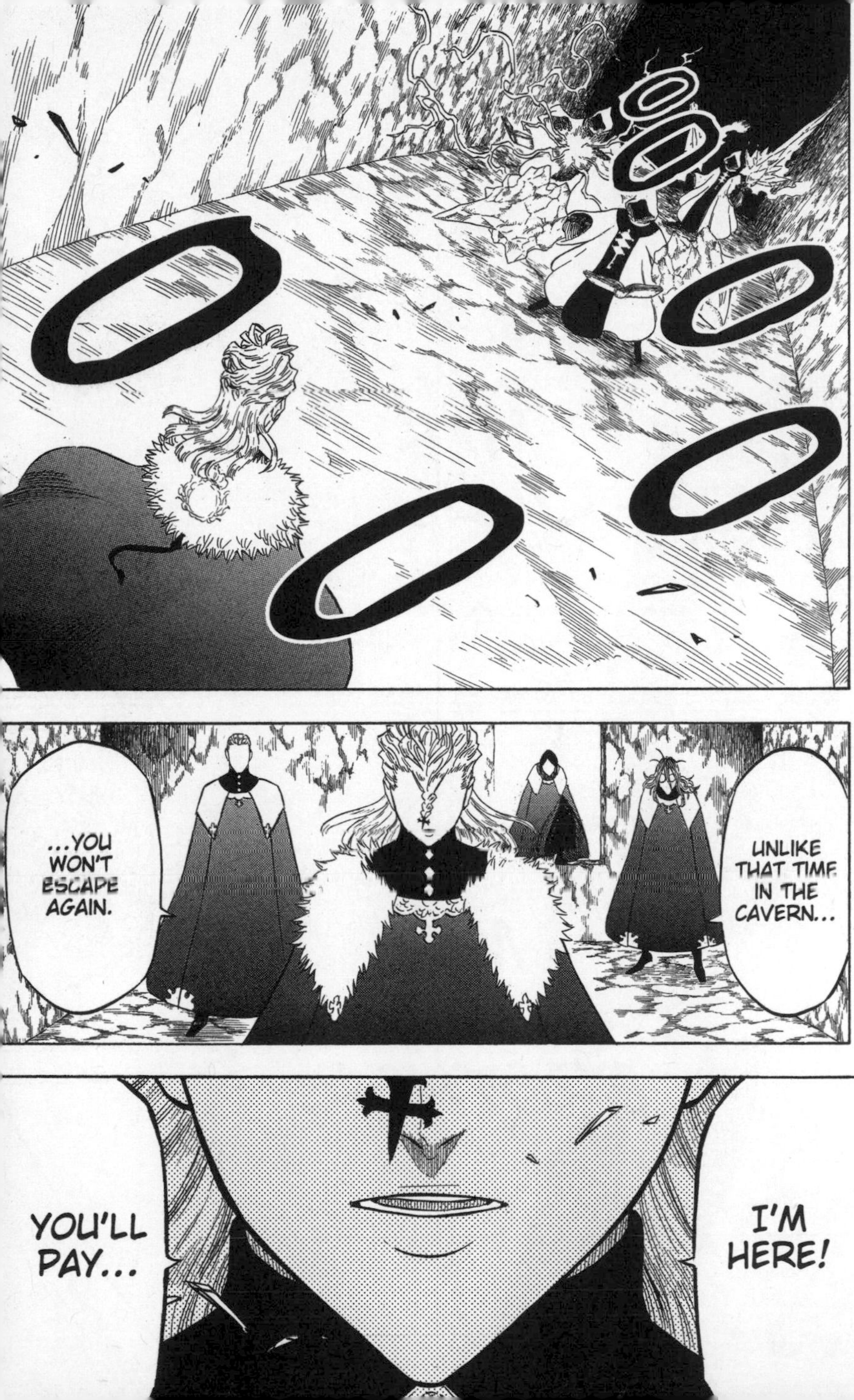
UNLIKE THAT TIME IN THE CAVERN...
...YOU WON'T ESCAPE AGAIN.
I'M HERE!
YOU'LL PAY...

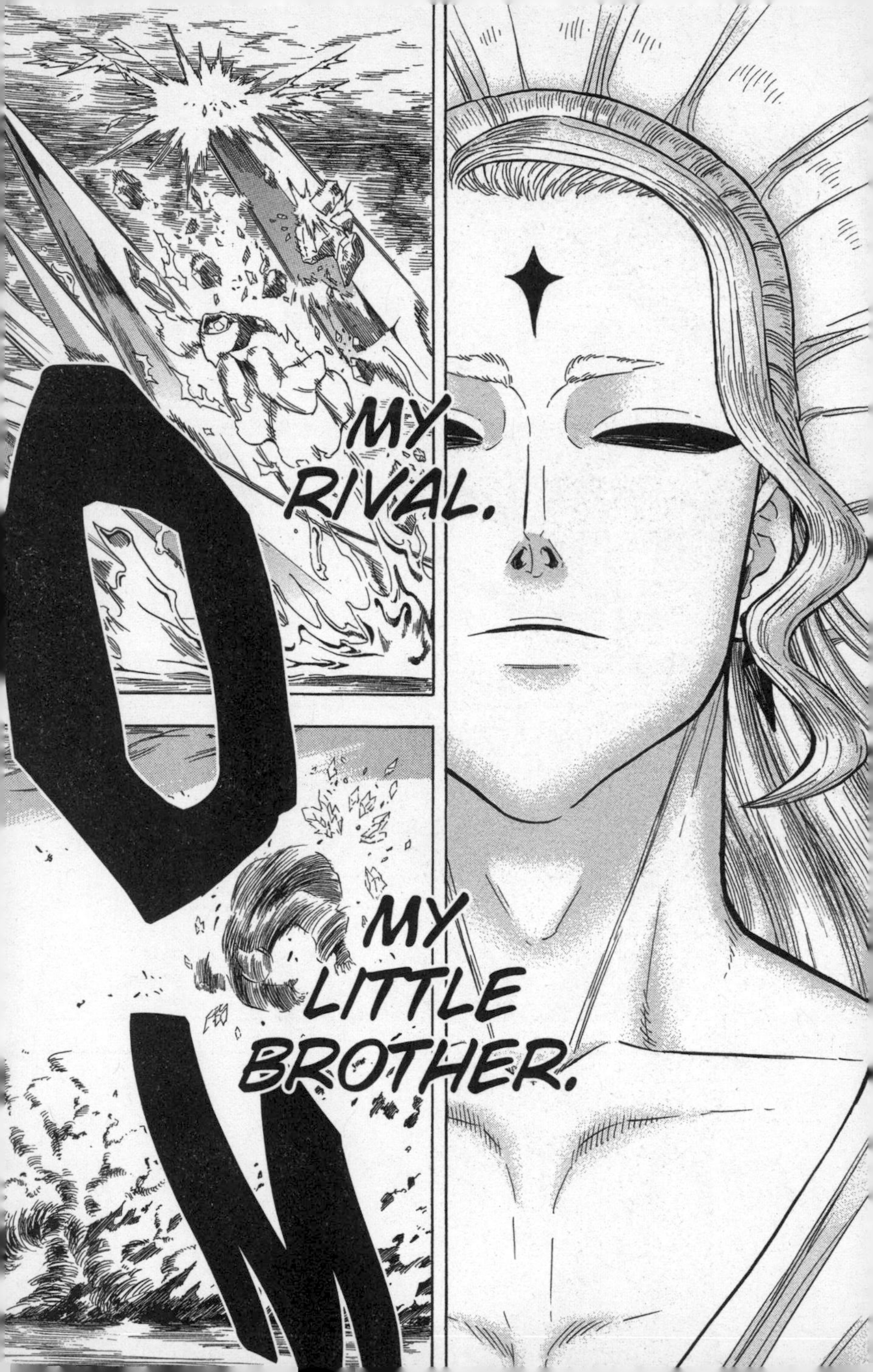
MY RIVAL.
MY LITTLE BROTHER.

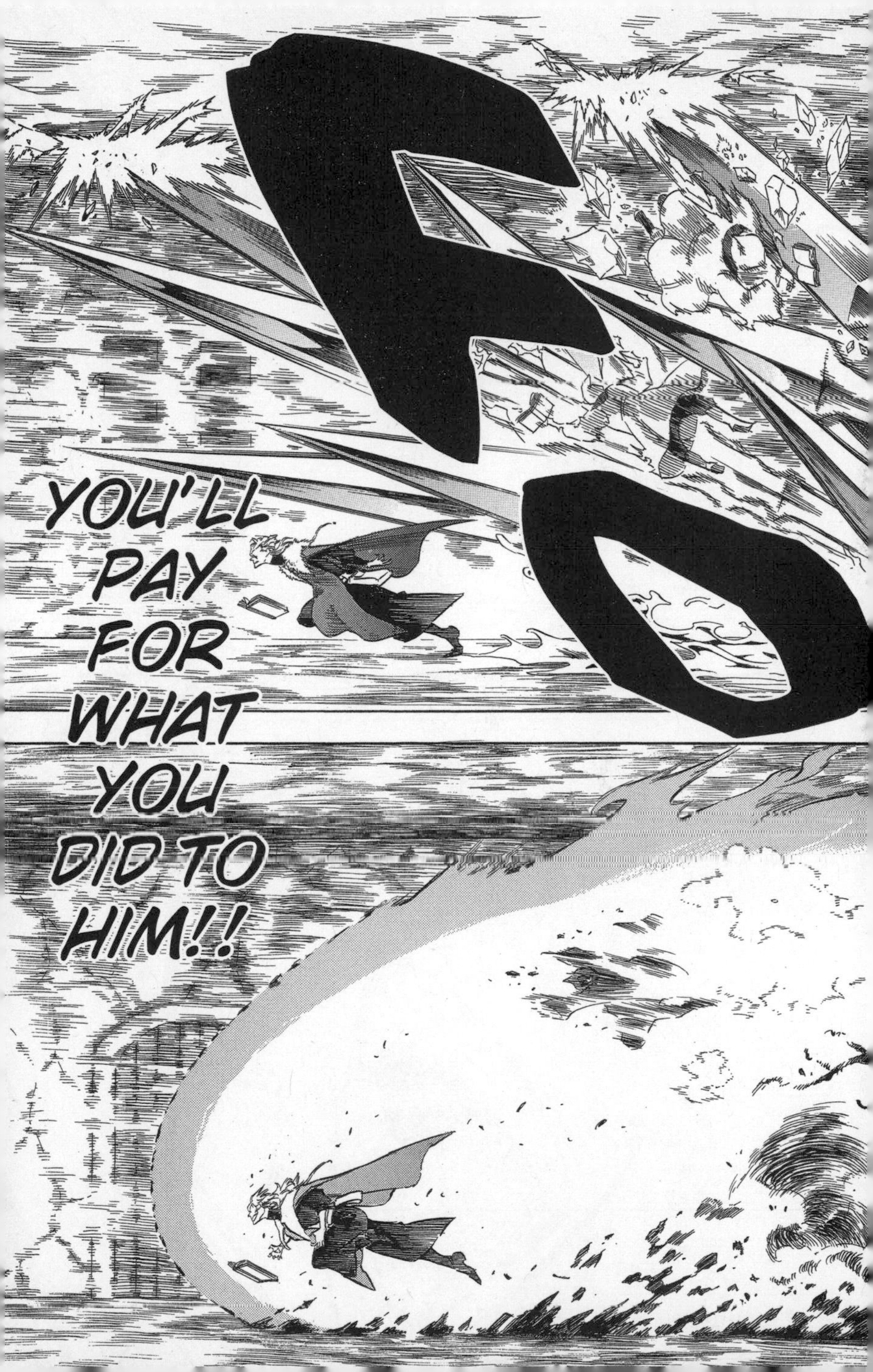
YOU'LL PAY FOR WHAT YOU DID TO HIM!!

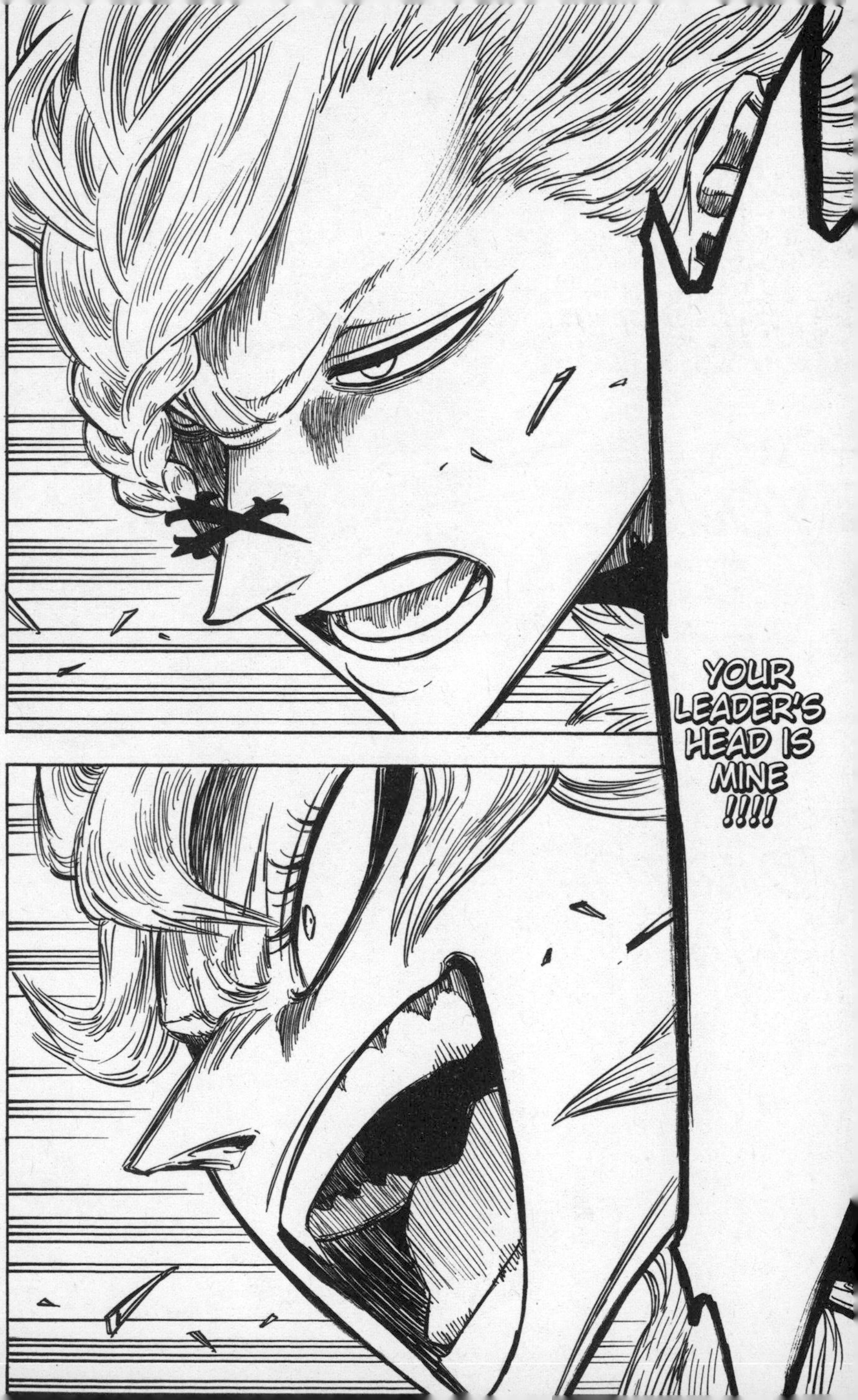
YOUR LEADER'S HEAD IS MINE !!!!

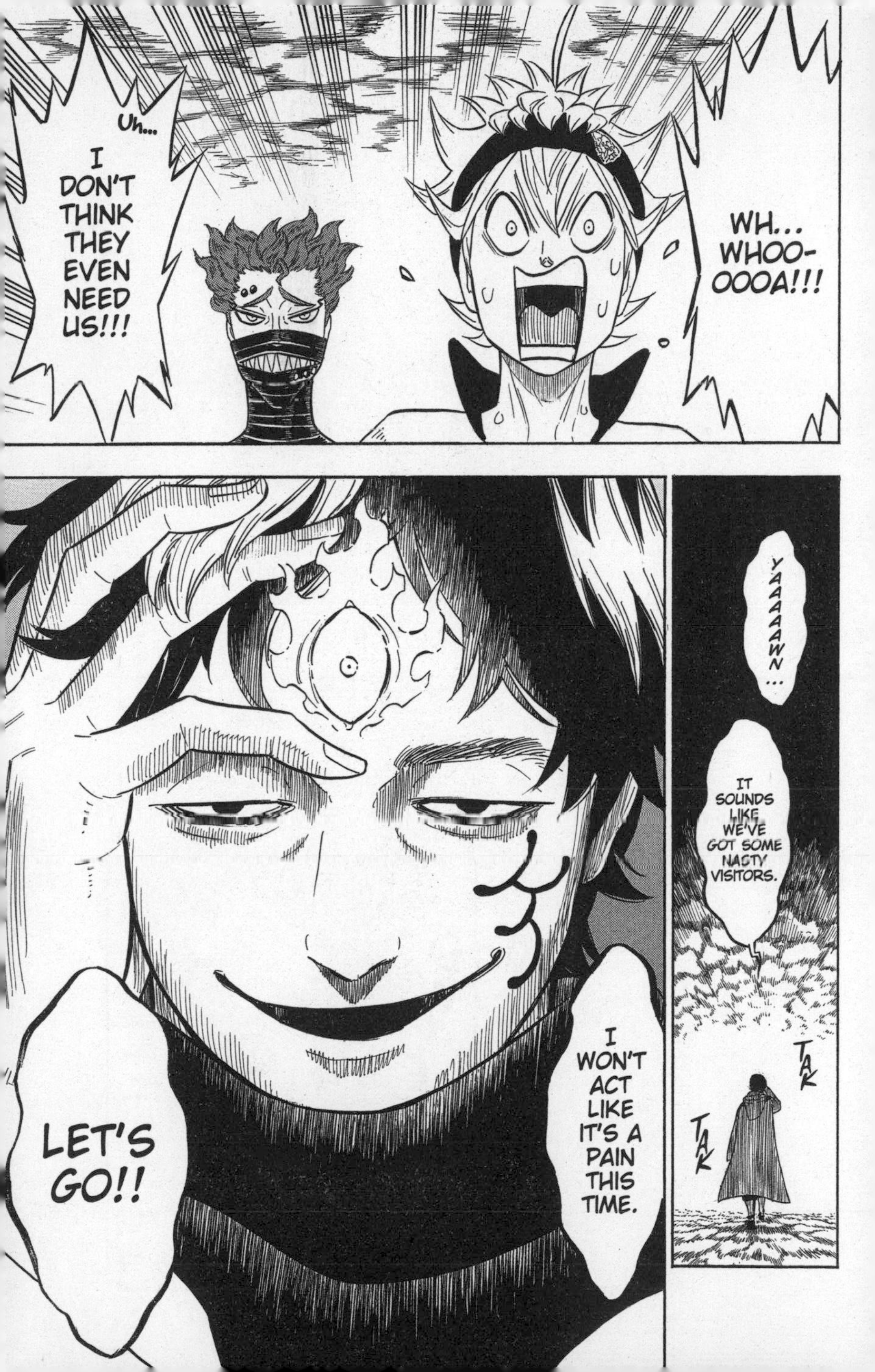
WH... WHOOO-OOOA!!!
Uh... I DON'T THINK THEY EVEN NEED US!!!
YAAAAAWN...
IT SOUNDS LIKE WE'VE GOT SOME NASTY VISITORS.
TAK
TAK
I WON'T ACT LIKE IT'S A PAIN THIS TIME.
LET'S GO!!

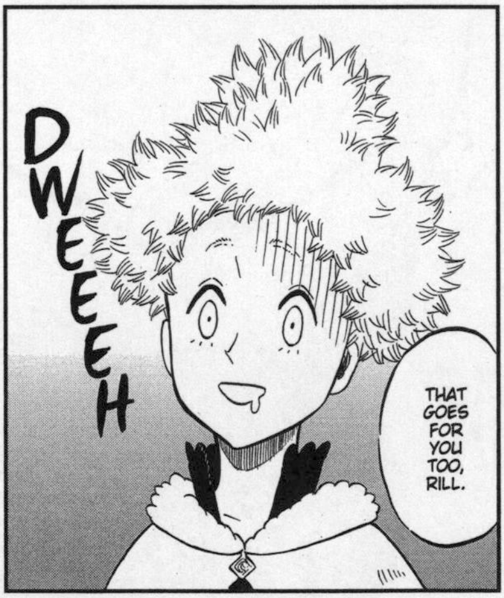
THAT GOES FOR YOU TOO, RILL.
DWEEEH

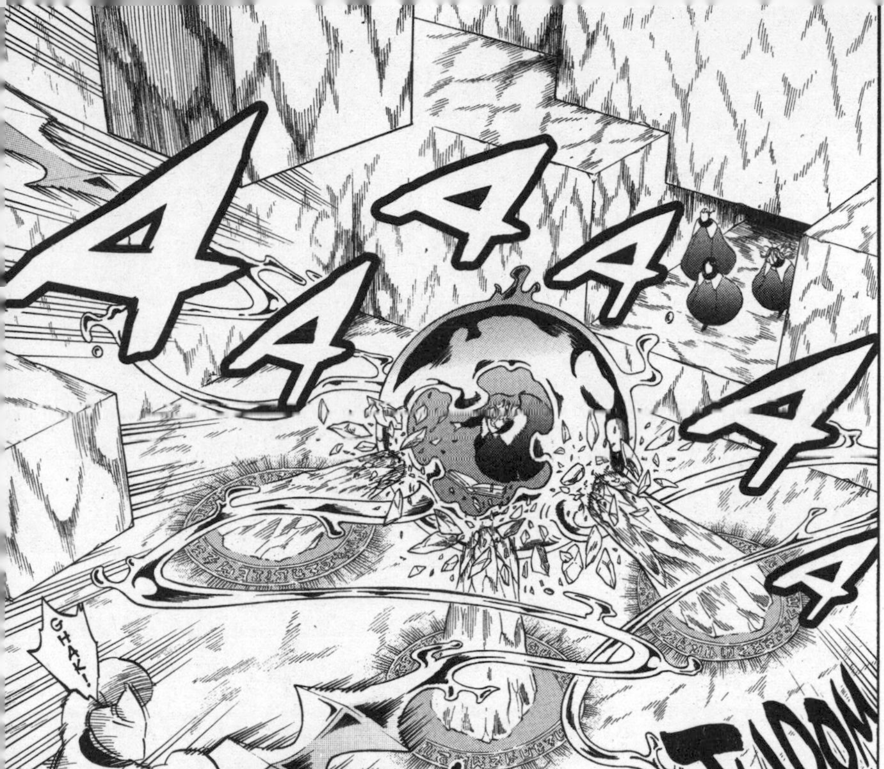
AAAAAAA
GHAK!
THOOM
THOOM
AAAGH!

Page 136: A Surging Advance

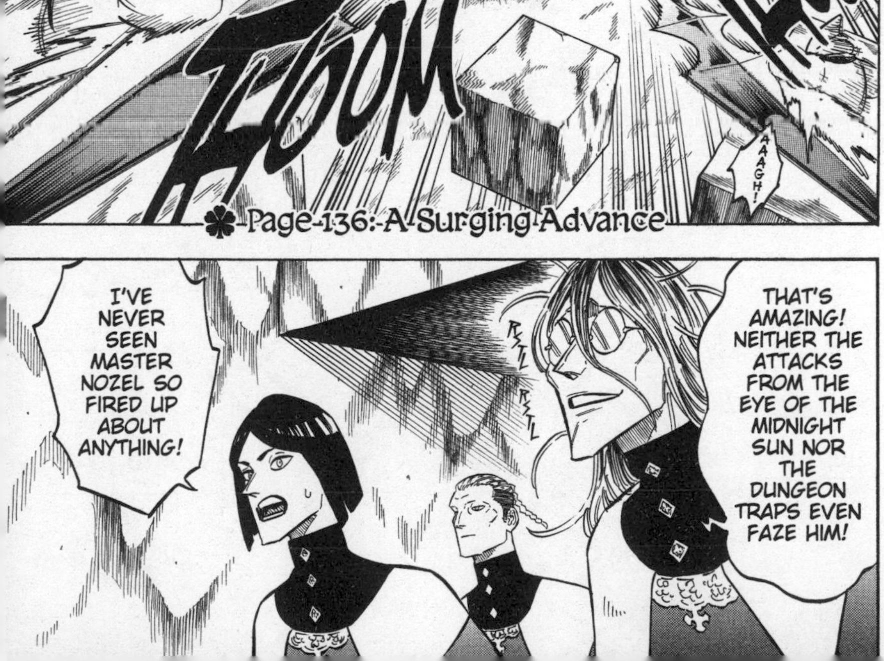
THAT'S AMAZING! NEITHER THE ATTACKS FROM THE EYE OF THE MIDNIGHT SUN NOR THE DUNGEON TRAPS EVEN FAZE HIM!
RSTL RSTL
I'VE NEVER SEEN MASTER NOZEL SO FIRED UP ABOUT ANYTHING!

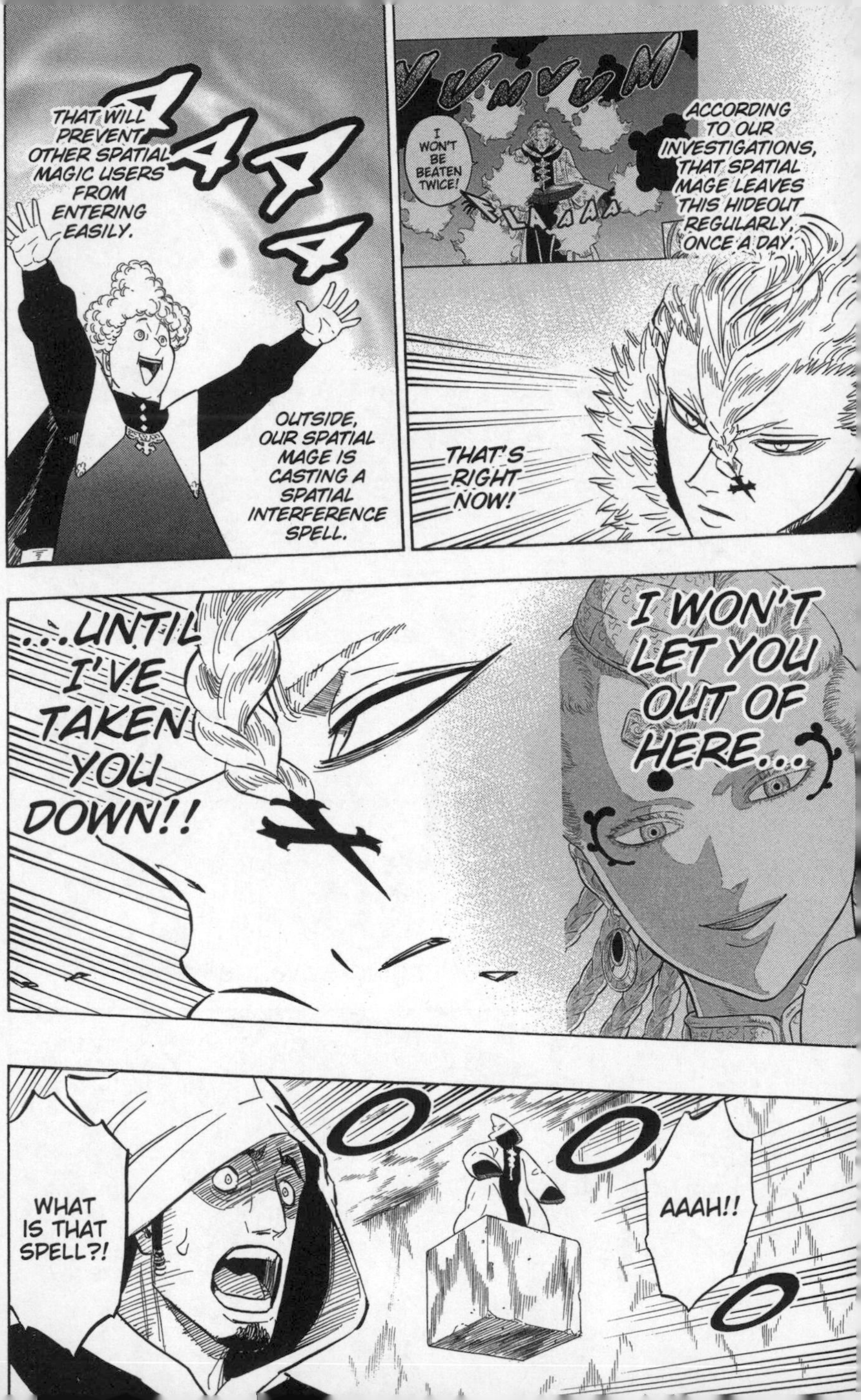
VVUMMVUM
I WON'T BE BEATEN TWICE!
ACCORDING TO OUR INVESTIGATIONS, THAT SPATIAL MAGE LEAVES THIS HIDEOUT REGULARLY, ONCE A DAY.
THAT'S RIGHT NOW!
AAAA
OUTSIDE, OUR SPATIAL MAGE IS CASTING A SPATIAL INTERFERENCE SPELL.
THAT WILL PREVENT OTHER SPATIAL MAGIC USERS FROM ENTERING EASILY.
I WON'T LET YOU OUT OF HERE...
...UNTIL I'VE TAKEN YOU DOWN!!
AAAH!!
WHAT IS THAT SPELL?!

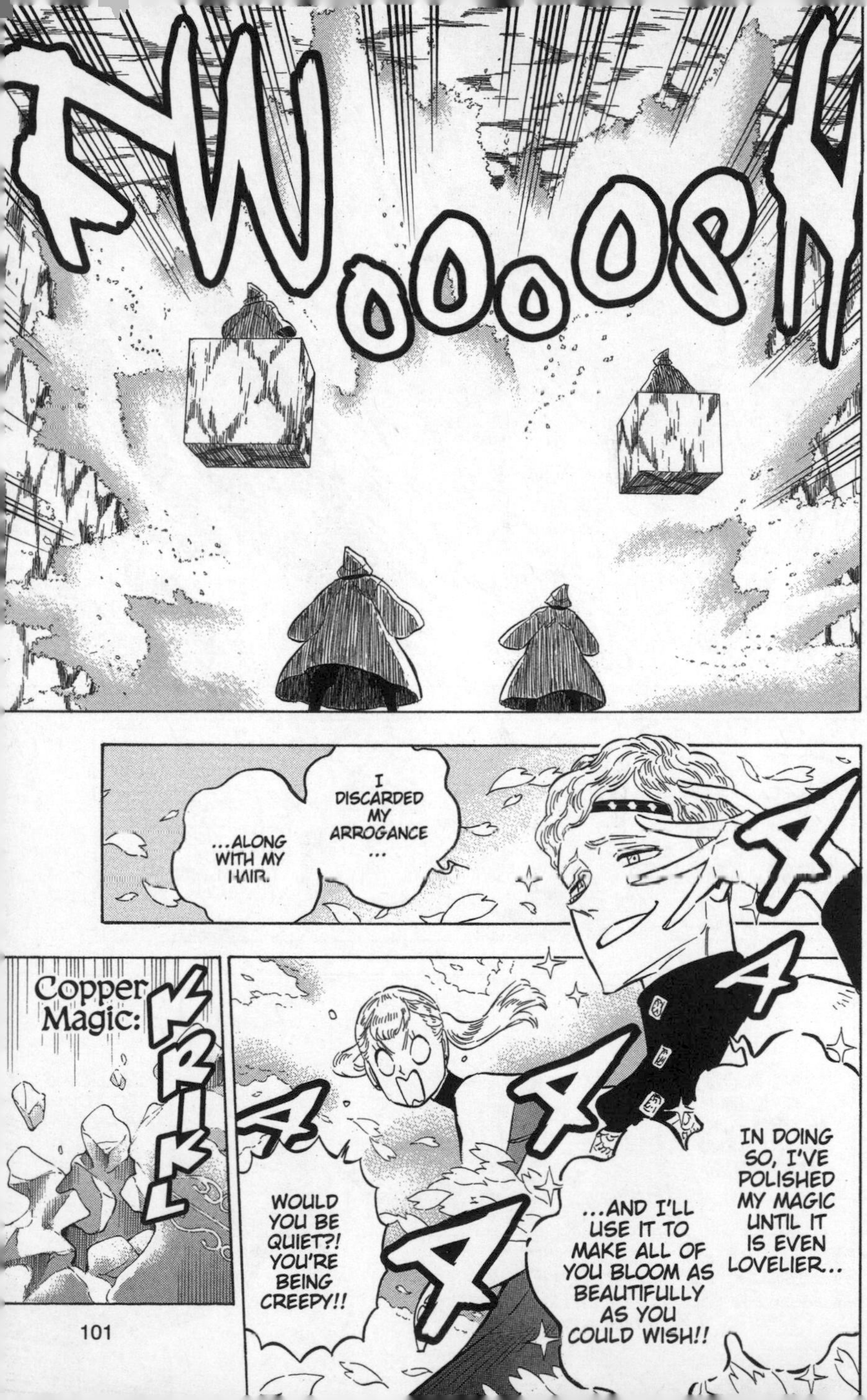
FWOOOOSH
I DISCARDED MY ARROGANCE...
...ALONG WITH MY HAIR.
AAAAA
IN DOING SO, I'VE POLISHED MY MAGIC UNTIL IT IS EVEN LOVELIER...
...AND I'LL USE IT TO MAKE ALL OF YOU BLOOM AS BEAUTIFULLY AS YOU COULD WISH!!
WOULD YOU BE QUIET?! YOU'RE BEING CREEPY!!
Copper Magic:
KRIKL

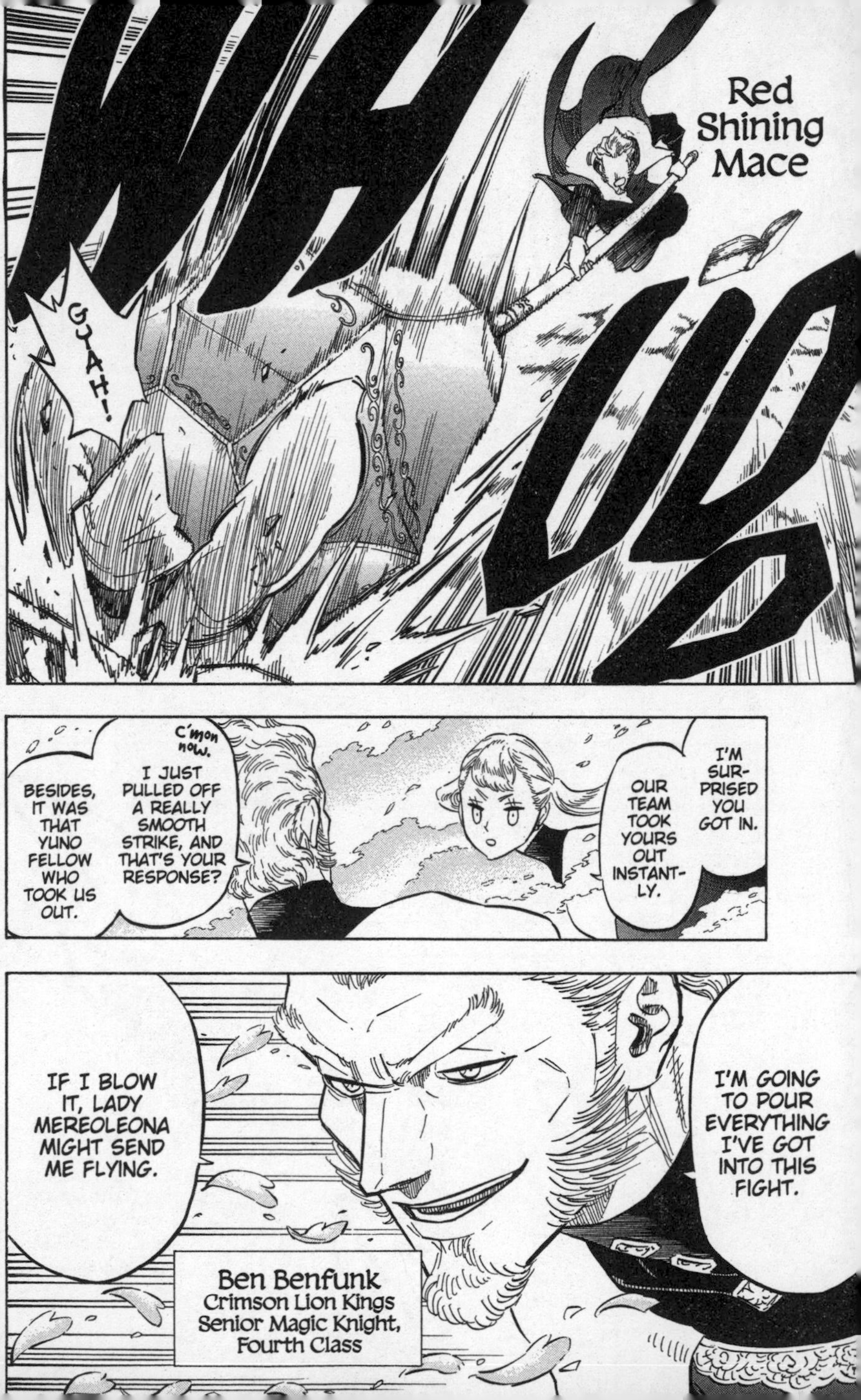
Red Shining Mace
GYAH!
I'M SURPRISED YOU GOT IN.
OUR TEAM TOOK YOURS OUT INSTANTLY.
C'mon now.
I JUST PULLED OFF A REALLY SMOOTH STRIKE, AND THAT'S YOUR RESPONSE?
BESIDES, IT WAS THAT YUNO FELLOW WHO TOOK US OUT.
I'M GOING TO POUR EVERYTHING I'VE GOT INTO THIS FIGHT.
IF I BLOW IT, LADY MEREOLEONA MIGHT SEND ME FLYING.
Ben Benfunk
Crimson Lion Kings
Senior Magic Knight, Fourth Class

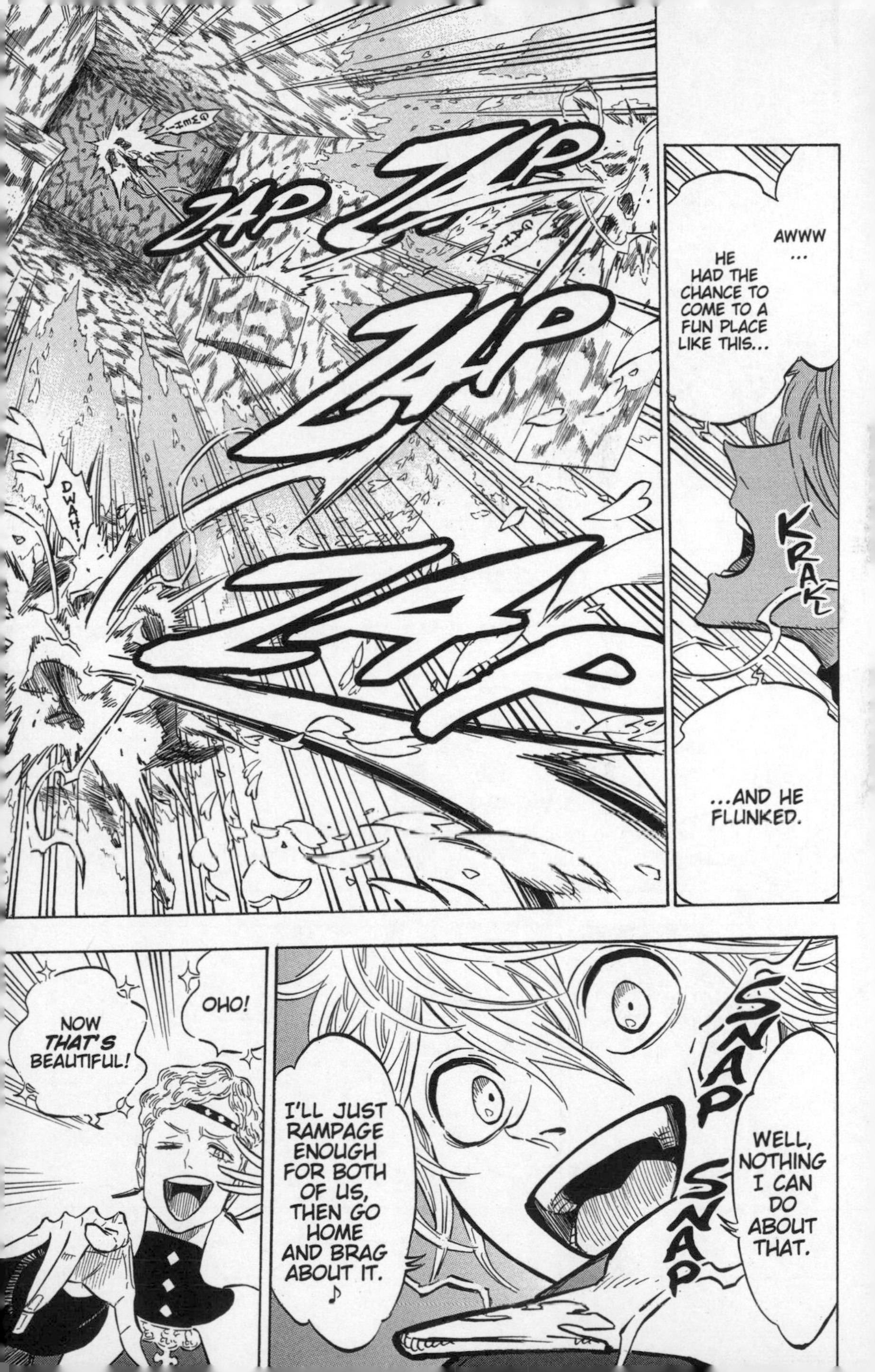
AWWW...
HE HAD THE CHANCE TO COME TO A FUN PLACE LIKE THIS...
KRAKL
...AND HE FLUNKED.
ZAP
ZAP
ZAP
ZAP
DWAH!
WELL, NOTHING I CAN DO ABOUT THAT.
SNAP SNAP
I'LL JUST RAMPAGE ENOUGH FOR BOTH OF US, THEN GO HOME AND BRAG ABOUT IT. ♪
OHO!
NOW THAT'S BEAUTIFUL!

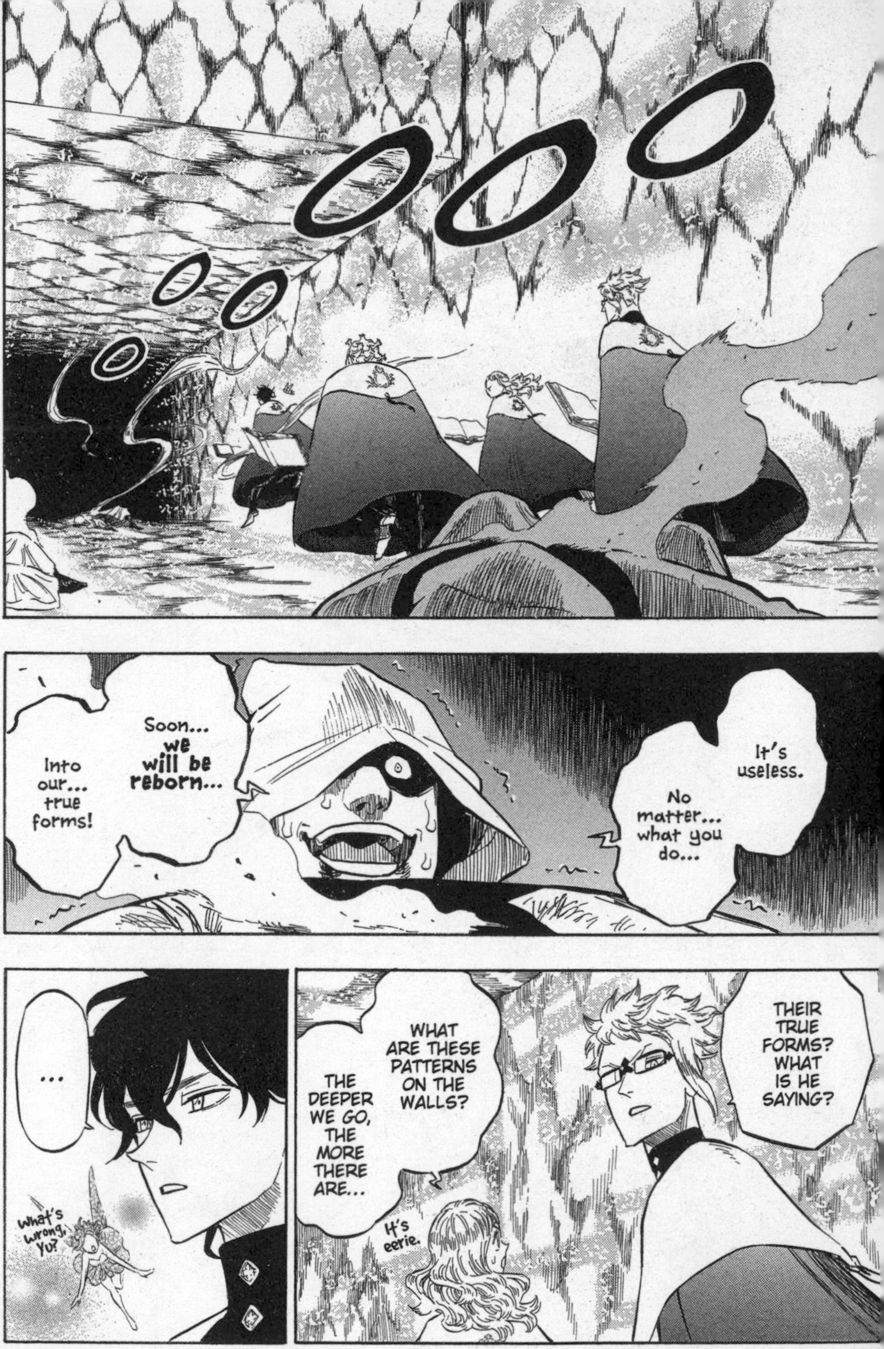
It's useless.
No matter... what you do...
Soon... we will be reborn...
Into our... true forms!
THEIR TRUE FORMS? WHAT IS HE SAYING?
WHAT ARE THESE PATTERNS ON THE WALLS?
THE DEEPER WE GO, THE MORE THERE ARE...
It's eerie.
...
What's wrong, Yu?

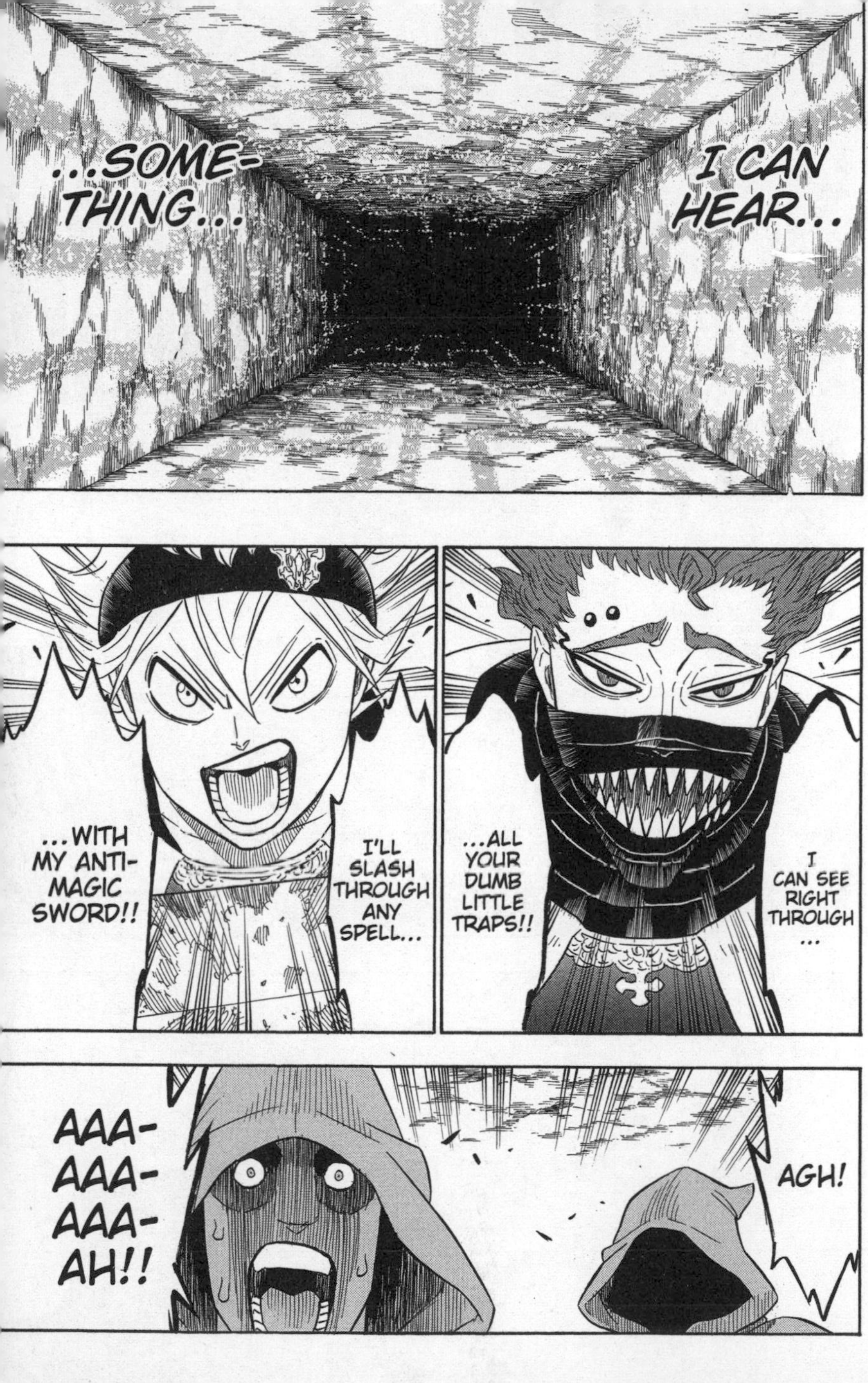
I CAN HEAR...
...SOME-THING...
I CAN SEE RIGHT THROUGH ...
...ALL YOUR DUMB LITTLE TRAPS!!
I'LL SLASH THROUGH ANY SPELL...
...WITH MY ANTI-MAGIC SWORD!!
AGH!
AAA-AAA-AAA-AH!!

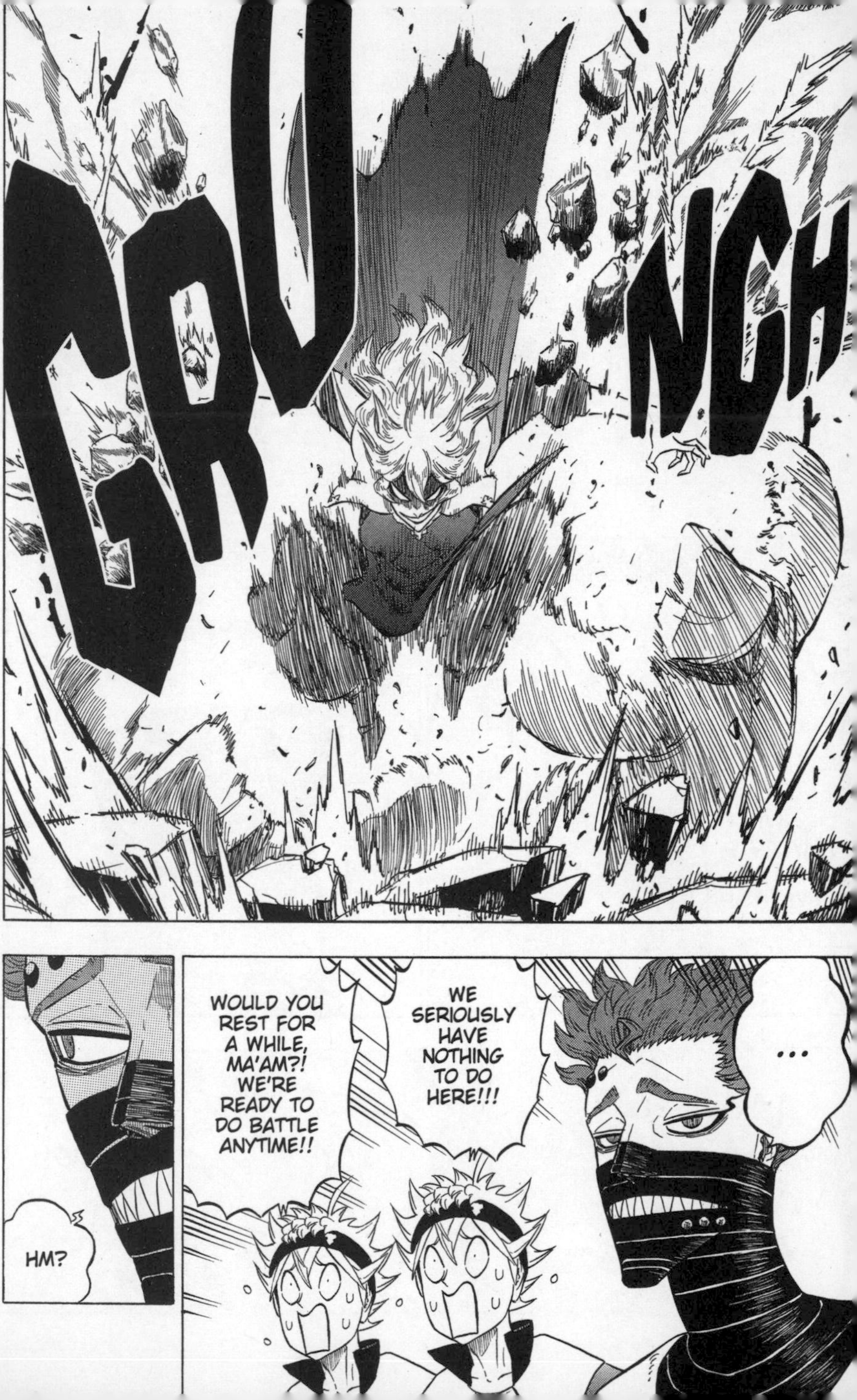
CRUNCH
...
WE SERIOUSLY HAVE NOTHING TO DO HERE!!!
WOULD YOU REST FOR A WHILE, MA'AM?! WE'RE READY TO DO BATTLE ANYTIME!!
HM?

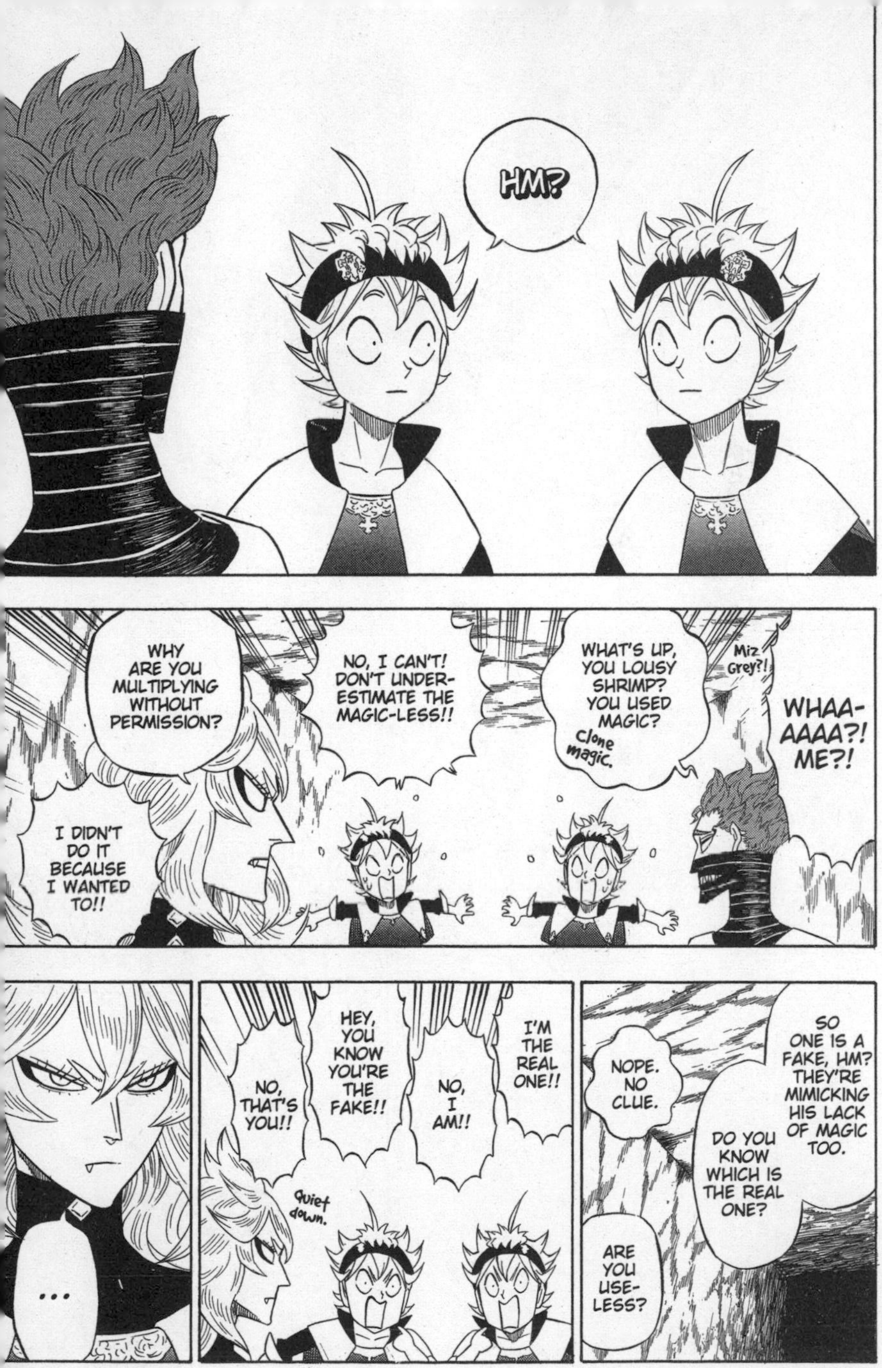
HM?
WHAA-AAAA?! ME?!
Miz Grey?!
WHAT'S UP, YOU LOUSY SHRIMP? YOU USED MAGIC?
Clone magic.
NO, I CAN'T! DON'T UNDER-ESTIMATE THE MAGIC-LESS!!
WHY ARE YOU MULTIPLYING WITHOUT PERMISSION?
I DIDN'T DO IT BECAUSE I WANTED TO!!
SO ONE IS A FAKE, HM? THEY'RE MIMICKING HIS LACK OF MAGIC TOO.
DO YOU KNOW WHICH IS THE REAL ONE?
NOPE. NO CLUE.
ARE YOU USE-LESS?
I'M THE REAL ONE!!
NO, I AM!!
HEY, YOU KNOW YOU'RE THE FAKE!!
NO, THAT'S YOU!!
Quiet down.
...

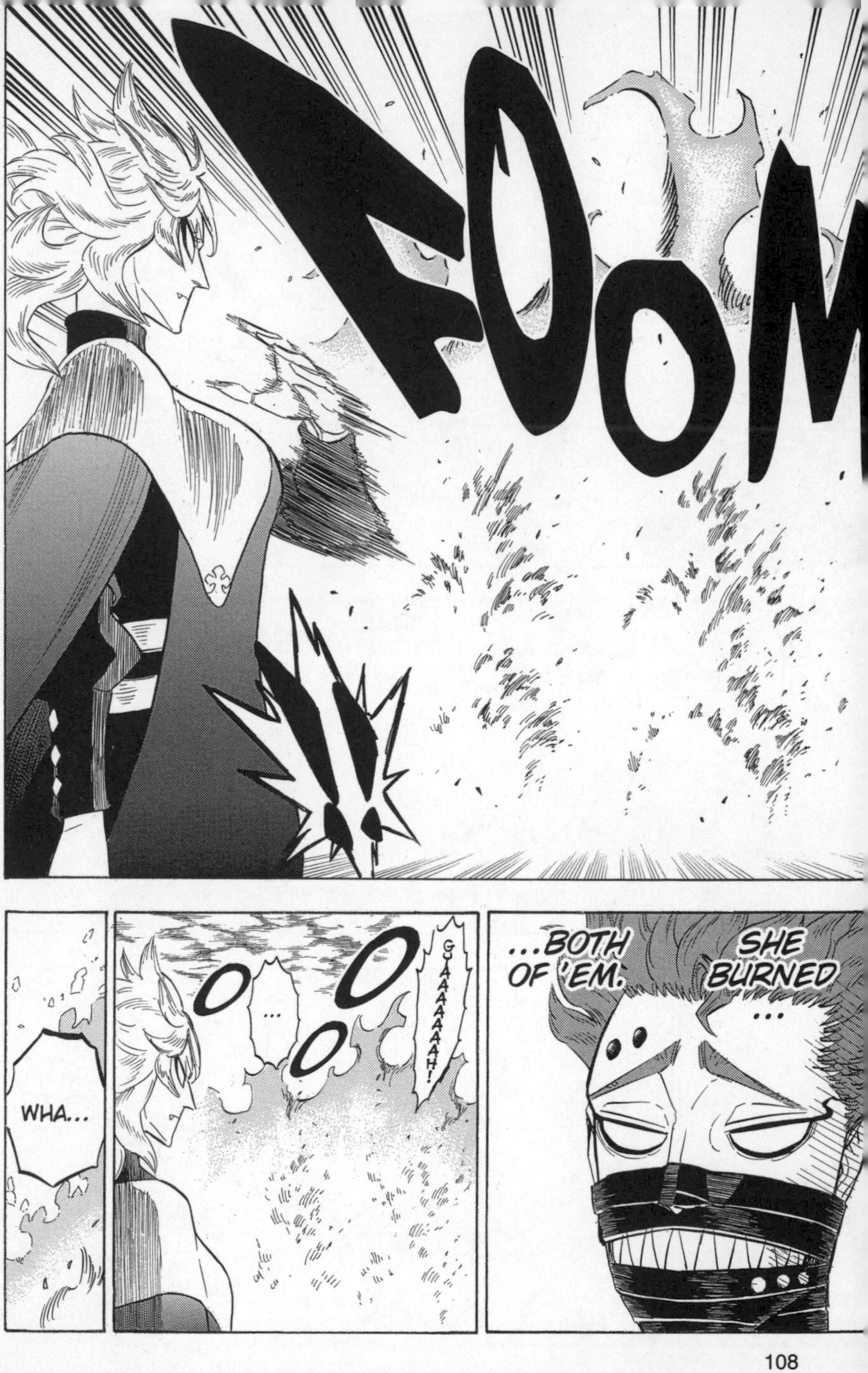
FOOM
SHE BURNED ...
...BOTH OF 'EM.
GUAAAAAAAH!
...
WHA...

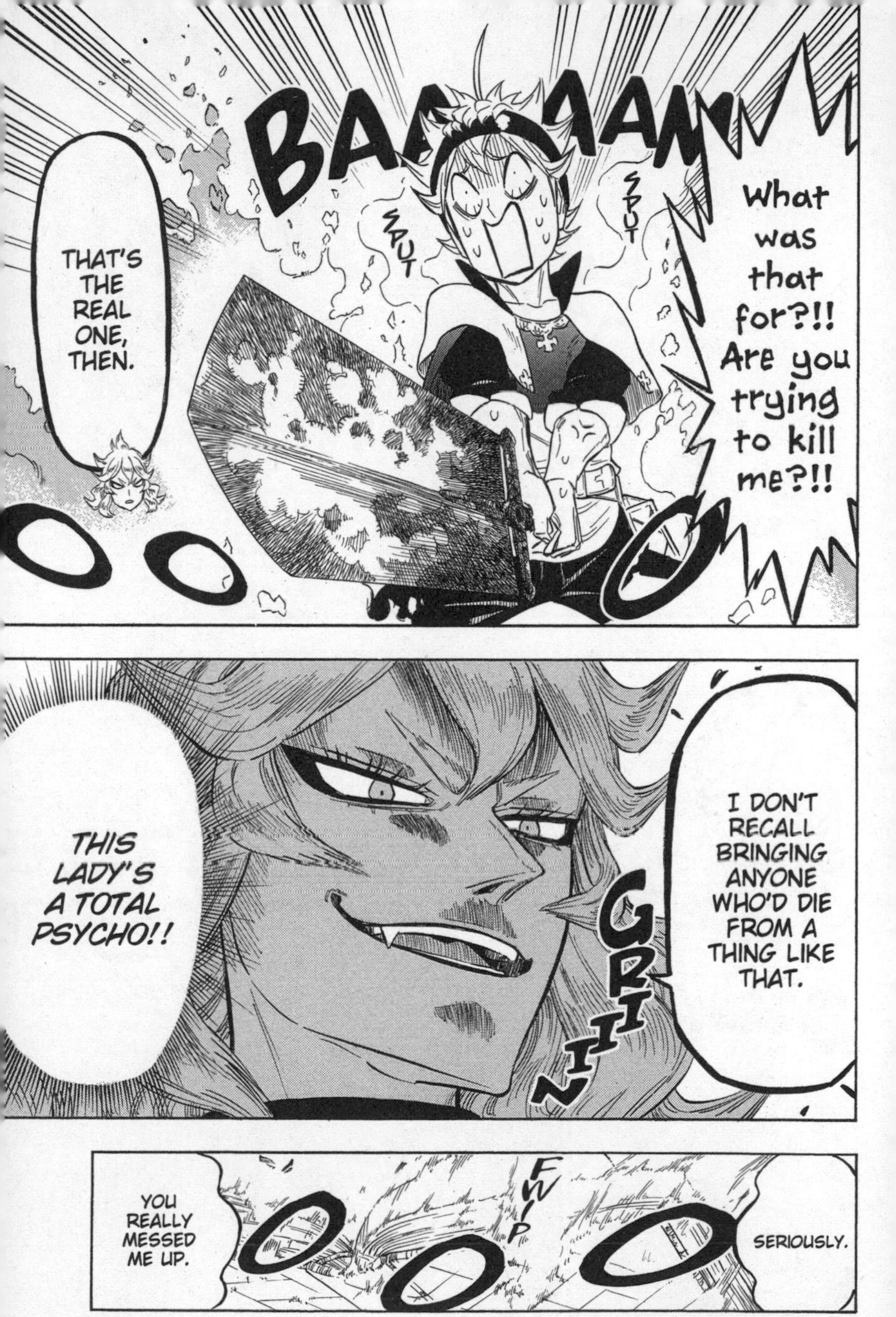
BAAAAAM
What was that for?!! Are you trying to kill me?!!
SPUT
SPUT
THAT'S THE REAL ONE, THEN.
I DON'T RECALL BRINGING ANYONE WHO'D DIE FROM A THING LIKE THAT.
GRIIIIN
THIS LADY'S A TOTAL PSYCHO!!
SERIOUSLY.
FWIP
YOU REALLY MESSED ME UP.

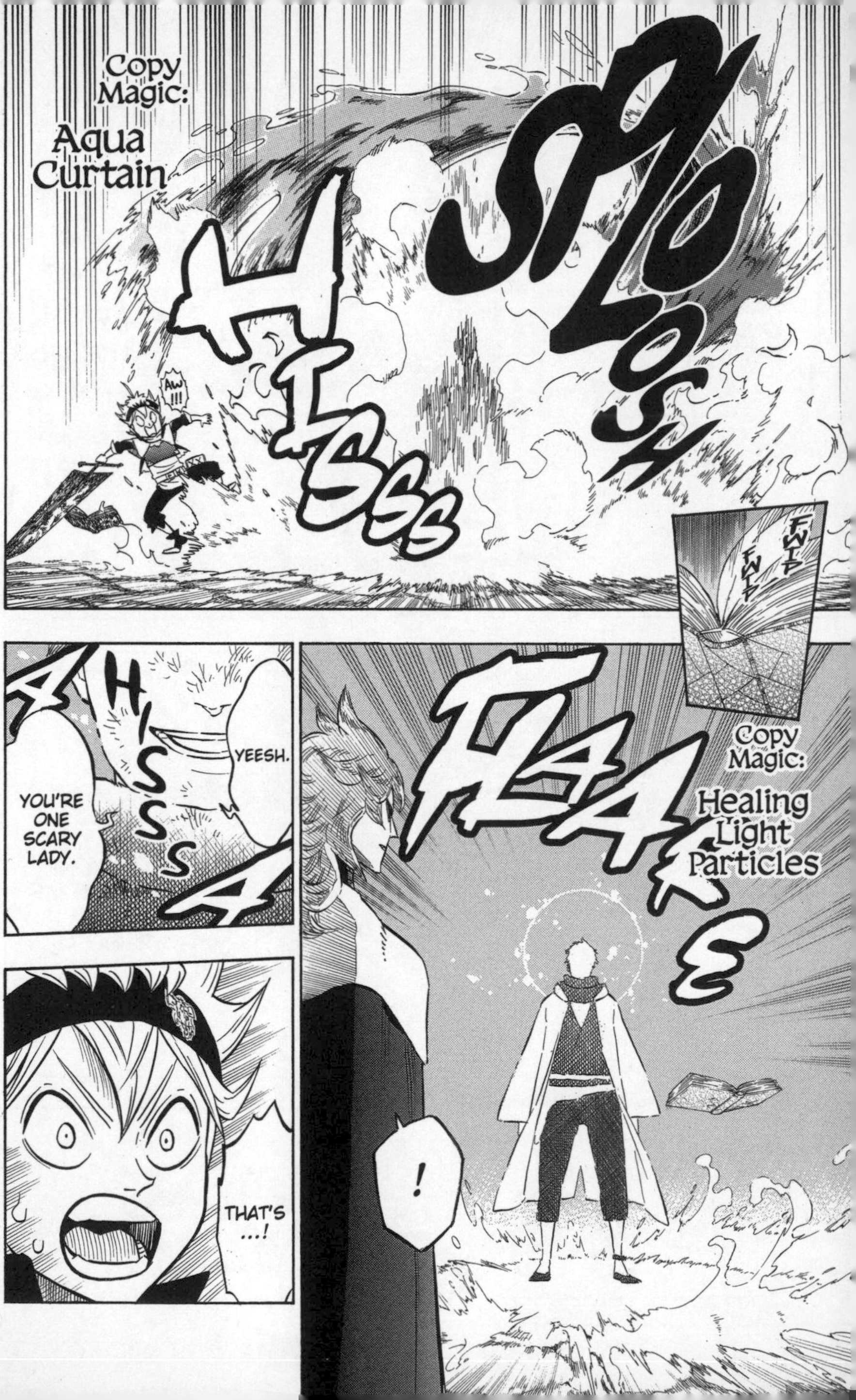

Copy Magic: Aqua Curtain
SPLOOSH
HISSS
AW!!!
FWIP FWIP
Copy Magic: Healing Light Particles
FLAKE
!
HISSS
YEESH.
YOU'RE ONE SCARY LADY.
THAT'S ...!

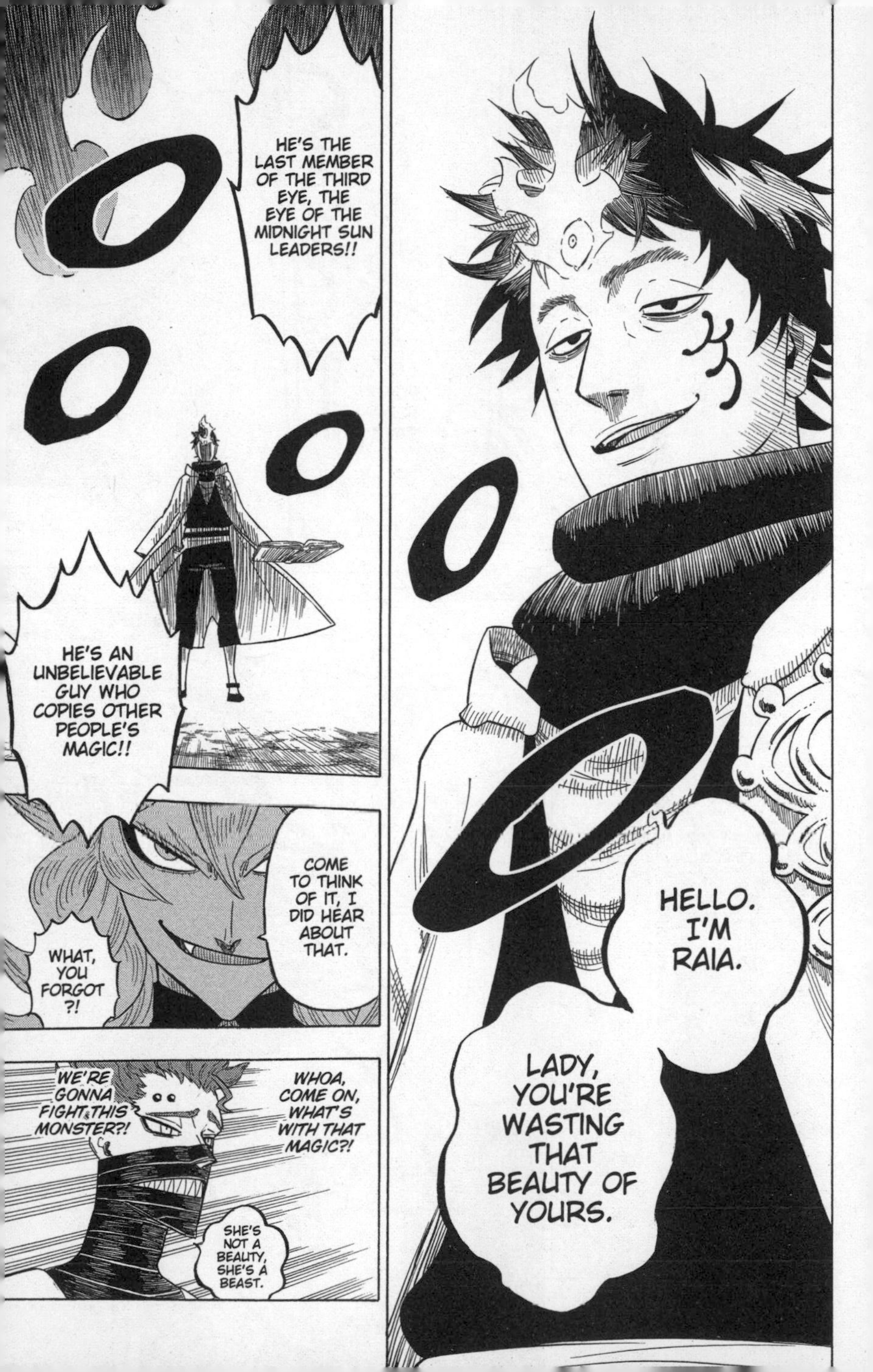
HELLO. I'M RAIA.
LADY, YOU'RE WASTING THAT BEAUTY OF YOURS.
HE'S THE LAST MEMBER OF THE THIRD EYE, THE EYE OF THE MIDNIGHT SUN LEADERS!!
HE'S AN UNBELIEVABLE GUY WHO COPIES OTHER PEOPLE'S MAGIC!!
COME TO THINK OF IT, I DID HEAR ABOUT THAT.
WHAT, YOU FORGOT?!
WHOA, COME ON, WHAT'S WITH THAT MAGIC?!
WE'RE GONNA FIGHT THIS MONSTER?!
SHE'S NOT A BEAUTY, SHE'S A BEAST.

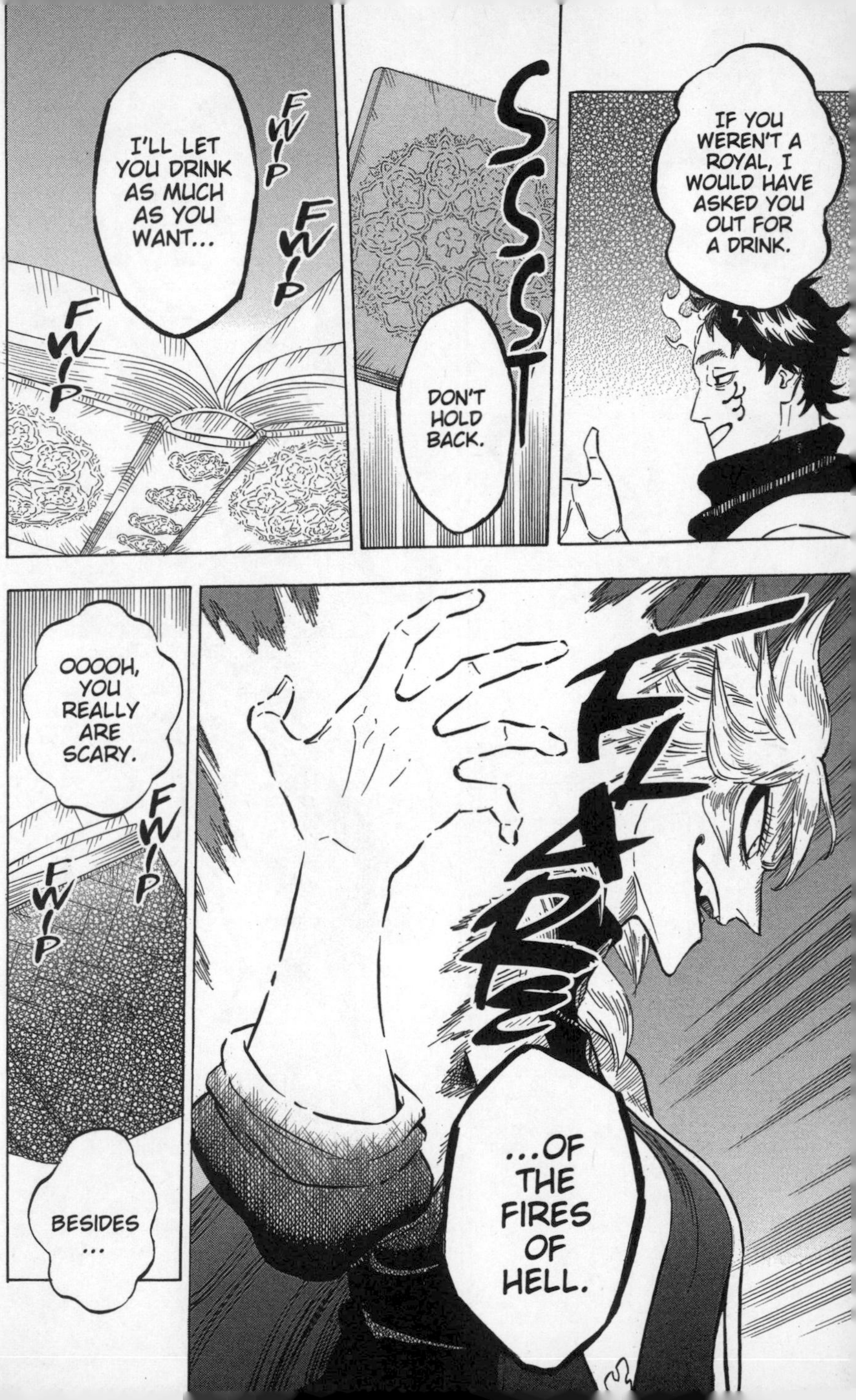
IF YOU WEREN'T A ROYAL, I WOULD HAVE ASKED YOU OUT FOR A DRINK.
SSSST
DON'T HOLD BACK.
I'LL LET YOU DRINK AS MUCH AS YOU WANT...
FWIP
FWIP
FWIP
...OF THE FIRES OF HELL.
OOOOH, YOU REALLY ARE SCARY.
FWIP
FWIP
BESIDES ...

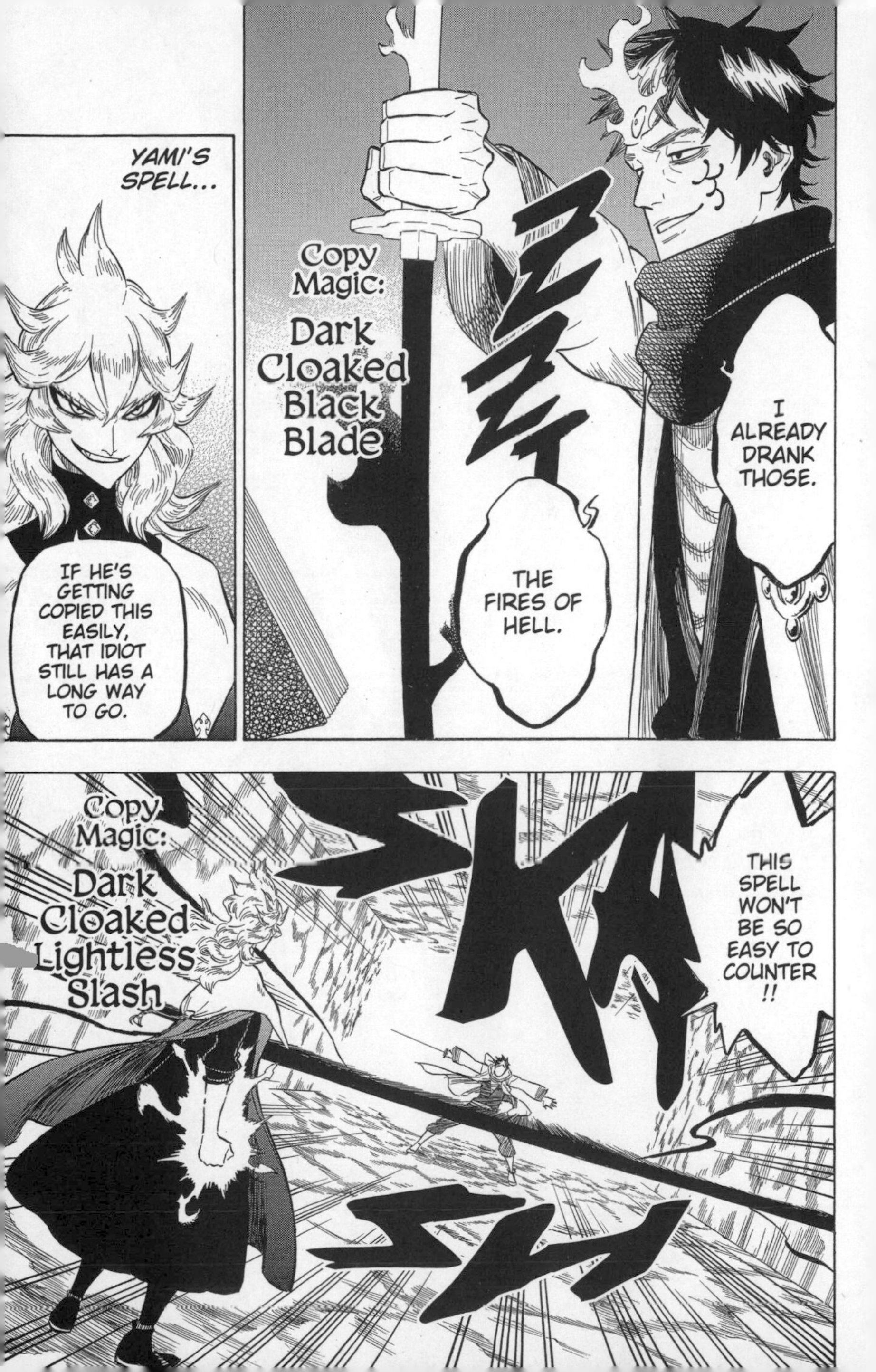
Copy Magic:
Dark Cloaked Black Blade
I ALREADY DRANK THOSE.
THE FIRES OF HELL.
YAMI'S SPELL...
IF HE'S GETTING COPIED THIS EASILY, THAT IDIOT STILL HAS A LONG WAY TO GO.
THIS SPELL WON'T BE SO EASY TO COUNTER !!
Copy Magic:
Dark Cloaked Lightless Slash

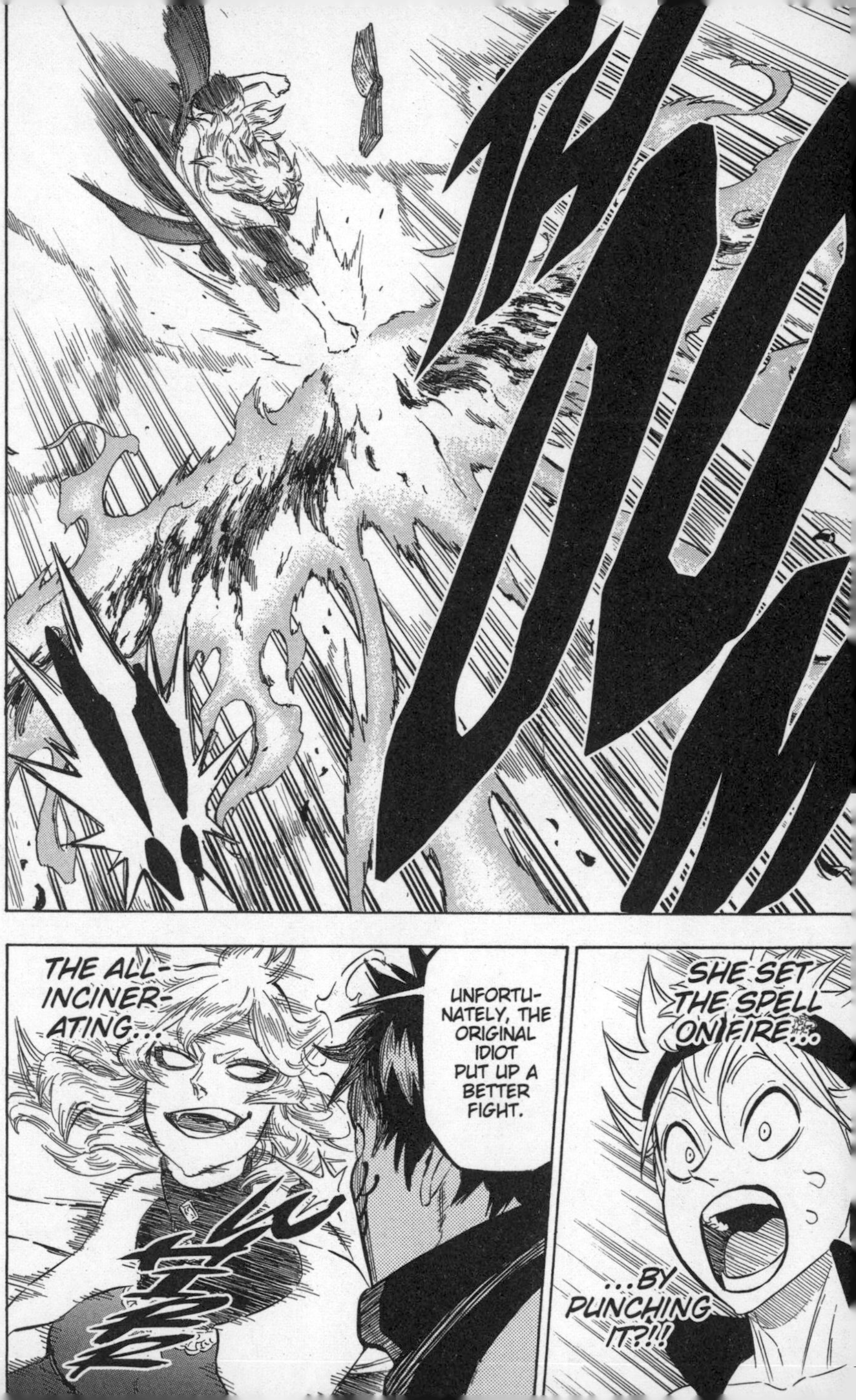
SHE SET THE SPELL ON FIRE...
...BY PUNCHING IT?!!
UNFORTUNATELY, THE ORIGINAL IDIOT PUT UP A BETTER FIGHT.
THE ALL-INCINERATING...

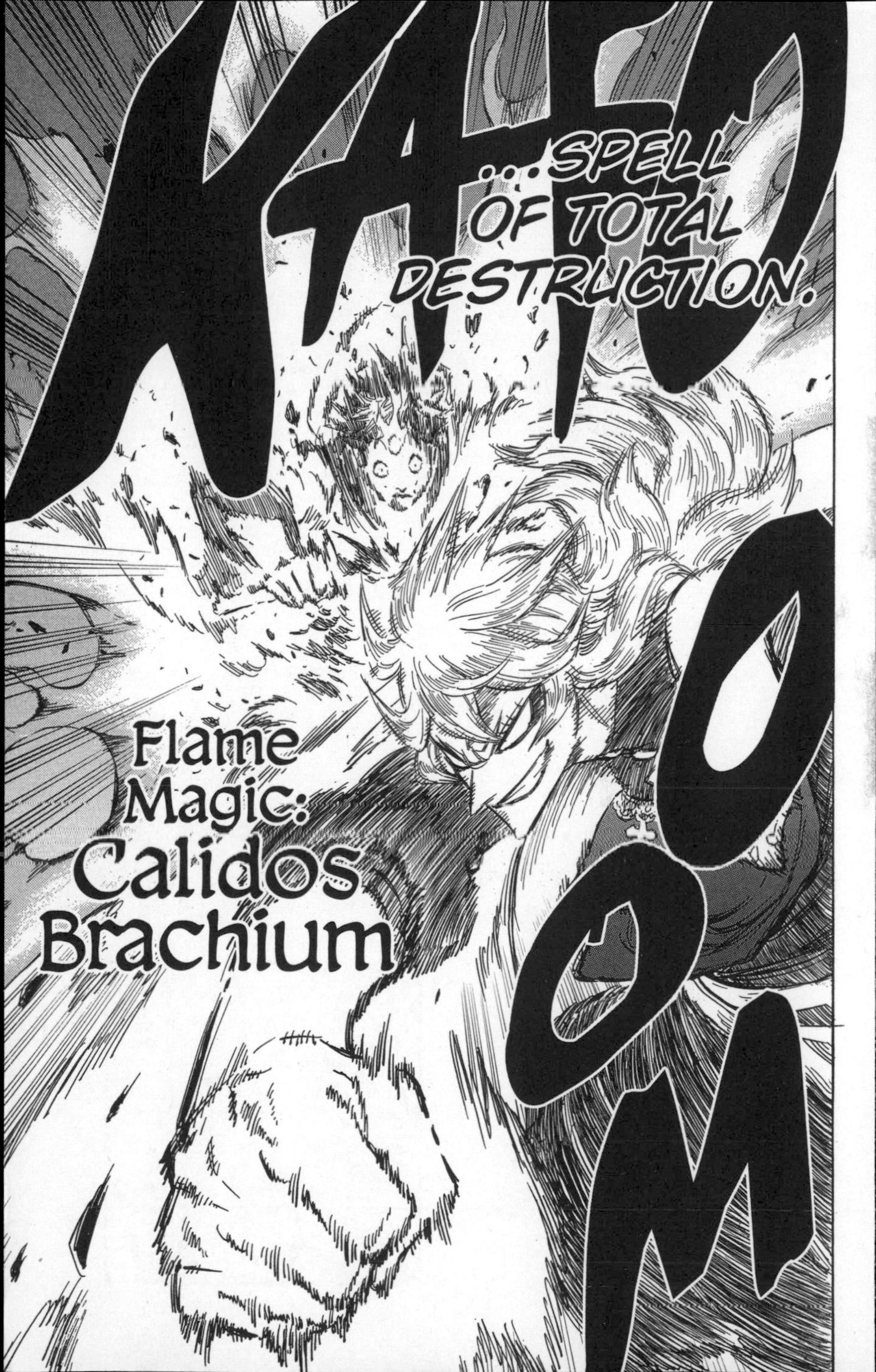

KA-BOOM
...SPELL OF TOTAL DESTRUCTION.
Flame Magic: Calidos Brachium

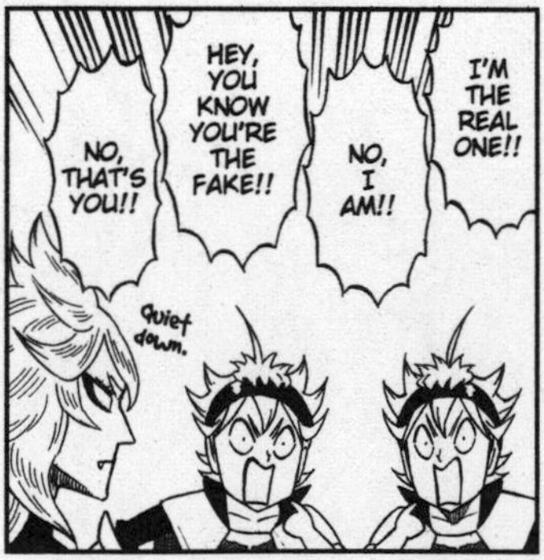
I'M THE REAL ONE!!
NO, I AM!!
HEY, YOU KNOW YOU'RE THE FAKE!!
NO, THAT'S YOU!!
Quiet down.

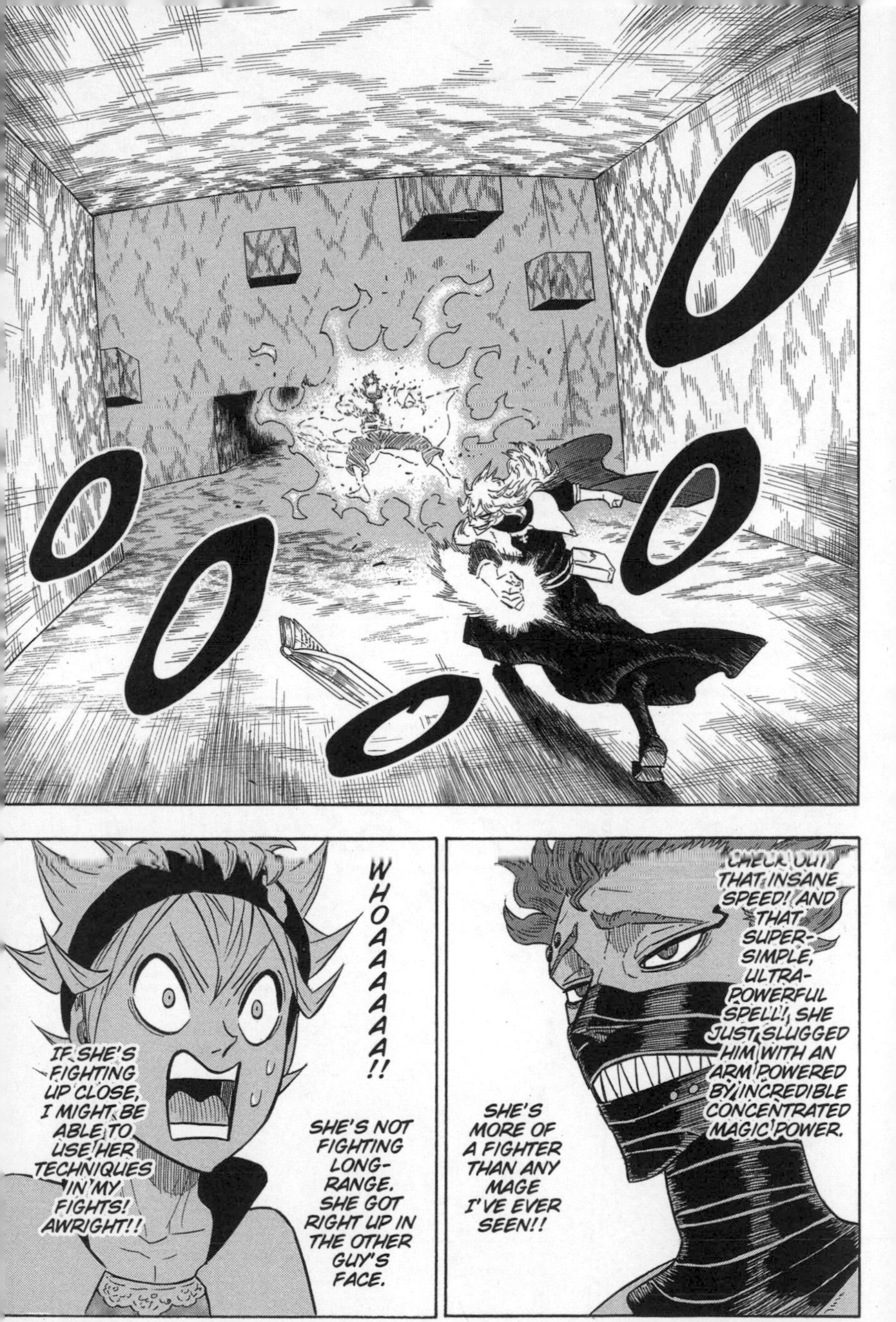
CHECK OUT THAT INSANE SPEED! AND THAT SUPER-SIMPLE, ULTRA-POWERFUL SPELL!, SHE JUST SLUGGED HIM WITH AN ARM POWERED BY INCREDIBLE CONCENTRATED MAGIC POWER.
SHE'S MORE OF A FIGHTER THAN ANY MAGE I'VE EVER SEEN!!
WHOAAAAAAAAA!!
SHE'S NOT FIGHTING LONG-RANGE. SHE GOT RIGHT UP IN THE OTHER GUY'S FACE.
IF SHE'S FIGHTING UP CLOSE, I MIGHT BE ABLE TO USE HER TECHNIQUES IN MY FIGHTS! AWRIGHT!!

Page 137: Mereoleona vs. Raia the Disloyal

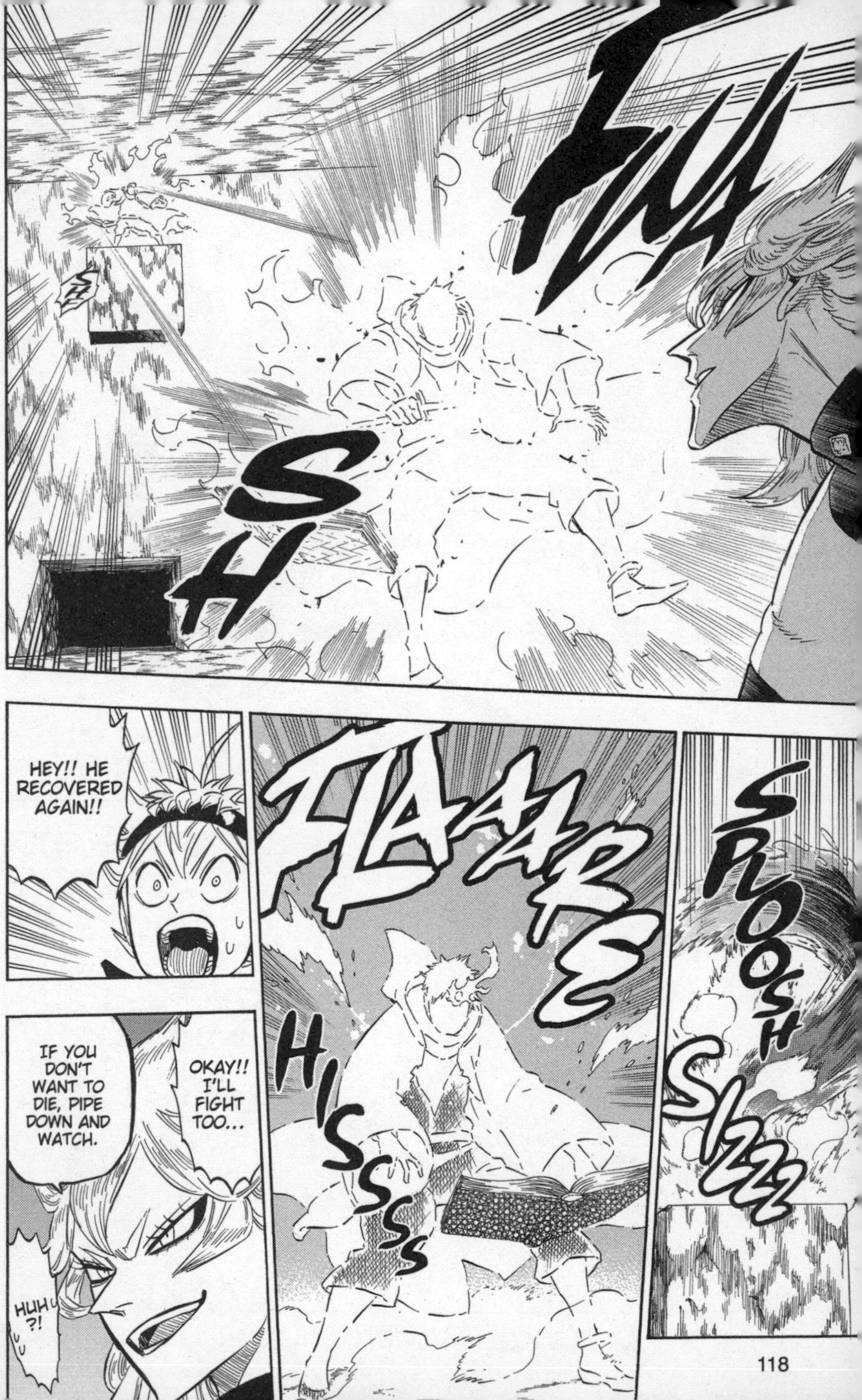
SH
SPLOOSH
SIZZZ
FLAARE
HISSSSS
HEY!! HE RECOVERED AGAIN!!
OKAY!! I'LL FIGHT TOO...
IF YOU DON'T WANT TO DIE, PIPE DOWN AND WATCH.
HUH ?!

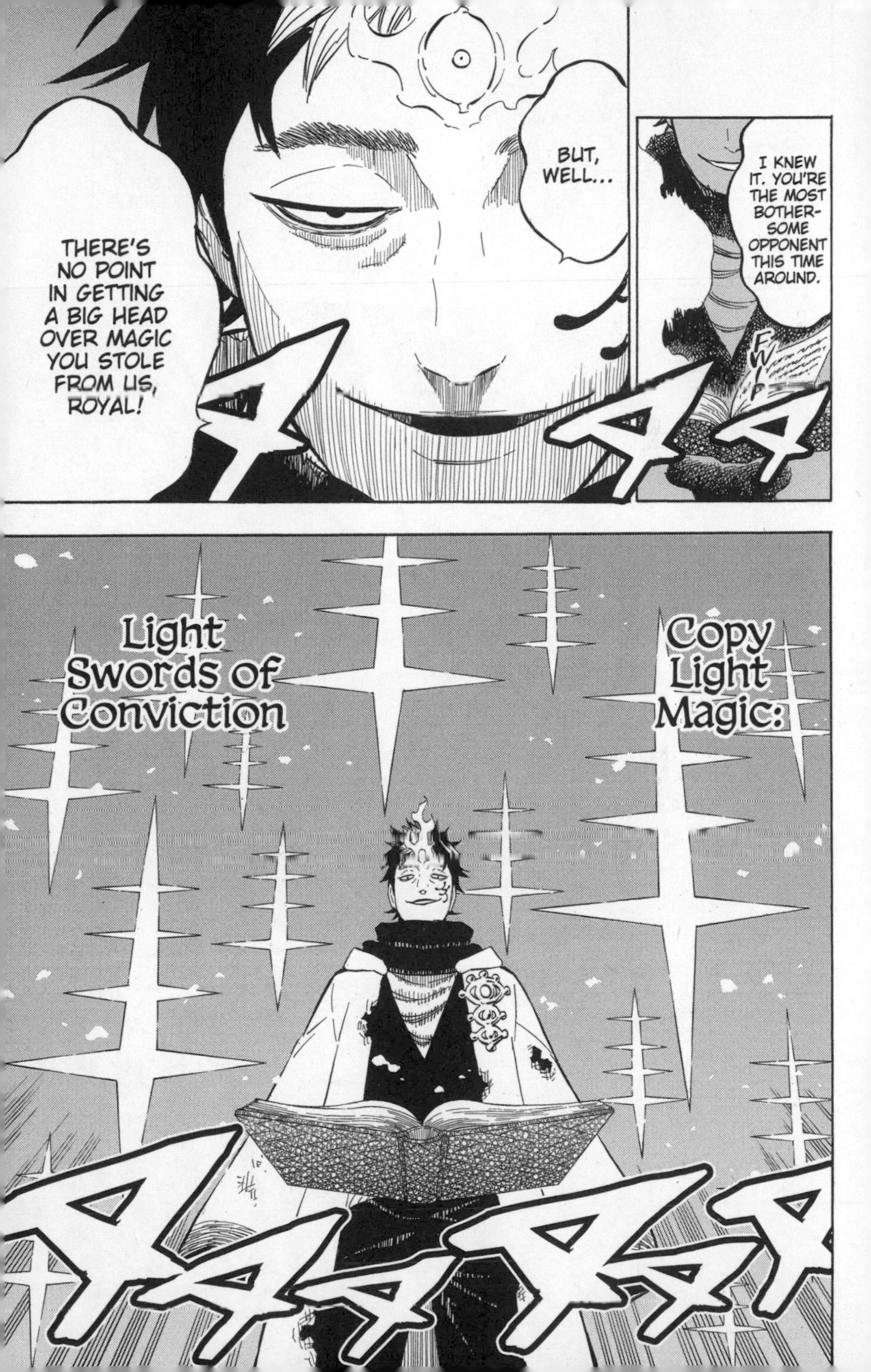
I KNEW IT. YOU'RE THE MOST BOTHER-SOME OPPONENT THIS TIME AROUND.
FWIP
BUT, WELL...
THERE'S NO POINT IN GETTING A BIG HEAD OVER MAGIC YOU STOLE FROM US, ROYAL!
Copy Light Magic:
Light Swords of Conviction

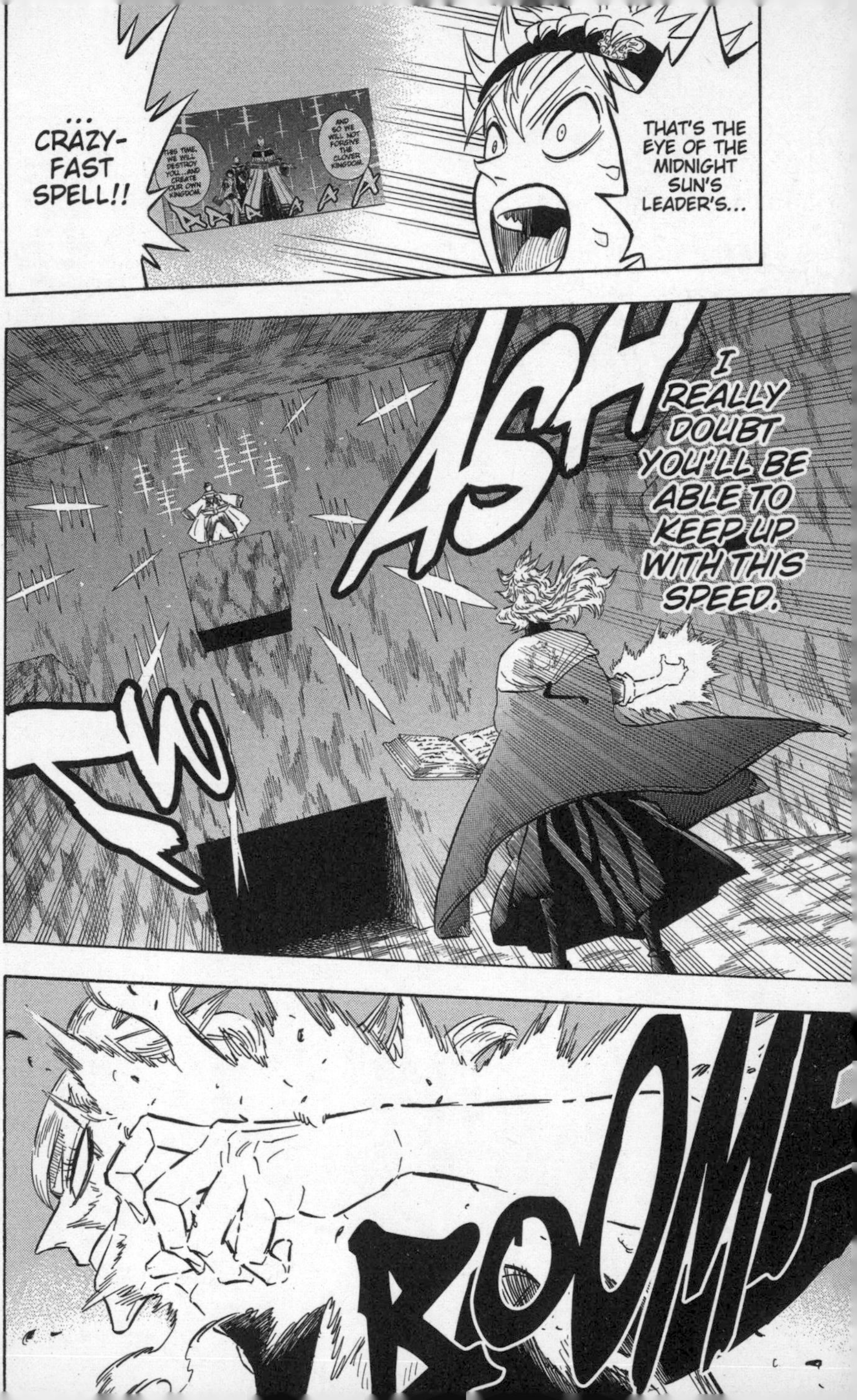
THAT'S THE EYE OF THE MIDNIGHT SUN'S LEADER'S...
AND SO WE WILL NOT FORGIVE THE CLOVER KINGDOM.
THIS TIME, WE WILL DESTROY YOU...AND CREATE OUR OWN KINGDOM.
...CRAZY-FAST SPELL!!
ASH
I REALLY DOUBT YOU'LL BE ABLE TO KEEP UP WITH THIS SPEED.
BOOM

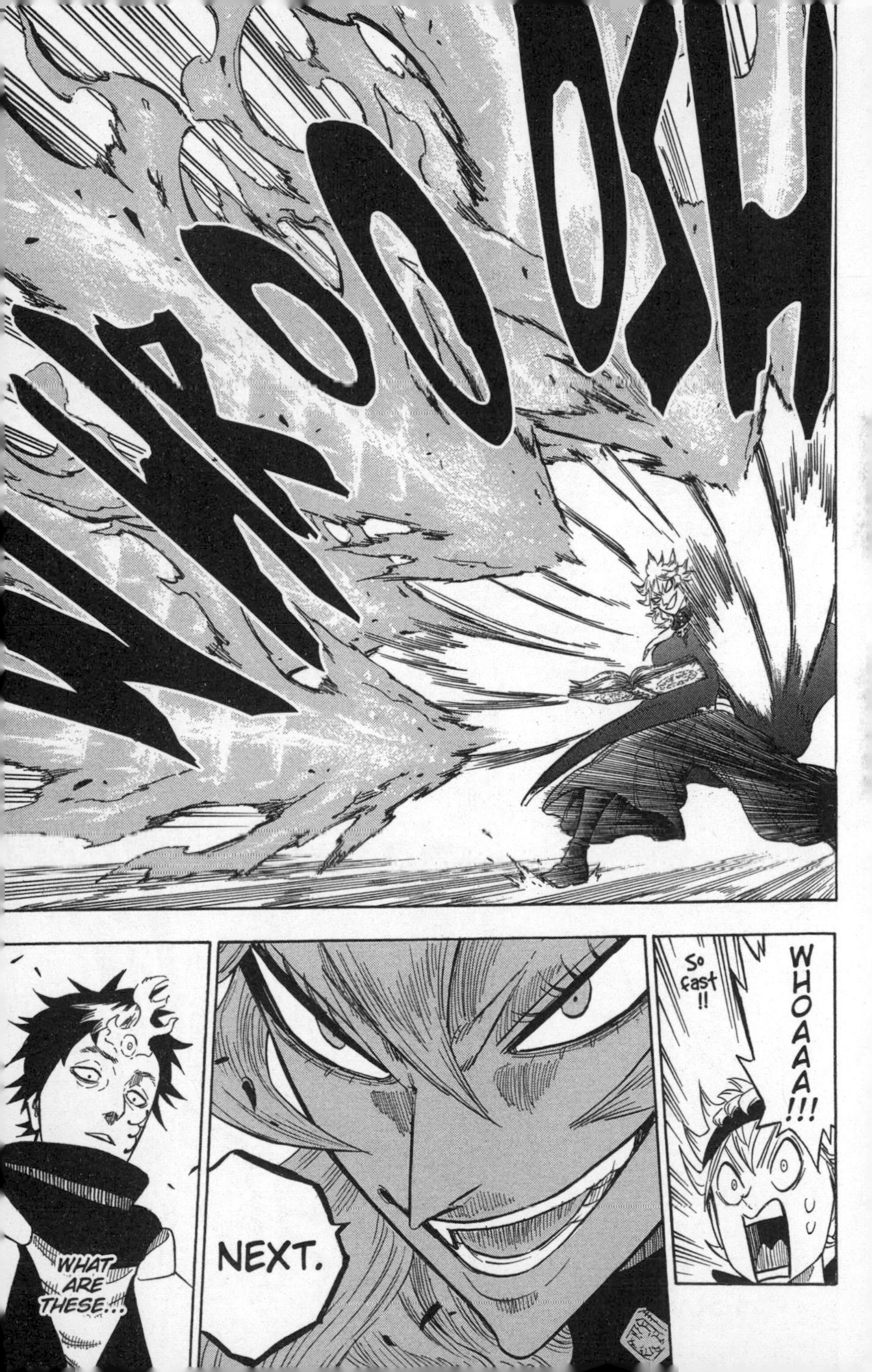
WHOAAA!!!
So fast!!
NEXT.
WHAT ARE THESE...

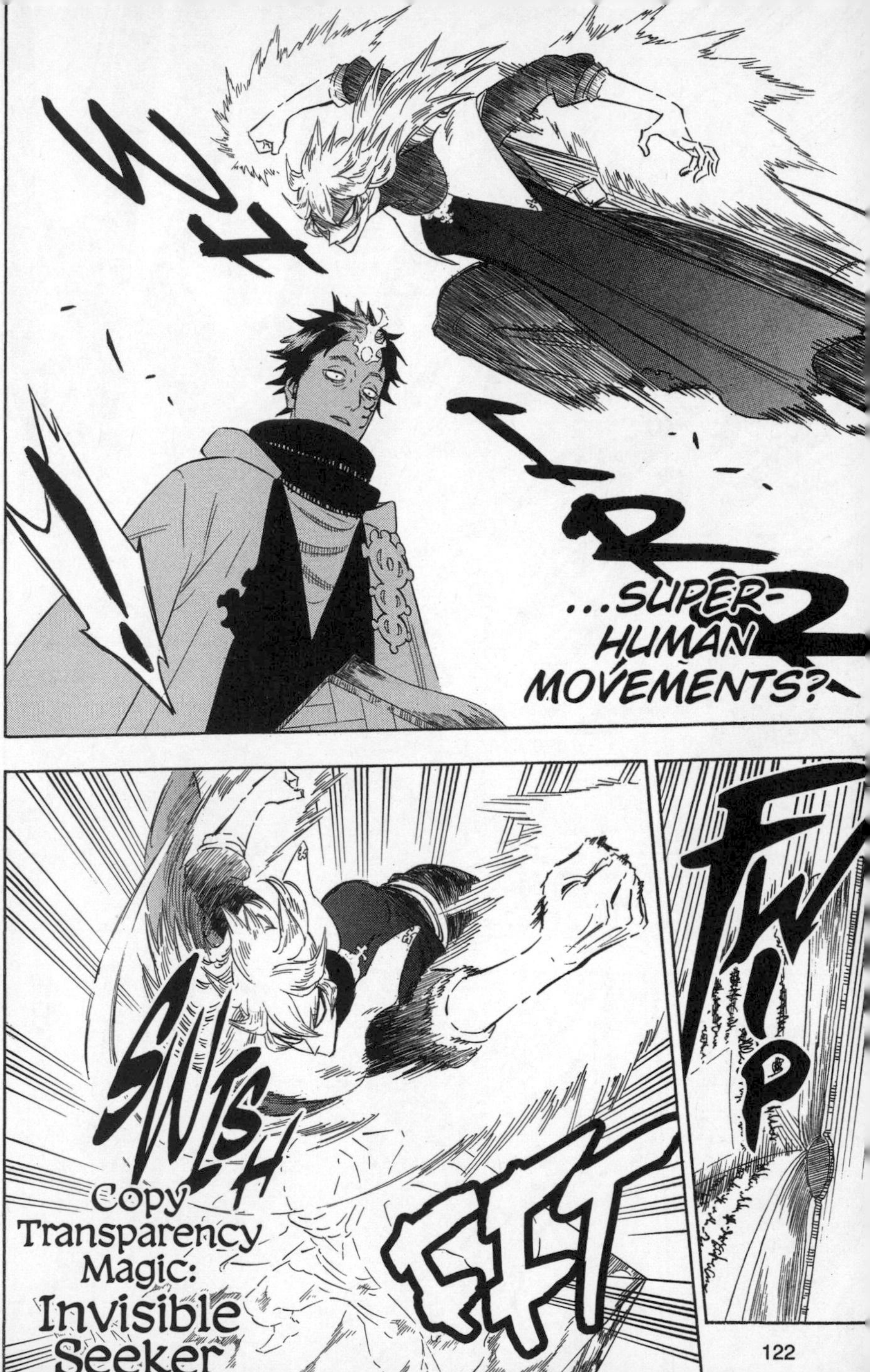
...SUPER-HUMAN MOVEMENTS?
FWIP
SWISH
Copy Transparency Magic: Invisible Seeker

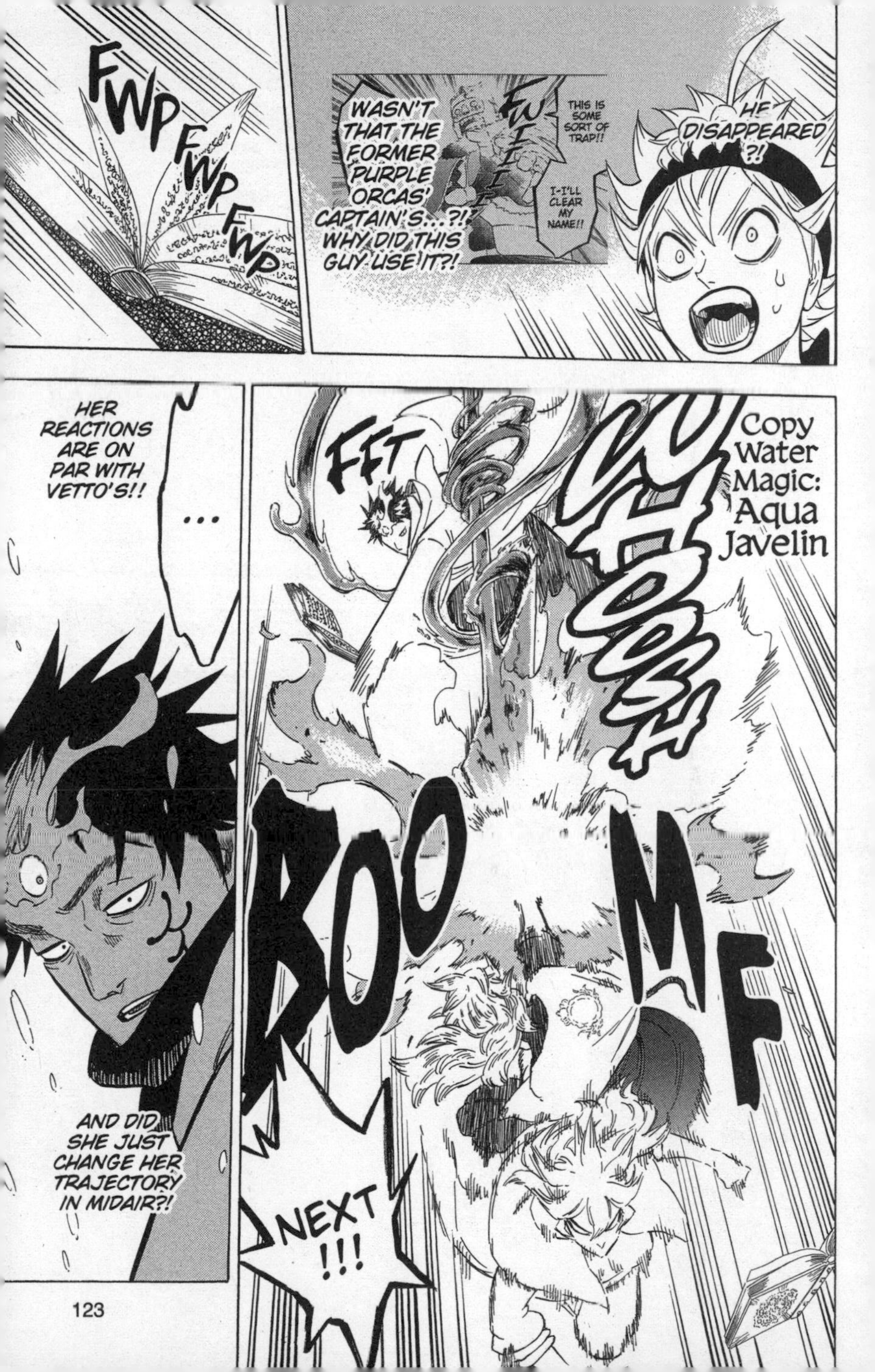
HE DISAPPEARED?!
WASN'T THAT THE FORMER PURPLE ORCAS' CAPTAIN'S...?! WHY DID THIS GUY USE IT?!
THIS IS SOME SORT OF TRAP!!
I-I'LL CLEAR MY NAME!!
FWP FWP FWP FWP
Copy Water Magic: Aqua Javelin
WHOOSH
FFT
BOOMF
NEXT!!!
HER REACTIONS ARE ON PAR WITH VETTO'S!!
...
AND DID SHE JUST CHANGE HER TRAJECTORY IN MIDAIR?!

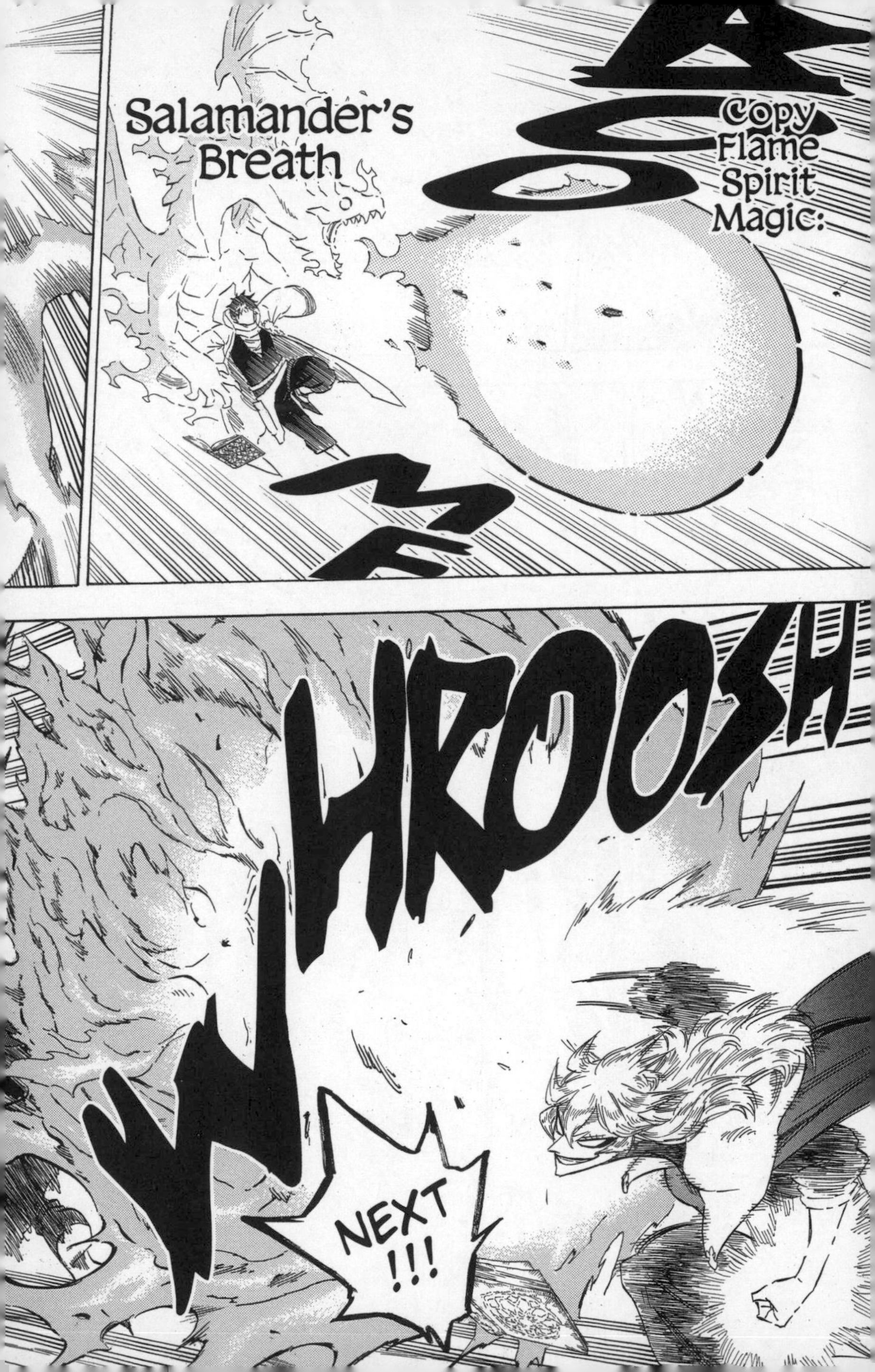
Copy Flame Spirit Magic:
Salamander's Breath
WHROOSH
NEXT !!!

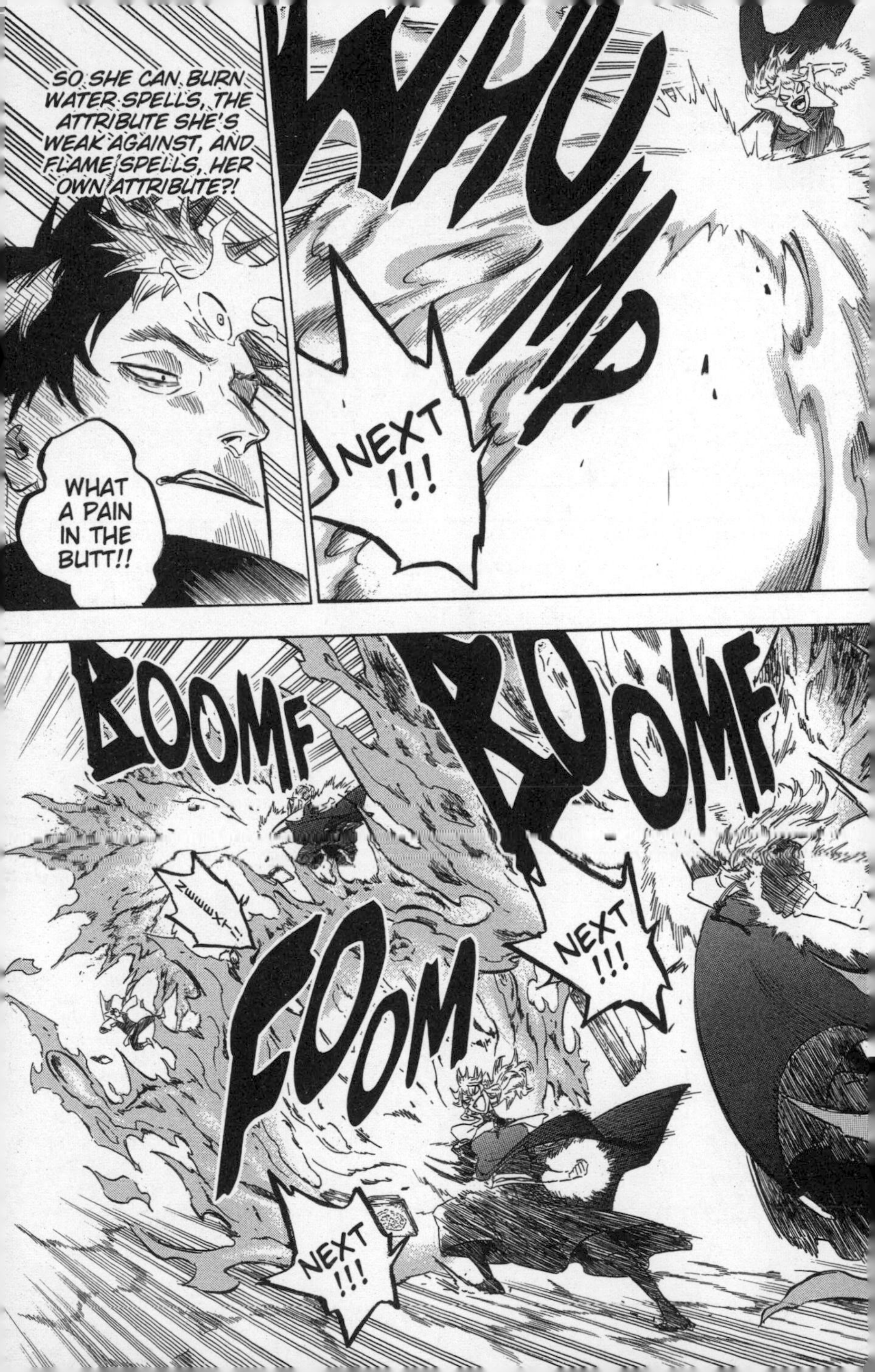
WHUMP
NEXT!!!
SO SHE CAN BURN WATER SPELLS, THE ATTRIBUTE SHE'S WEAK AGAINST, AND FLAME SPELLS, HER OWN ATTRIBUTE?!
WHAT A PAIN IN THE BUTT!!
BOOMF
BOOMF
NEXT!!!
FOOM
NEXT!!!

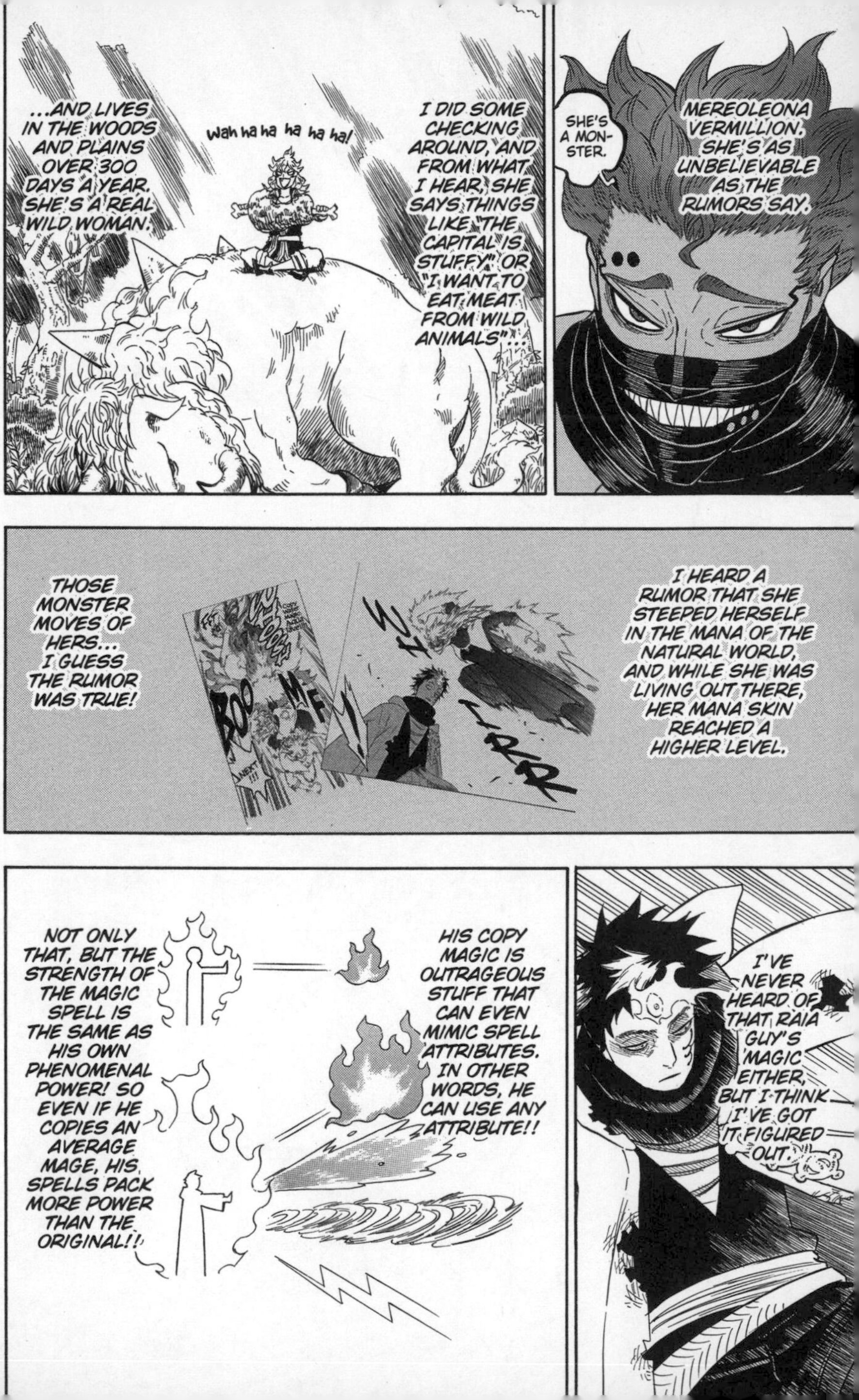
MEREOLEONA VERMILLION. SHE'S AS UNBELIEVABLE AS THE RUMORS SAY.
SHE'S A MONSTER.
I DID SOME CHECKING AROUND, AND FROM WHAT I HEAR, SHE SAYS THINGS LIKE "THE CAPITAL IS STUFFY" OR "I WANT TO EAT MEAT FROM WILD ANIMALS"...
Wah ha ha ha ha ha!
...AND LIVES IN THE WOODS AND PLAINS OVER 300 DAYS A YEAR. SHE'S A REAL WILD WOMAN.
I HEARD A RUMOR THAT SHE STEEPED HERSELF IN THE MANA OF THE NATURAL WORLD, AND WHILE SHE WAS LIVING OUT THERE, HER MANA SKIN REACHED A HIGHER LEVEL.
THOSE MONSTER MOVES OF HERS... I GUESS THE RUMOR WAS TRUE!
I'VE NEVER HEARD OF THAT RAIA GUY'S MAGIC EITHER, BUT I THINK I'VE GOT IT FIGURED OUT.
HIS COPY MAGIC IS OUTRAGEOUS STUFF THAT CAN EVEN MIMIC SPELL ATTRIBUTES. IN OTHER WORDS, HE CAN USE ANY ATTRIBUTE!!
NOT ONLY THAT, BUT THE STRENGTH OF THE MAGIC SPELL IS THE SAME AS HIS OWN PHENOMENAL POWER! SO EVEN IF HE COPIES AN AVERAGE MAGE, HIS SPELLS PACK MORE POWER THAN THE ORIGINAL!!

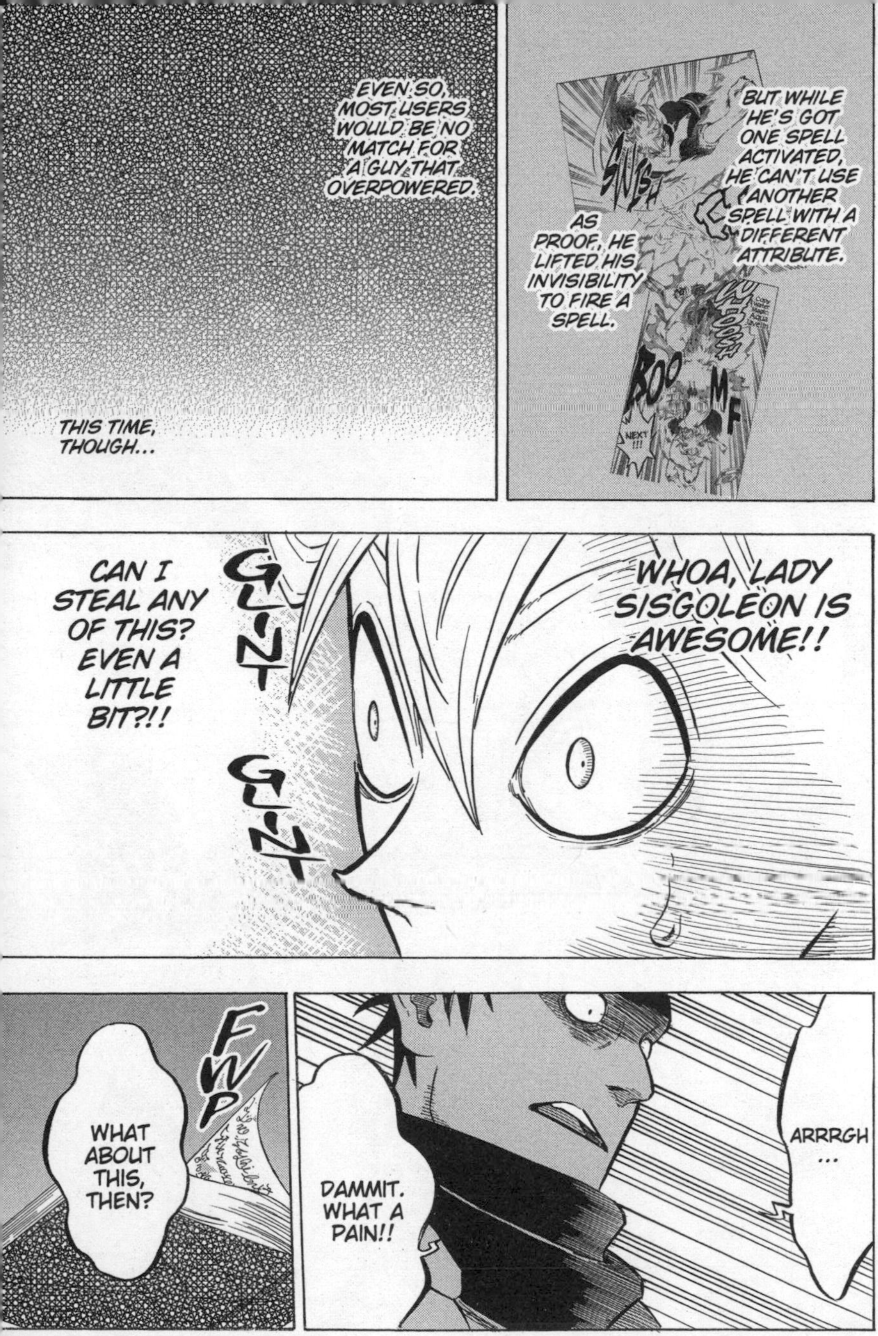
BUT WHILE HE'S GOT ONE SPELL ACTIVATED, HE CAN'T USE ANOTHER SPELL WITH A DIFFERENT ATTRIBUTE.
AS PROOF, HE LIFTED HIS INVISIBILITY TO FIRE A SPELL.
BOOMF
EVEN SO, MOST USERS WOULD BE NO MATCH FOR A GUY THAT OVERPOWERED.
THIS TIME, THOUGH...
WHOA, LADY SISGOLEON IS AWESOME!!
GLINT
GLINT
CAN I STEAL ANY OF THIS? EVEN A LITTLE BIT?!!
ARRRGH...
DAMMIT. WHAT A PAIN!!
FWP
WHAT ABOUT THIS, THEN?

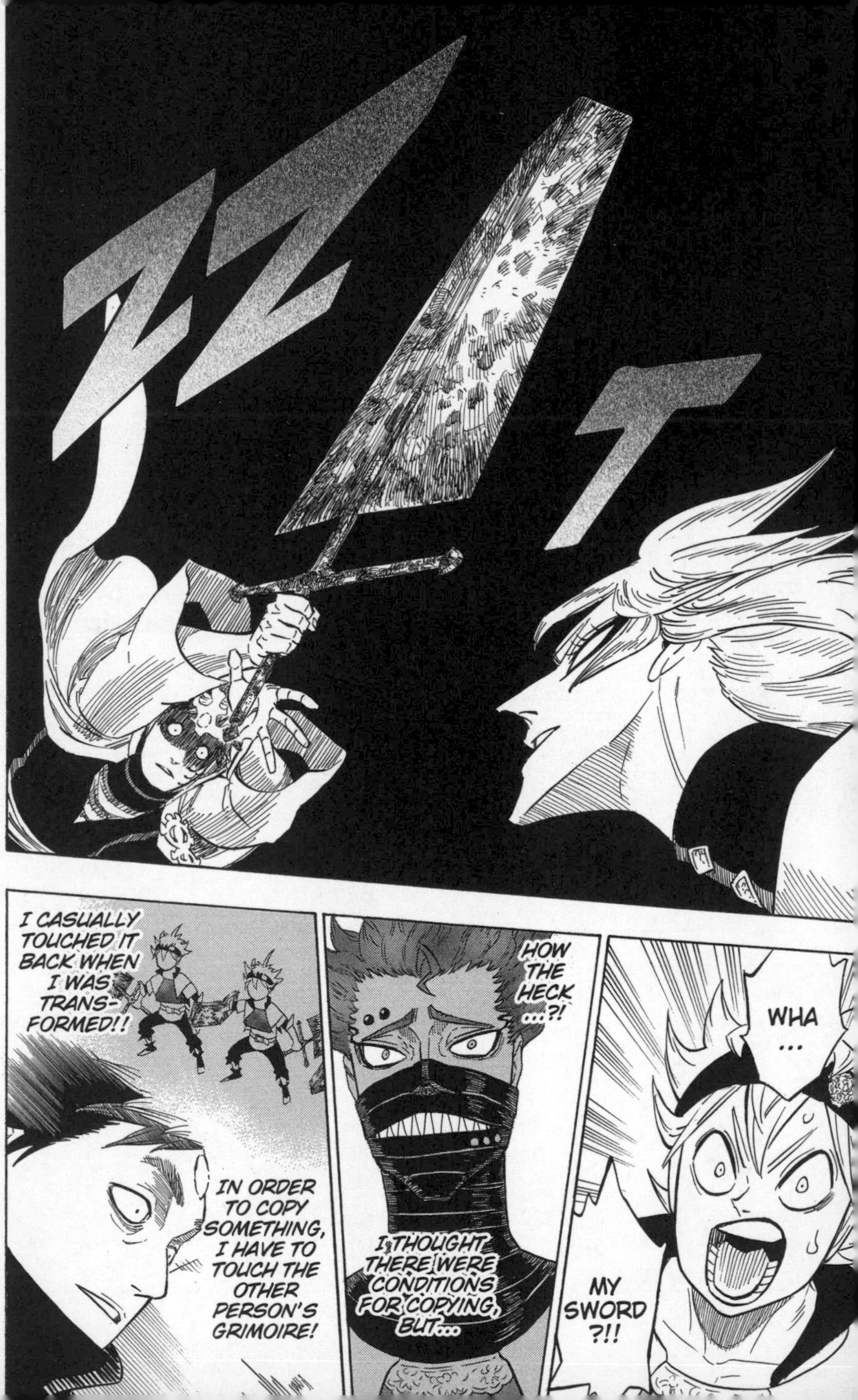
ZZZAT
WHA...
MY SWORD?!!
HOW THE HECK...?!
I THOUGHT THERE WERE CONDITIONS FOR COPYING, BUT...
I CASUALLY TOUCHED IT BACK WHEN I WAS TRANS-FORMED!!
IN ORDER TO COPY SOMETHING, I HAVE TO TOUCH THE OTHER PERSON'S GRIMOIRE!

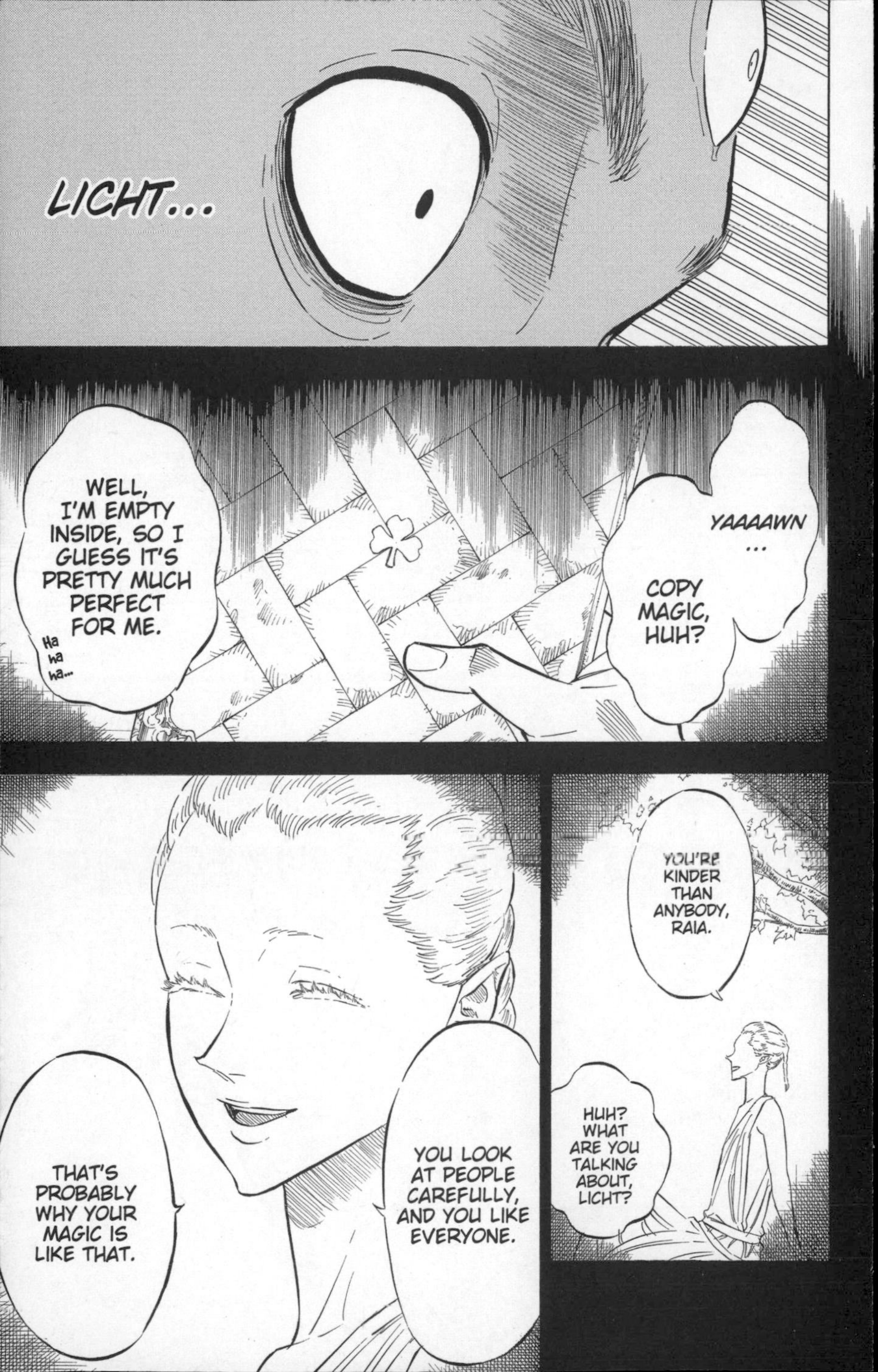
LICHT...
YAAAAWN...
COPY MAGIC, HUH?
WELL, I'M EMPTY INSIDE, SO I GUESS IT'S PRETTY MUCH PERFECT FOR ME.
Ha ha ha...
YOU'RE KINDER THAN ANYBODY, RAIA.
HUH? WHAT ARE YOU TALKING ABOUT, LICHT?
YOU LOOK AT PEOPLE CAREFULLY, AND YOU LIKE EVERYONE.
THAT'S PROBABLY WHY YOUR MAGIC IS LIKE THAT.

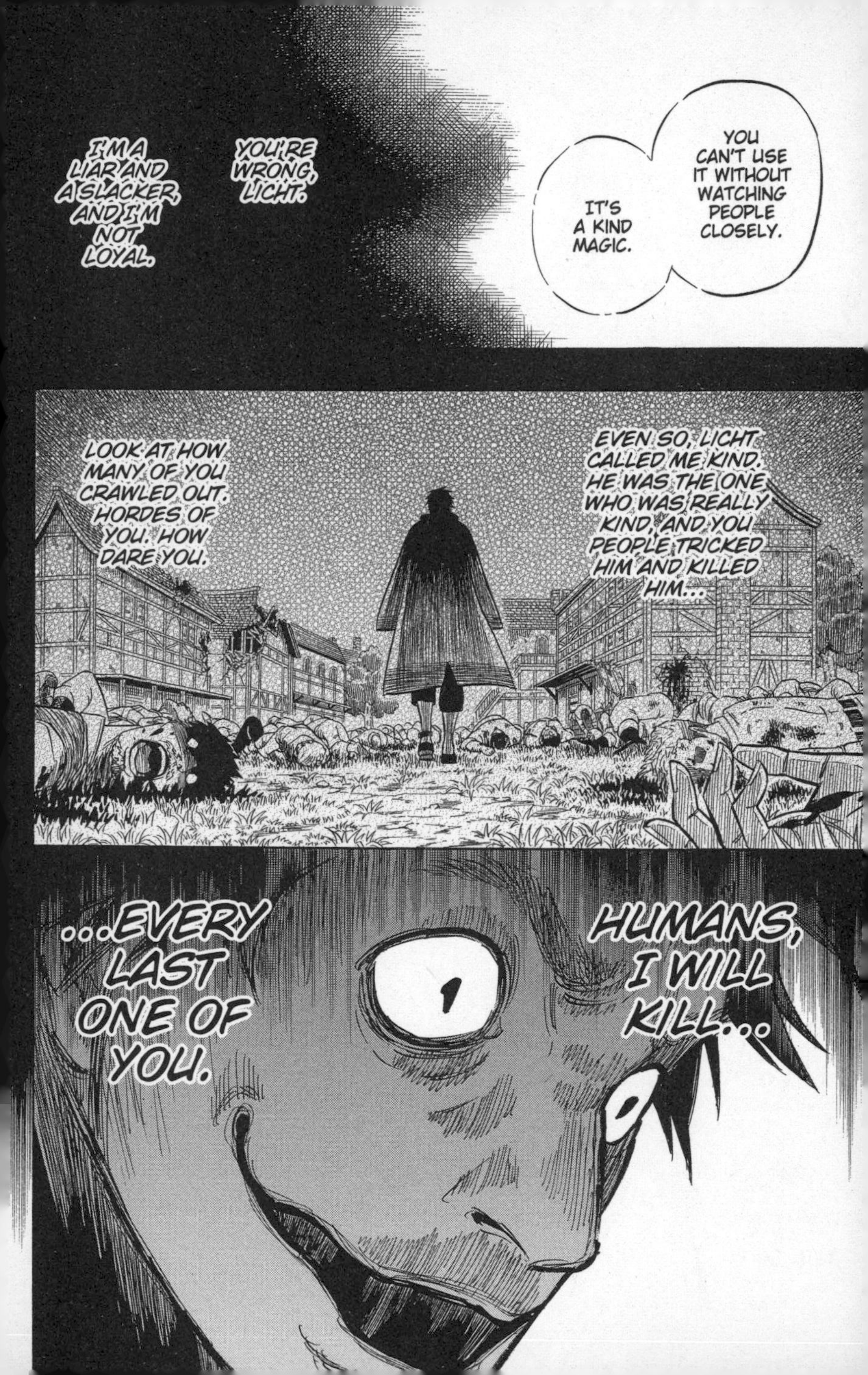
YOU CAN'T USE IT WITHOUT WATCHING PEOPLE CLOSELY.
IT'S A KIND MAGIC.
YOU'RE WRONG, LICHT.
I'M A LIAR AND A SLACKER, AND I'M NOT LOYAL.
EVEN SO, LICHT CALLED ME KIND. HE WAS THE ONE WHO WAS REALLY KIND, AND YOU PEOPLE TRICKED HIM AND KILLED HIM...
LOOK AT HOW MANY OF YOU CRAWLED OUT. HORDES OF YOU. HOW DARE YOU.
HUMANS, I WILL KILL...
...EVERY LAST ONE OF YOU.

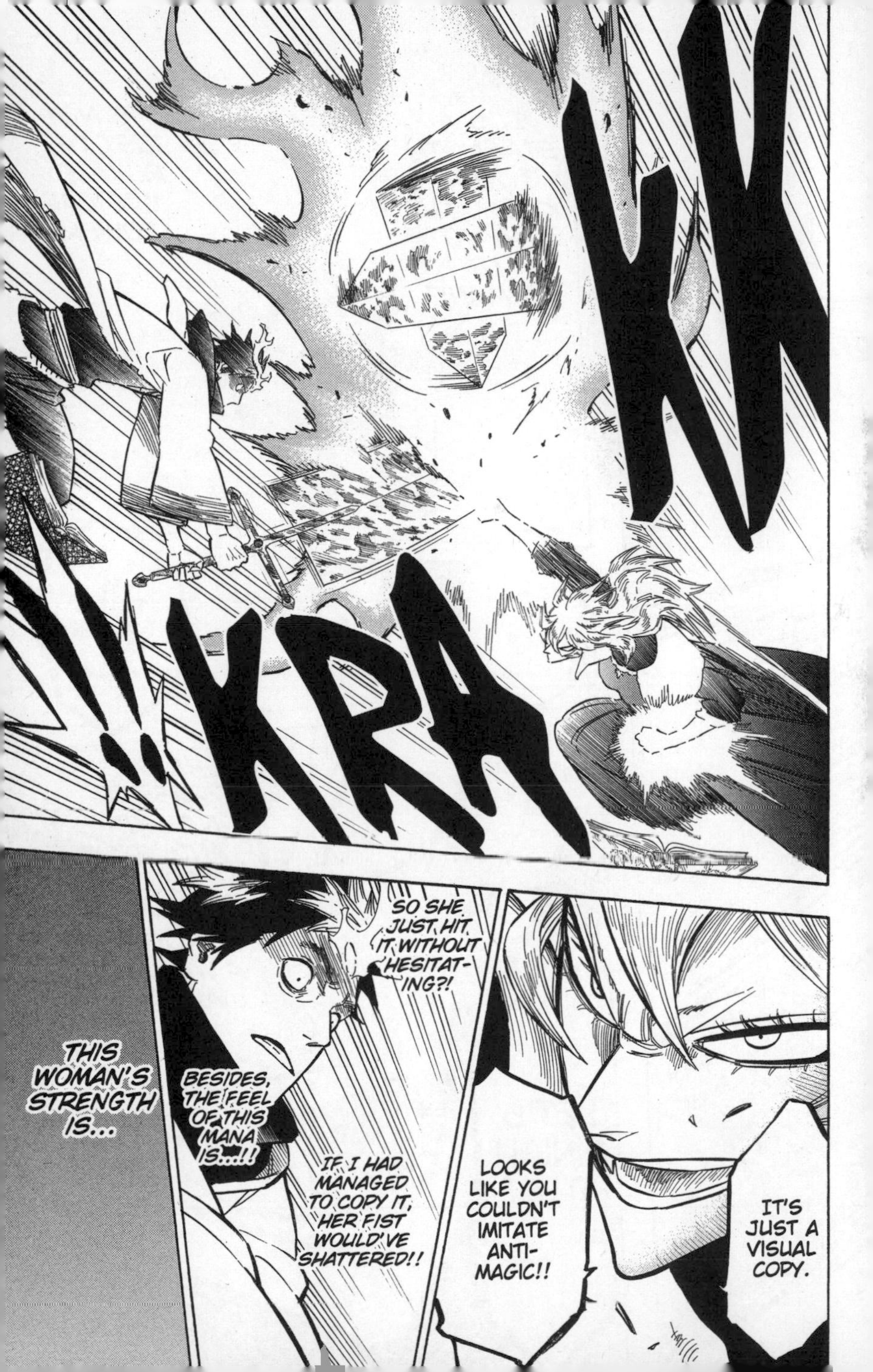
KRAKK!!
IT'S JUST A VISUAL COPY.
LOOKS LIKE YOU COULDN'T IMITATE ANTI-MAGIC!!
SO SHE JUST HIT IT WITHOUT HESITATING?!
IF I HAD MANAGED TO COPY IT, HER FIST WOULD'VE SHATTERED!!
BESIDES, THE FEEL OF THIS MANA IS...!!
THIS WOMAN'S STRENGTH IS...

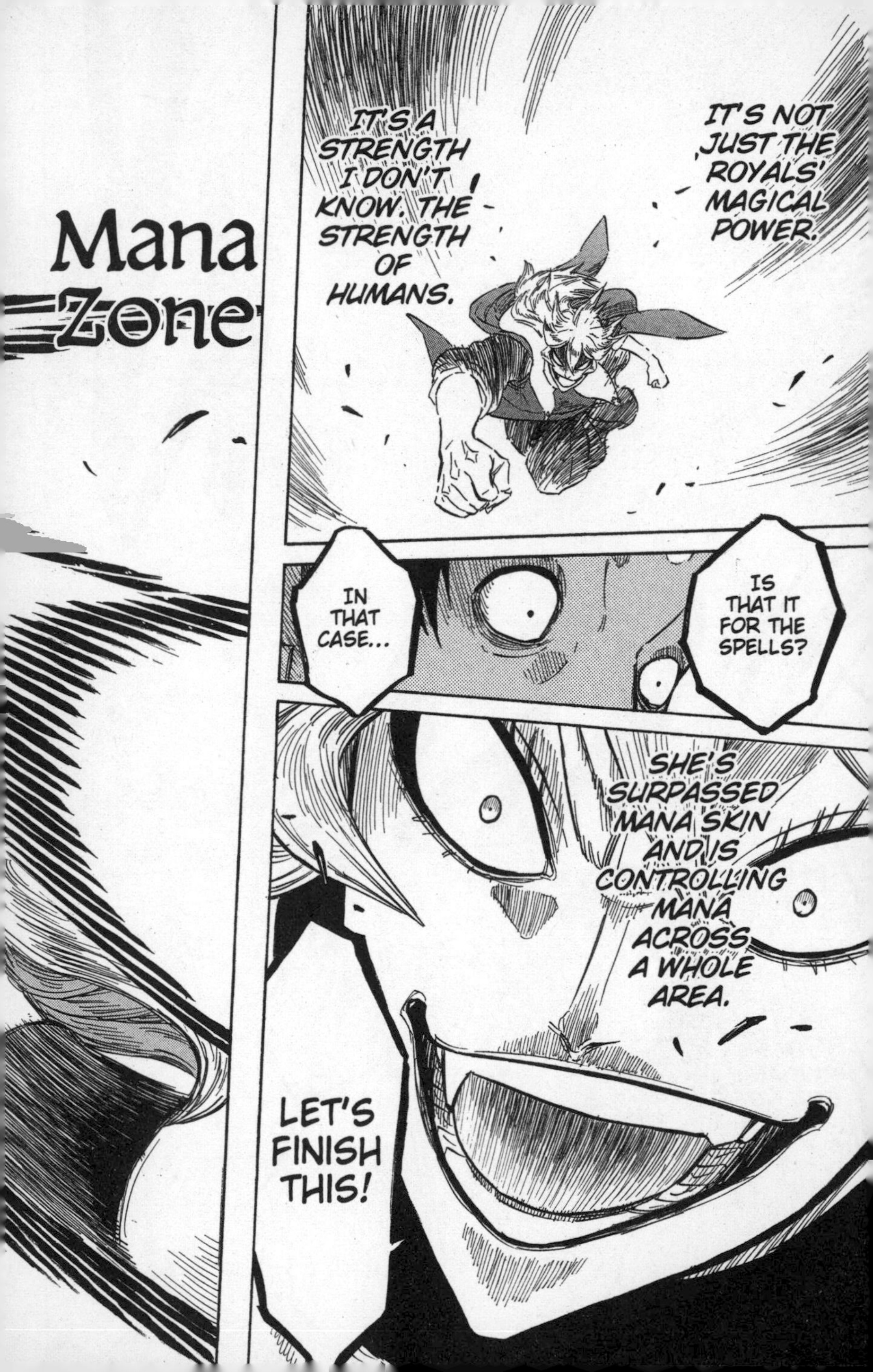
IT'S NOT JUST THE ROYALS' MAGICAL POWER.
IT'S A STRENGTH I DON'T KNOW. THE STRENGTH OF HUMANS.
IS THAT IT FOR THE SPELLS?
IN THAT CASE...
SHE'S SURPASSED MANA SKIN AND IS CONTROLLING MANA ACROSS A WHOLE AREA.
LET'S FINISH THIS!
Mana Zone

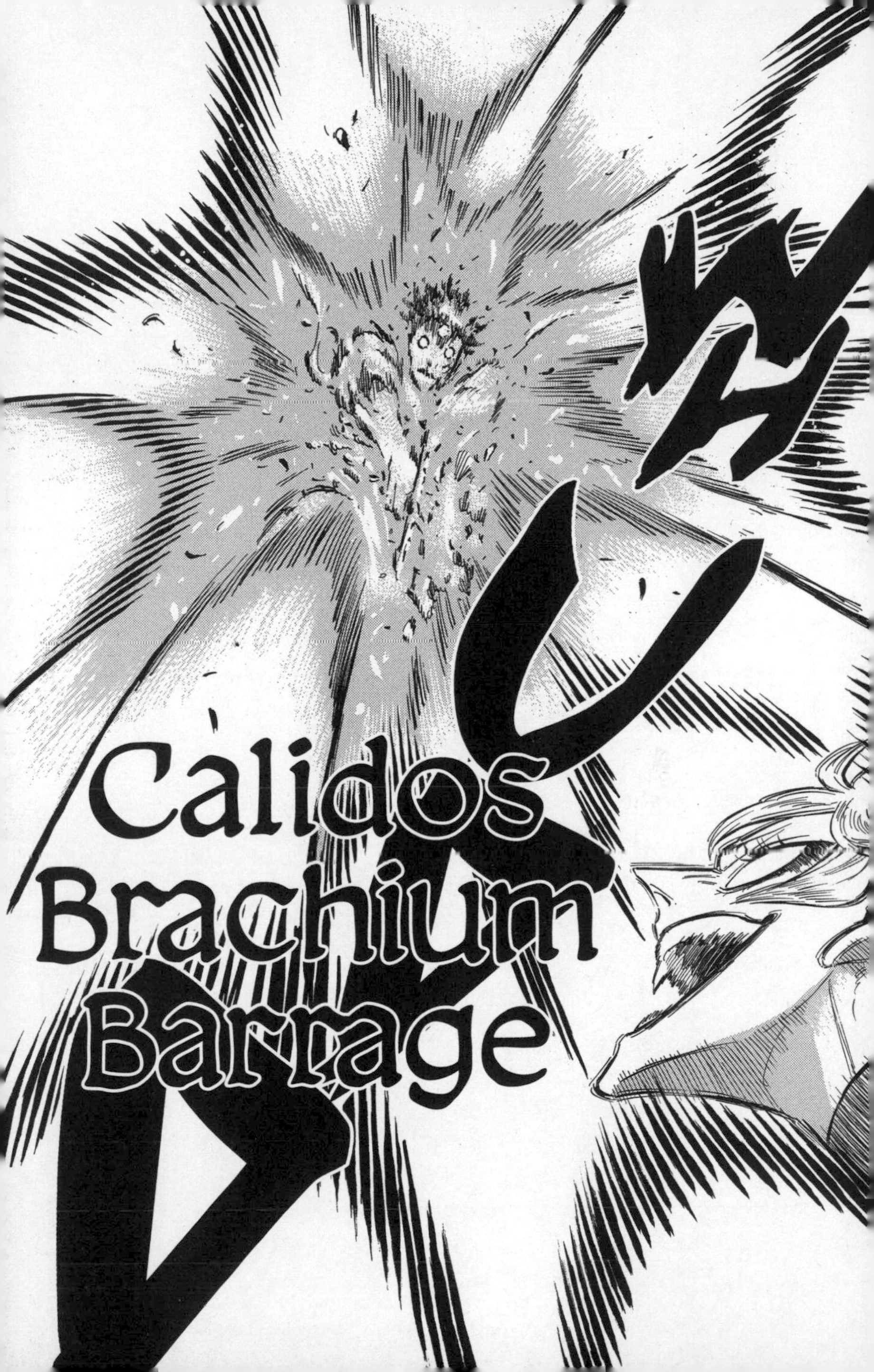
Calidos Brachium Barrage

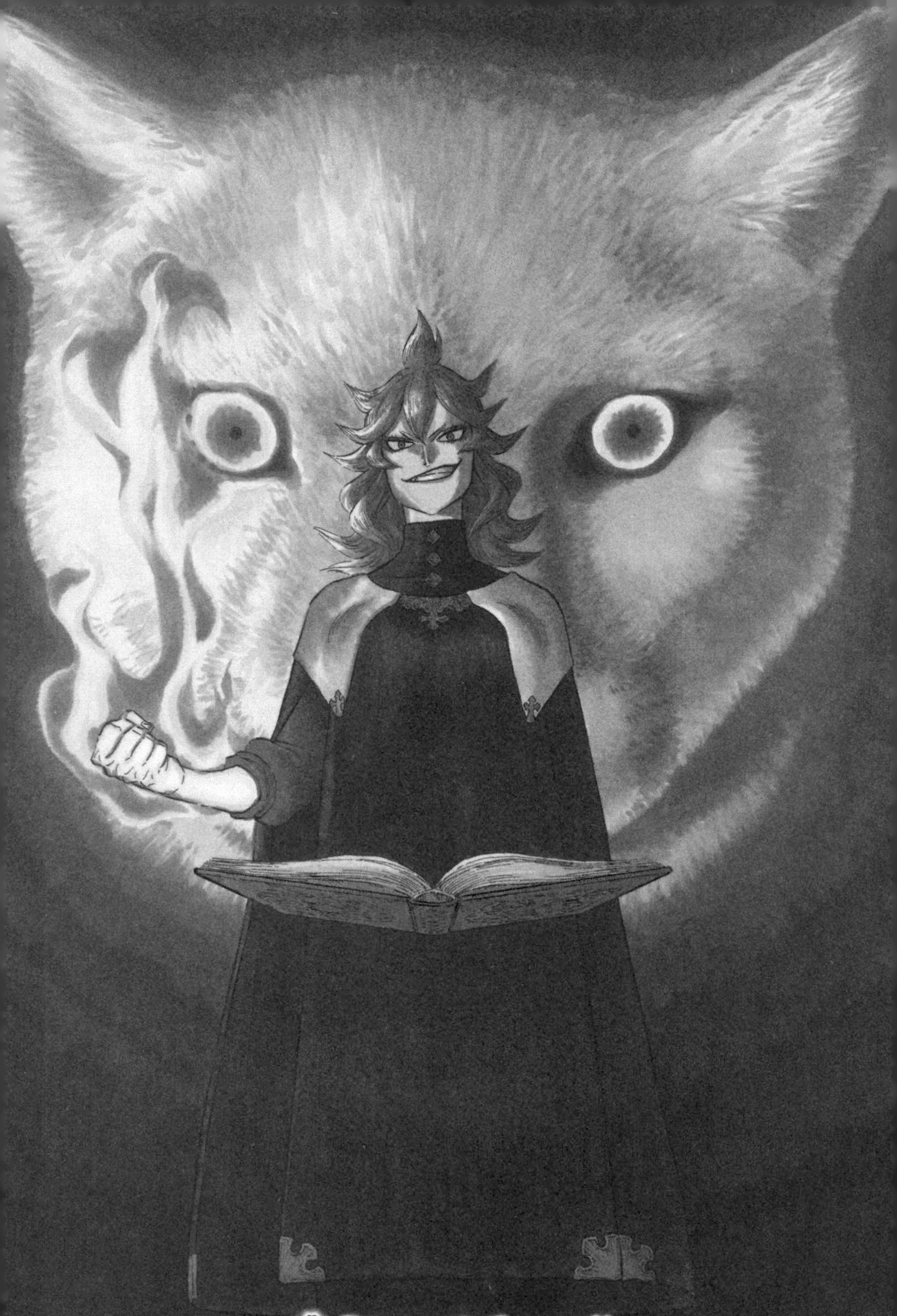

Page 138: Assault

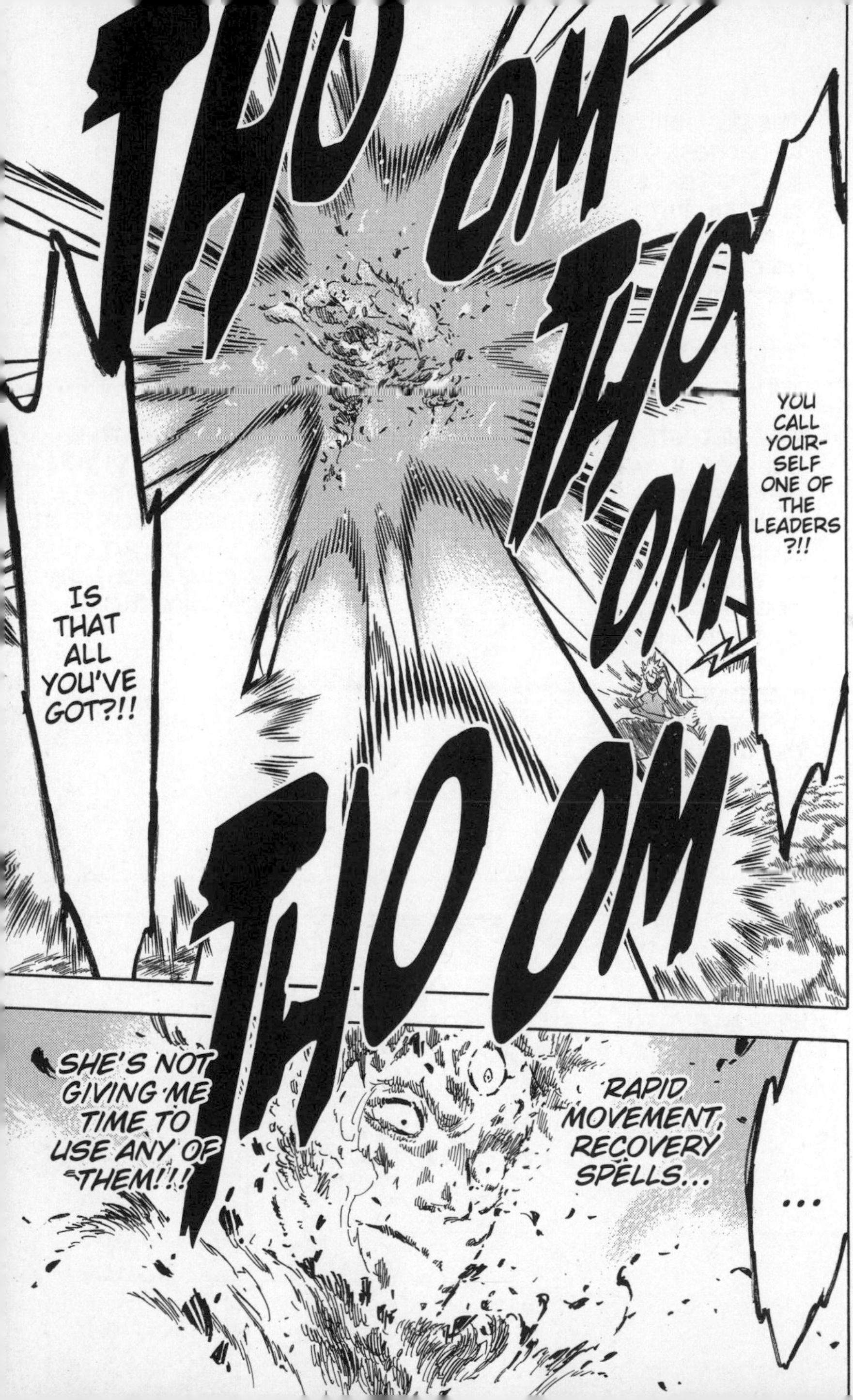
THOOM
THOOM
YOU CALL YOUR-SELF ONE OF THE LEADERS ?!!
IS THAT ALL YOU'VE GOT?!!
THOOM
...
RAPID MOVEMENT, RECOVERY SPELLS...
SHE'S NOT GIVING ME TIME TO USE ANY OF THEM!!!

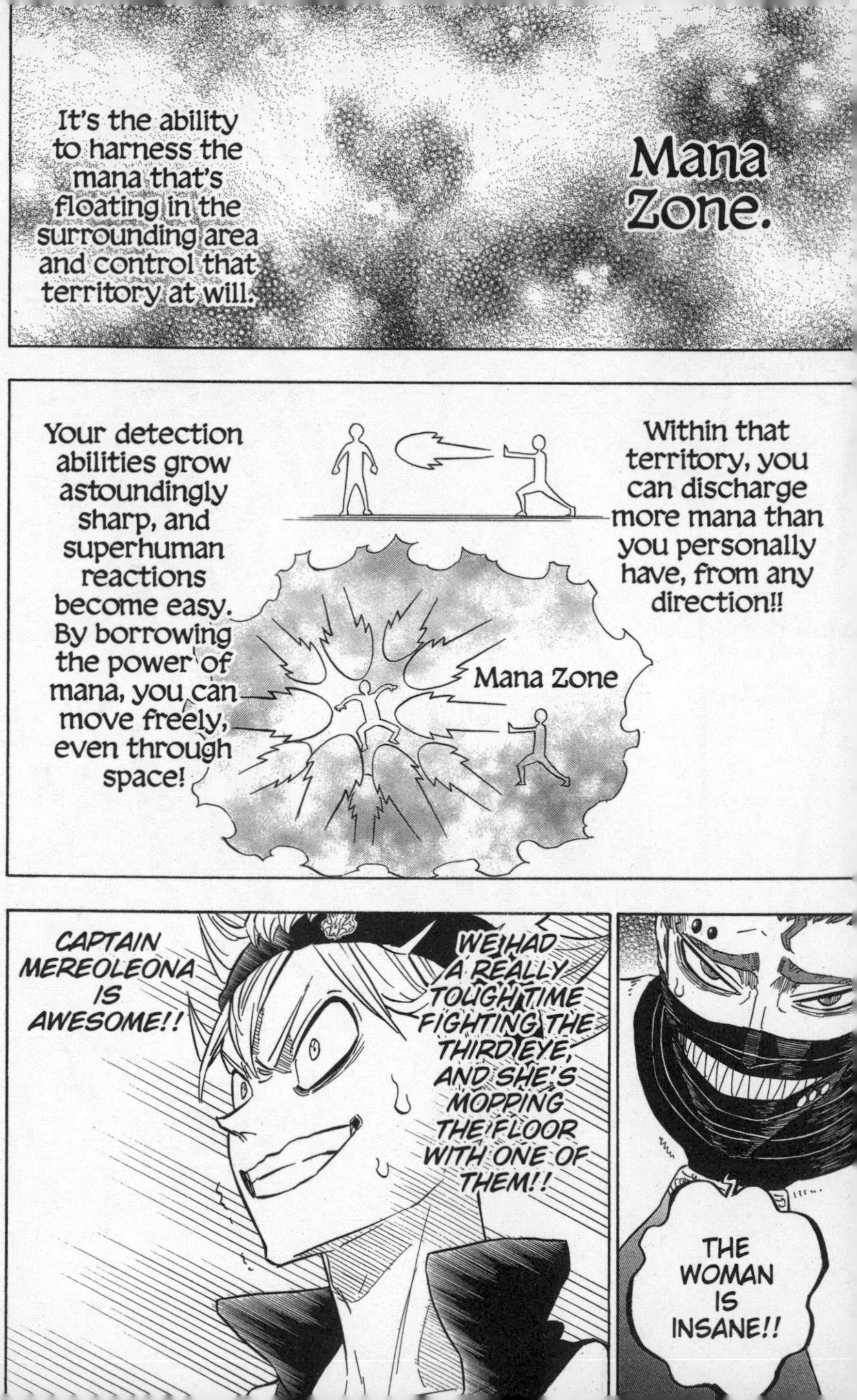
Mana Zone.
It's the ability to harness the mana that's floating in the surrounding area and control that territory at will.
Within that territory, you can discharge more mana than you personally have, from any direction!!
Mana Zone
Your detection abilities grow astoundingly sharp, and superhuman reactions become easy. By borrowing the power of mana, you can move freely, even through space!
THE WOMAN IS INSANE!!
WE HAD A REALLY TOUGH TIME FIGHTING THE THIRD EYE, AND SHE'S MOPPING THE FLOOR WITH ONE OF THEM!!
CAPTAIN MEREOLEONA IS AWESOME!!

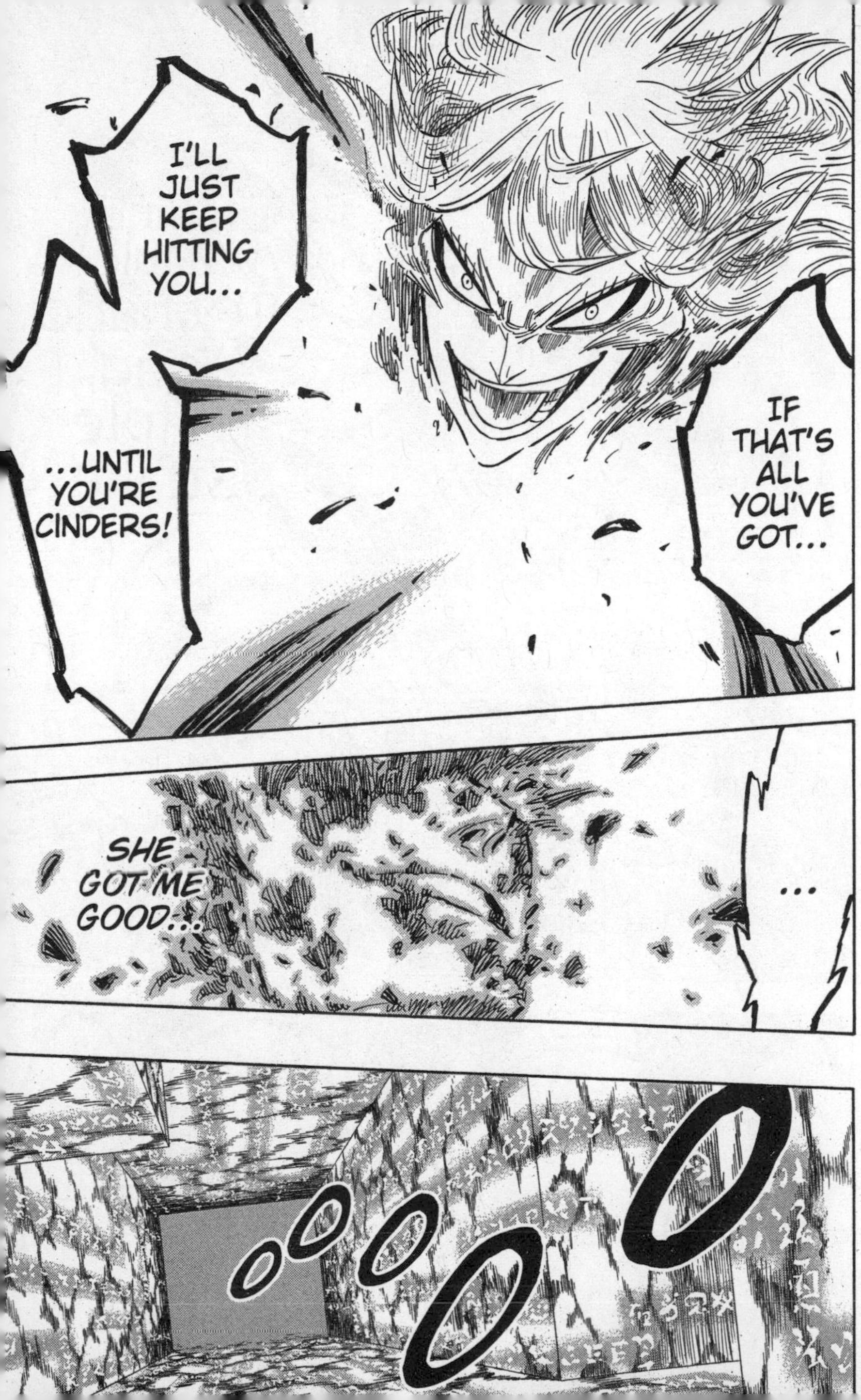
IF THAT'S ALL YOU'VE GOT...
I'LL JUST KEEP HITTING YOU...
...UNTIL YOU'RE CINDERS!
...
SHE GOT ME GOOD...

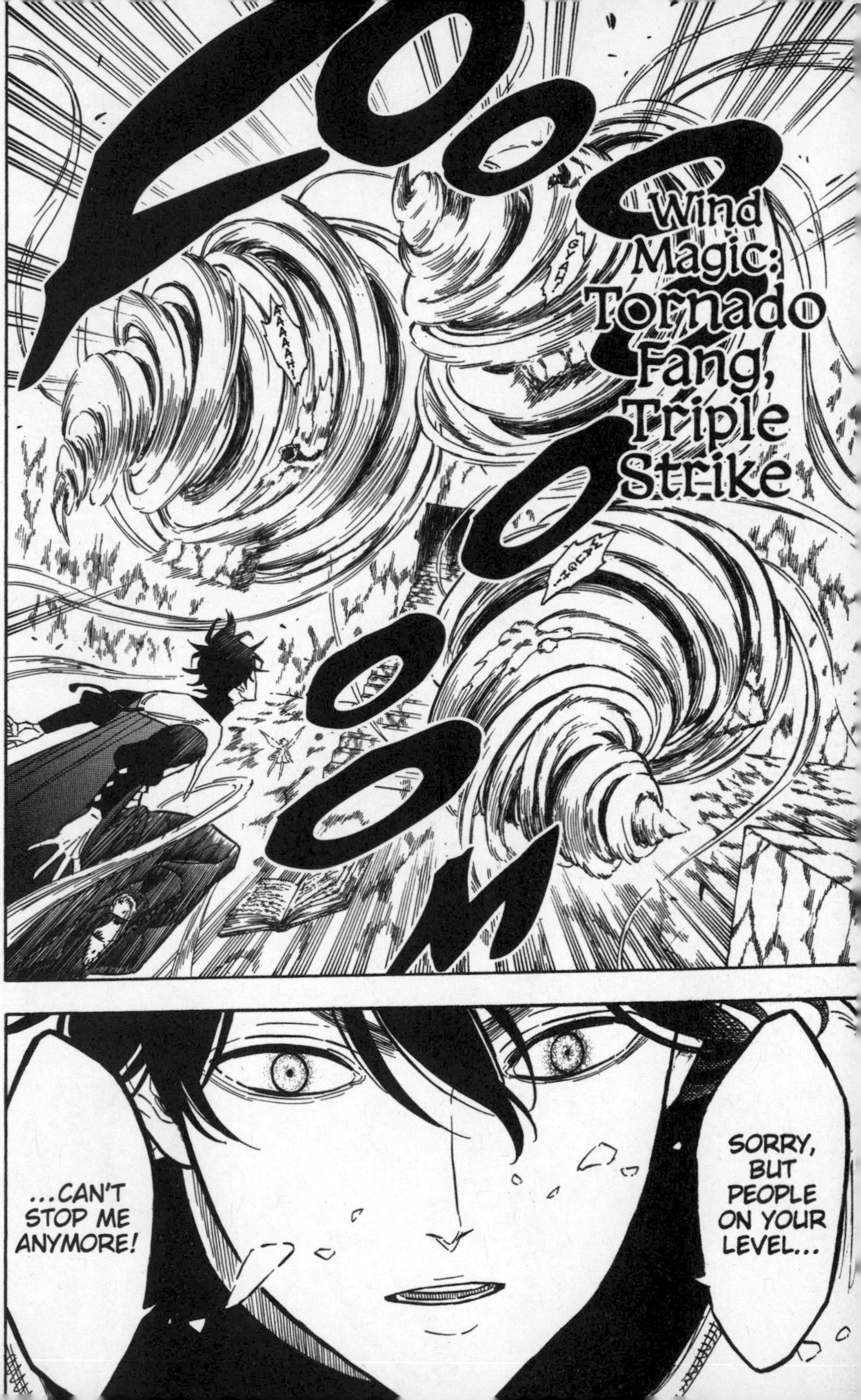
Wind Magic: Tornado Fang, Triple Strike
ZOOOOOOOOM
GYAH!
AAAAAH!
WAUGH!
SORRY, BUT PEOPLE ON YOUR LEVEL...
...CAN'T STOP ME ANYMORE!

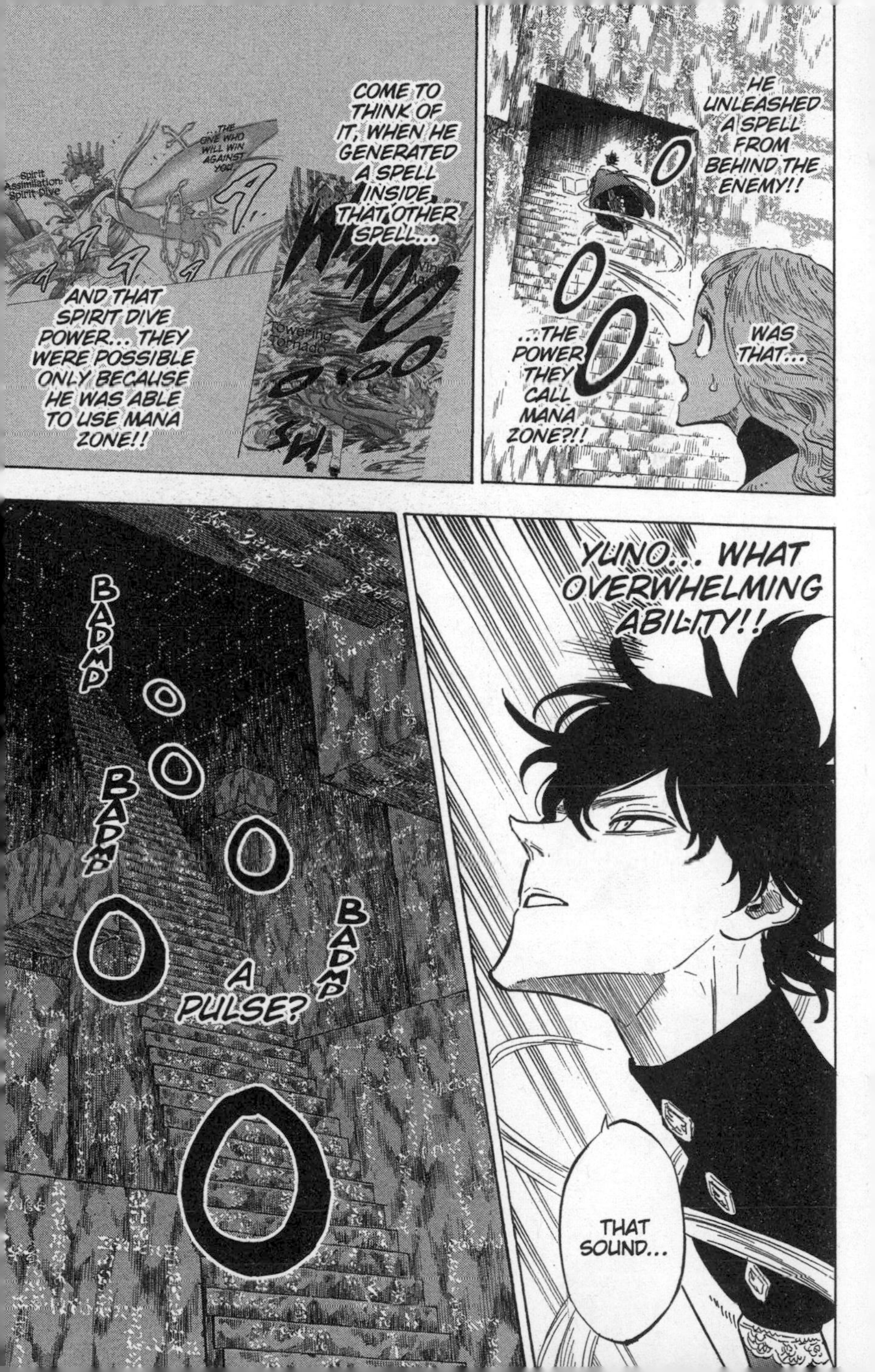
HE UNLEASHED A SPELL FROM BEHIND THE ENEMY!!
WAS THAT...
...THE POWER THEY CALL MANA ZONE?!!
COME TO THINK OF IT, WHEN HE GENERATED A SPELL INSIDE THAT OTHER SPELL...
Towering Tornado
...THE ONE WHO WILL WIN AGAINST YOU!
Spirit Assimilation: Spirit Dive
AND THAT SPIRIT DIVE POWER... THEY WERE POSSIBLE ONLY BECAUSE HE WAS ABLE TO USE MANA ZONE!!
YUNO... WHAT OVERWHELMING ABILITY!!
THAT SOUND...
BADMP
BADMP
BADMP
A PULSE?

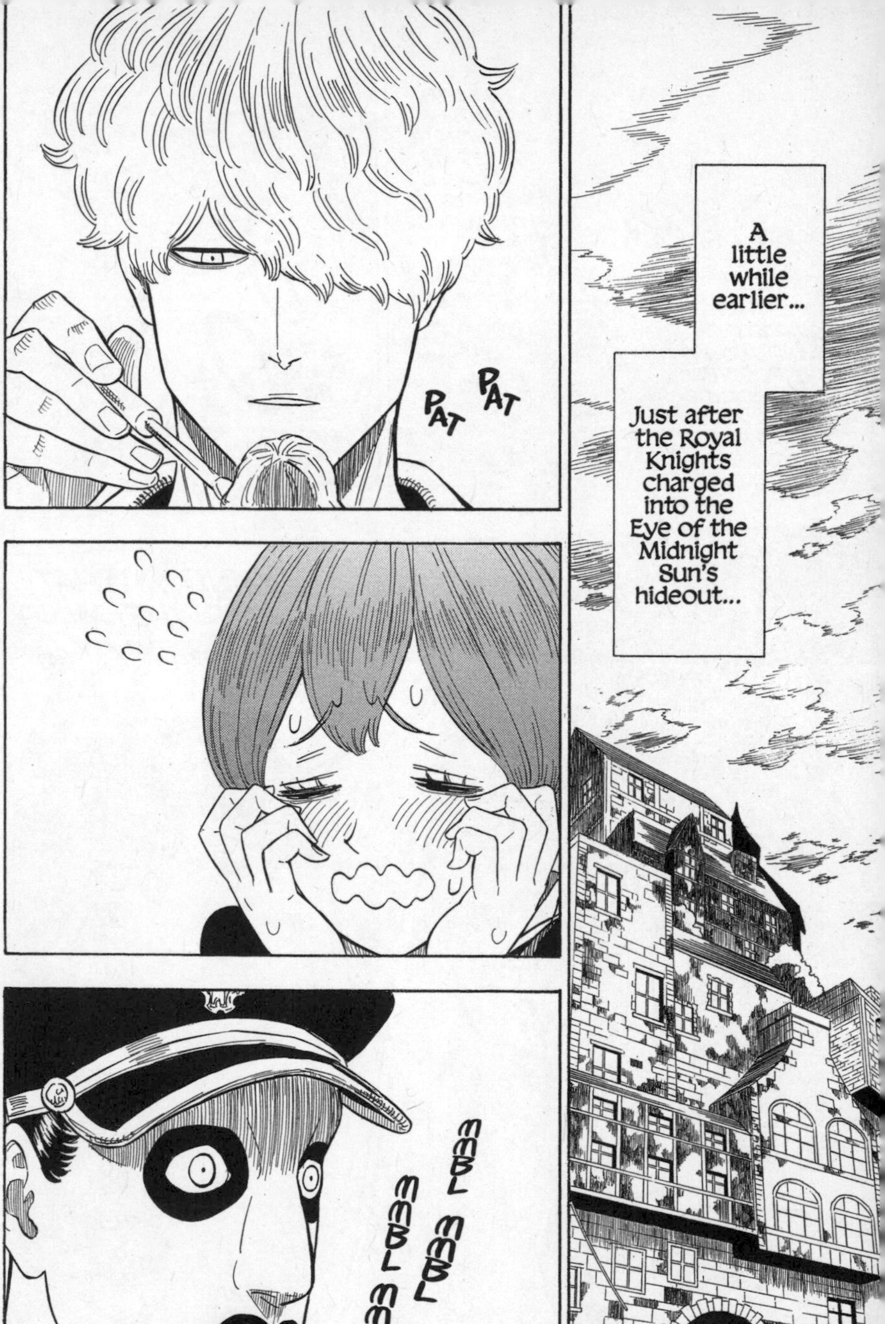
A little while earlier...
Just after the Royal Knights charged into the Eye of the Midnight Sun's hideout...
PAT
PAT
MMBL
MMBL
MMBL
MMBL

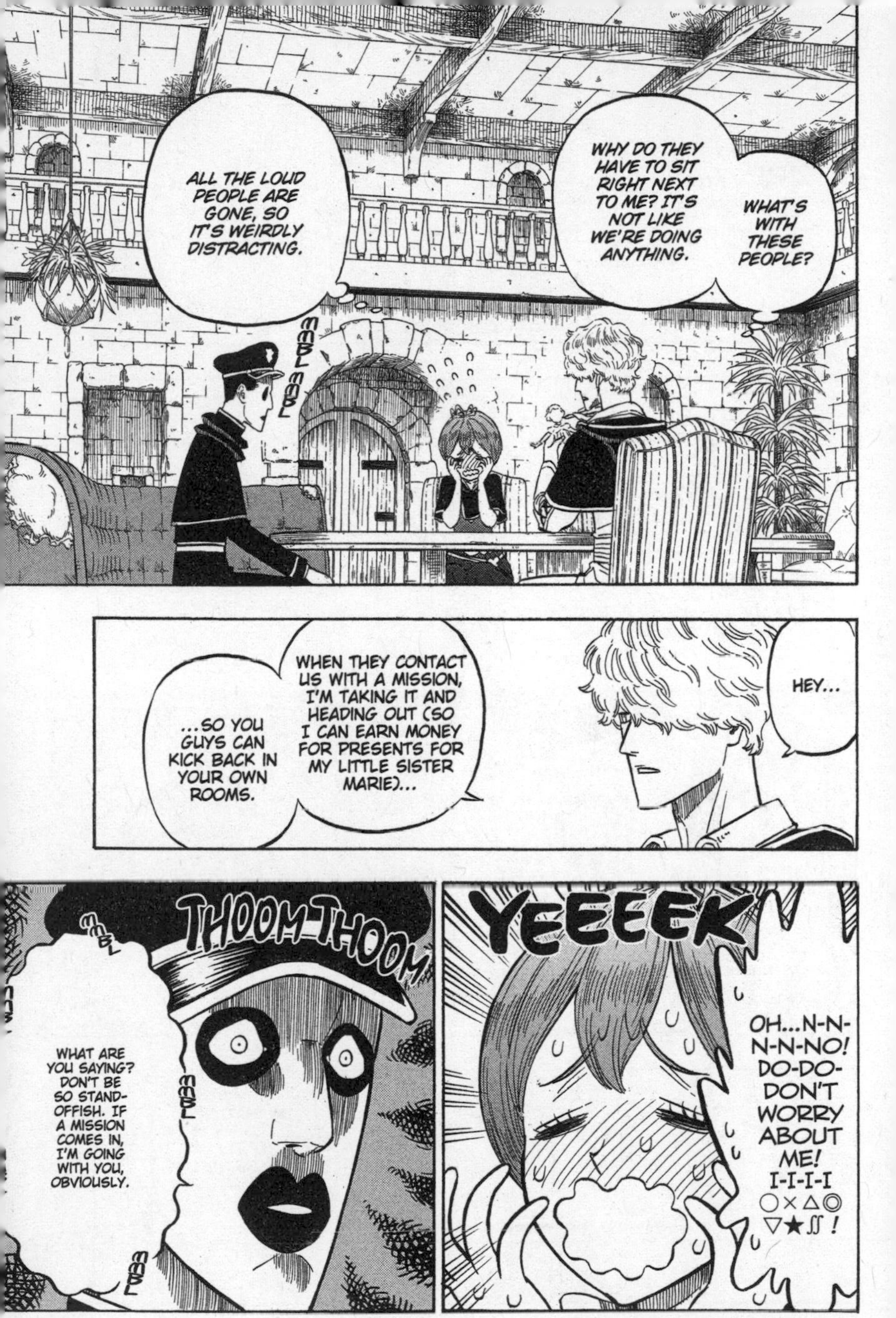
WHAT'S WITH THESE PEOPLE?
WHY DO THEY HAVE TO SIT RIGHT NEXT TO ME? IT'S NOT LIKE WE'RE DOING ANYTHING.
ALL THE LOUD PEOPLE ARE GONE, SO IT'S WEIRDLY DISTRACTING.
MMBL MMBL
HEY...
WHEN THEY CONTACT US WITH A MISSION, I'M TAKING IT AND HEADING OUT (SO I CAN EARN MONEY FOR PRESENTS FOR MY LITTLE SISTER MARIE)...
...SO YOU GUYS CAN KICK BACK IN YOUR OWN ROOMS.
YEEEEK
OH...N-N-N-N-NO! DO-DO-DON'T WORRY ABOUT ME! I-I-I-I ○×△◎▽★ʃʃ!
THOOM THOOM
MMBL
WHAT ARE YOU SAYING? DON'T BE SO STAND-OFFISH. IF A MISSION COMES IN, I'M GOING WITH YOU, OBVIOUSLY.
MMBL
MMBL

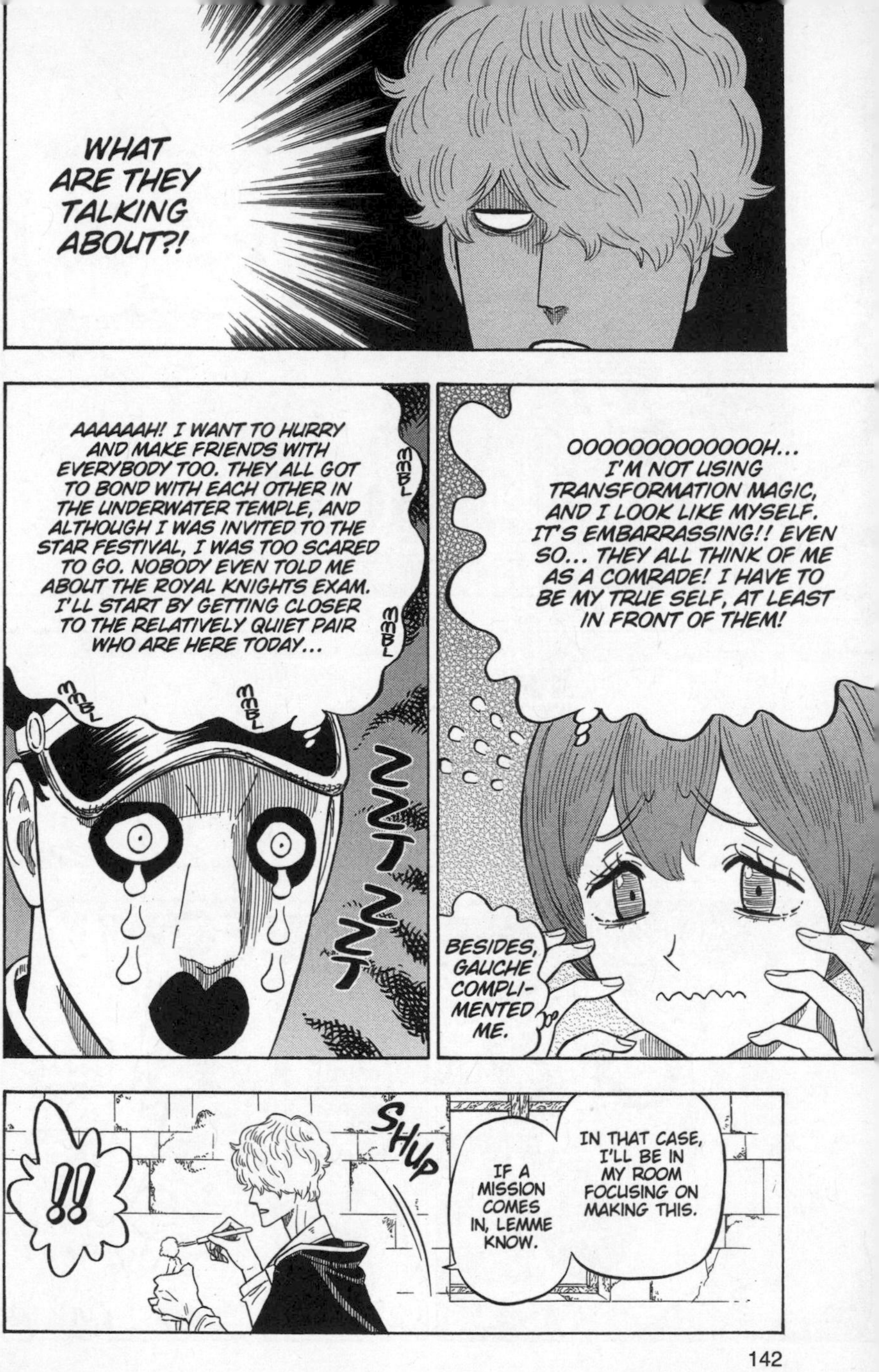
WHAT ARE THEY TALKING ABOUT?!
OOOOOOOOOOOOOH... I'M NOT USING TRANSFORMATION MAGIC, AND I LOOK LIKE MYSELF. IT'S EMBARRASSING!! EVEN SO... THEY ALL THINK OF ME AS A COMRADE! I HAVE TO BE MY TRUE SELF, AT LEAST IN FRONT OF THEM!
BESIDES, GAUCHE COMPLIMENTED ME.
AAAAAAH! I WANT TO HURRY AND MAKE FRIENDS WITH EVERYBODY TOO. THEY ALL GOT TO BOND WITH EACH OTHER IN THE UNDERWATER TEMPLE, AND ALTHOUGH I WAS INVITED TO THE STAR FESTIVAL, I WAS TOO SCARED TO GO. NOBODY EVEN TOLD ME ABOUT THE ROYAL KNIGHTS EXAM. I'LL START BY GETTING CLOSER TO THE RELATIVELY QUIET PAIR WHO ARE HERE TODAY...
MMBL
MMBL
MMBL
MMBL
ZZZT ZZZT
IN THAT CASE, I'LL BE IN MY ROOM FOCUSING ON MAKING THIS.
IF A MISSION COMES IN, LEMME KNOW.
SHUP
!!

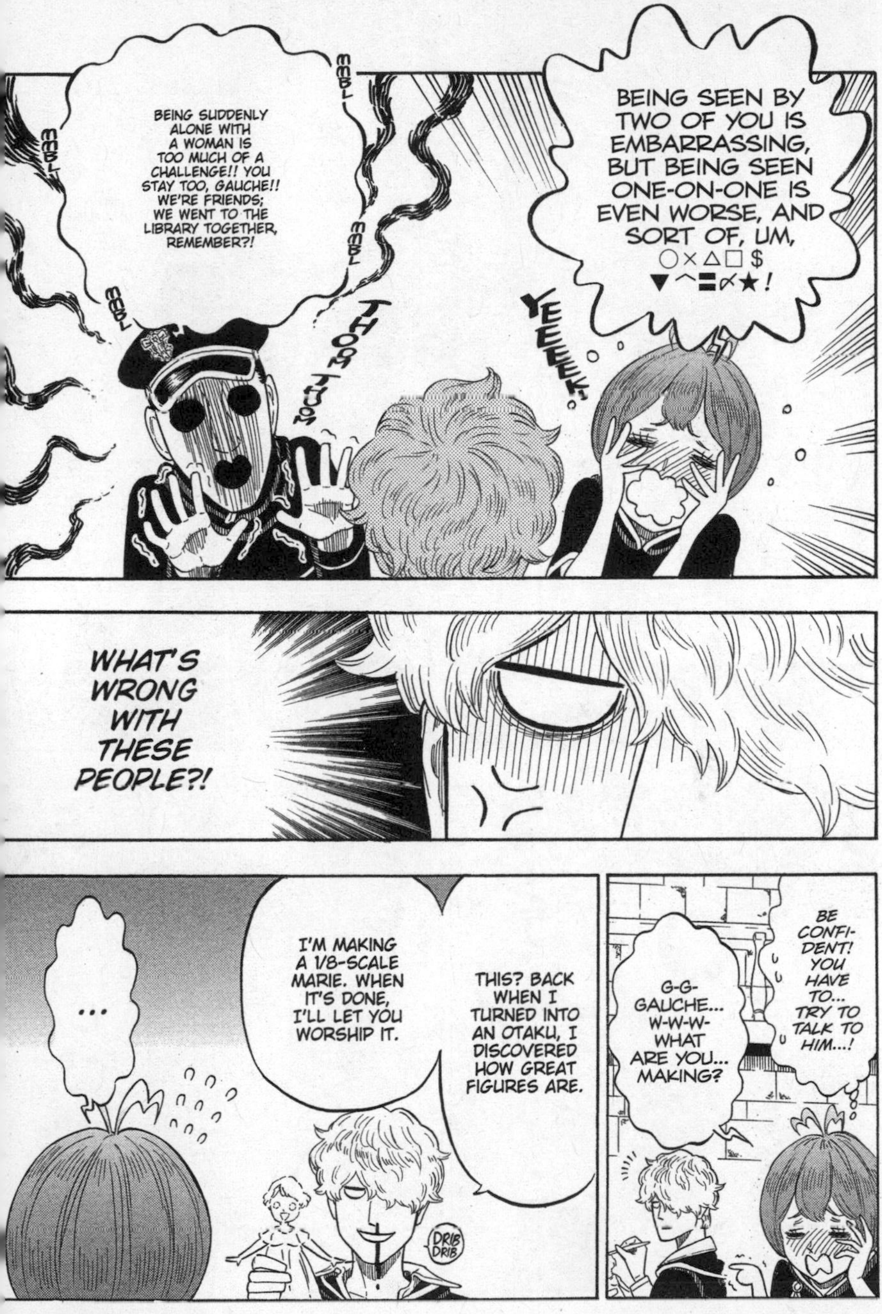

BEING SEEN BY TWO OF YOU IS EMBARRASSING, BUT BEING SEEN ONE-ON-ONE IS EVEN WORSE, AND SORT OF, UM, ○×△□ $ ▼⌒〓∝★!
YEEEEK!
THOOM THOOM
MMBL MMBL MMBL MMBL
BEING SUDDENLY ALONE WITH A WOMAN IS TOO MUCH OF A CHALLENGE!! YOU STAY TOO, GAUCHE!! WE'RE FRIENDS; WE WENT TO THE LIBRARY TOGETHER, REMEMBER?!
WHAT'S WRONG WITH THESE PEOPLE?!
BE CONFIDENT! YOU HAVE TO... TRY TO TALK TO HIM...!
G-G-GAUCHE... W-W-WHAT ARE YOU... MAKING?
THIS? BACK WHEN I TURNED INTO AN OTAKU, I DISCOVERED HOW GREAT FIGURES ARE.
I'M MAKING A 1/8-SCALE MARIE. WHEN IT'S DONE, I'LL LET YOU WORSHIP IT.
DRIB DRIB
...

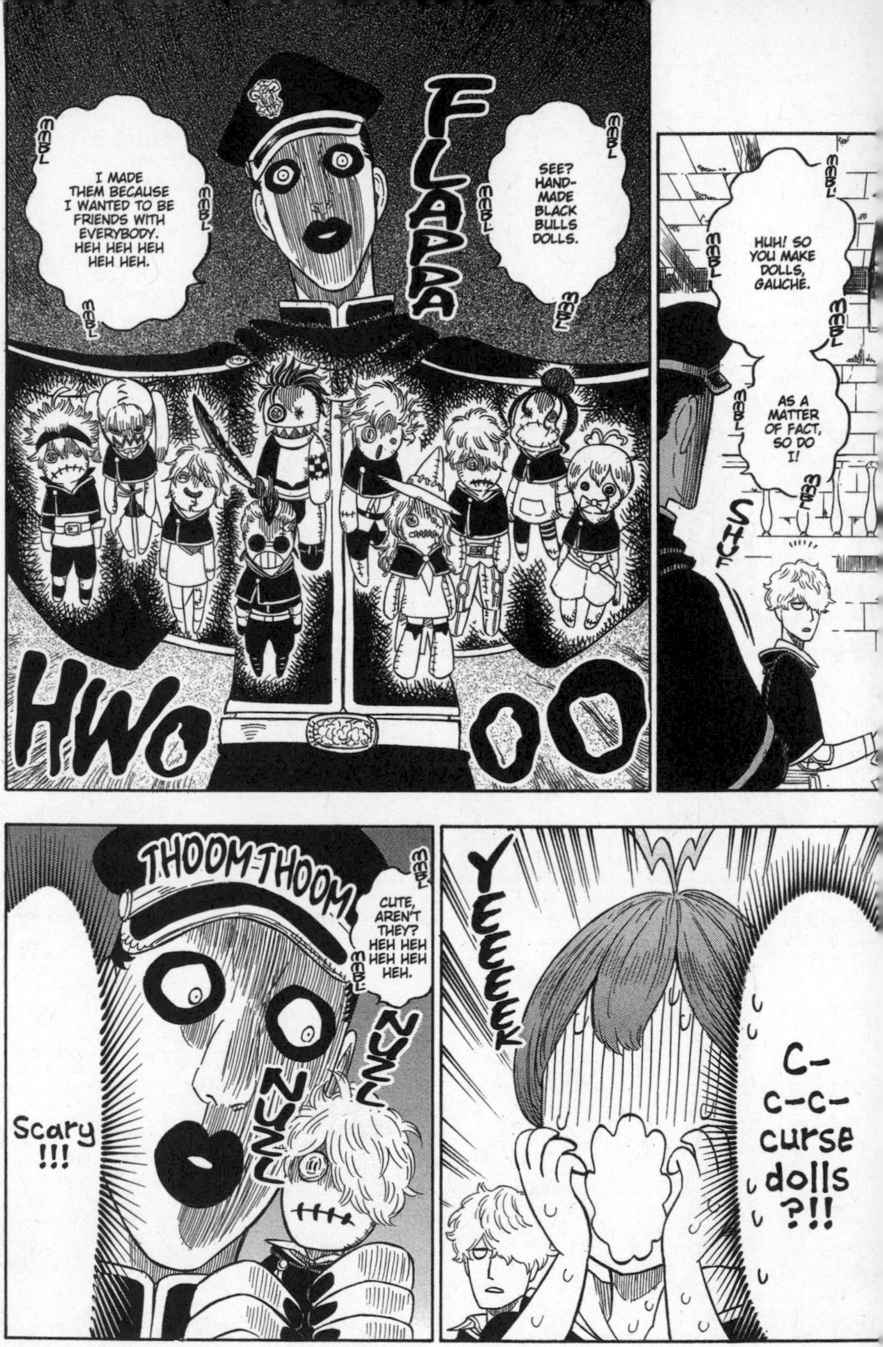
MMBL
HUH! SO YOU MAKE DOLLS, GAUCHE.
MMBL
AS A MATTER OF FACT, SO DO I!
MMBL
SHUF
FLAPPA
MMBL
SEE? HAND-MADE BLACK BULLS DOLLS.
MMBL
I MADE THEM BECAUSE I WANTED TO BE FRIENDS WITH EVERYBODY. HEH HEH HEH HEH HEH.
MMBL
HWOOO
YEEEEK
C-C-C-curse dolls?!!
THOOM-THOOM
MMBL
CUTE, AREN'T THEY? HEH HEH HEH HEH HEH.
NUZL NUZL
Scary!!!

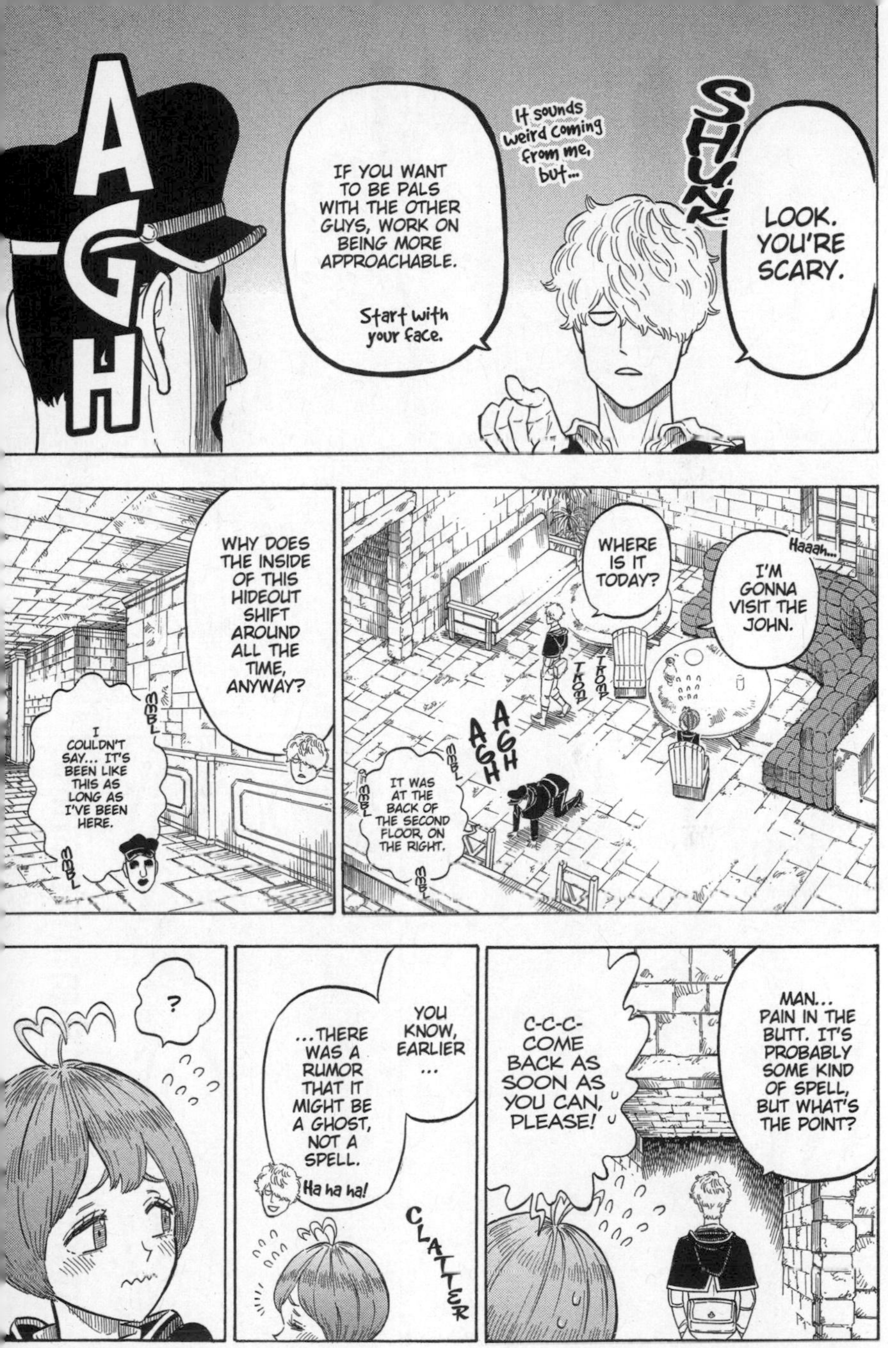
SHUNK
LOOK. YOU'RE SCARY.
It sounds weird coming from me, but...
IF YOU WANT TO BE PALS WITH THE OTHER GUYS, WORK ON BEING MORE APPROACHABLE.
Start with your face.
AGH
Haaah...
I'M GONNA VISIT THE JOHN.
WHERE IS IT TODAY?
TROMP TROMP
AGH AGH
MMBL
IT WAS AT THE BACK OF THE SECOND FLOOR, ON THE RIGHT.
MMBL
MMBL
WHY DOES THE INSIDE OF THIS HIDEOUT SHIFT AROUND ALL THE TIME, ANYWAY?
MMBL
I COULDN'T SAY... IT'S BEEN LIKE THIS AS LONG AS I'VE BEEN HERE.
MMBL
MAN... PAIN IN THE BUTT. IT'S PROBABLY SOME KIND OF SPELL, BUT WHAT'S THE POINT?
C-C-C-COME BACK AS SOON AS YOU CAN, PLEASE!
YOU KNOW, EARLIER...
...THERE WAS A RUMOR THAT IT MIGHT BE A GHOST, NOT A SPELL.
Ha ha ha!
CLATTER
?

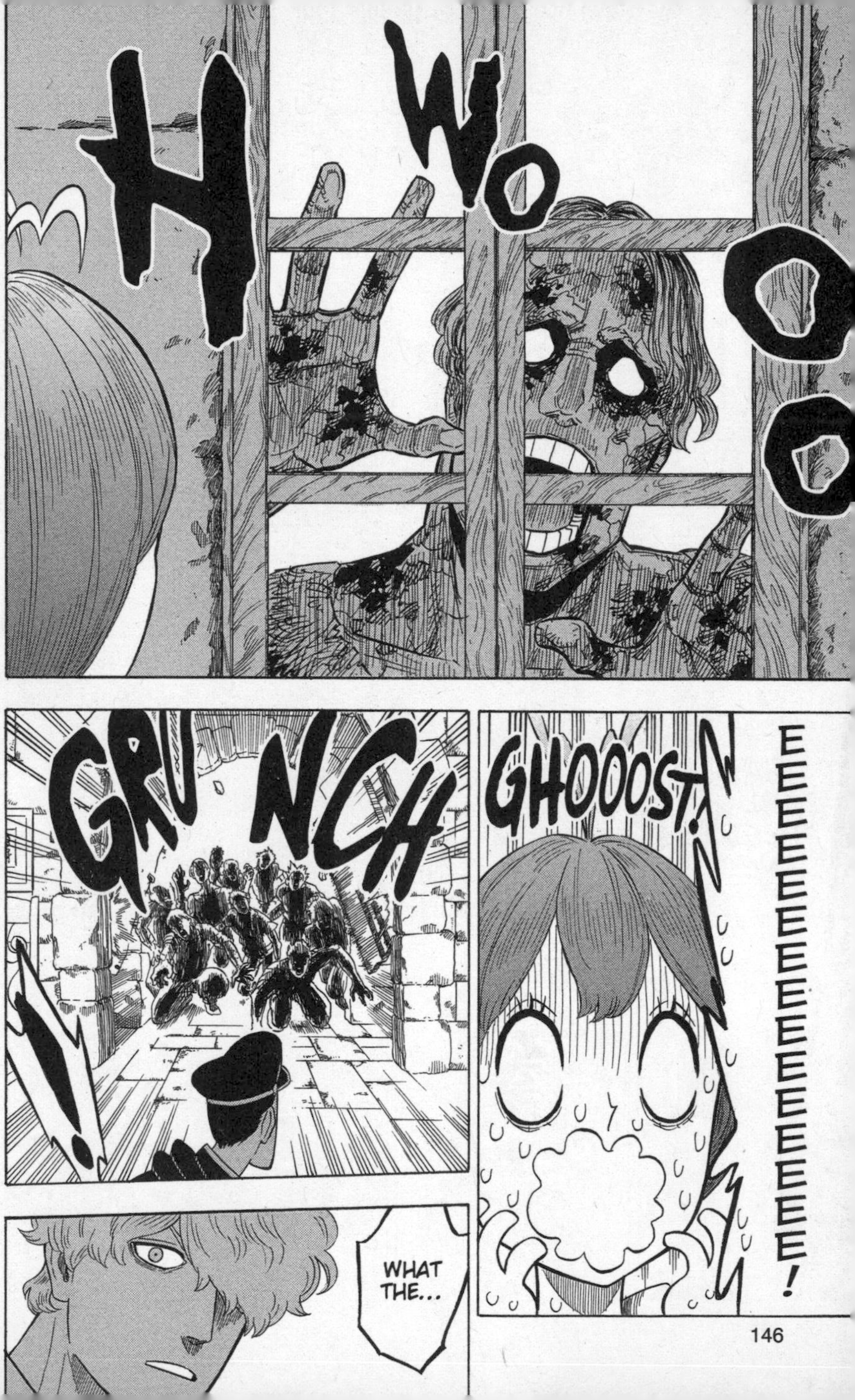
HWOOOO
GHOOOST!
EEEEEEEEEEEEEEEEE!
GRUNCH
!
WHAT THE...

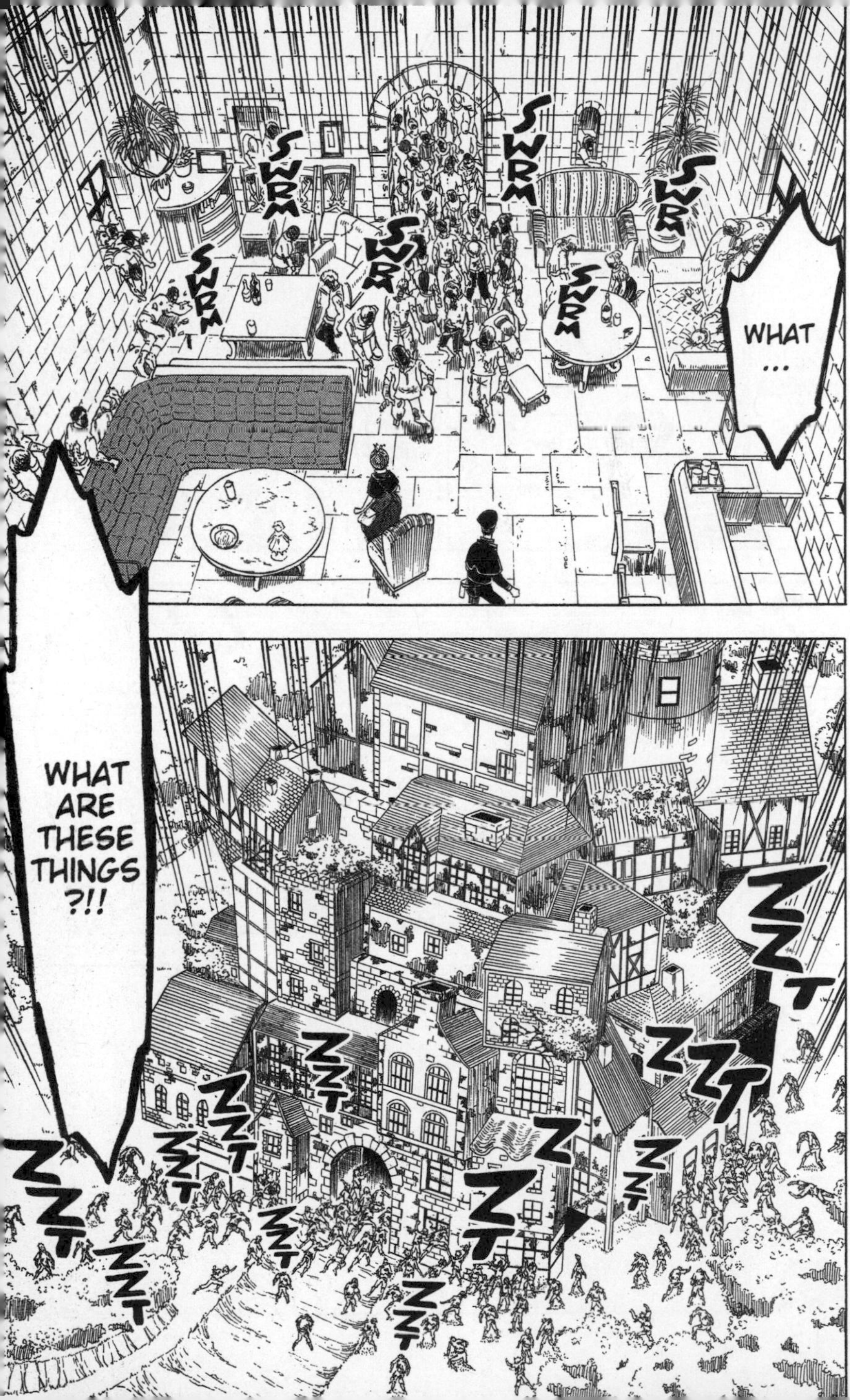
SWRM
SWRM
SWRM
SWRM
SWRM
SWRM
WHAT ...
WHAT ARE THESE THINGS?!!
ZZZT
ZZZT
ZZZT
ZZZT
ZZZT
ZZZT
ZZZT
ZZZT
ZZZT

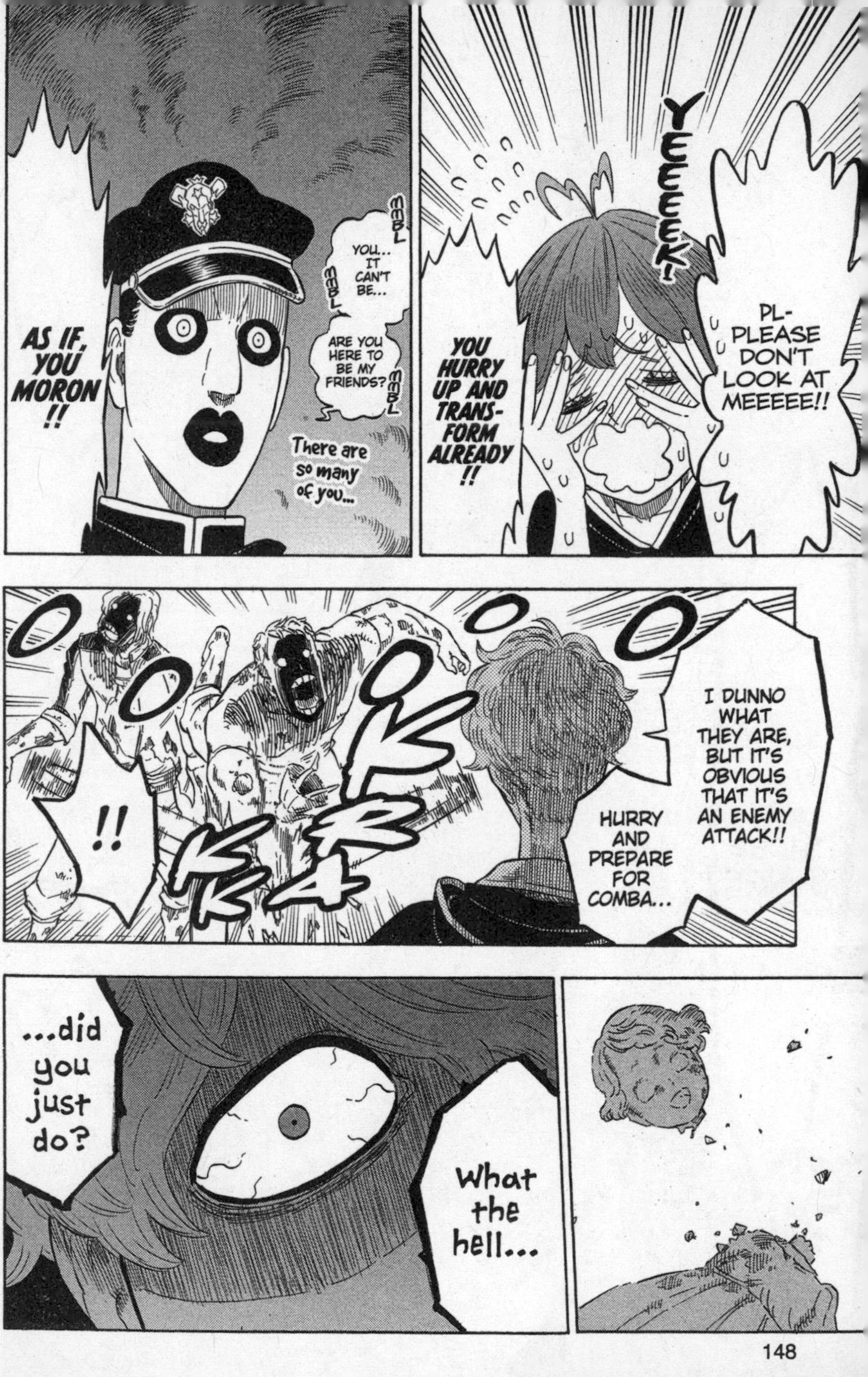
YEEEEEK!
PL-PLEASE DON'T LOOK AT MEEEEE!!
YOU HURRY UP AND TRANS-FORM ALREADY!!
MMBL
YOU... IT CAN'T BE...
MMBL
ARE YOU HERE TO BE MY FRIENDS?
MMBL
There are so many of you...
AS IF, YOU MORON!!
I DUNNO WHAT THEY ARE, BUT IT'S OBVIOUS THAT IT'S AN ENEMY ATTACK!!
HURRY AND PREPARE FOR COMBA...
!!
What the hell...
...did you just do?

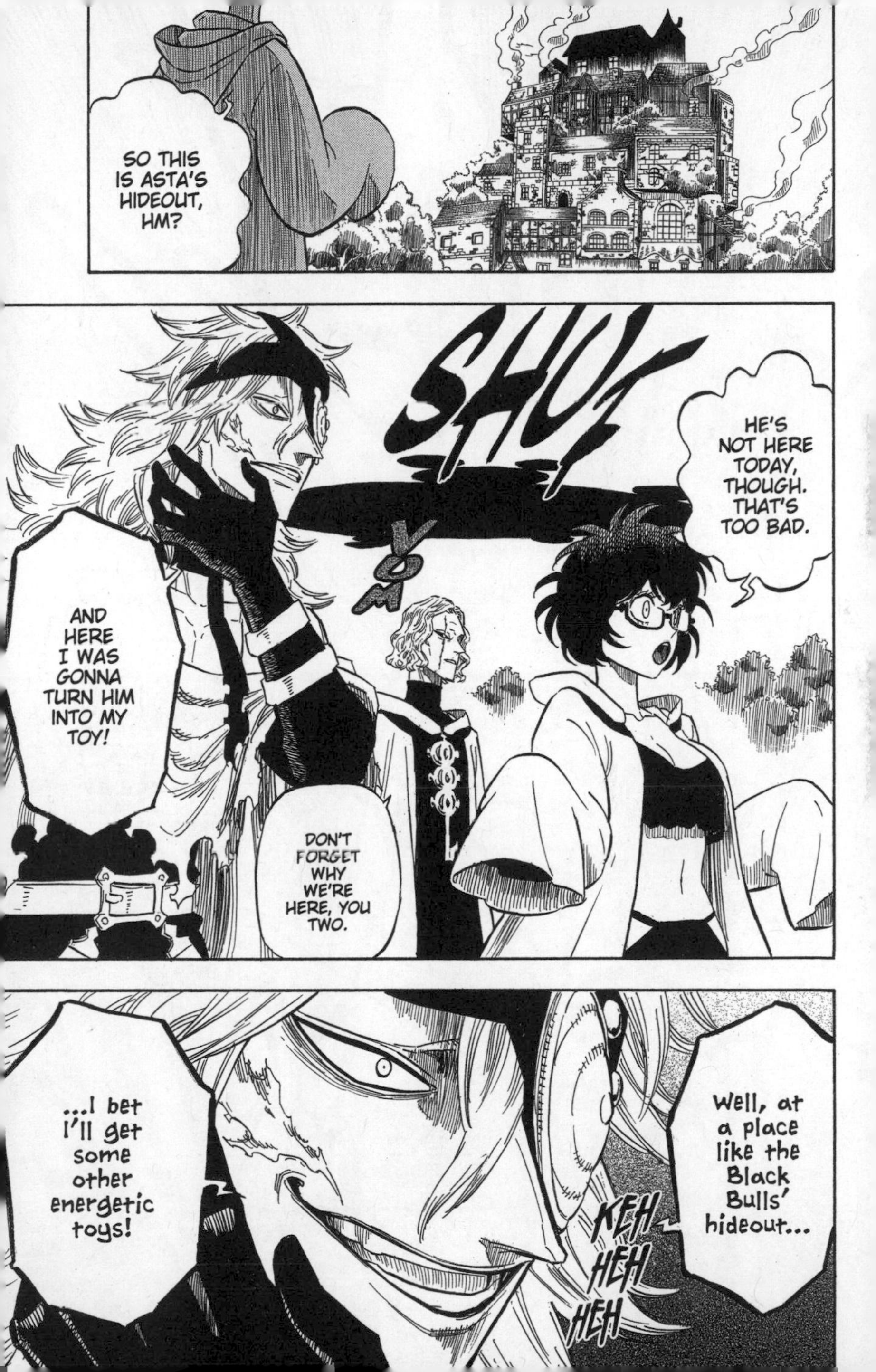
SO THIS IS ASTA'S HIDEOUT, HM?
HE'S NOT HERE TODAY, THOUGH. THAT'S TOO BAD.
SHU
VOM
AND HERE I WAS GONNA TURN HIM INTO MY TOY!
DON'T FORGET WHY WE'RE HERE, YOU TWO.
Well, at a place like the Black Bulls' hideout...
KEH HEH HEH HEH
...I bet I'll get some other energetic toys!

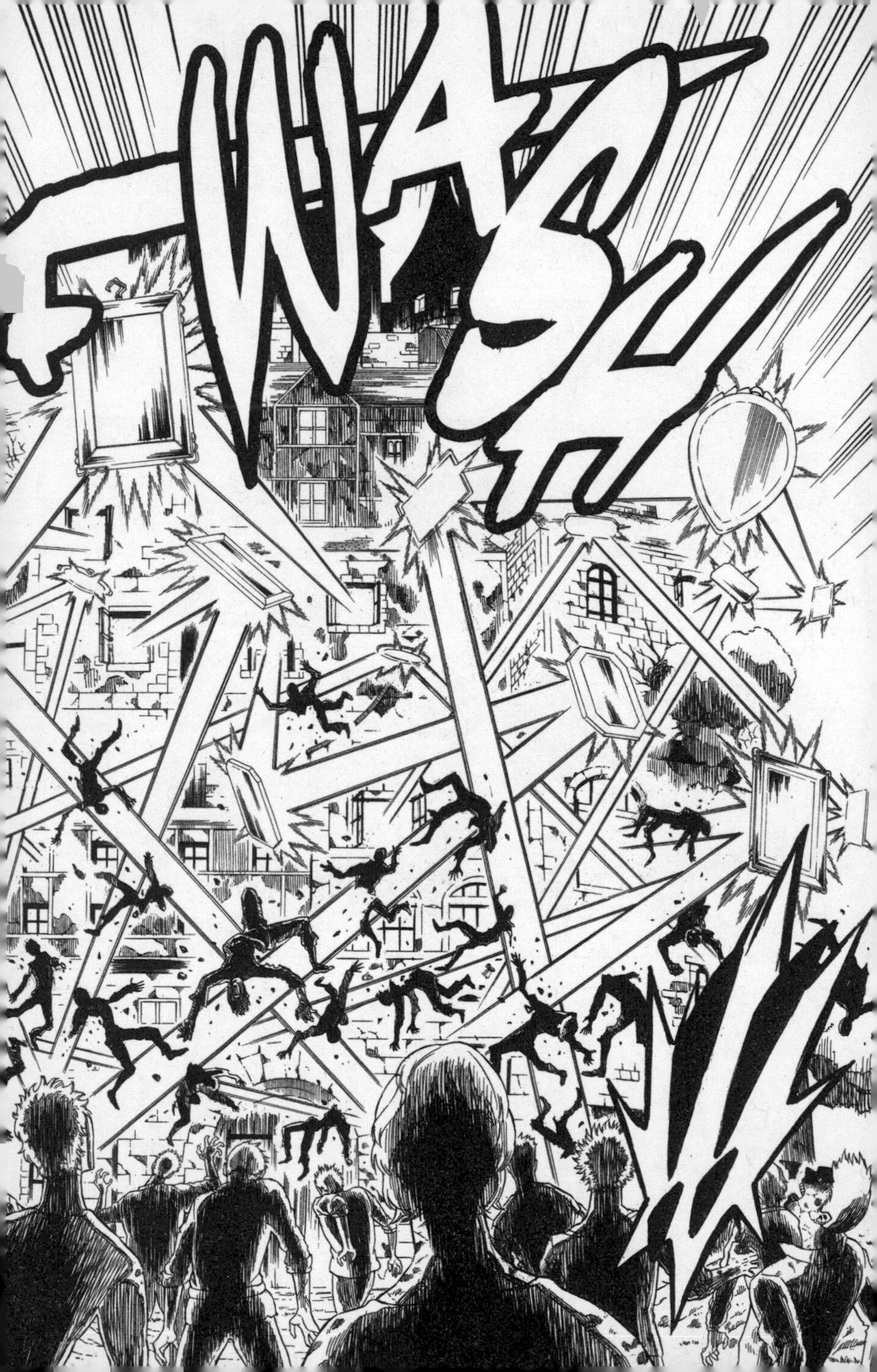
FWASH!!

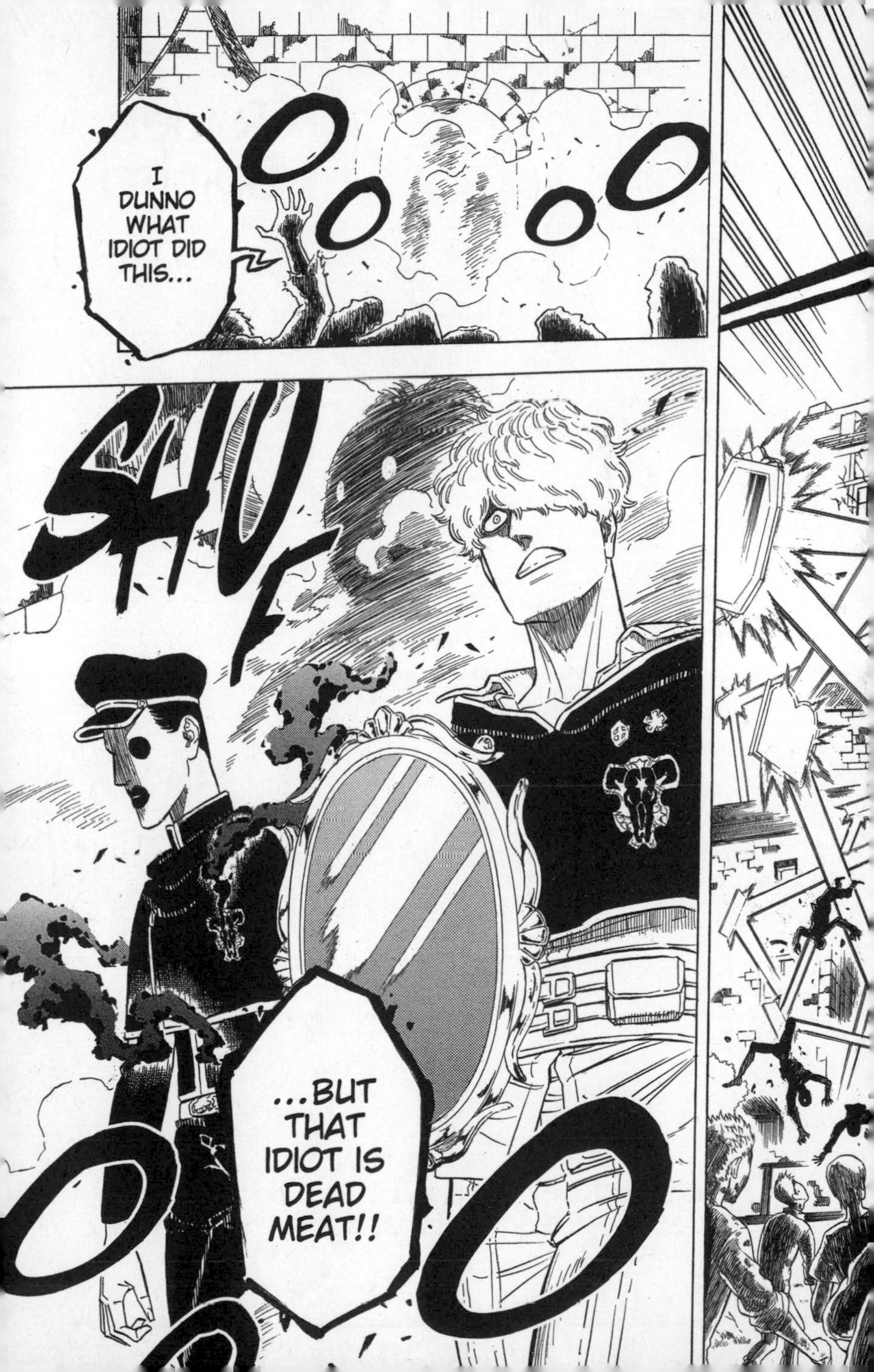
OOOOO
I DUNNO WHAT IDIOT DID THIS...
SHU
...BUT THAT IDIOT IS DEAD MEAT!!
OOOO

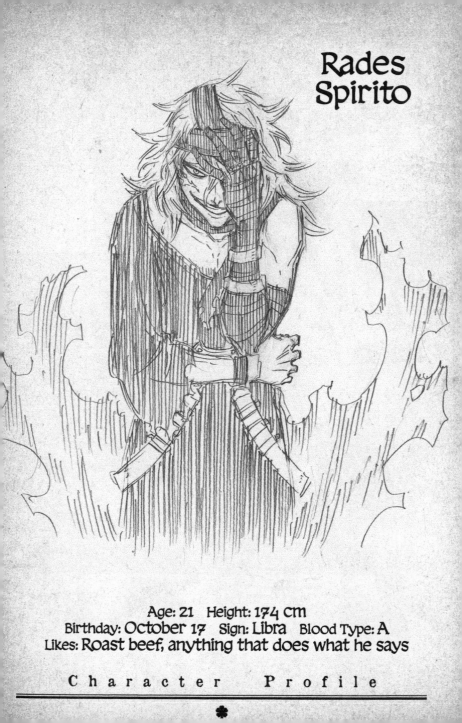

Rades Spirito

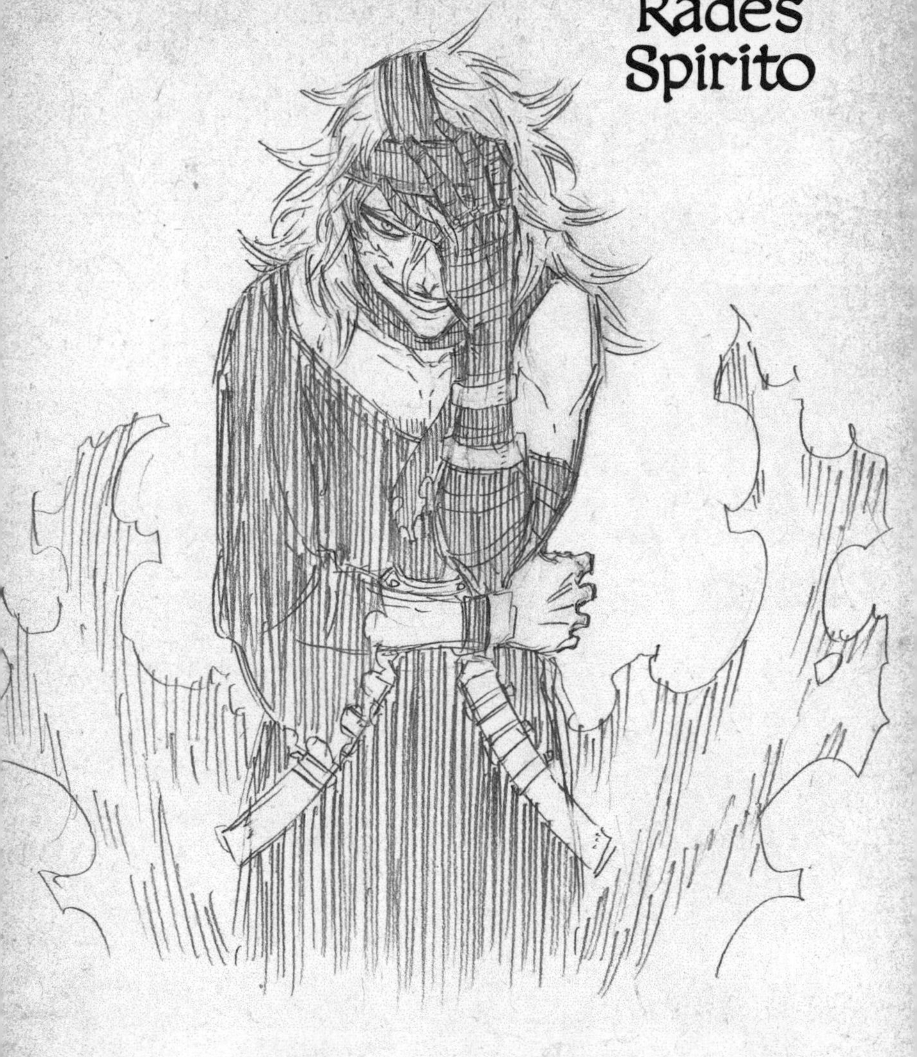

Age: 21 Height: 174 cm
Birthday: October 17 Sign: Libra Blood Type: A
Likes: Roast beef, anything that does what he says

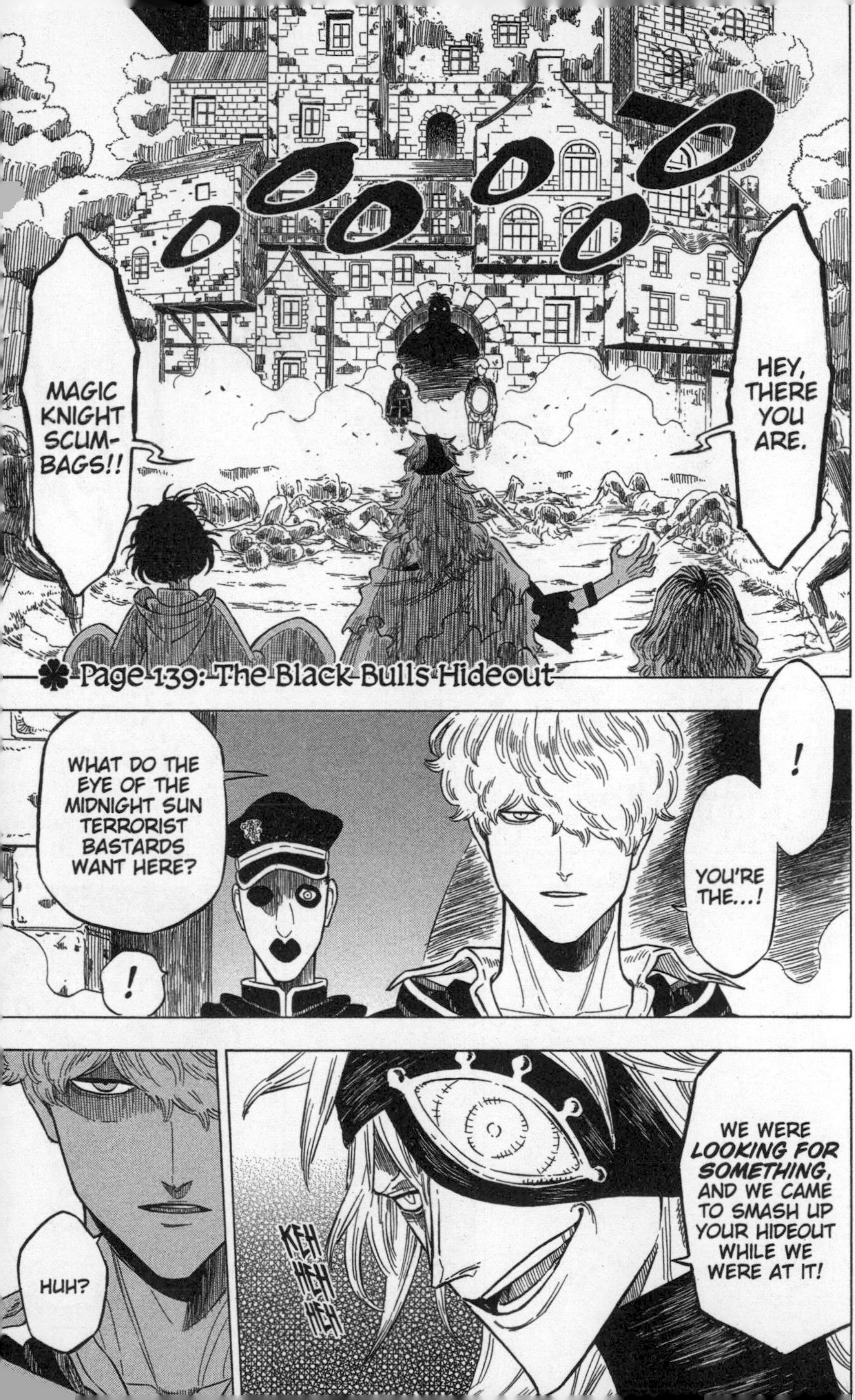
HEY, THERE YOU ARE.
MAGIC KNIGHT SCUM-BAGS!!
Page 139: The Black Bulls Hideout
!
YOU'RE THE...!
WHAT DO THE EYE OF THE MIDNIGHT SUN TERRORIST BASTARDS WANT HERE?
!
WE WERE *LOOKING FOR SOMETHING*, AND WE CAME TO SMASH UP YOUR HIDEOUT WHILE WE WERE AT IT!
KEH HEH HEH
HUH?

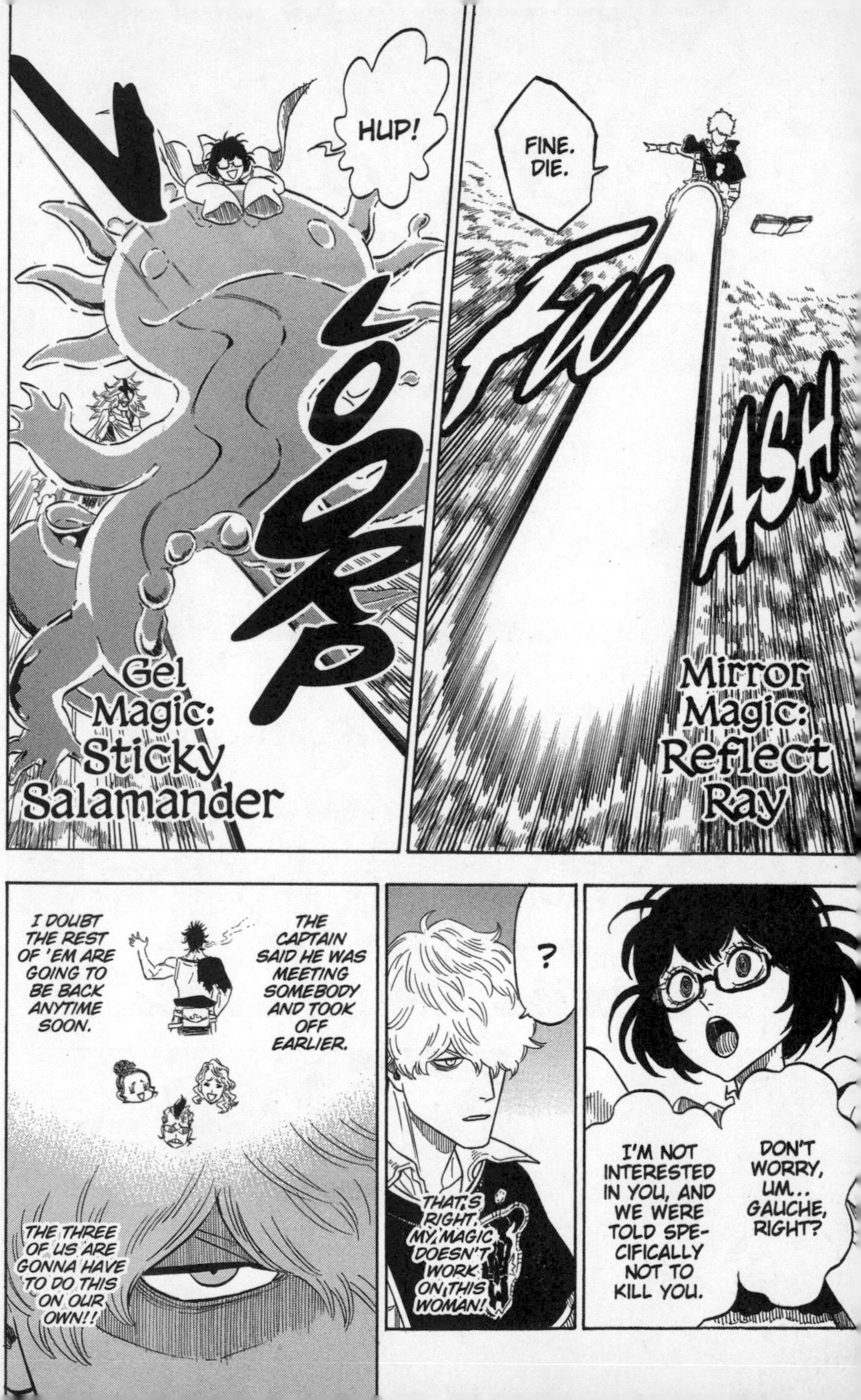
FINE. DIE.
Mirror Magic: Reflect Ray
HUP!
Gel Magic: Sticky Salamander
DON'T WORRY, UM... GAUCHE, RIGHT?
I'M NOT INTERESTED IN YOU, AND WE WERE TOLD SPE-CIFICALLY NOT TO KILL YOU.
?
THAT'S RIGHT. MY MAGIC DOESN'T WORK ON THIS WOMAN!
THE CAPTAIN SAID HE WAS MEETING SOMEBODY AND TOOK OFF EARLIER.
I DOUBT THE REST OF 'EM ARE GOING TO BE BACK ANYTIME SOON.
THE THREE OF US ARE GONNA HAVE TO DO THIS ON OUR OWN!!

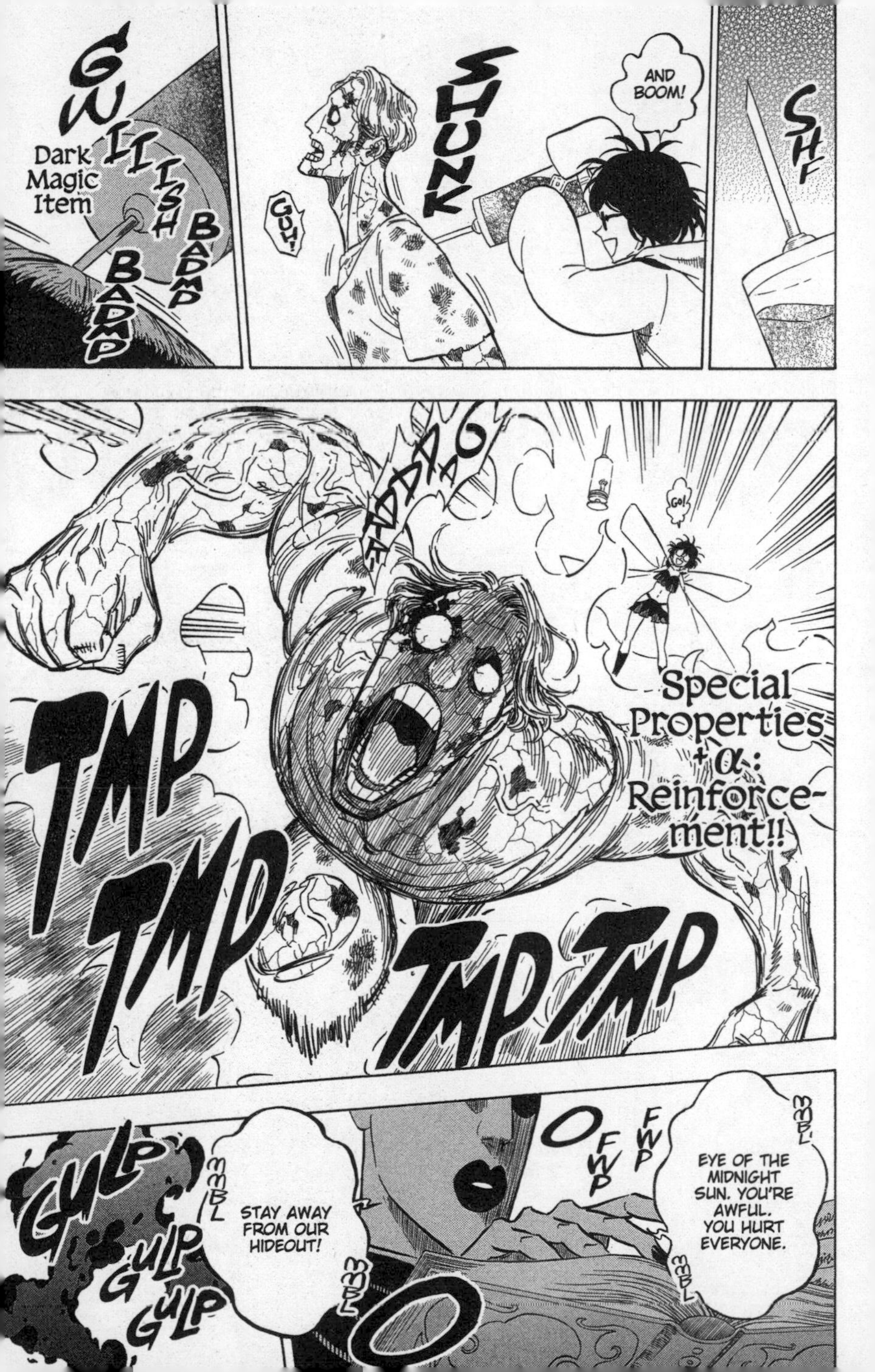
SHF
AND BOOM!
SHUNK
GUH!
GWIIISH
Dark Magic Item
BADMP
BADMP
GO!
Special Properties +α: Reinforcement!!
TMP TMP
TMP TMP
MMBL
EYE OF THE MIDNIGHT SUN. YOU'RE AWFUL. YOU HURT EVERYONE.
MMBL
FWP FWP
FWP FWP
MMBL
STAY AWAY FROM OUR HIDEOUT!
MMBL
GULP
GULP
GULP

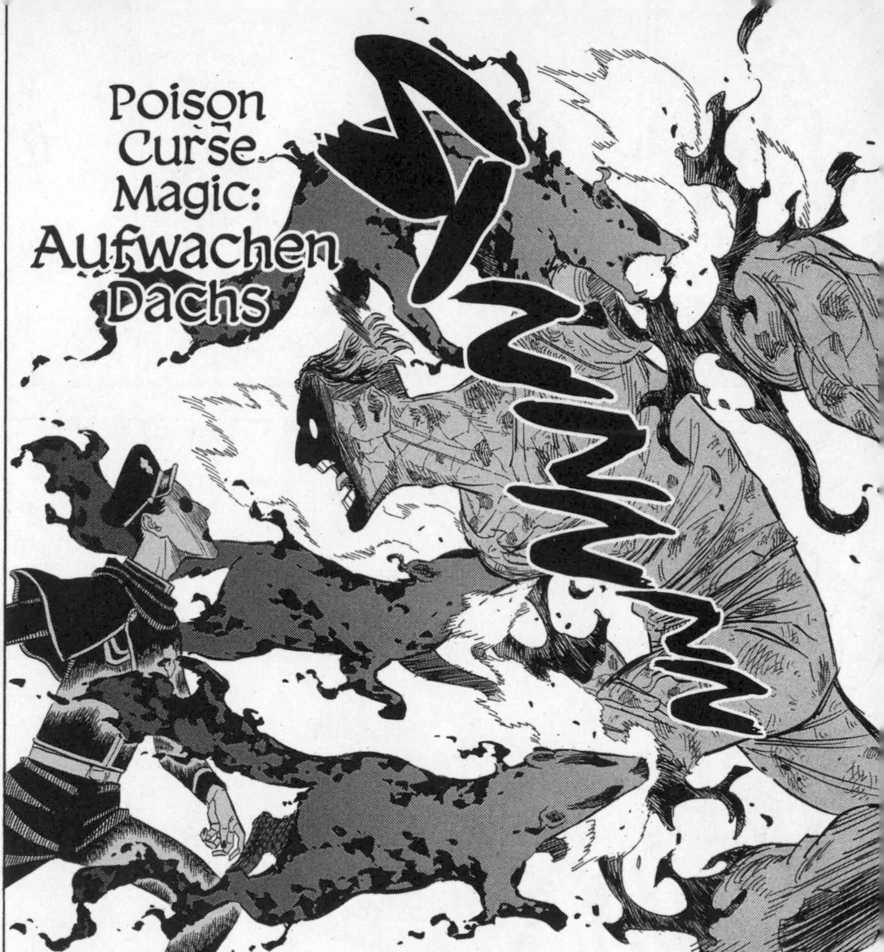
Poison Curse Magic: Aufwachen Dachs
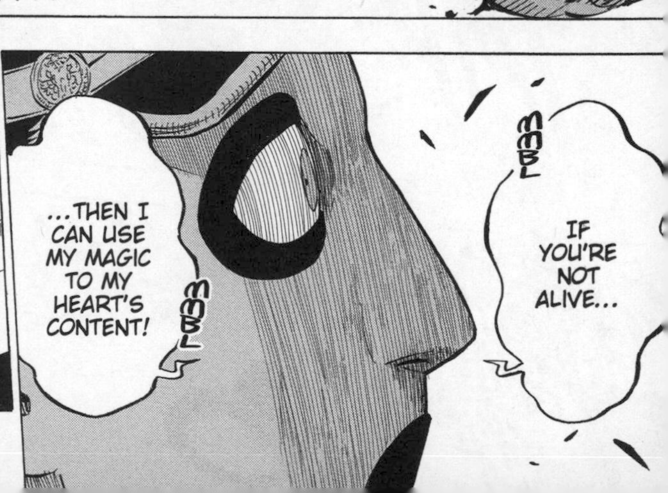
MMBL
IF YOU'RE NOT ALIVE...
...THEN I CAN USE MY MAGIC TO MY HEART'S CONTENT!
MMBL
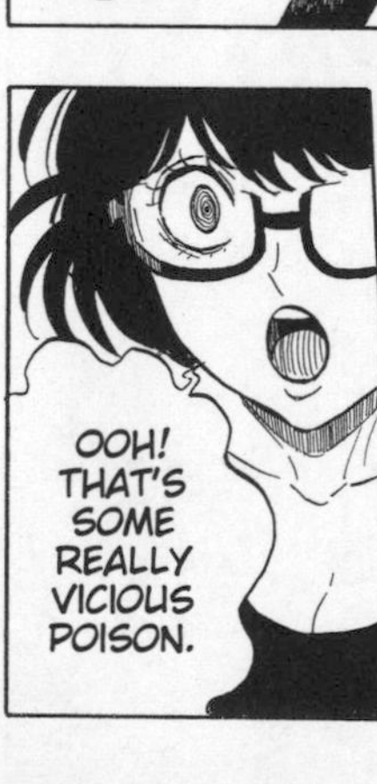
OOH! THAT'S SOME REALLY VICIOUS POISON.

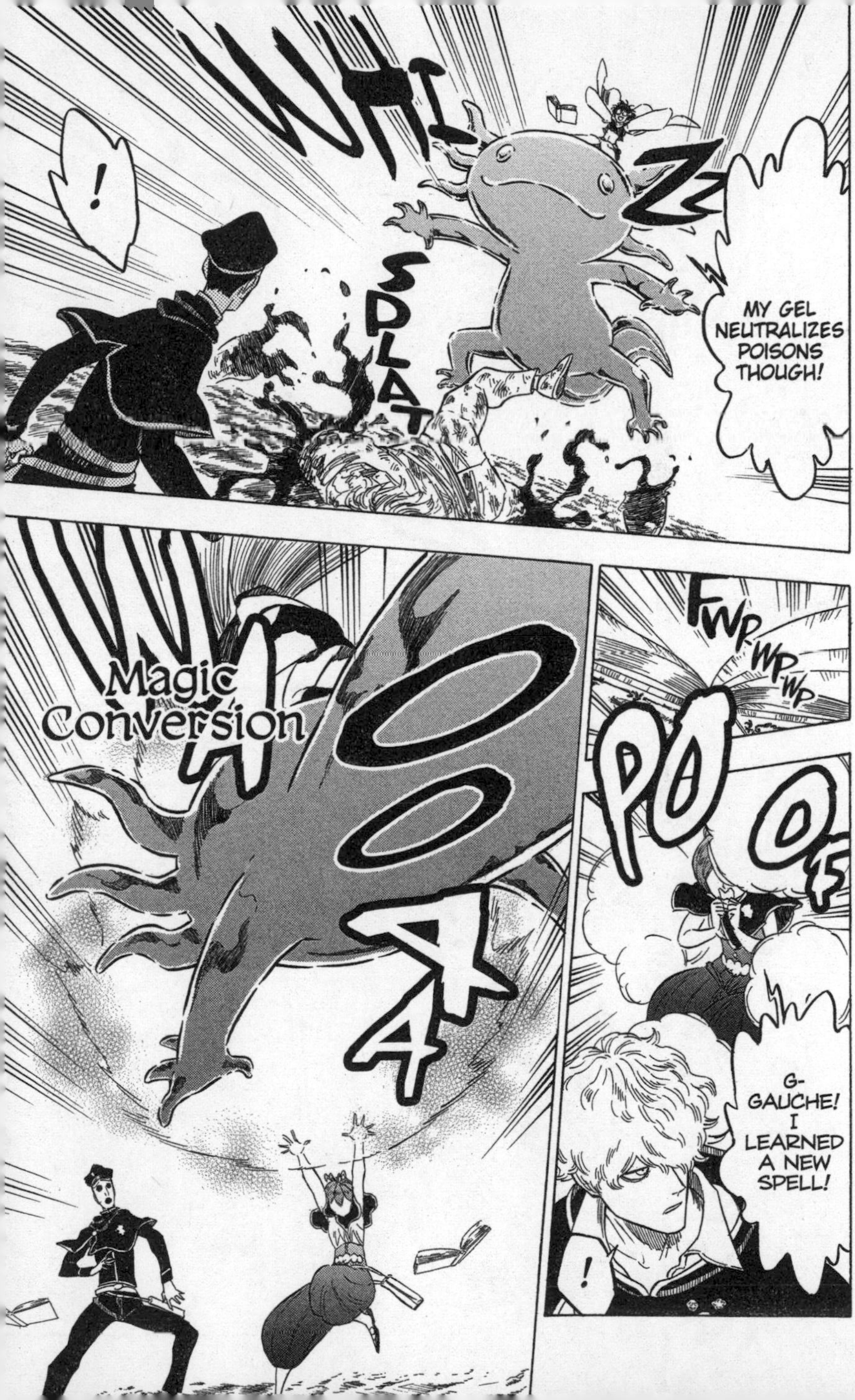
MY GEL NEUTRALIZES POISONS THOUGH!
WHIZZ
SPLAT
!
FWP-WP-WP
POOF
G-GAUCHE! I LEARNED A NEW SPELL!
!
Magic Conversion

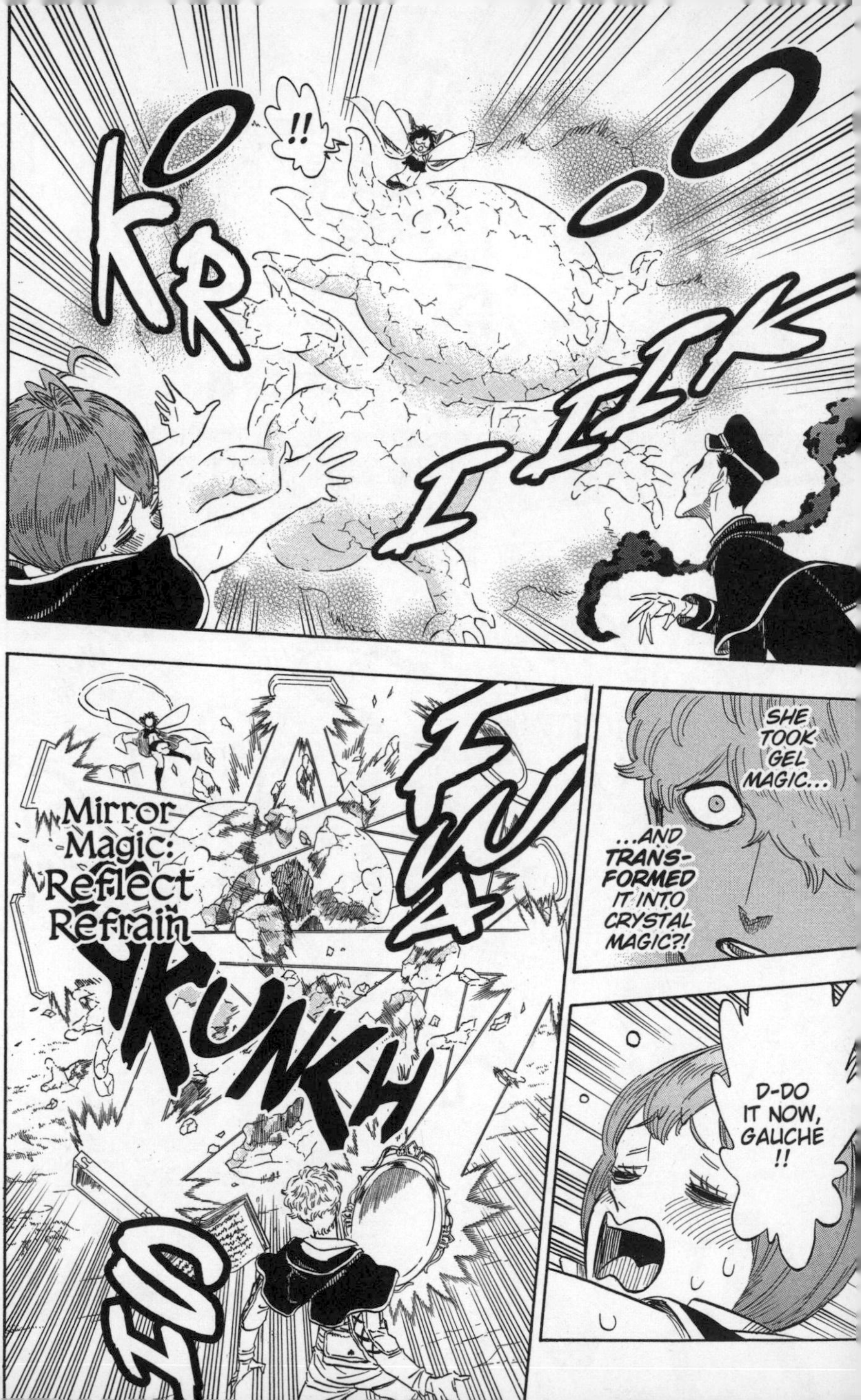
!!
SHE TOOK GEL MAGIC...
...AND TRANS-FORMED IT INTO CRYSTAL MAGIC?!
D-DO IT NOW, GAUCHE!!
Mirror Magic: Reflect Refrain
KUNKH

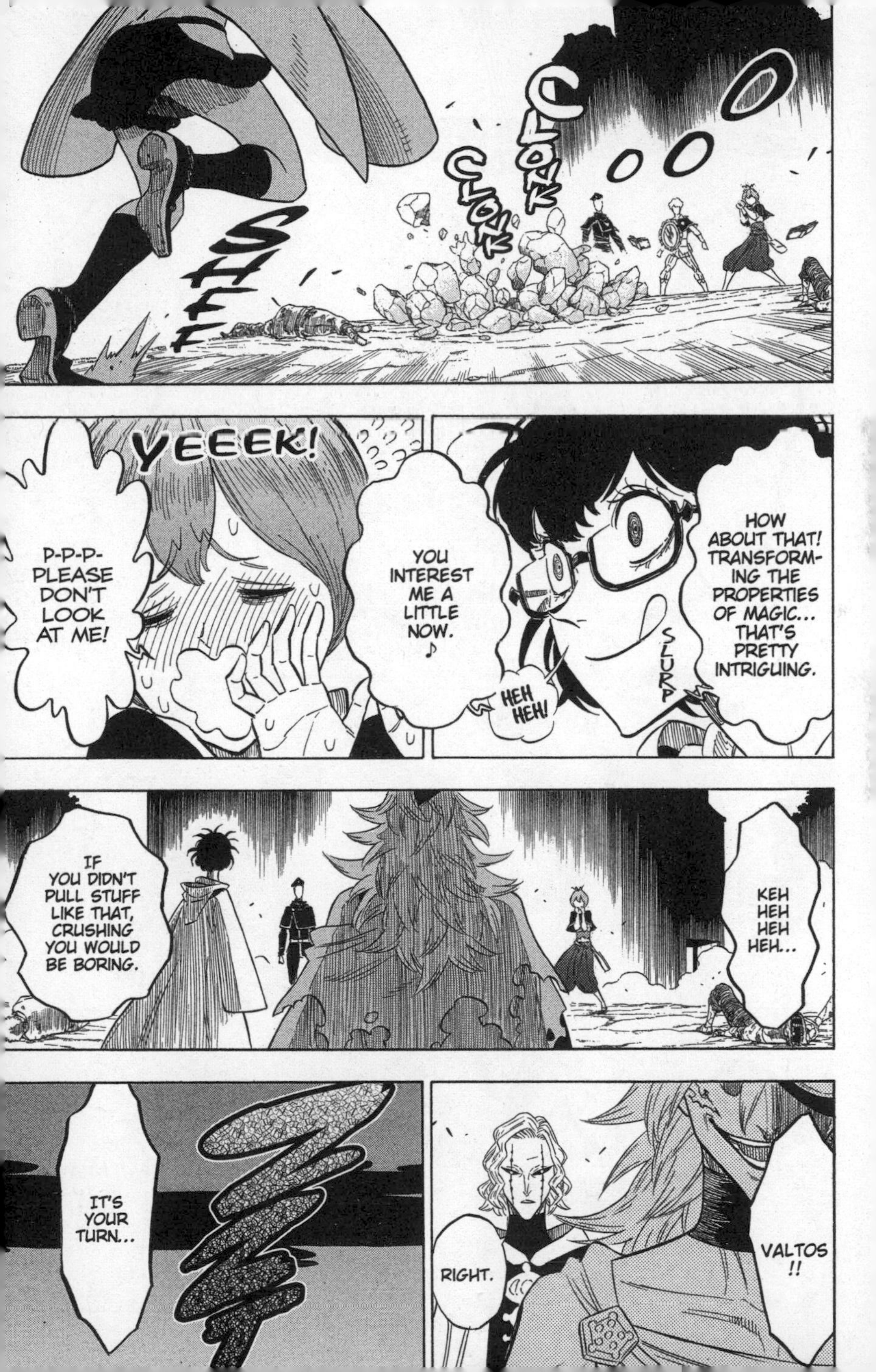
CLONK
CLONK
SHFFF
HOW ABOUT THAT! TRANSFORMING THE PROPERTIES OF MAGIC... THAT'S PRETTY INTRIGUING.
SLURP
YOU INTEREST ME A LITTLE NOW. ♪
HEH HEH!
YEEEK!
P-P-P-PLEASE DON'T LOOK AT ME!
KEH HEH HEH HEH...
IF YOU DIDN'T PULL STUFF LIKE THAT, CRUSHING YOU WOULD BE BORING.
VALTOS!!
RIGHT.
IT'S YOUR TURN...

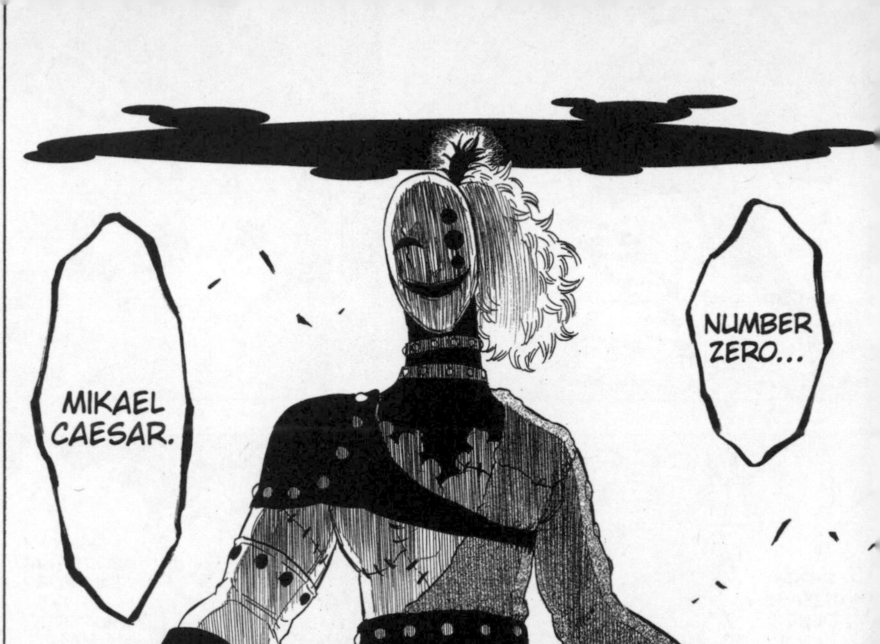
NUMBER ZERO...
MIKAEL CAESAR.
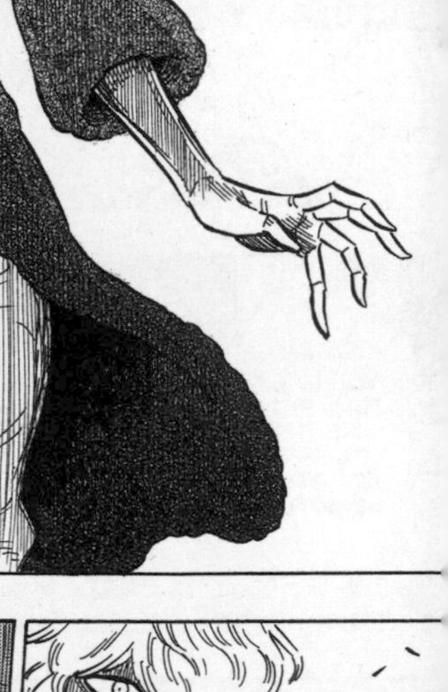
WHAT IS THAT NASTY THING?
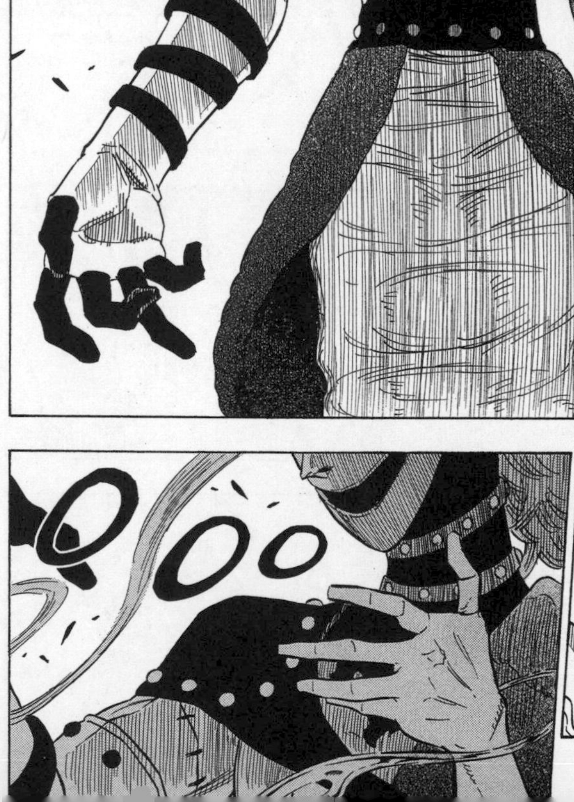

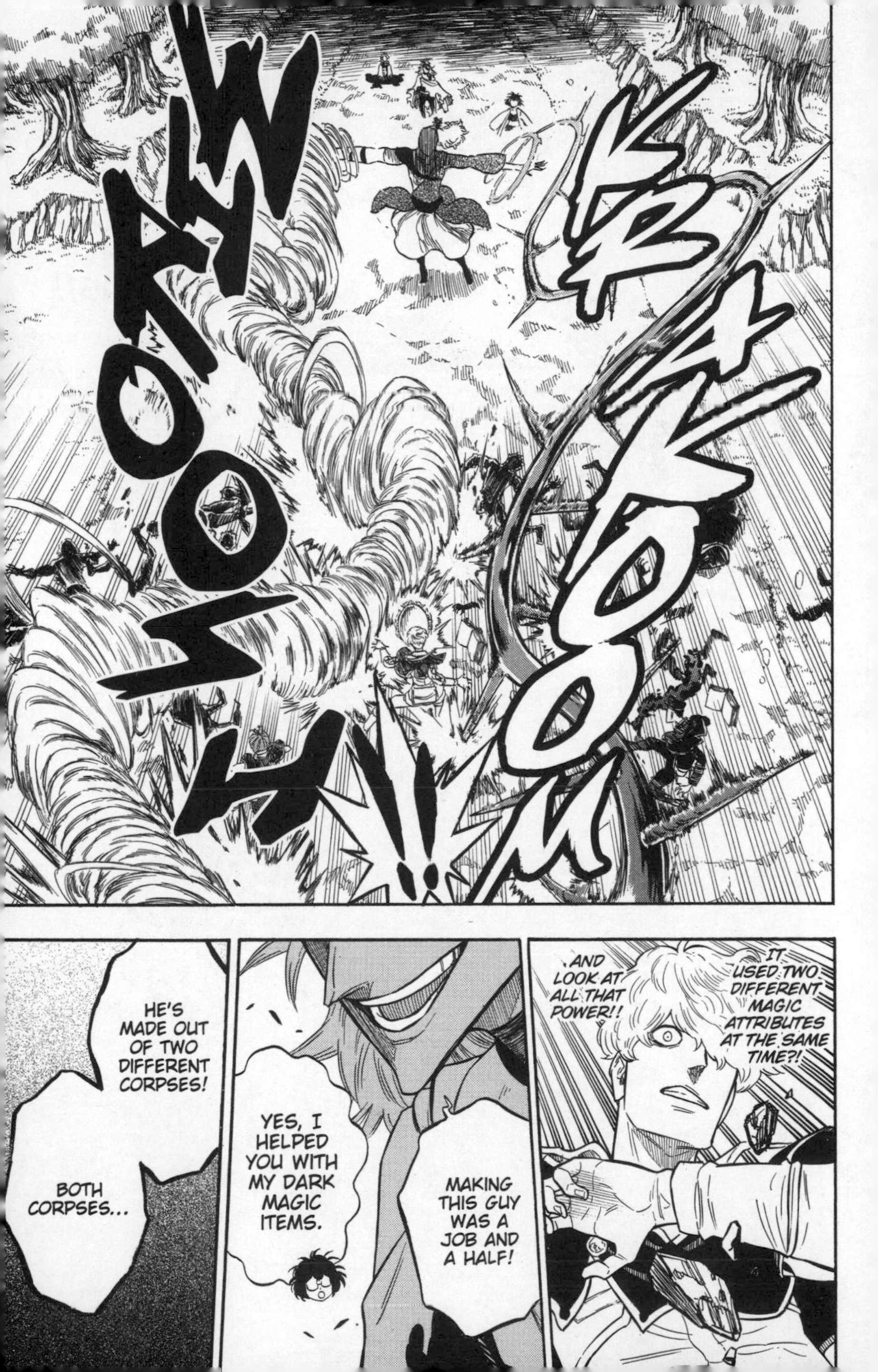
IT USED TWO DIFFERENT MAGIC ATTRIBUTES AT THE SAME TIME?!
AND LOOK AT ALL THAT POWER!!
MAKING THIS GUY WAS A JOB AND A HALF!
YES, I HELPED YOU WITH MY DARK MAGIC ITEMS.
HE'S MADE OUT OF TWO DIFFERENT CORPSES!
BOTH CORPSES...

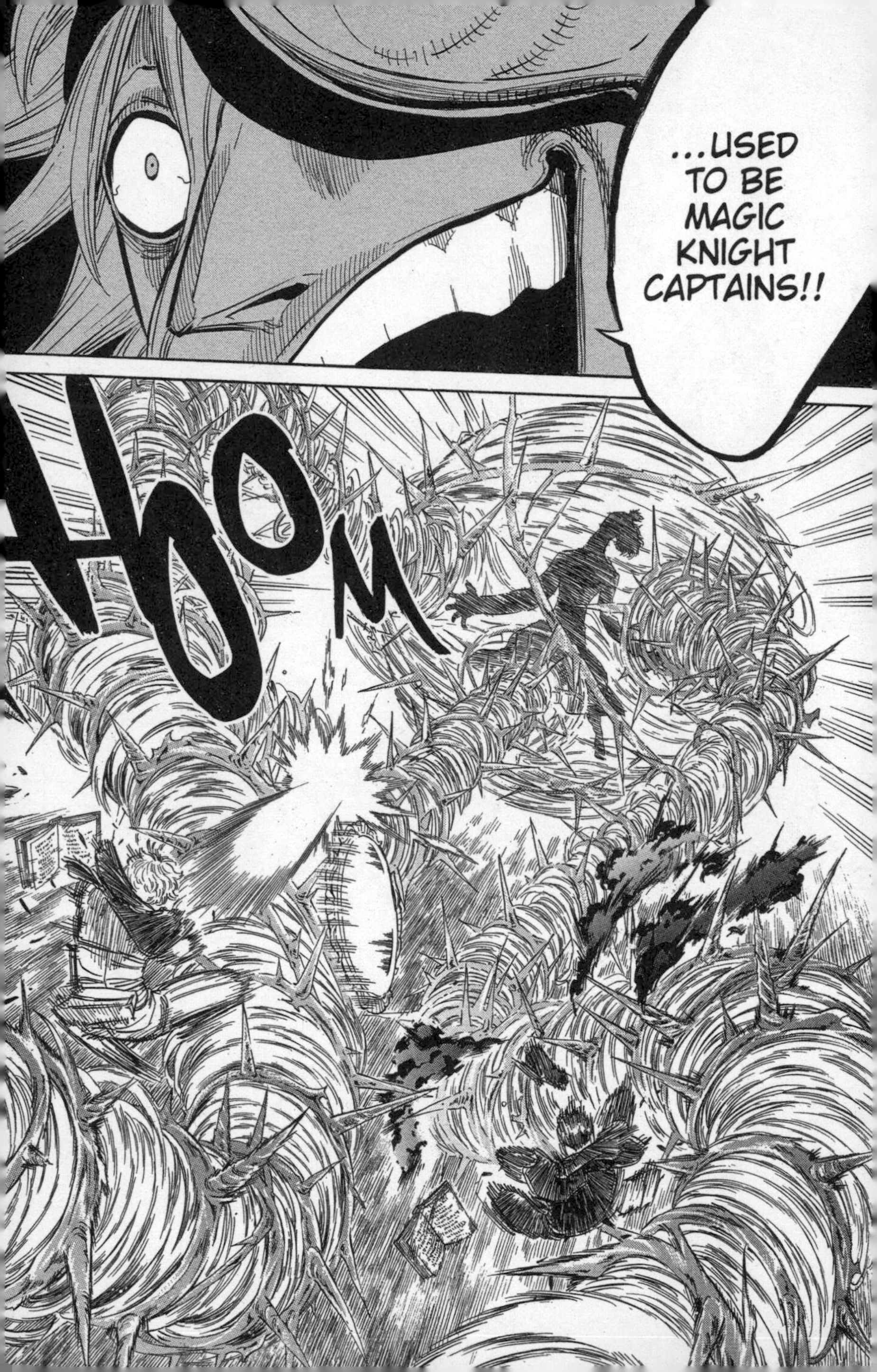
...USED TO BE MAGIC KNIGHT CAPTAINS!!
HOOM

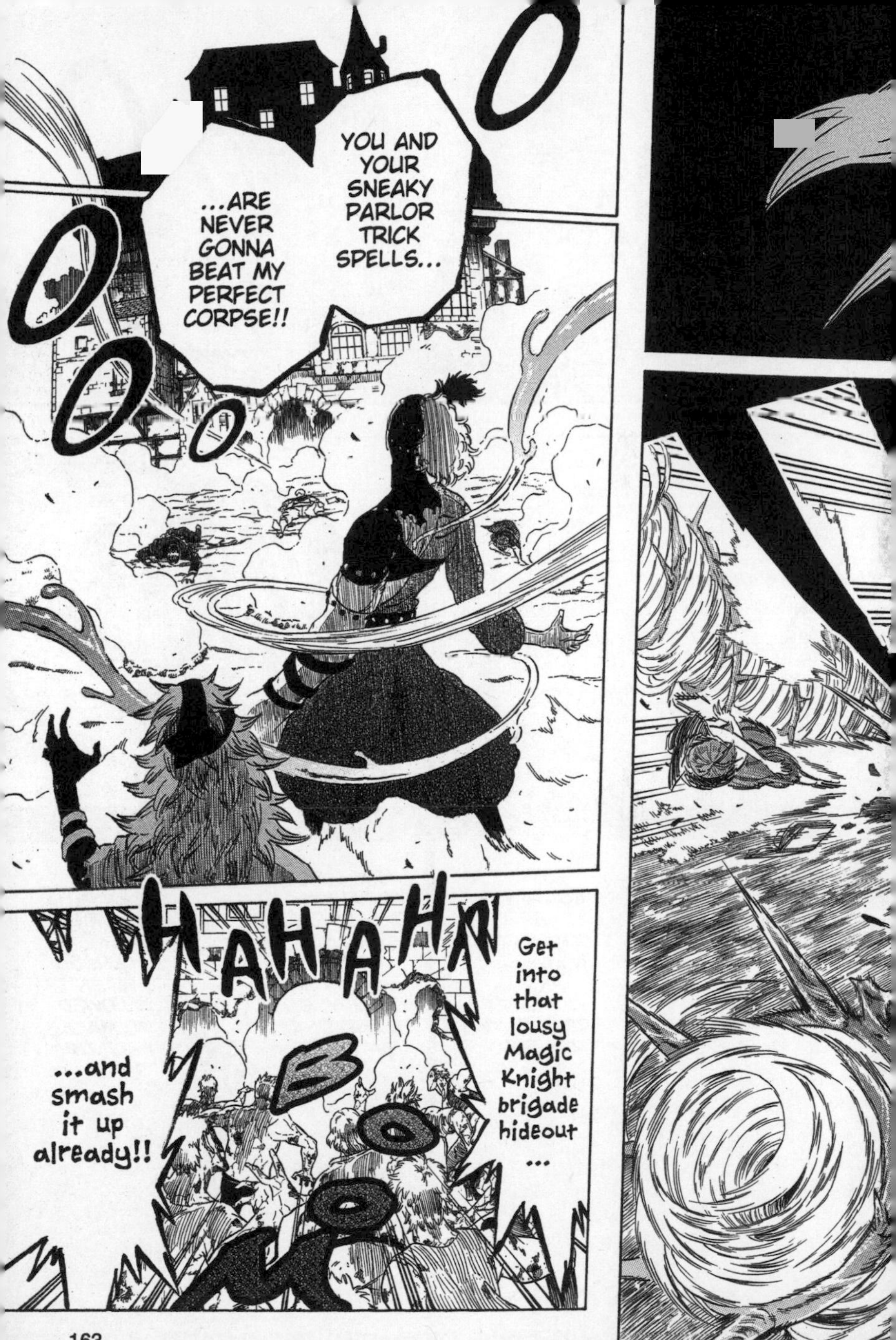
YOU AND YOUR SNEAKY PARLOR TRICK SPELLS...
...ARE NEVER GONNA BEAT MY PERFECT CORPSE!!
HAHAHA
Get into that lousy Magic Knight brigade hideout...
...and smash it up already!!
BOOM

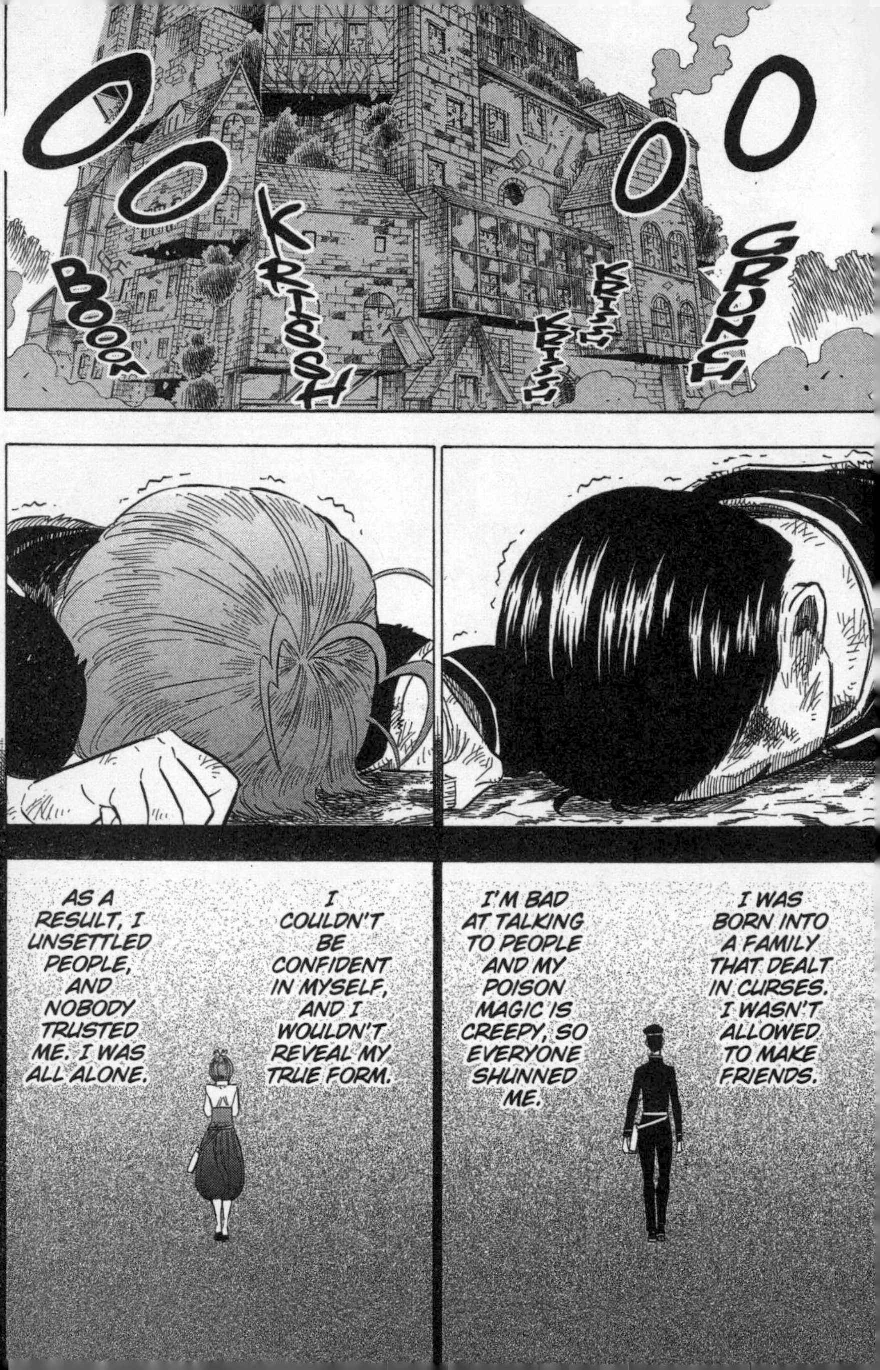
GRUNCH
KRISSH
BOOOM
I WAS BORN INTO A FAMILY THAT DEALT IN CURSES. I WASN'T ALLOWED TO MAKE FRIENDS.
I'M BAD AT TALKING TO PEOPLE AND MY POISON MAGIC IS CREEPY, SO EVERYONE SHUNNED ME.
I COULDN'T BE CONFIDENT IN MYSELF, AND I WOULDN'T REVEAL MY TRUE FORM.
AS A RESULT, I UNSETTLED PEOPLE, AND NOBODY TRUSTED ME. I WAS ALL ALONE.

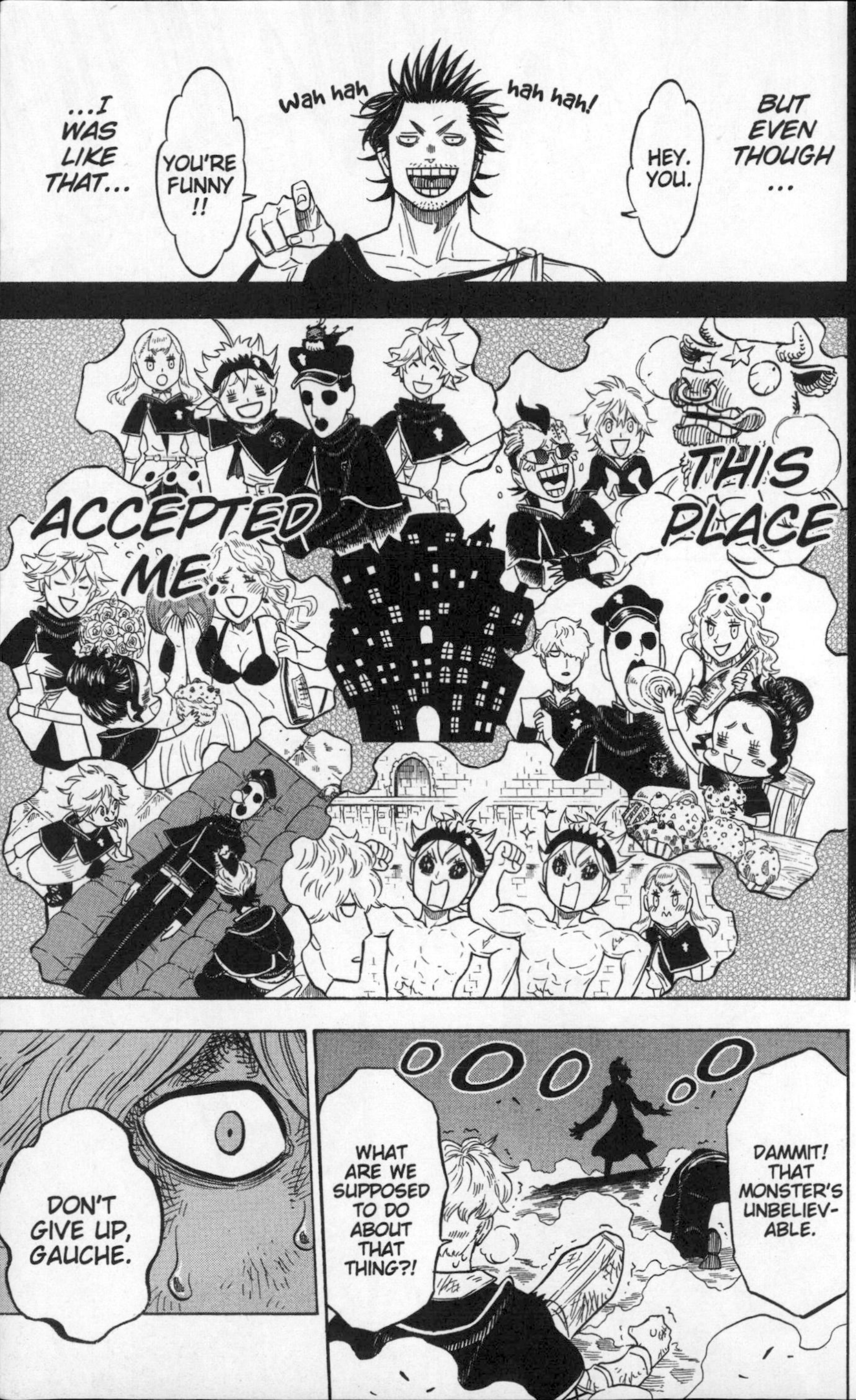
BUT EVEN THOUGH...
HEY. YOU.
Wah hah hah hah!
YOU'RE FUNNY!!
...I WAS LIKE THAT...
THIS PLACE
ACCEPTED ME.
DAMMIT! THAT MONSTER'S UNBELIEV-ABLE.
WHAT ARE WE SUPPOSED TO DO ABOUT THAT THING?!
DON'T GIVE UP, GAUCHE.

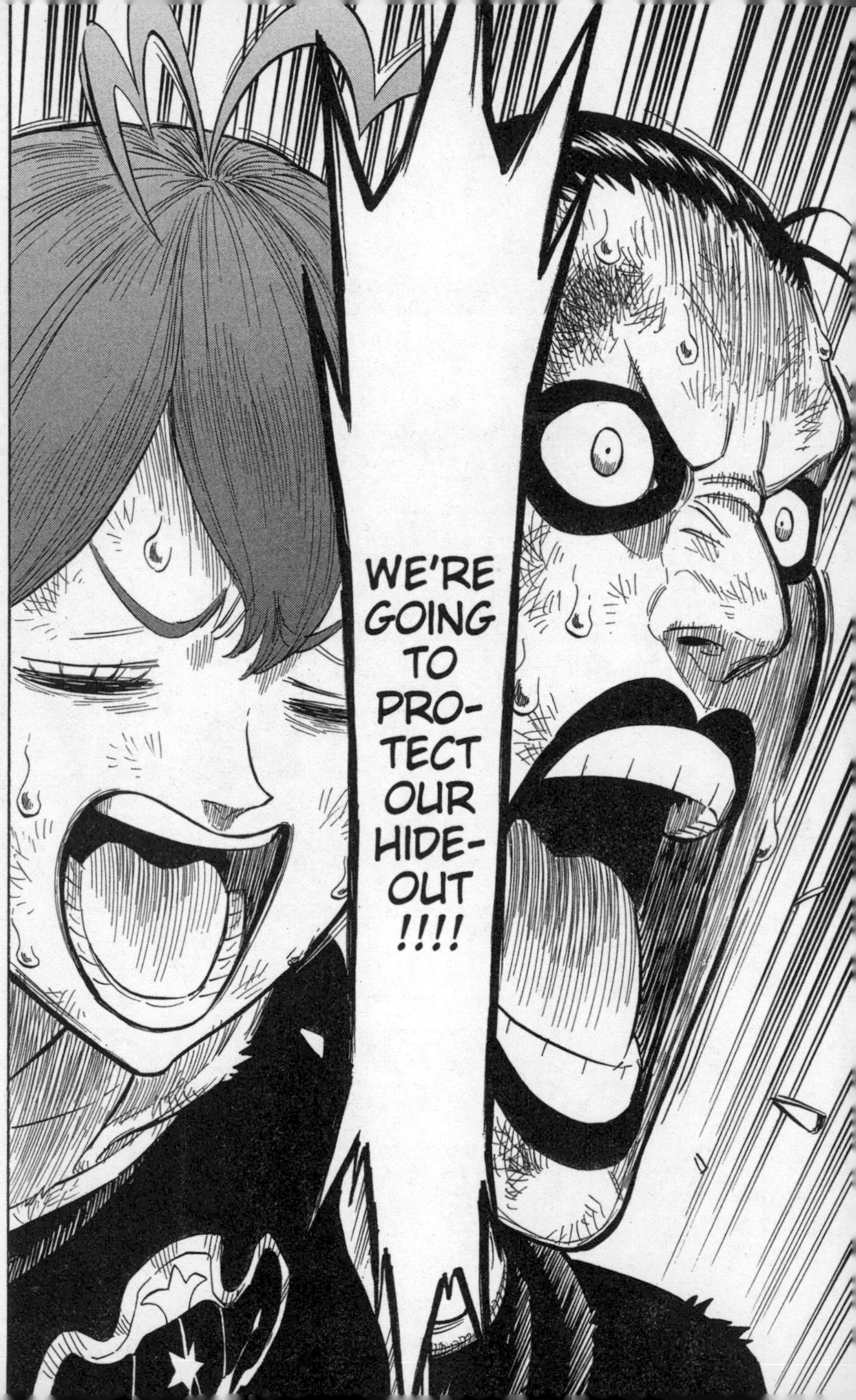
WE'RE GOING TO PROTECT OUR HIDEOUT !!!!

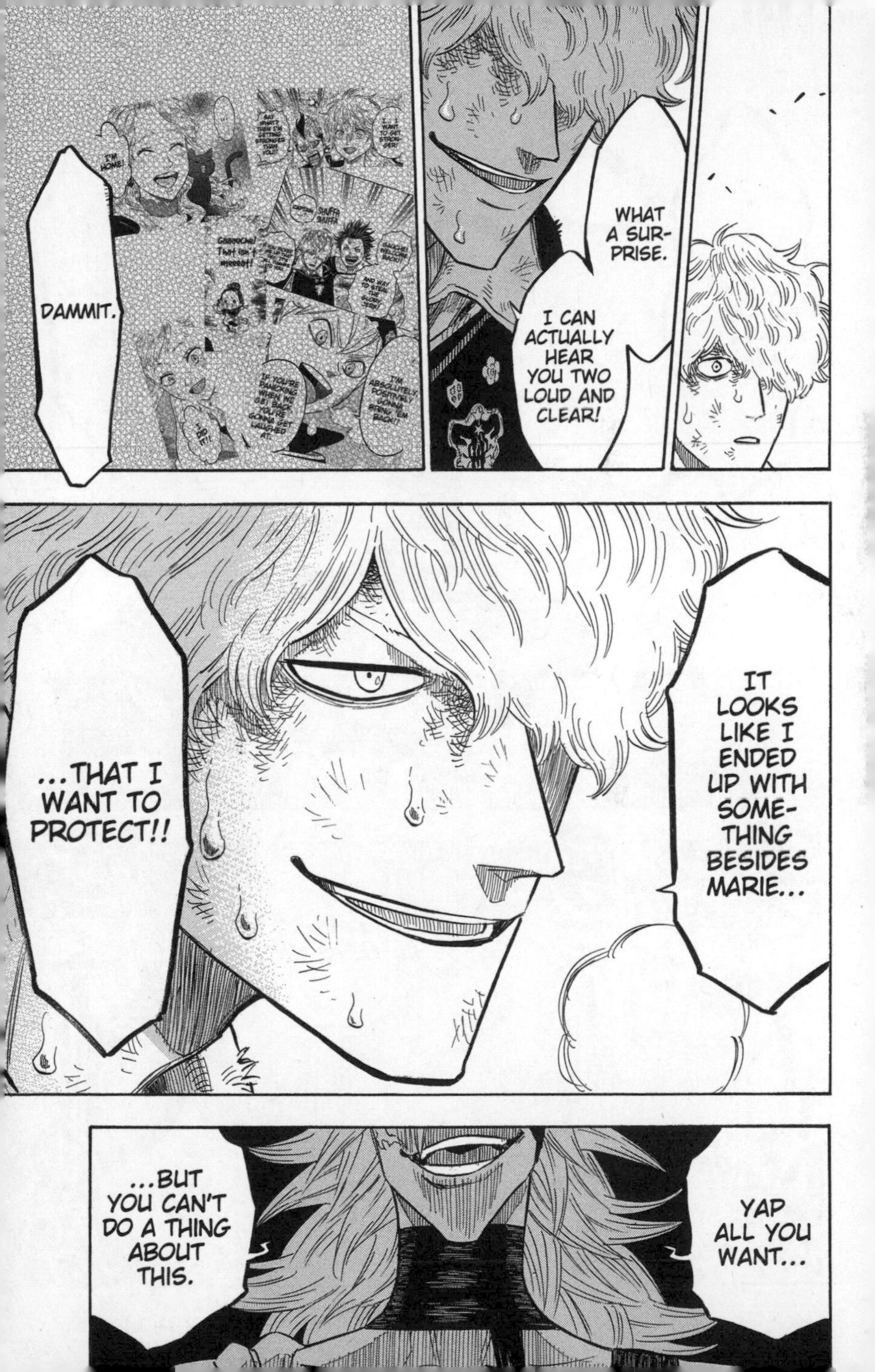
WHAT A SURPRISE.
I CAN ACTUALLY HEAR YOU TWO LOUD AND CLEAR!
I... I WANT TO GET STRONGER!
SAY WHAT?! THEN I'M GETTING STRONGER THAN YOU!!
I'M HOME!
GAUCHE! WELCOME BACK!!
AND WAY TO STEAL THE GLORY, JERK!
CAPTAIN
SHUFFA SHUFFA
Gaaauche! That isn't meeeat!
I'M ABSOLUTELY, POSITIVELY GONNA BRING 'EM BACK!!
IF YOU'RE PANICKING WHEN WE GET BACK, YOU'RE GONNA GET LAUGHED AT.
I DID IT!!
DAMMIT.
IT LOOKS LIKE I ENDED UP WITH SOMETHING BESIDES MARIE...
...THAT I WANT TO PROTECT!!
YAP ALL YOU WANT...
...BUT YOU CAN'T DO A THING ABOUT THIS.

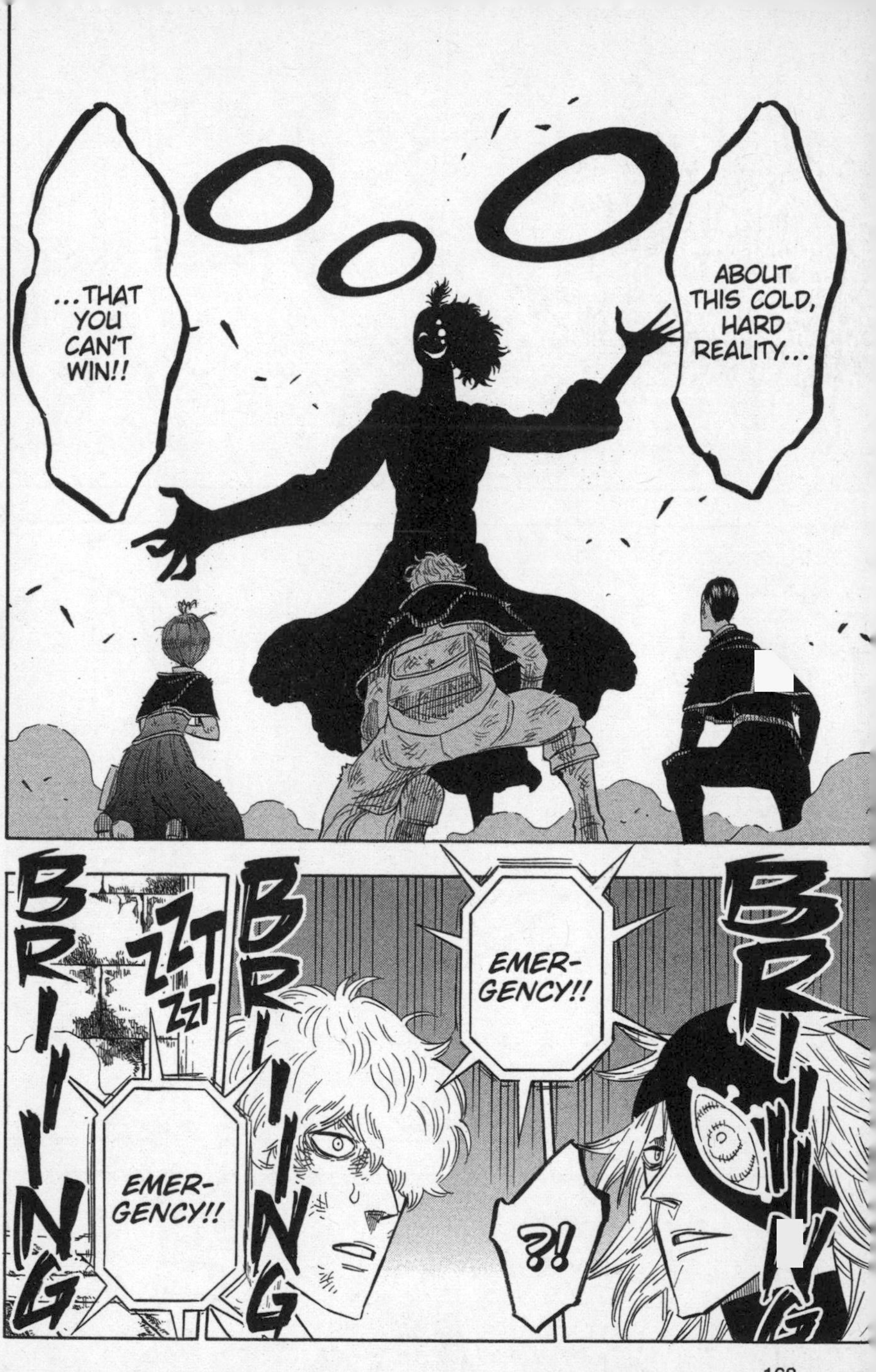
ABOUT THIS COLD, HARD REALITY...
...THAT YOU CAN'T WIN!!
?!
EMERGENCY!!
BRIIING
EMERGENCY!!
BRIIING
ZZT ZZT

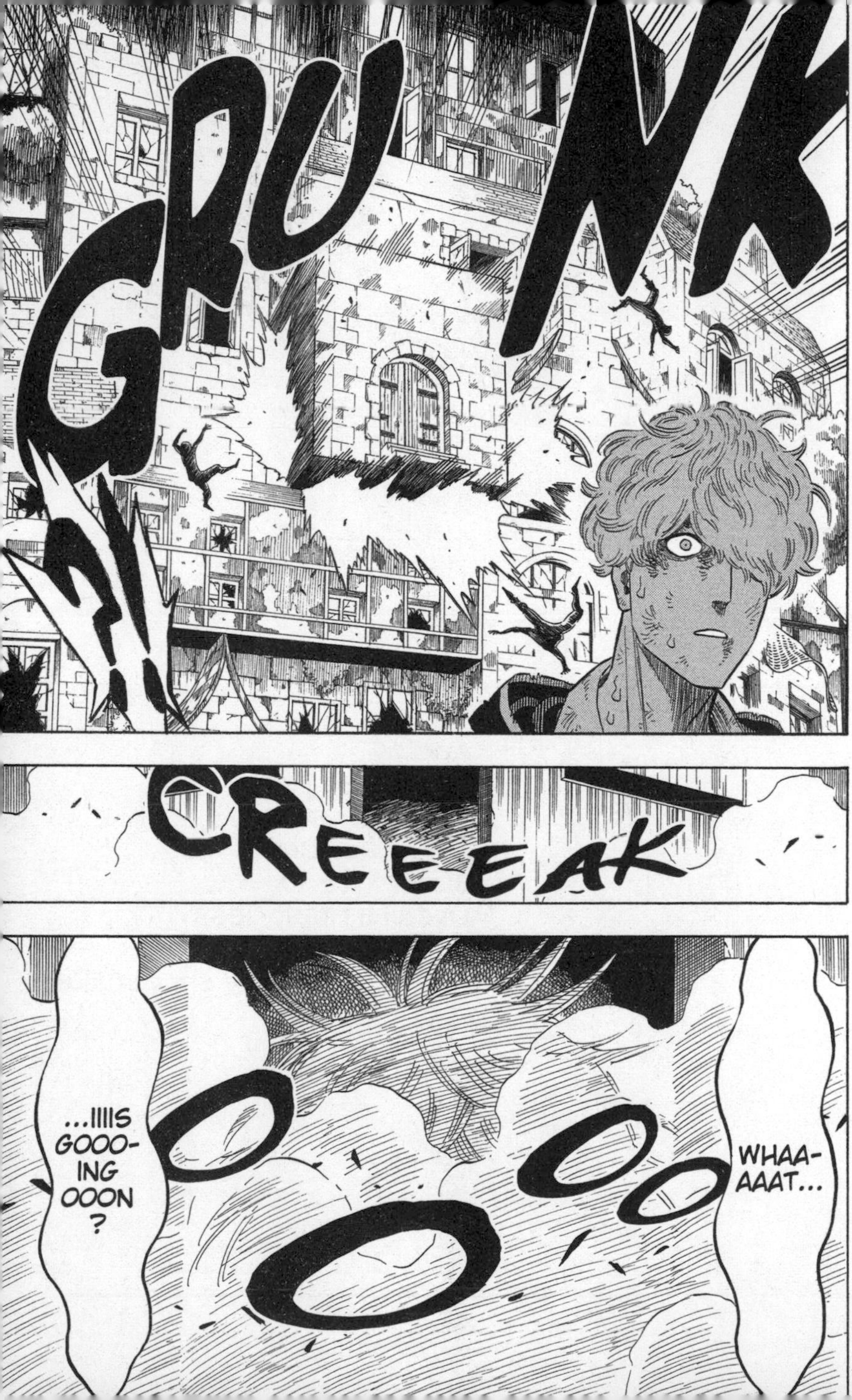
GRUNK
CREEEAK
WHAA-AAAT...
OOOO
...IIIIS GOOO-ING OOON?

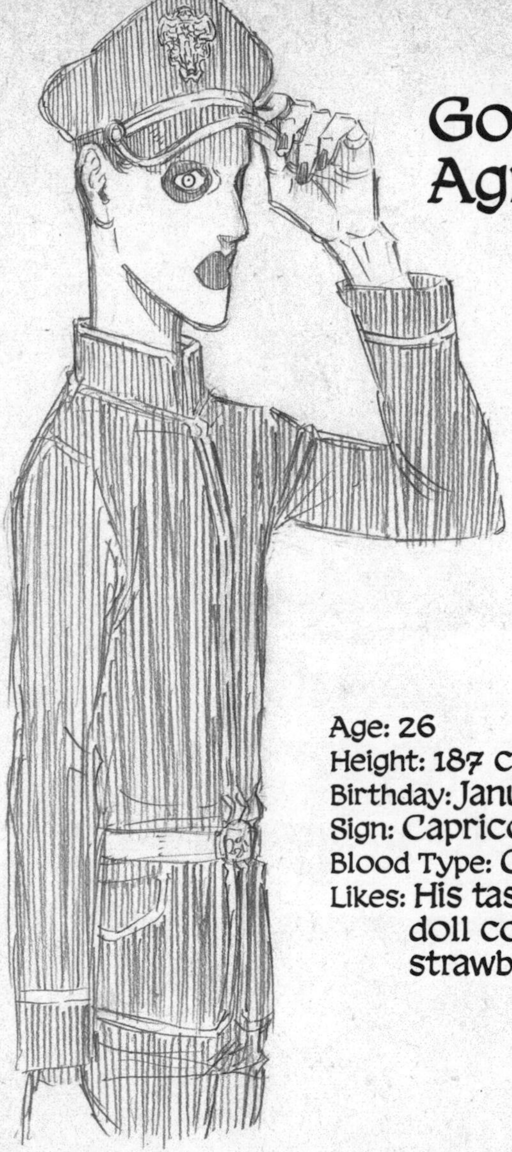

Gordon Agrippa

Age: 26
Height: 187 cm
Birthday: January 13
Sign: Capricorn
Blood Type: O
Likes: His tasteless doll collection, strawberry shortcake

Character Profile

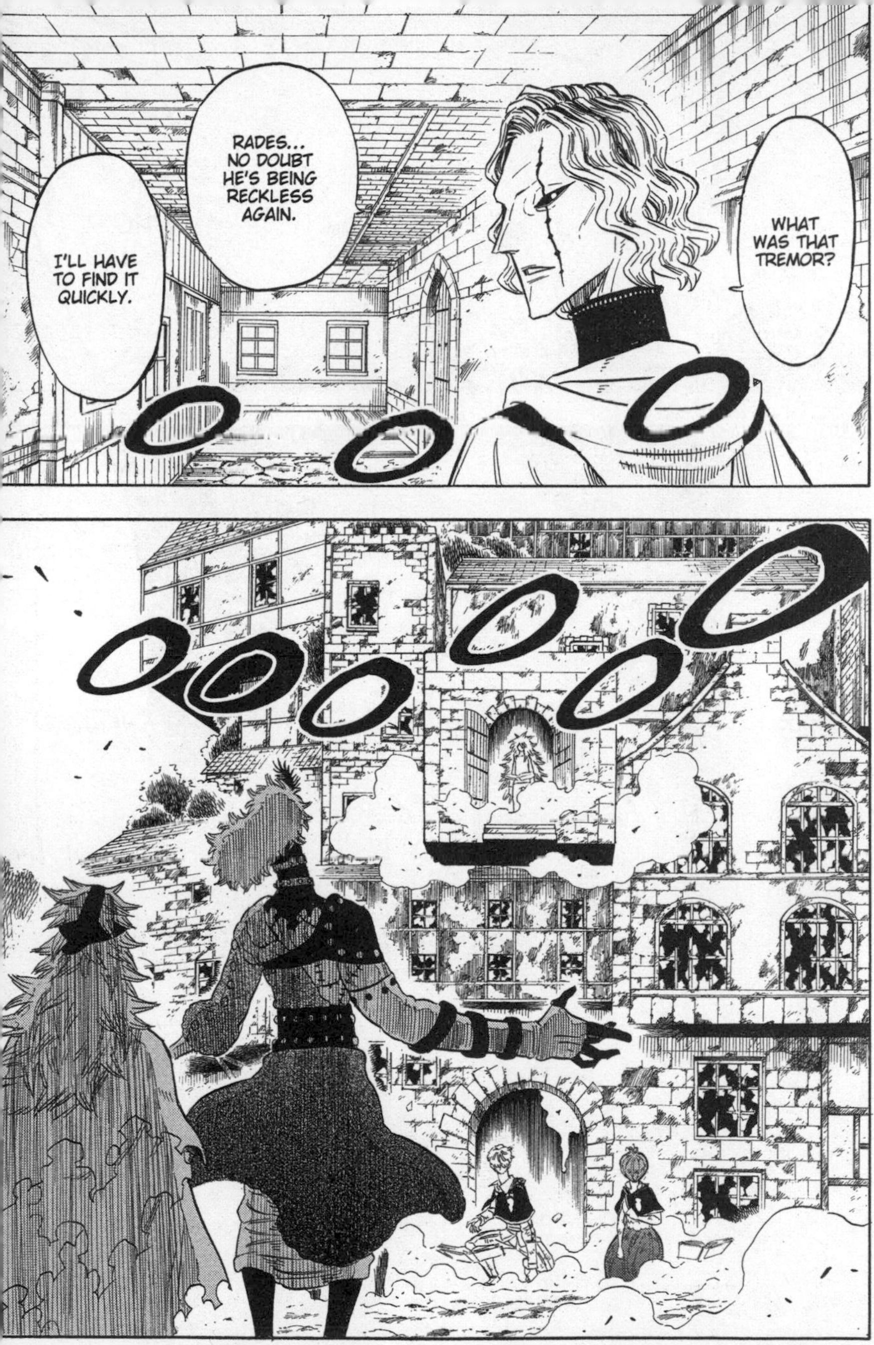
WHAT WAS THAT TREMOR?
RADES... NO DOUBT HE'S BEING RECKLESS AGAIN.
I'LL HAVE TO FIND IT QUICKLY.

Page 140: You Probably Don't Know, But...

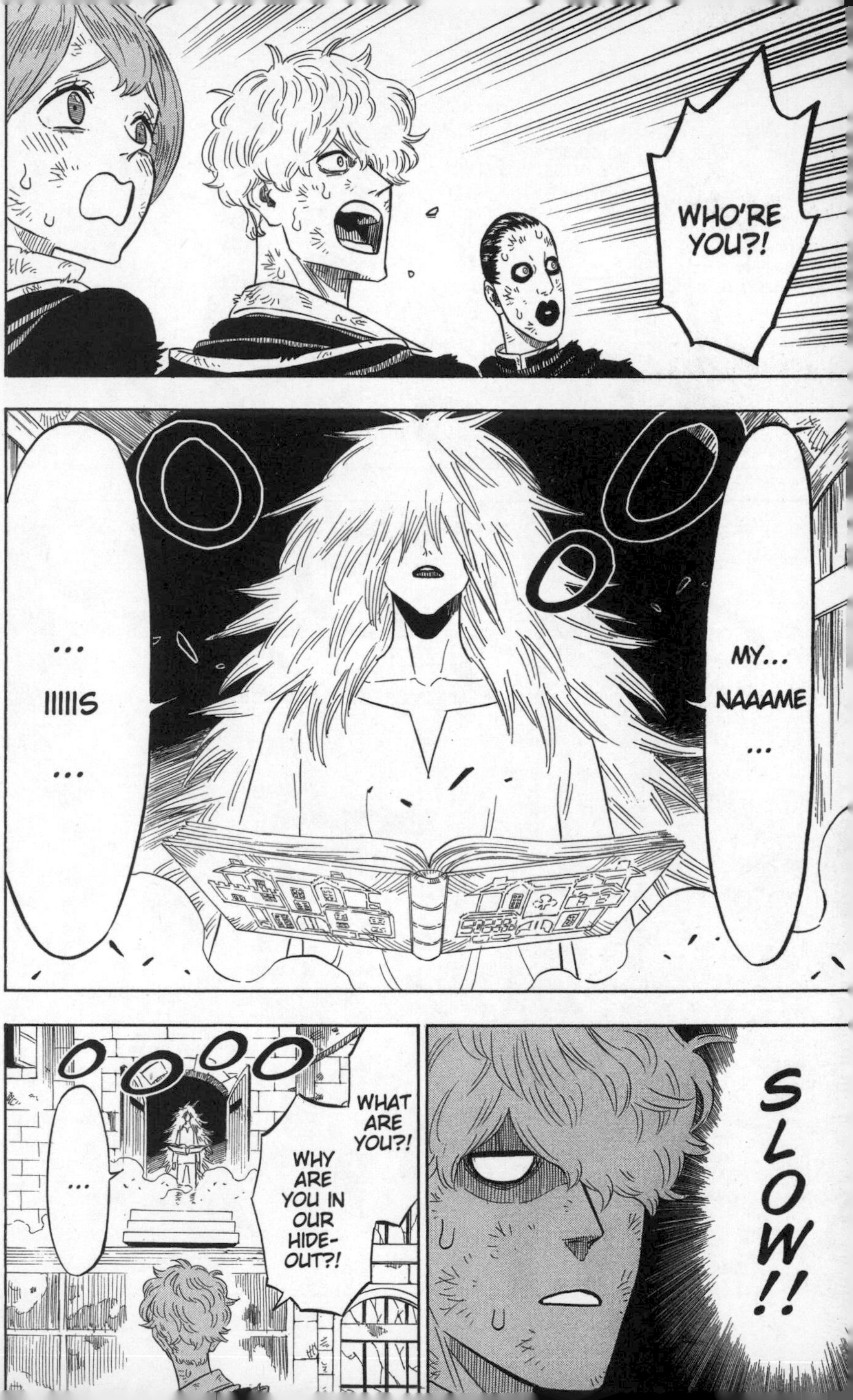
WHO'RE YOU?!
MY... NAAAME ...
... IIIIIS ...
OOO
SLOW!!
WHAT ARE YOU?!
WHY ARE YOU IN OUR HIDE-OUT?!
OOOO
...

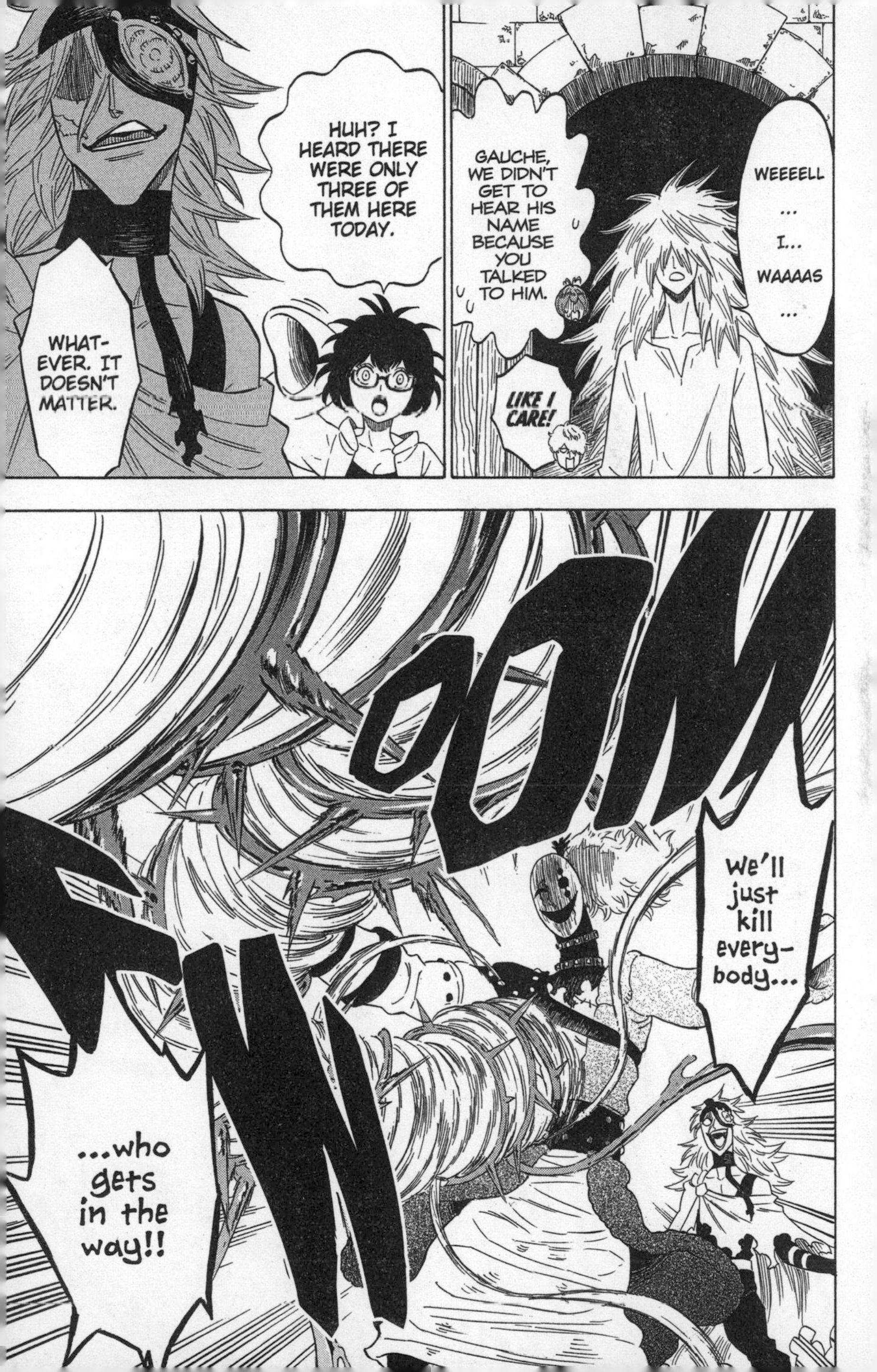
WEEEELL ... I... WAAAAS ...
GAUCHE, WE DIDN'T GET TO HEAR HIS NAME BECAUSE YOU TALKED TO HIM.
LIKE I CARE!
HUH? I HEARD THERE WERE ONLY THREE OF THEM HERE TODAY.
WHAT-EVER. IT DOESN'T MATTER.
We'll just kill every-body...
WOOM
...who gets in the way!!

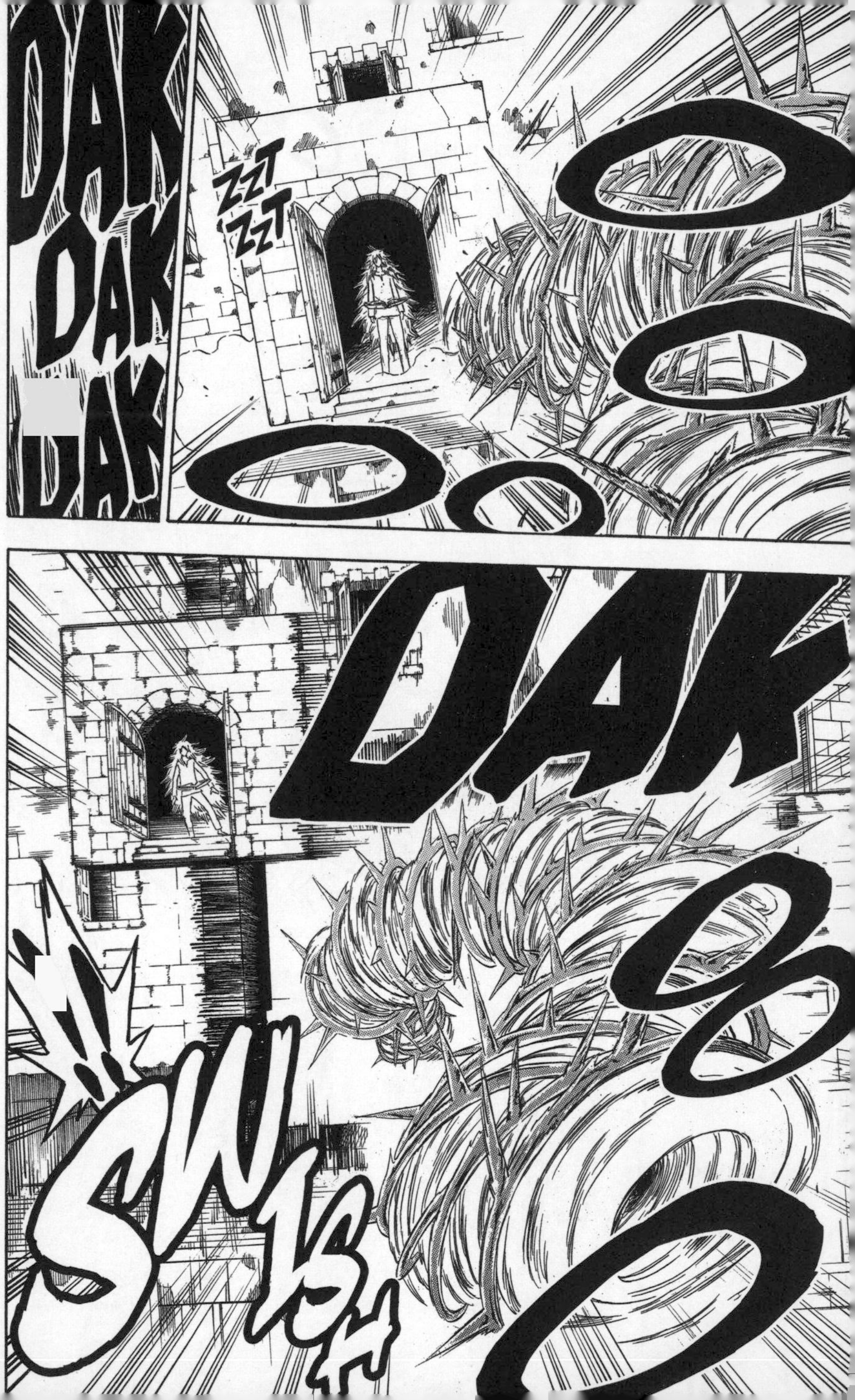
ZZT ZZT
DAK DAK DAK
DAK
SWISH

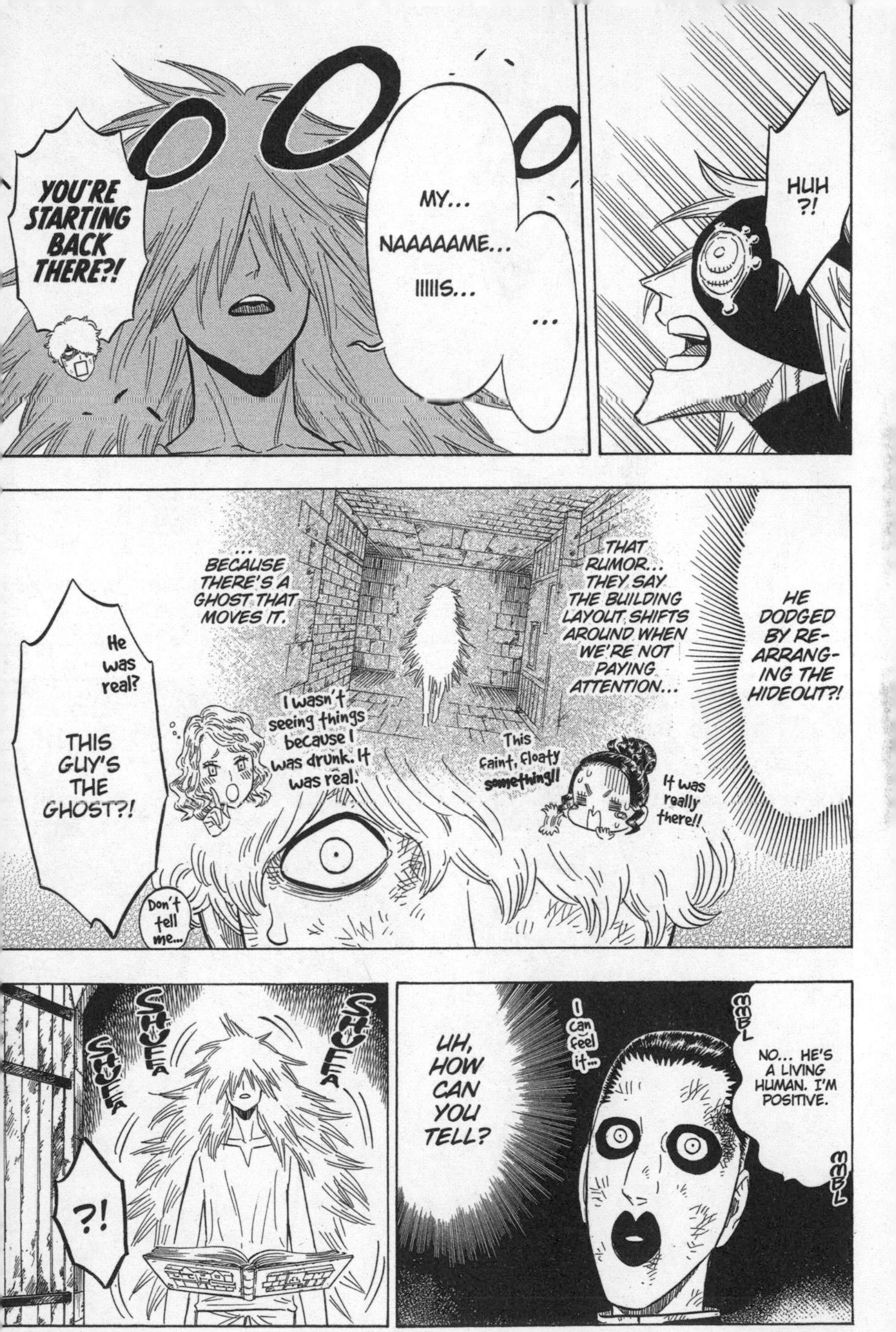
HUH ?!
MY... NAAAAAME... IIIIIS... ...
YOU'RE STARTING BACK THERE?!
HE DODGED BY RE-ARRANG-ING THE HIDEOUT?!
THAT RUMOR... THEY SAY THE BUILDING LAYOUT SHIFTS AROUND WHEN WE'RE NOT PAYING ATTENTION...
... BECAUSE THERE'S A GHOST THAT MOVES IT.
It was really there!!
This faint, floaty something!!
I wasn't seeing things because I was drunk. It was real.
He was real?
THIS GUY'S THE GHOST?!
Don't tell me...
MMBL
NO... HE'S A LIVING HUMAN. I'M POSITIVE.
MMBL
I can feel it...
UH, HOW CAN YOU TELL?
SHUFFA
SHUFFA
SHUFFA
?!

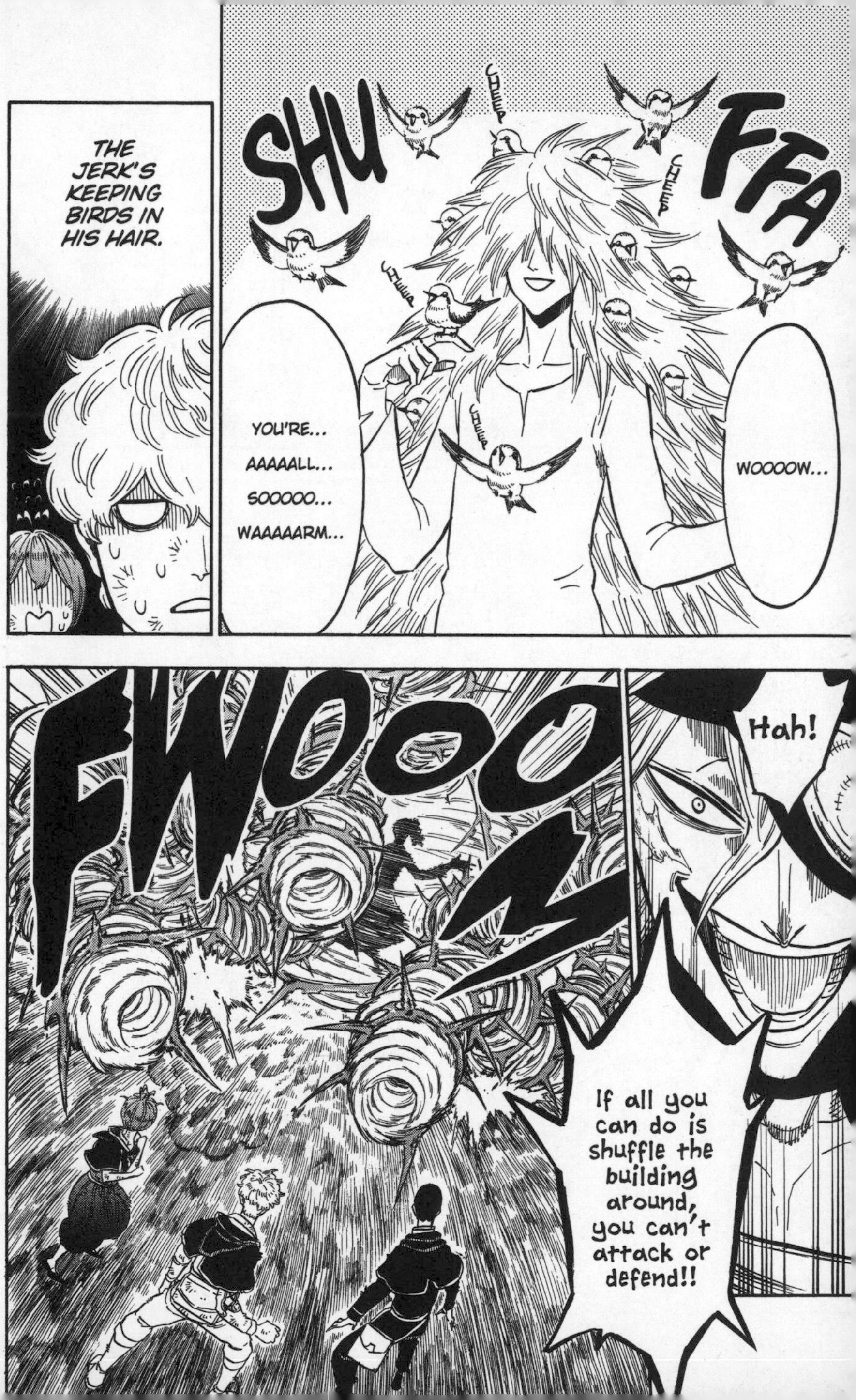
SHU FFA
CHEEP
CHEEP
CHEEP
CHEEP
WOOOOW...
YOU'RE... AAAAALL... SOOOOO... WAAAAARM...
THE JERK'S KEEPING BIRDS IN HIS HAIR.
Hah!
If all you can do is shuffle the building around, you can't attack or defend!!
FWOOO

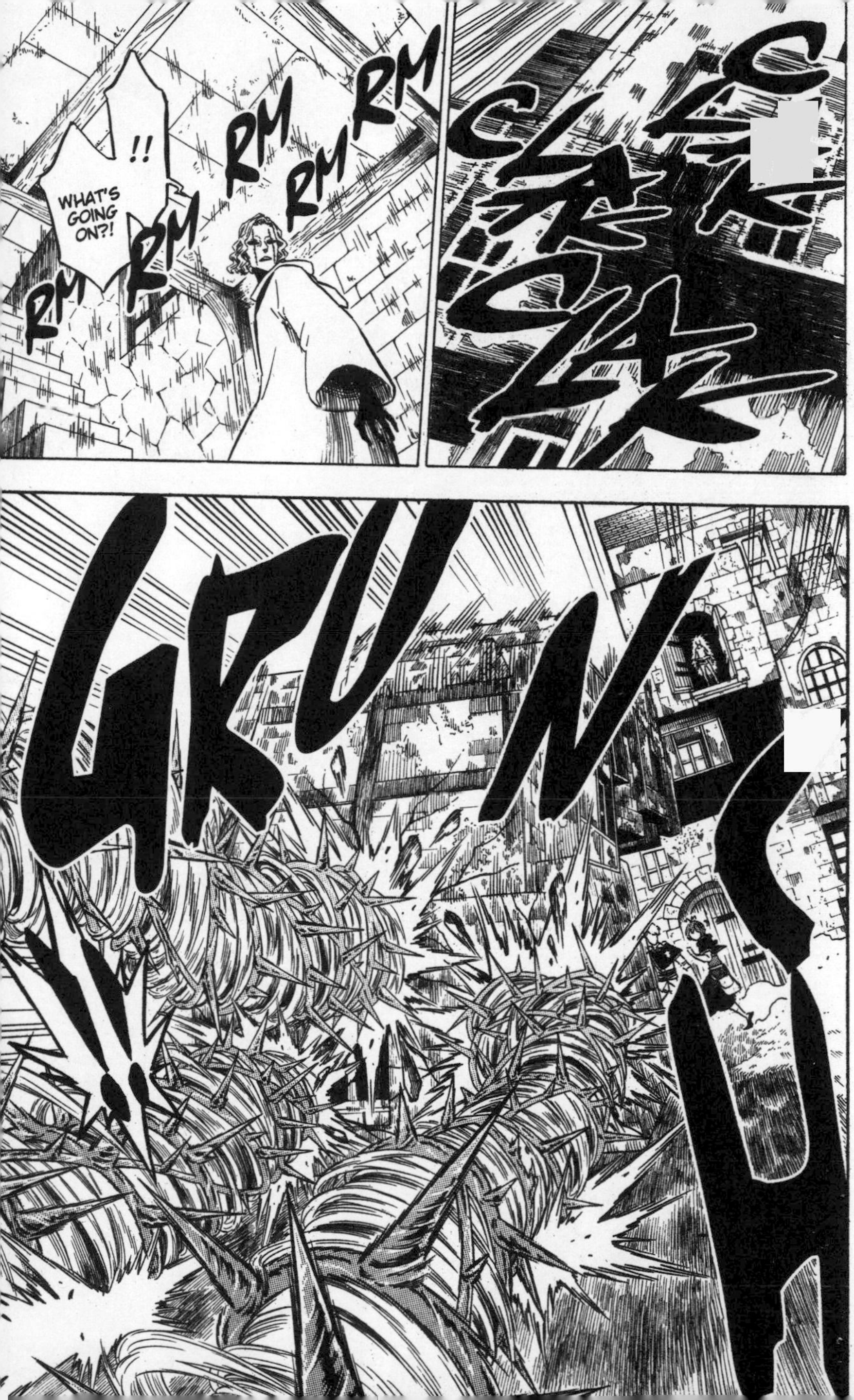
CLAK
CLAK
RM RM RM RM RM RM
!!
WHAT'S GOING ON?!
GRUNK
!!

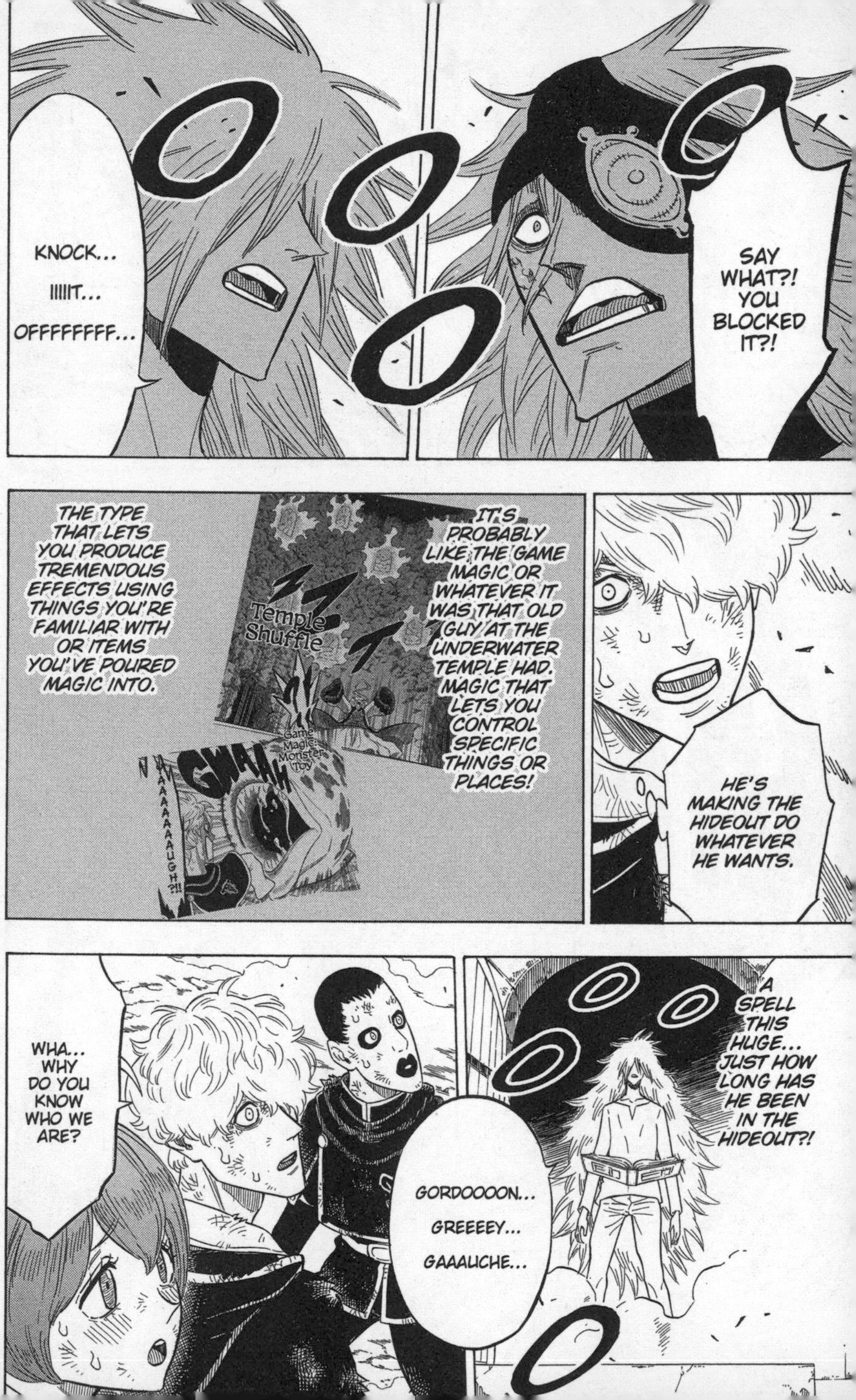
SAY WHAT?! YOU BLOCKED IT?!
KNOCK... IIIIIT... OFFFFFFFF...
HE'S MAKING THE HIDEOUT DO WHATEVER HE WANTS.
IT'S PROBABLY LIKE THE GAME MAGIC OR WHATEVER IT WAS THAT OLD GUY AT THE UNDERWATER TEMPLE HAD. MAGIC THAT LETS YOU CONTROL SPECIFIC THINGS OR PLACES!
Temple Shuffle
Game Magic: Monster Toy
GWAAAH
THE TYPE THAT LETS YOU PRODUCE TREMENDOUS EFFECTS USING THINGS YOU'RE FAMILIAR WITH OR ITEMS YOU'VE POURED MAGIC INTO.
A SPELL THIS HUGE... JUST HOW LONG HAS HE BEEN IN THE HIDEOUT?!
GORDOOOON... GREEEEY... GAAAUCHE...
WHA... WHY DO YOU KNOW WHO WE ARE?

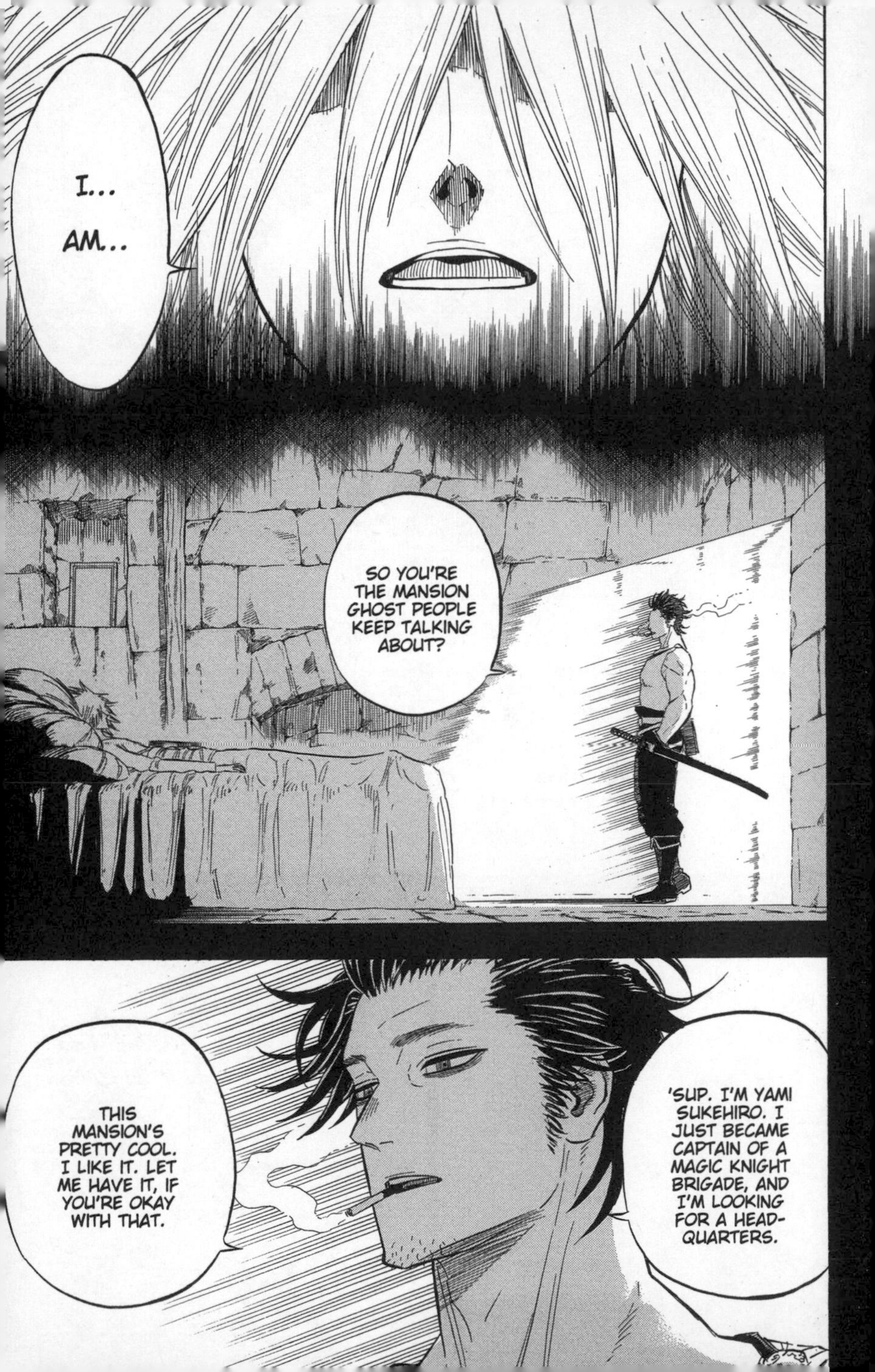
I... AM...
SO YOU'RE THE MANSION GHOST PEOPLE KEEP TALKING ABOUT?
'SUP. I'M YAMI SUKEHIRO. I JUST BECAME CAPTAIN OF A MAGIC KNIGHT BRIGADE, AND I'M LOOKING FOR A HEAD-QUARTERS.
THIS MANSION'S PRETTY COOL. I LIKE IT. LET ME HAVE IT, IF YOU'RE OKAY WITH THAT.

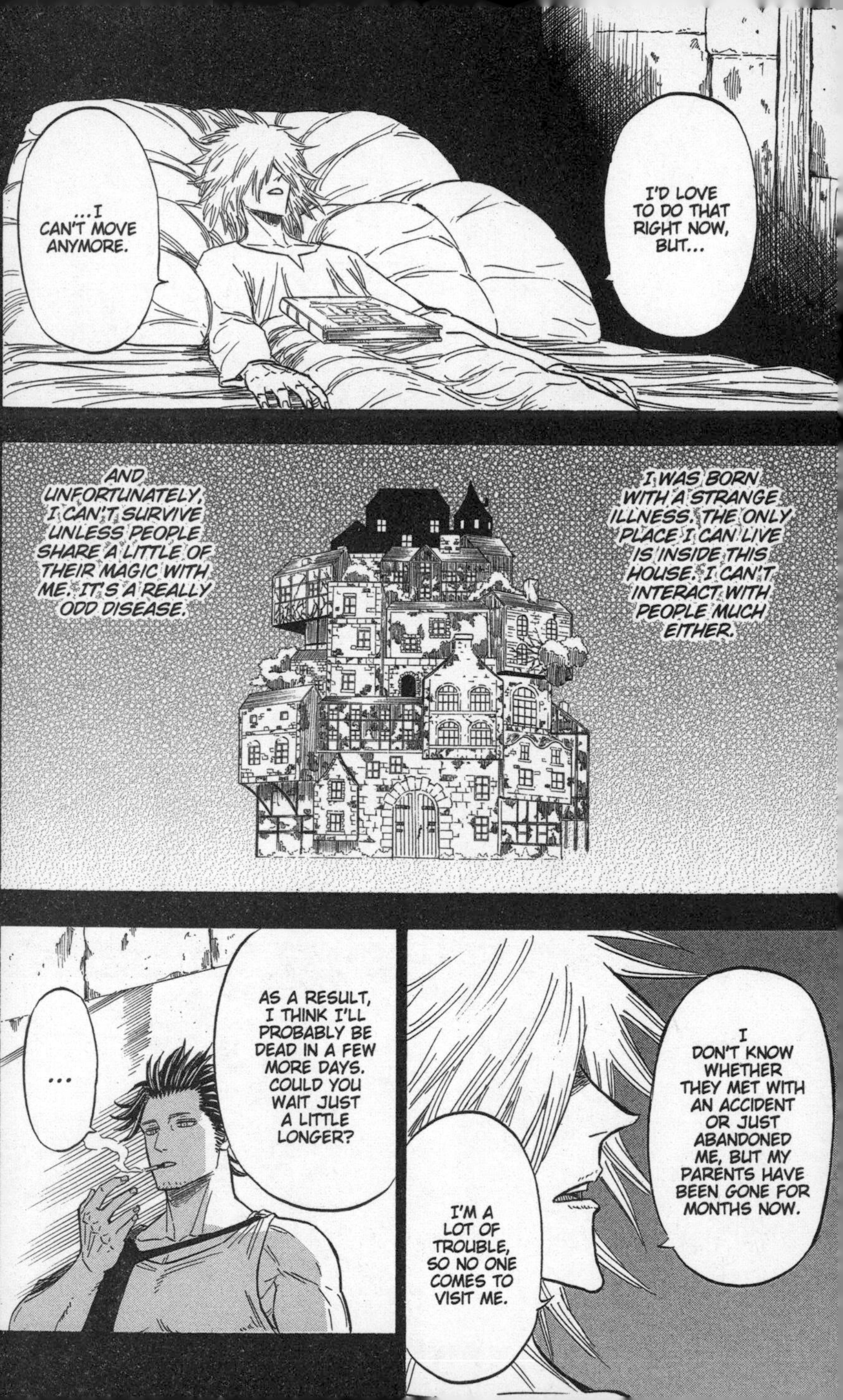
I'D LOVE TO DO THAT RIGHT NOW, BUT...
...I CAN'T MOVE ANYMORE.
I WAS BORN WITH A STRANGE ILLNESS. THE ONLY PLACE I CAN LIVE IS INSIDE THIS HOUSE. I CAN'T INTERACT WITH PEOPLE MUCH EITHER.
AND UNFORTUNATELY, I CAN'T SURVIVE UNLESS PEOPLE SHARE A LITTLE OF THEIR MAGIC WITH ME. IT'S A REALLY ODD DISEASE.
I DON'T KNOW WHETHER THEY MET WITH AN ACCIDENT OR JUST ABANDONED ME, BUT MY PARENTS HAVE BEEN GONE FOR MONTHS NOW.
I'M A LOT OF TROUBLE, SO NO ONE COMES TO VISIT ME.
AS A RESULT, I THINK I'LL PROBABLY BE DEAD IN A FEW MORE DAYS. COULD YOU WAIT JUST A LITTLE LONGER?
...

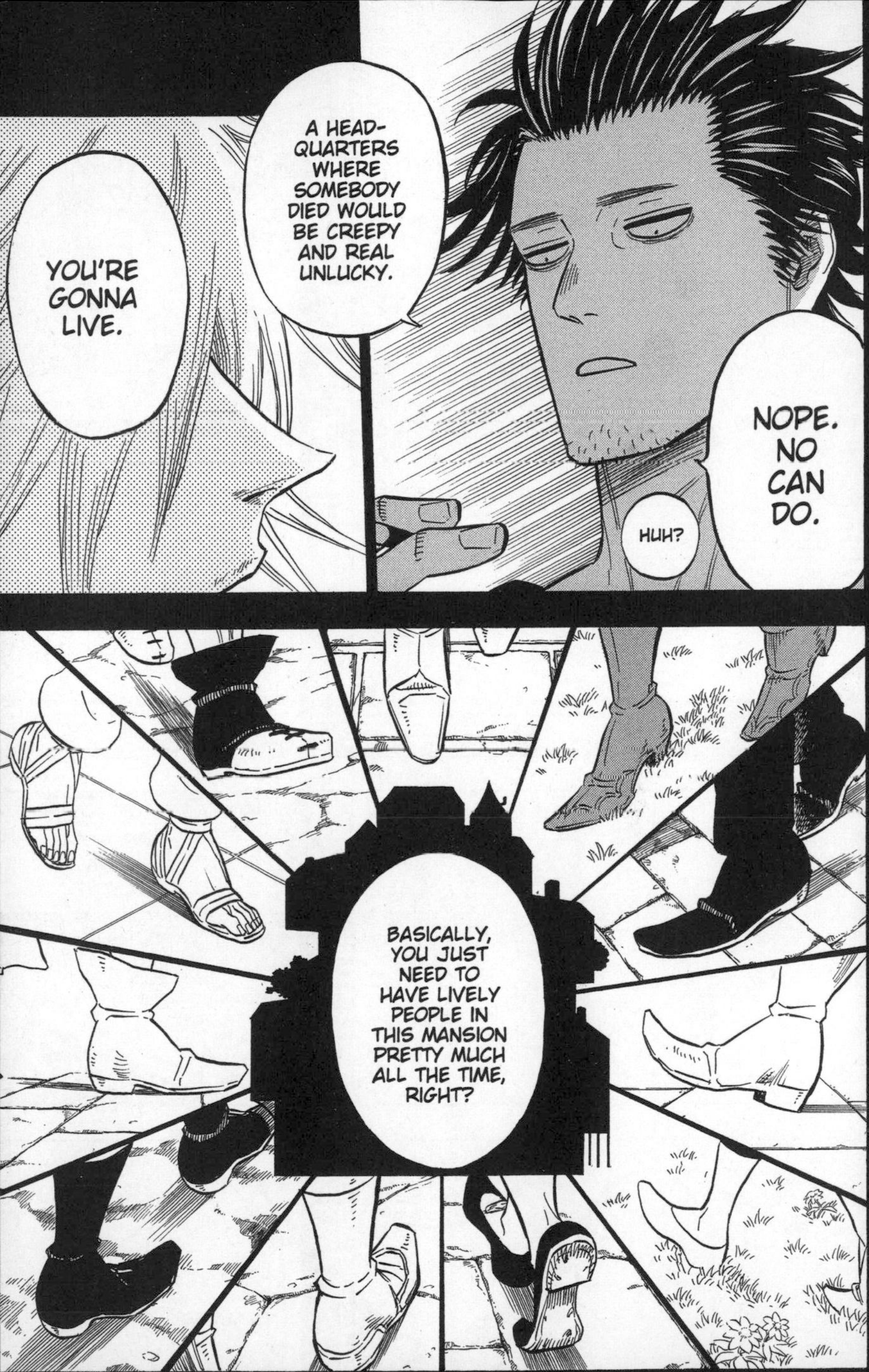
NOPE. NO CAN DO.
HUH?
A HEAD-QUARTERS WHERE SOMEBODY DIED WOULD BE CREEPY AND REAL UNLUCKY.
YOU'RE GONNA LIVE.
BASICALLY, YOU JUST NEED TO HAVE LIVELY PEOPLE IN THIS MANSION PRETTY MUCH ALL THE TIME, RIGHT?

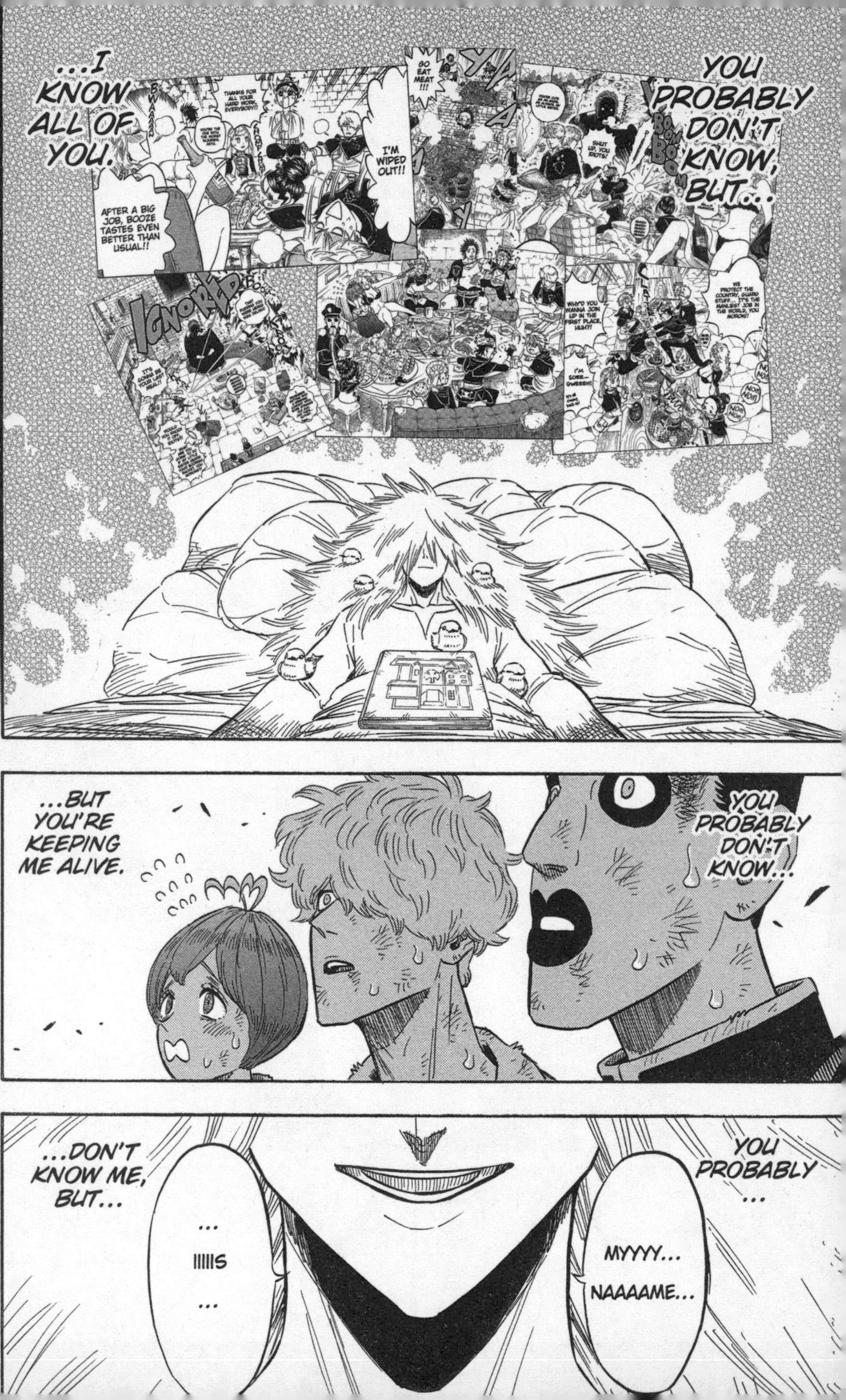
YOU PROBABLY DON'T KNOW, BUT...
...I KNOW ALL OF YOU.
GO EAT MEAT!!!
I'M WIPED OUT!!
THANKS FOR ALL YOUR HARD WORK, EVERYBODY!!
AFTER A BIG JOB, BOOZE TASTES EVEN BETTER THAN USUAL!!
SHUT UP, YOU IDIOTS!
WE PROTECT THE COUNTRY, GUARD STUFF... IT'S THE MANLIEST JOB IN THE WORLD, YOU MORON!!
WHY'D YOU WANNA JOIN UP IN THE FIRST PLACE, HUH?!
I'M SORR—GWEEEH!!
IGNORED
YOU PROBABLY DON'T KNOW...
...BUT YOU'RE KEEPING ME ALIVE.
YOU PROBABLY...
MYYYY... NAAAAME...
... IIIIIS ...
...DON'T KNOW ME, BUT...

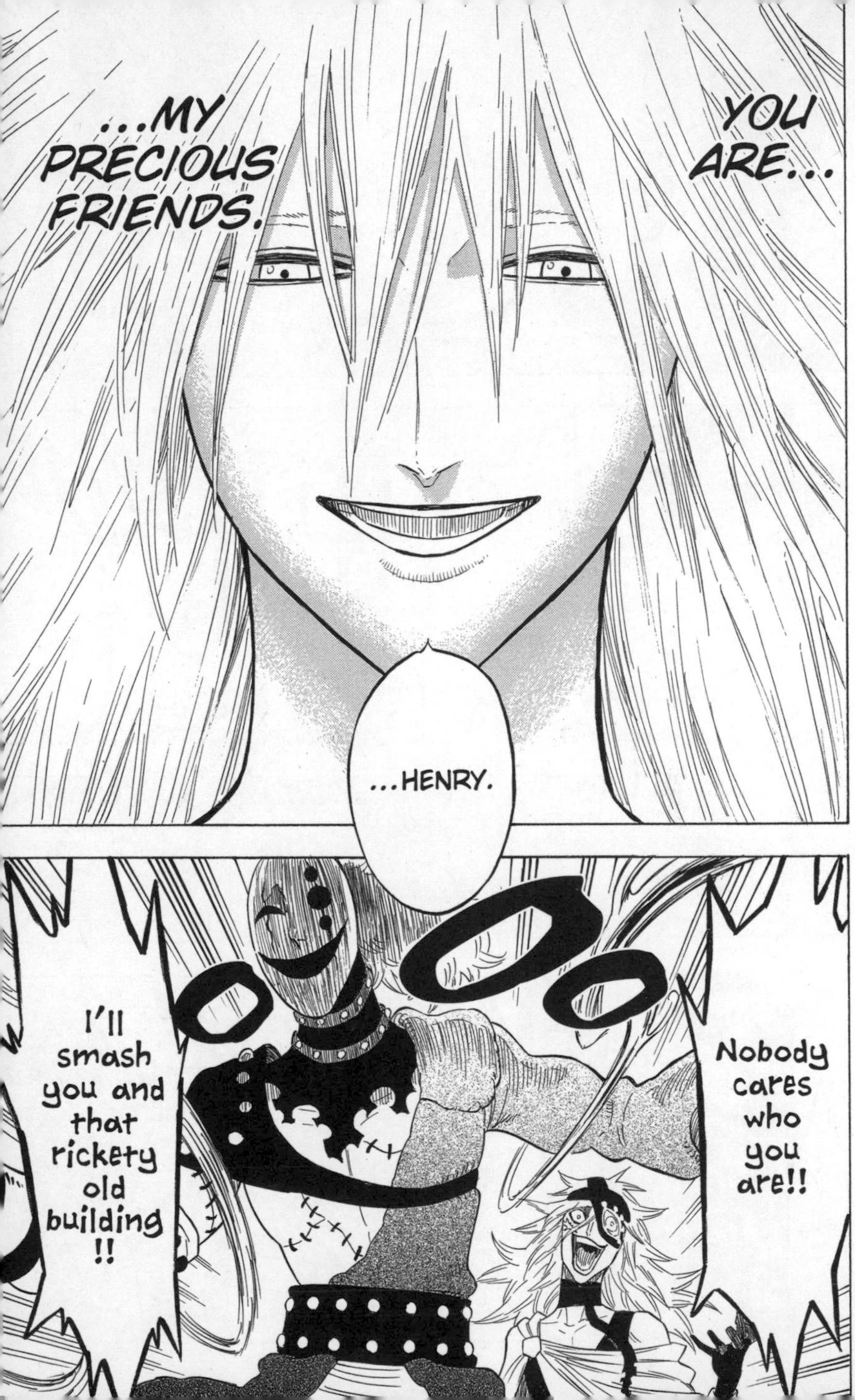
YOU ARE...
...MY PRECIOUS FRIENDS.
...HENRY.
Nobody cares who you are!!
I'll smash you and that rickety old building!!

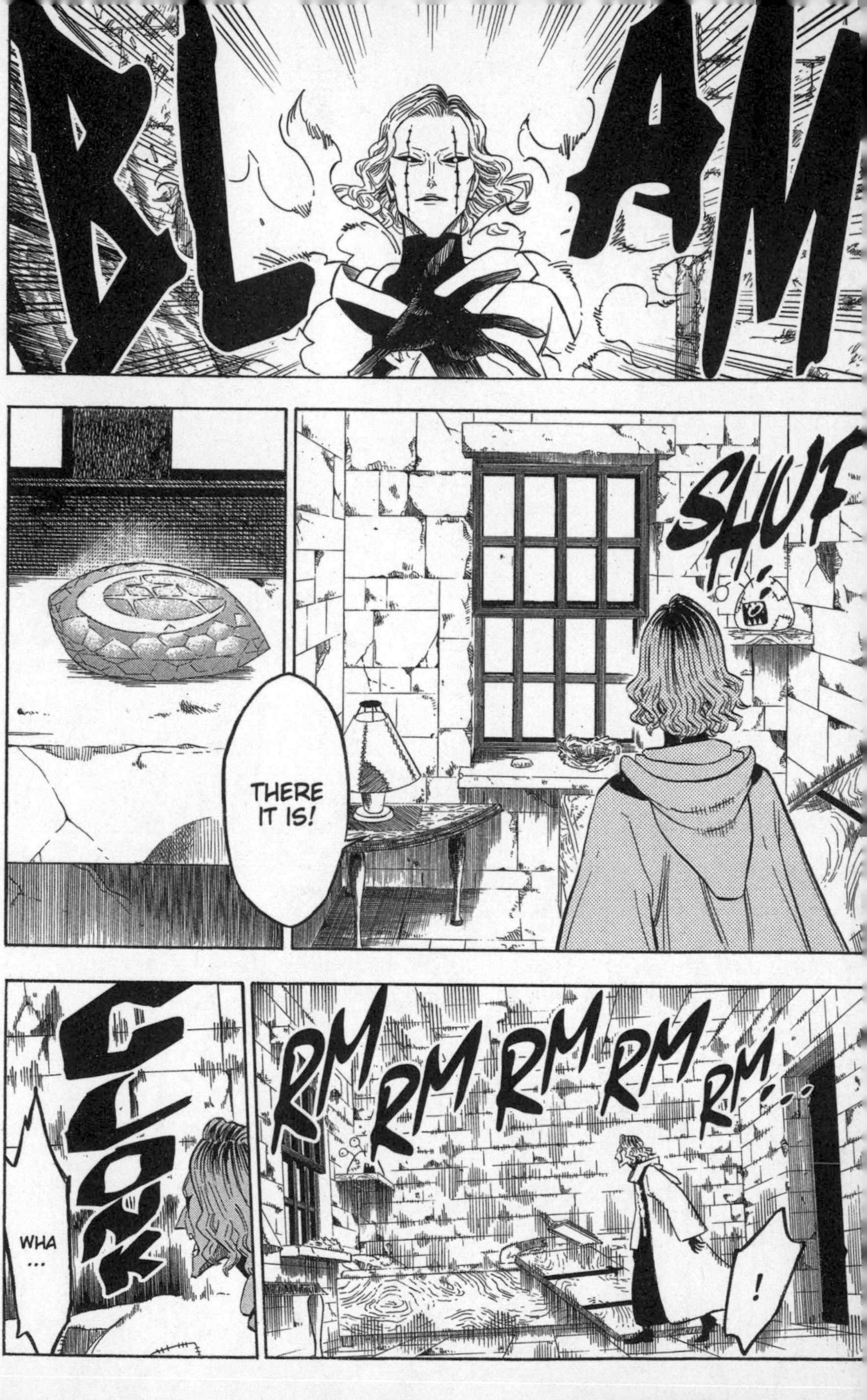
BLAM
SHUF
THERE IT IS!
RM RM RM RM RM...
!
WHA...

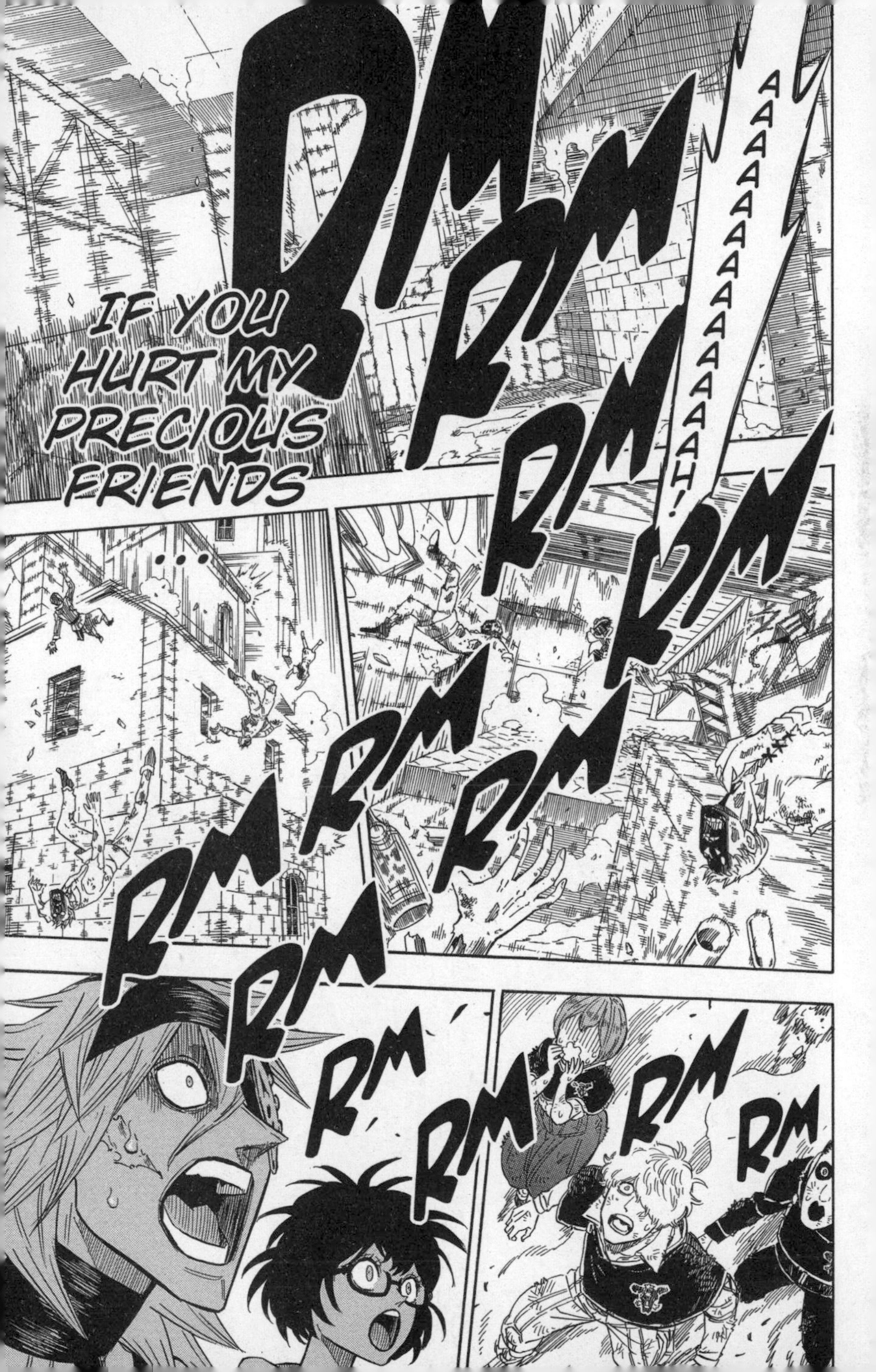
AAAAAAAAAAAAAAH!
DMM
RM RM RM
IF YOU HURT MY PRECIOUS FRIENDS
...
RM RM RM RM RM
RM RM RM RM RM

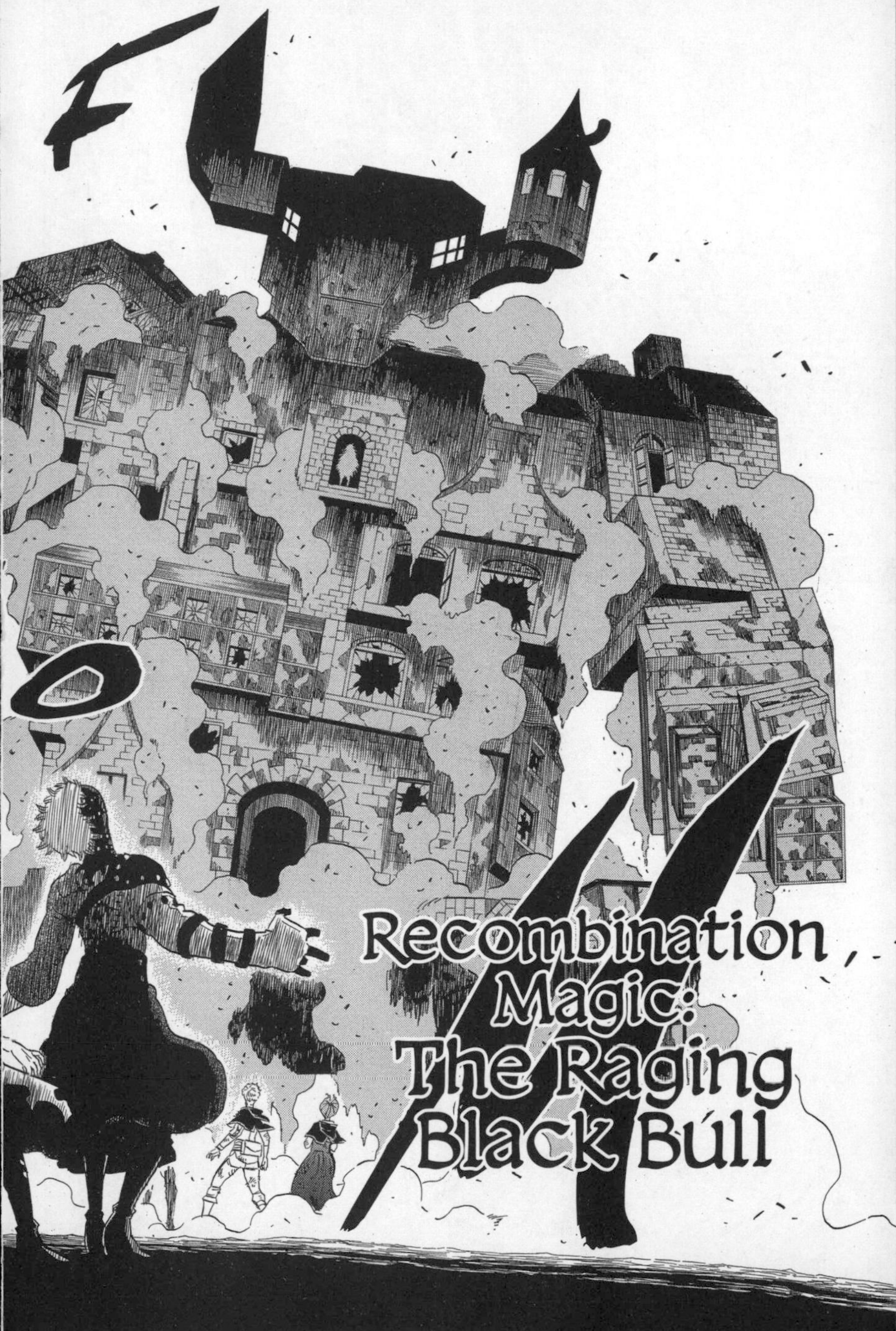
Recombination Magic: The Raging Black Bull

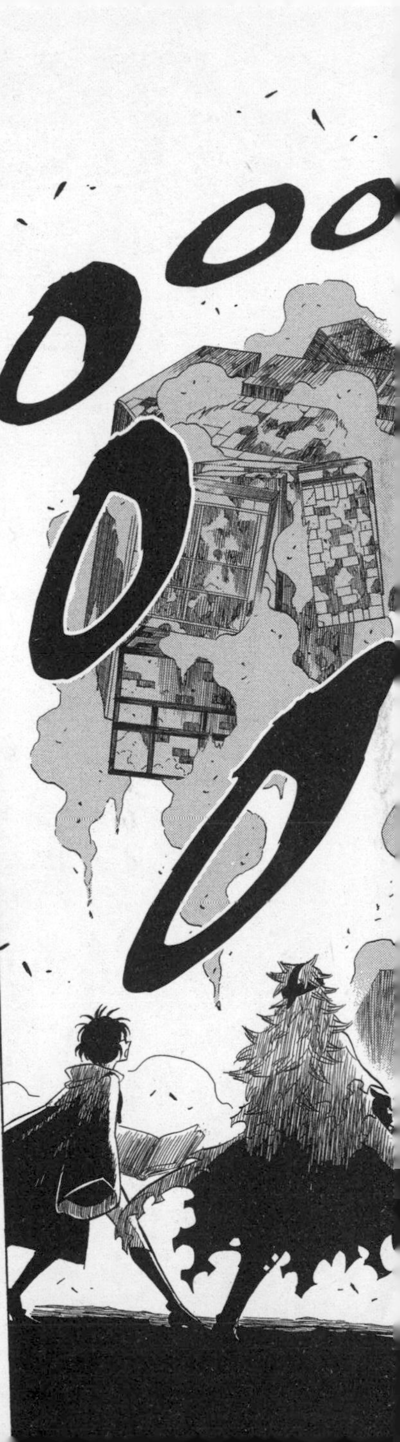

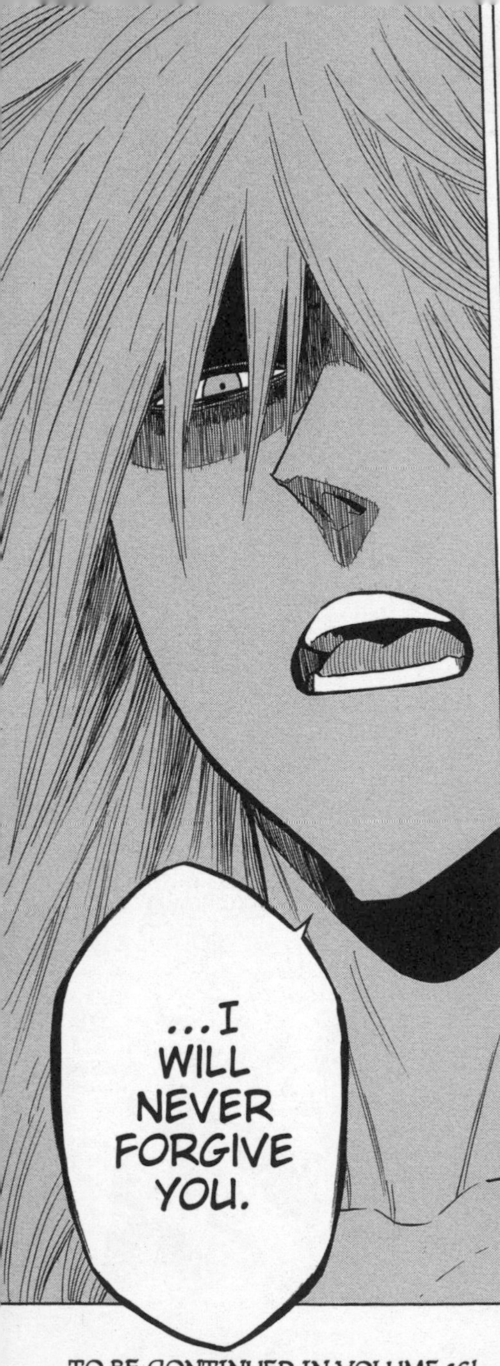
...I WILL NEVER FORGIVE YOU.

TO BE CONTINUED IN VOLUME 16!

The Blank Page Brigade

This volume's topic:
What have you spent money on lately?

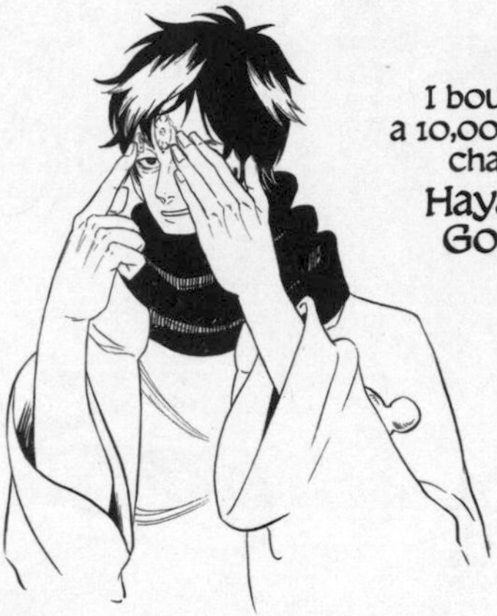

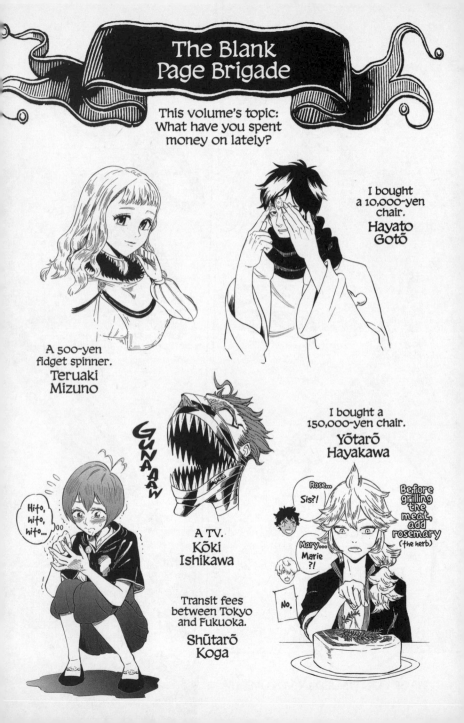

I bought a 10,000-yen chair.

Hayato Gotō

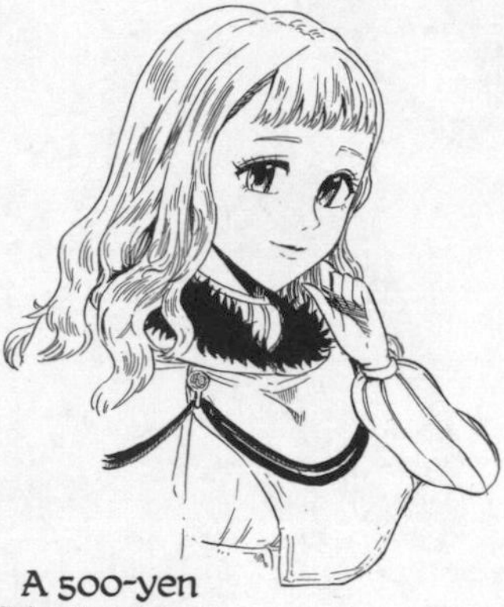

A 500-yen fidget spinner.

Teruaki Mizuno

I bought a 150,000-yen chair.

Yōtarō Hayakawa

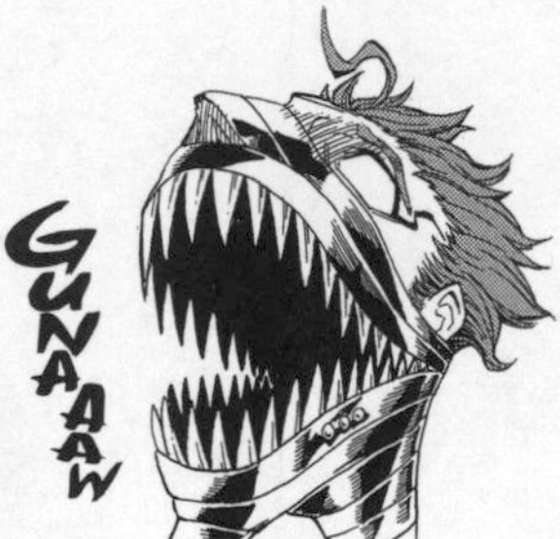
GUNAAAW

A TV.

Kōki Ishikawa

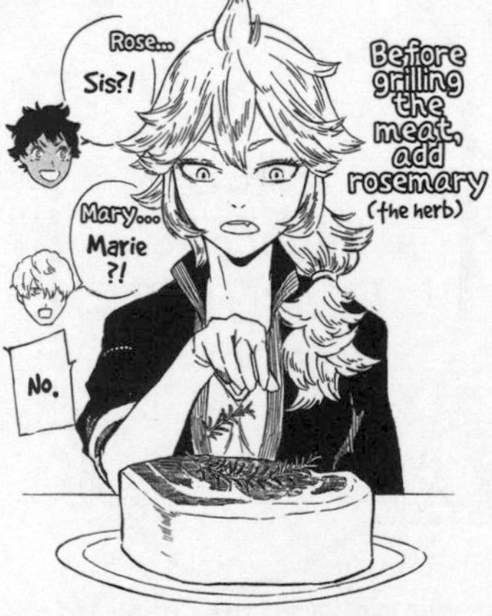
Before grilling the meat, add rosemary (the herb)
Rose...
Sis?!
Mary...
Marie ?!
No.

Transit fees between Tokyo and Fukuoka.

Shūtarō Koga

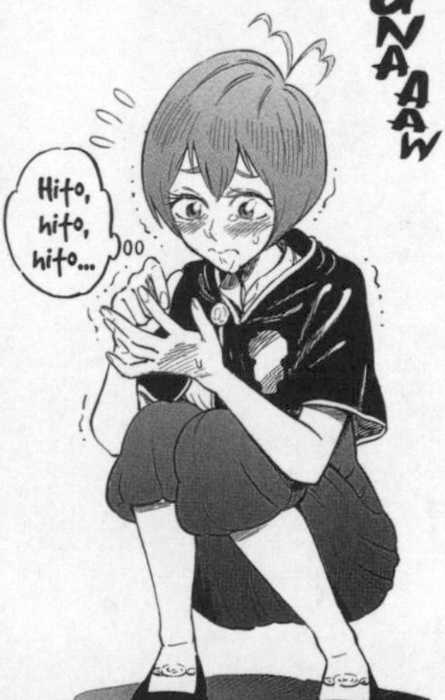
Hito, hito, hito...

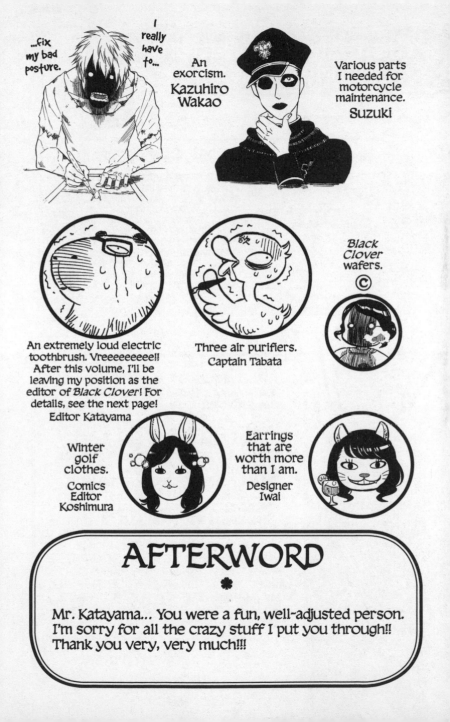

Various parts I needed for motorcycle maintenance.
Suzuki

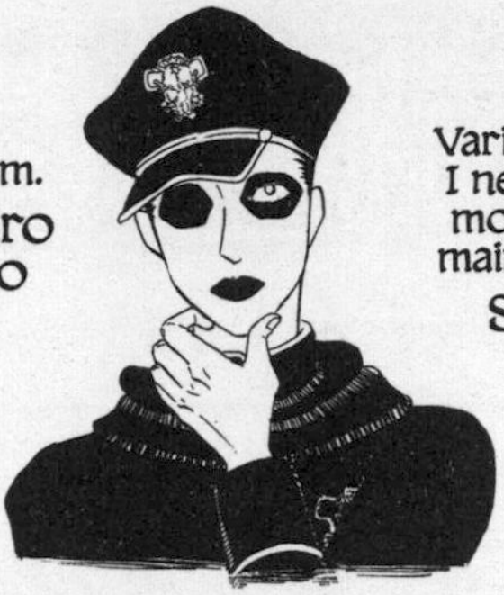

An exorcism.
Kazuhiro Wakao

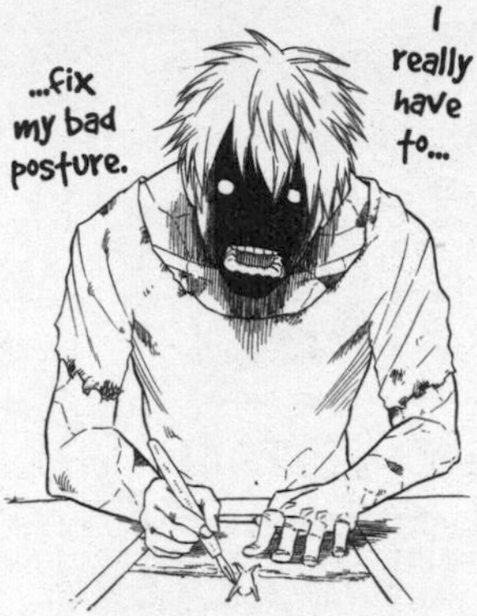
I really have to...
...fix my bad posture.

Black Clover wafers.
©

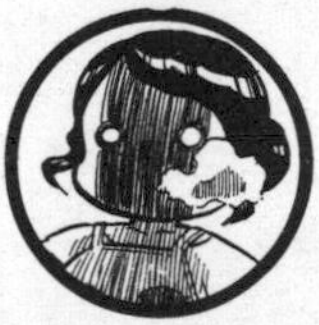

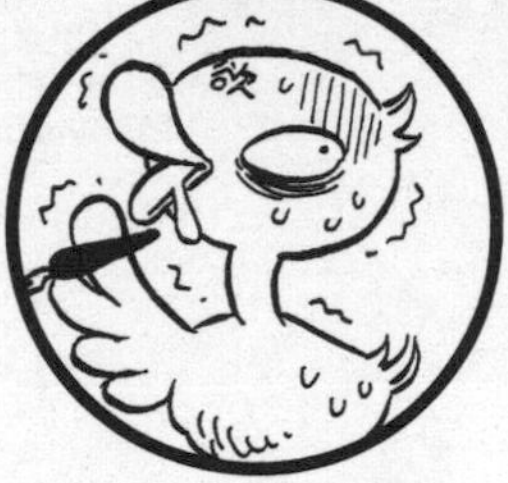

Three air purifiers.
Captain Tabata

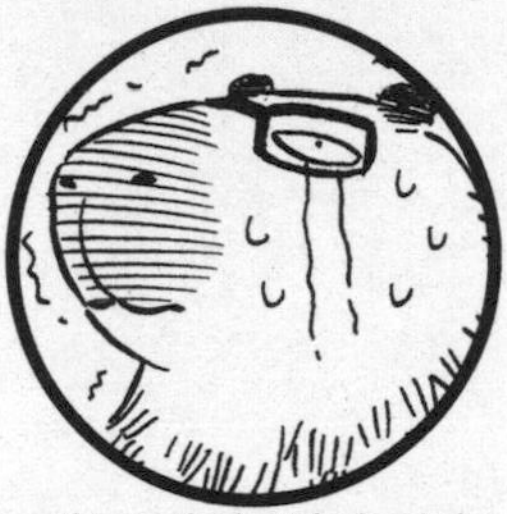

An extremely loud electric toothbrush. Vreeeeeeeee!! After this volume, I'll be leaving my position as the editor of *Black Clover*! For details, see the next page!
Editor Katayama

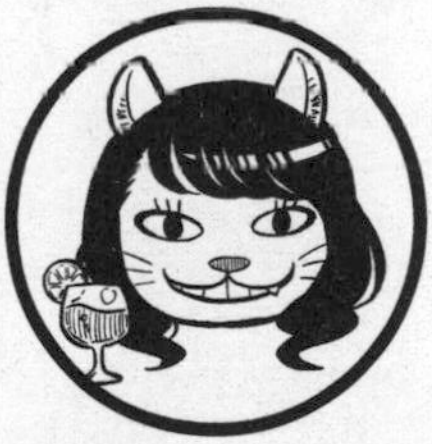

Earrings that are worth more than I am.
Designer Iwai

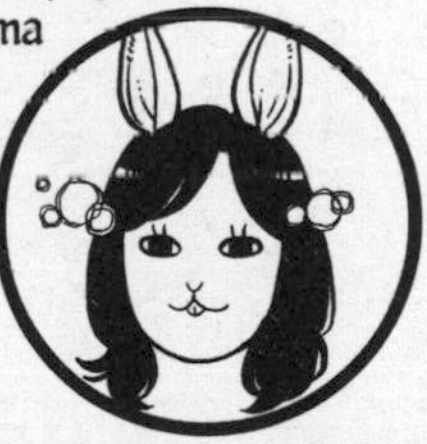

Winter golf clothes.
Comics Editor Koshimura

AFTERWORD

Mr. Katayama... You were a fun, well-adjusted person. I'm sorry for all the crazy stuff I put you through!! Thank you very, very much!!!

The Teary Graduation Article Brigade

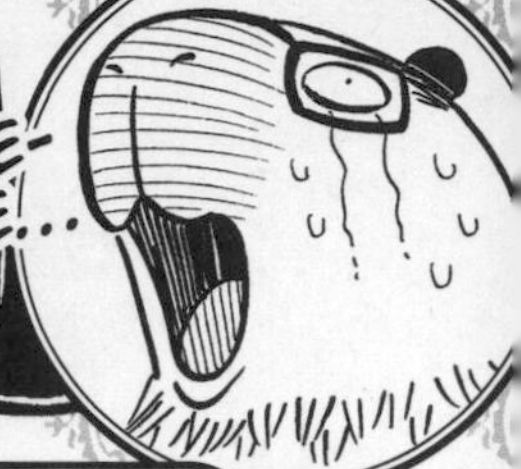
BYE-BYE...

who's leaving the series after this volume!

WHO IS KATAYAMA, ANYWAY?

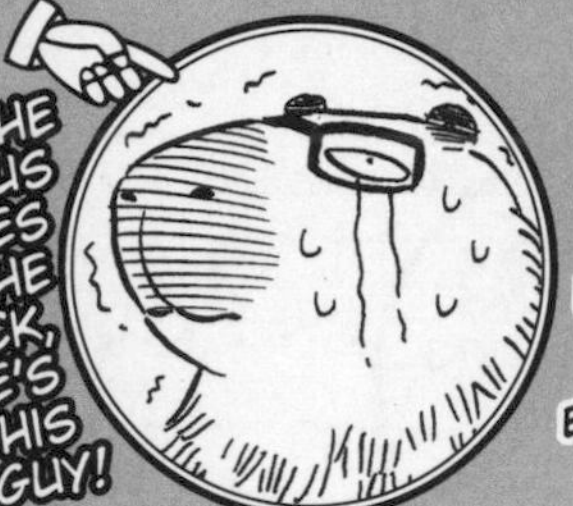
IN THE BONUS PAGES AT THE BACK, HE'S THIS GUY!

BLACK CLOVER'S EDITOR. HE JOINED SHUEISHA IN 2010, AND WAS ASSIGNED TO THE *WEEKLY SHONEN JUMP* EDITORIAL DEPARTMENT THAT SAME YEAR. HE'S BEEN *BLACK CLOVER'S* EDITOR SINCE IT BEGAN IN 2015, AND HE SUPERVISED EVERYTHING UP TO THE CHAPTERS INCLUDED IN THIS VOLUME, BUT NOW THE SERIES IS CHANGING EDITORS. HIS HOBBIES ARE VIDEO GAMES AND WATCHING MOVIES. HE'S SINGLE.

REVEALED IN THE COMICS FOR THE FIRST TIME: AN ACTUAL PHOTO OF KATAYAMA!

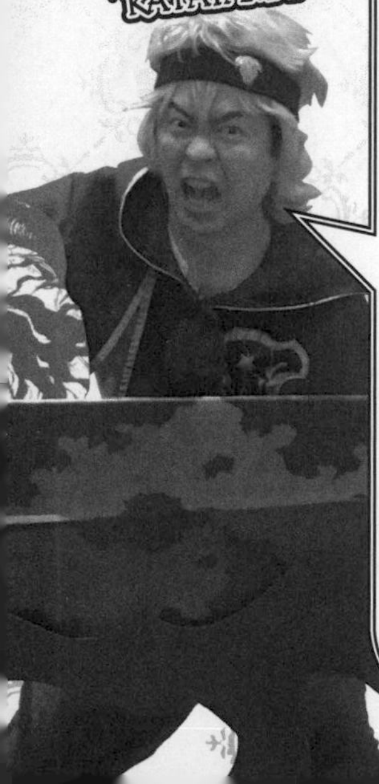

REMARKS FROM KATAYAMA

HELLO AND GOOD EVENING! THIS IS KATAYAMA OF *SHONEN JUMP*, AND I'M STEPPING DOWN FROM MY POST AS EDITOR OF *BLACK CLOVER*. I MET TABATA SENSEI IN 2014, AND HAVE KNOWN HIM FOR CLOSE TO FOUR YEARS. MY FIRST IMPRESSION OF HIM WAS, "HE'S TOO CHEERFUL!" HE'S A REALLY EASY PERSON TO TALK TO, AND OUR MEETINGS WERE ALWAYS FUN. THE SERIES IS CURRENTLY CHANGING EDITORS, AND TABATA SENSEI ABRUPTLY TOLD ME, "WE'VE GOT TWO EMPTY PAGES IN THE GRAPHIC NOVEL, SO PLEASE WRITE SOMETHING. ANYTHING'S FINE." THAT ADDED "HE'S TOO FREEWHEELING!" TO MY IMPRESSIONS OF HIM, BUT SINCE HE'S LEFT THIS JOB TO ME, I'LL DEFINITELY WRITE SOMETHING! AND SO, ON THE LEFT-HAND PAGE, I'VE ANNOUNCED MY PERSONAL *BLACK CLOVER* TOP THREES!

*PHOTO FROM JUMP FESTA 2018

SPECIAL BACK-OF-THE-VOLUME PROJECT!!

Goodbye, Editor Katayama!

This article is a feature on *Black Clover* editor Katayama,

KATAYAMA DECIDES! *BLACK CLOVER* TOP THREE LISTS!!

Favorite Chapter

1. **Page 23: The Distinguished Service Ceremony**
   I LIKE THE WAY ASTA YELLS, NOT FOR HIS OWN SAKE, BUT FOR NOELLE'S. THE EDITOR MEETING FOR THIS ONE WAS FUN TOO.
2. **Page 56: Three-Leaf Salute**
   THE UNEXPECTED BOND BETWEEN YAMI AND JULIUS! IT WAS A QUIETLY INTENSE CHAPTER THAT GAVE YOU A SENSE OF GUYS' FRIENDSHIPS AND THE MASTER/STUDENT RELATIONSHIP.
3. **Page 38: The One I've Set My Heart On**
   A...A MIXER?! I DIDN'T EXPECT THIS STORY, BUT IT'S A CUTE EPISODE THAT SHOWS ASTA'S DEVOTION.

Favorite Character

1. **Yami**
   EVERYTHING ABOUT HIM IS COOL, AND WHEN HE'S AROUND, THE STORY SHAPES UP.

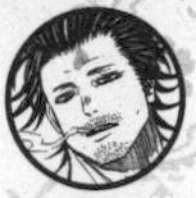

2. **Zora**
   THE SADDEST, MOST FIRED-UP GUY IN THE SERIES! AN UNUSUAL TYPE FOR *BLACK CLOVER*.

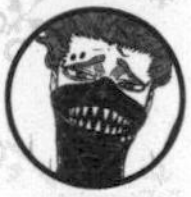

3. **Raia**
   AN OFFICIAL CHARACTER BASED ON AN ACTUAL ACTOR. THAT'S SUPER ORIGINAL! THANK YOU, MR. ARAI!

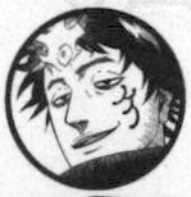

The Rough Parts of Being the Editor

1. **Waiting for manuscripts**
   AT THE LONGEST, I WAITED TEN HOURS AT THE OFFICE FOR THE MANUSCRIPT. WHICH IS FINE... AS LONG AS THE CHAPTER IS GOOD.
2. **Waiting for him to wake up**
   DURING EDITOR MEETINGS, EVERY ONCE IN A WHILE, TABATA SENSEI WOULD FALL ASLEEP. WHICH WAS FINE... AS LONG AS THAT CHAPTER TURNED OUT TO BE GOOD.
3. **Writing this article**
   TABATA SENSEI TOLD ME ABOUT THIS ARTICLE OUT OF THE BLUE, AND I'M CURRENTLY WRITING IT WITH NO HINTS WHATSOEVER. THIS ISN'T FINE!!

The Nice Parts of Being the Editor

1. **Mrs. Tabata's cooking**
   AT EVERY EDITOR MEETING, MRS. TABATA WOULD SERVE US DELICIOUS HOME-COOKED MEALS. SHE'S A GOD-DESS. A GODDESS OF NOURISHMENT.
2. **Playing with Amélie**
   AT EVERY MEETING, TABATA SENSEI'S DOG WOULD HELP ME DE-STRESS WITH HER ADORABLE LOOKS. SHE'S A GOD-DESS. A DOGGY GODDESS OF HEALING.
3. **Meeting Incredibly Brilliant People**
   GETTING TO MEET THE ANIME STAFF, HONOKA AKIMOTO, HIROFUMI ARAI AND OTHER FANTASTIC FOLKS.

In closing...

GETTING TO BE TABATA SENSEI'S EDITOR WAS A REALLY LUCKY BREAK FOR ME. SOMETIMES IT WAS FUN, SOMETIMES IT WAS ROUGH, BUT IT WAS ALWAYS REALLY AND TRULY RARE AND VALUABLE. IT MAY BE PRESUMPTUOUS OF ME, BUT IT FEELS AS THOUGH TABATA SENSEI AND I WERE "COMRADES IN ARMS" WHO FOUGHT OUR WAY THROUGH THE BATTLEFIELD OF *SHONEN JUMP*! THE EDITOR IS CHANGING, BUT I BET TOIDE, WHO'S TAKING OVER FOR ME, WILL WORK HARD AND MAKE THE SERIES EVEN MORE INTERESTING! I HOPE WE'LL GET TO WORK TOGETHER AGAIN SOMEDAY. THANK YOU VERY MUCH! —KATAYAMA

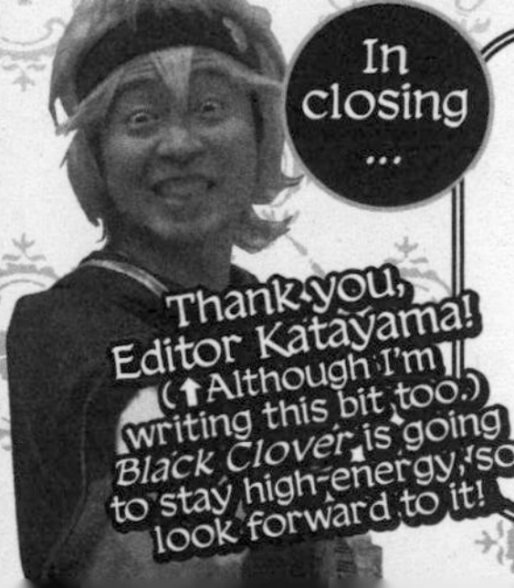
Thank you, Editor Katayama!
(↑Although I'm writing this bit too.)
Black Clover is going to stay high-energy, so look forward to it!

This is the rough sketch for the illustration at the beginning of Page 138! I was originally planning to leave Mereoleona's eyes white!

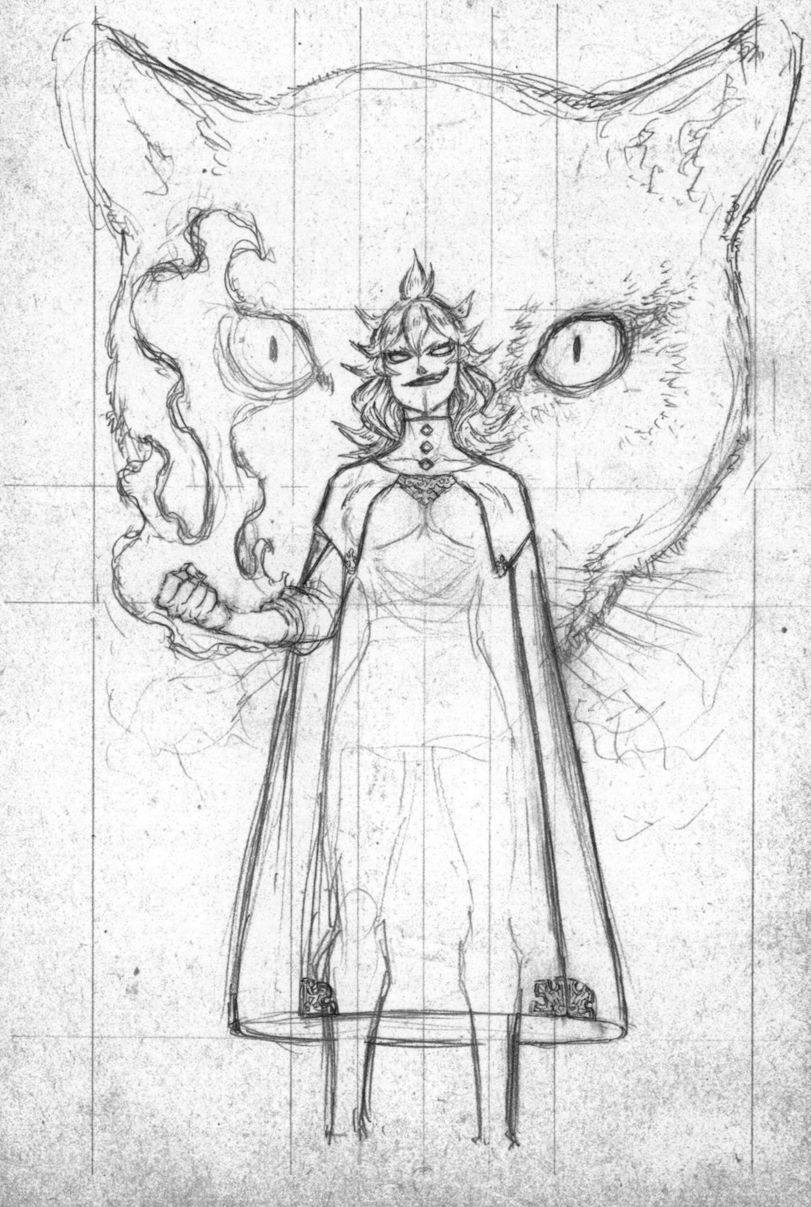

Special Bonus Materials

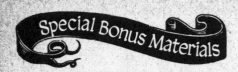

An early design sketch for Grey! This is what she looks like when she takes off her robe!

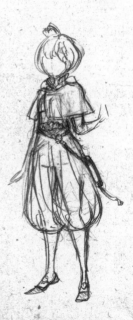

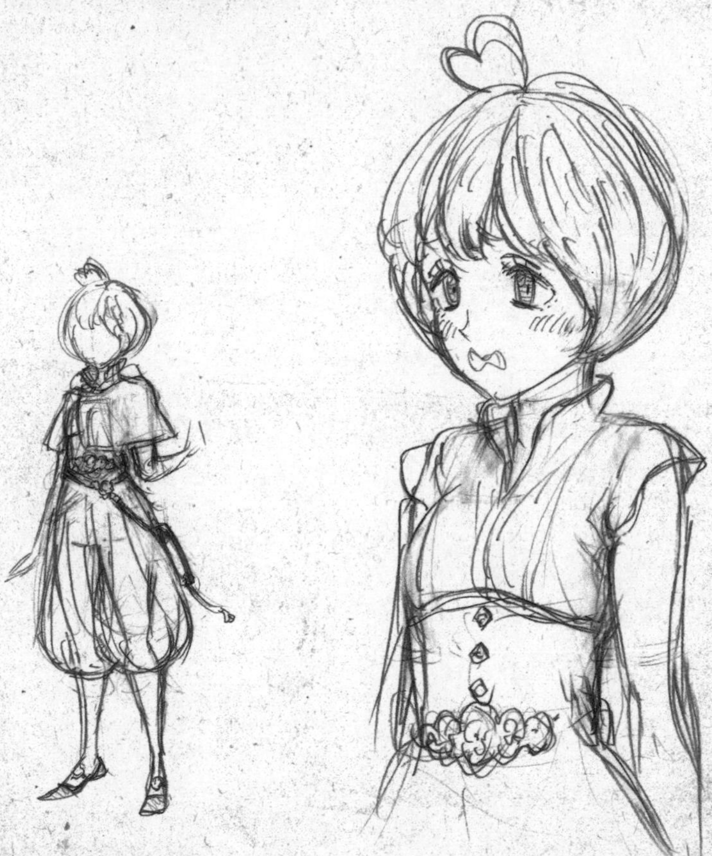

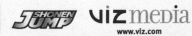

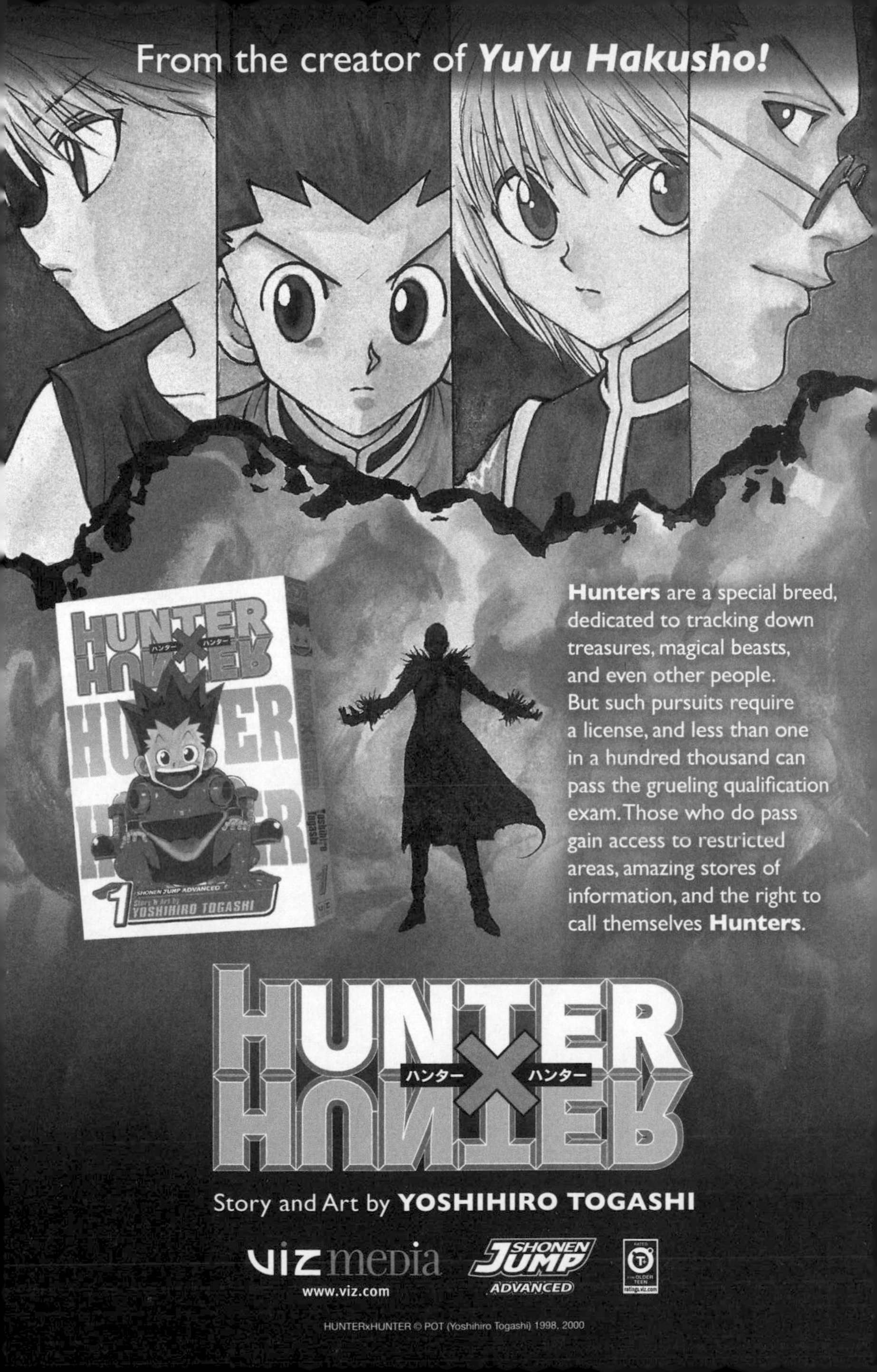
From the creator of *YuYu Hakusho!*
HUNTER ハンター × ハンター HUNTER
1 SHONEN JUMP ADVANCED Story & Art by YOSHIHIRO TOGASHI
Hunters are a special breed, dedicated to tracking down treasures, magical beasts, and even other people. But such pursuits require a license, and less than one in a hundred thousand can pass the grueling qualification exam. Those who do pass gain access to restricted areas, amazing stores of information, and the right to call themselves **Hunters**.
HUNTER ハンター × ハンター HUNTER
Story and Art by **YOSHIHIRO TOGASHI**
viz media
www.viz.com
SHONEN JUMP ADVANCED
T+ OLDER TEEN
ratings.viz.com
HUNTER×HUNTER © POT (Yoshihiro Togashi) 1998, 2000

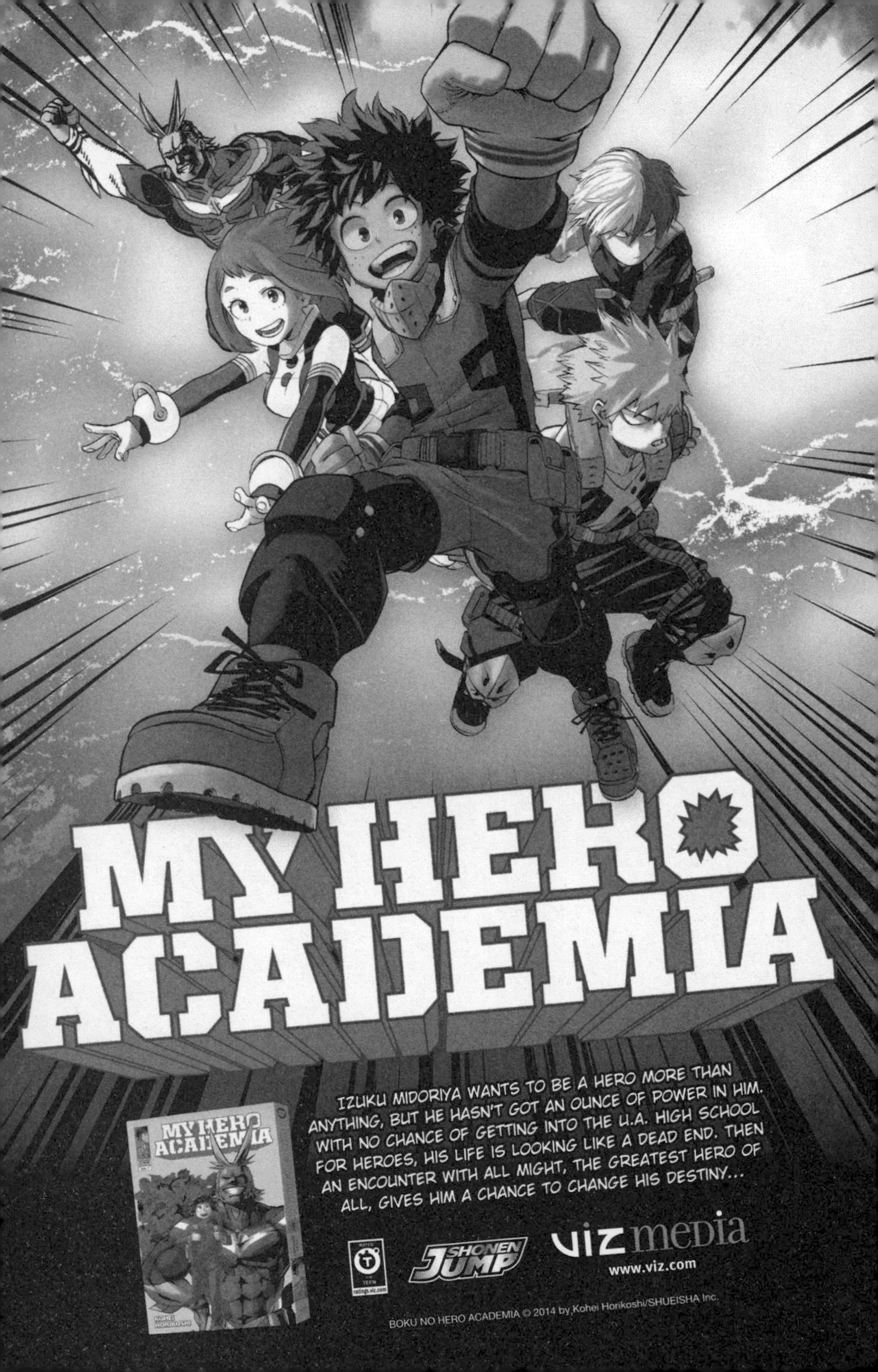
MY HERO ACADEMIA
IZUKU MIDORIYA WANTS TO BE A HERO MORE THAN ANYTHING, BUT HE HASN'T GOT AN OUNCE OF POWER IN HIM. WITH NO CHANCE OF GETTING INTO THE U.A. HIGH SCHOOL FOR HEROES, HIS LIFE IS LOOKING LIKE A DEAD END. THEN AN ENCOUNTER WITH ALL MIGHT, THE GREATEST HERO OF ALL, GIVES HIM A CHANCE TO CHANGE HIS DESTINY...
MY HERO ACADEMIA
KOHEI HORIKOSHI
RATED T TEEN
ratings.viz.com
SHONEN JUMP
VIZ media
www.viz.com
BOKU NO HERO ACADEMIA © 2014 by Kohei Horikoshi/SHUEISHA Inc.

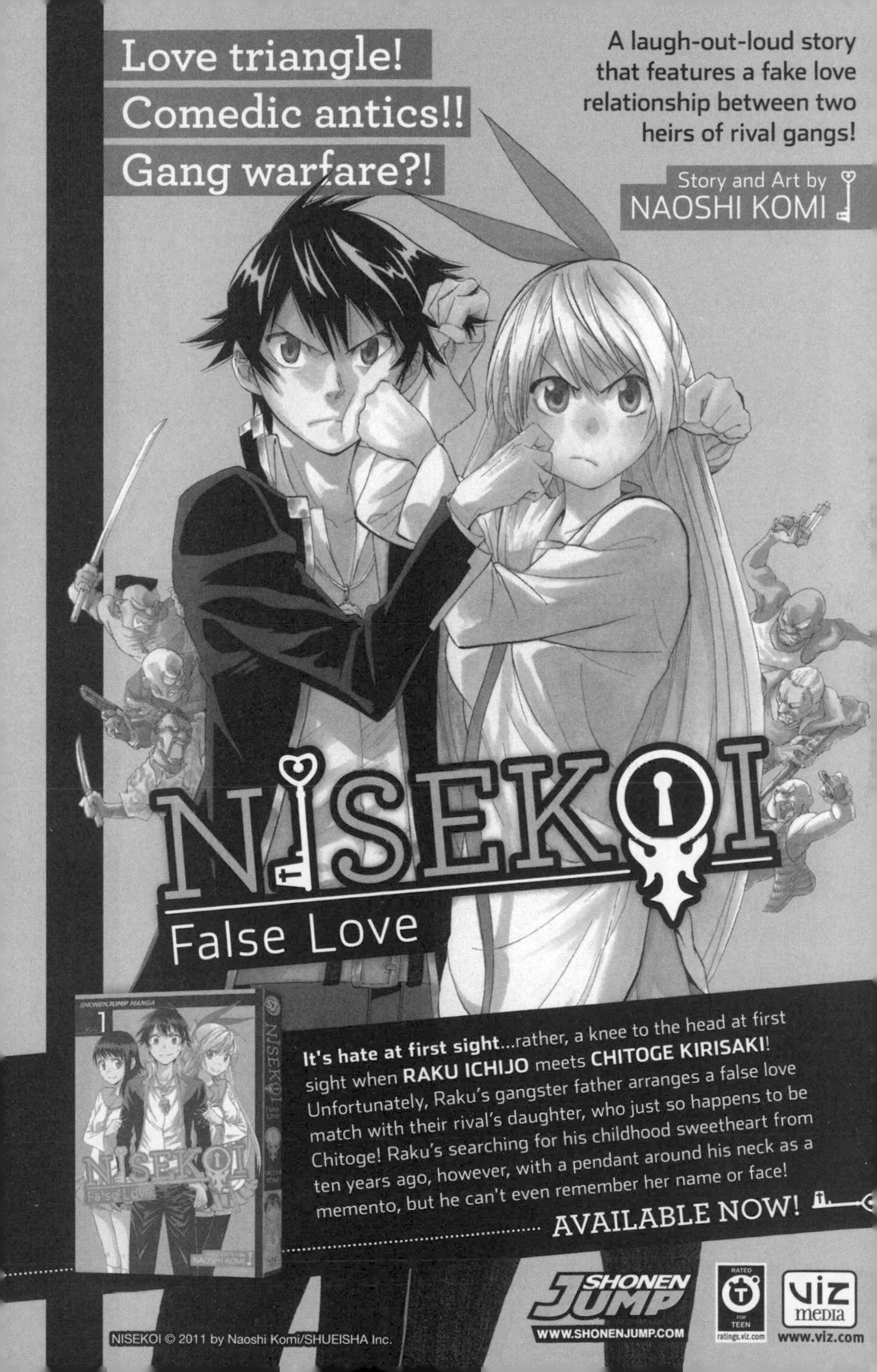
Love triangle!
Comedic antics!!
Gang warfare?!
A laugh-out-loud story that features a fake love relationship between two heirs of rival gangs!
Story and Art by
NAOSHI KOMI
NISEKOI
False Love
SHONENJUMP MANGA
VOL. 1
NISEKOI False Love
It's hate at first sight...rather, a knee to the head at first sight when RAKU ICHIJO meets CHITOGE KIRISAKI! Unfortunately, Raku's gangster father arranges a false love match with their rival's daughter, who just so happens to be Chitoge! Raku's searching for his childhood sweetheart from ten years ago, however, with a pendant around his neck as a memento, but he can't even remember her name or face!
AVAILABLE NOW!
SHONEN JUMP
WWW.SHONENJUMP.COM
RATED T FOR TEEN
ratings.viz.com
VIZ media
www.viz.com
NISEKOI © 2011 by Naoshi Komi/SHUEISHA Inc.

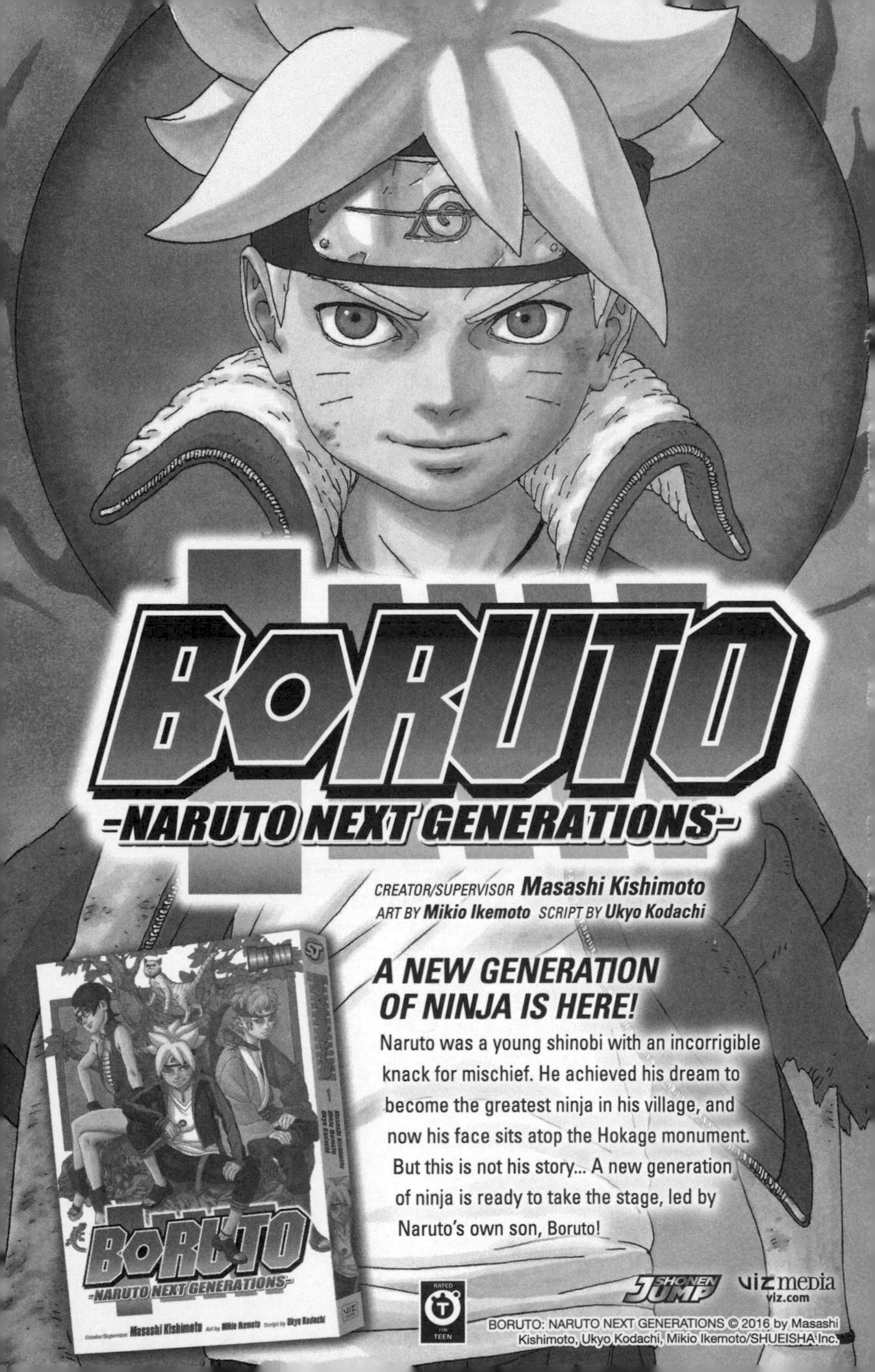
BORUTO
-NARUTO NEXT GENERATIONS-
CREATOR/SUPERVISOR Masashi Kishimoto
ART BY Mikio Ikemoto SCRIPT BY Ukyo Kodachi
A NEW GENERATION OF NINJA IS HERE!
Naruto was a young shinobi with an incorrigible knack for mischief. He achieved his dream to become the greatest ninja in his village, and now his face sits atop the Hokage monument. But this is not his story... A new generation of ninja is ready to take the stage, led by Naruto's own son, Boruto!
RATED T FOR TEEN
SHONEN JUMP
VIZ media
viz.com
BORUTO: NARUTO NEXT GENERATIONS © 2016 by Masashi Kishimoto, Ukyo Kodachi, Mikio Ikemoto/SHUEISHA Inc.

𝕾𝖙𝖔𝖕

YOU'RE READING
THE WRONG WAY!

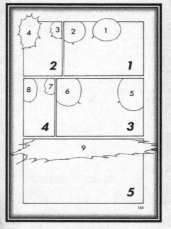

BLACK CLOVER

reads from right to left, starting
in the upper-right corner. Japanese
is read from right to left, meaning
that action, sound effects, and
word-balloon order are completely
reversed from English order.